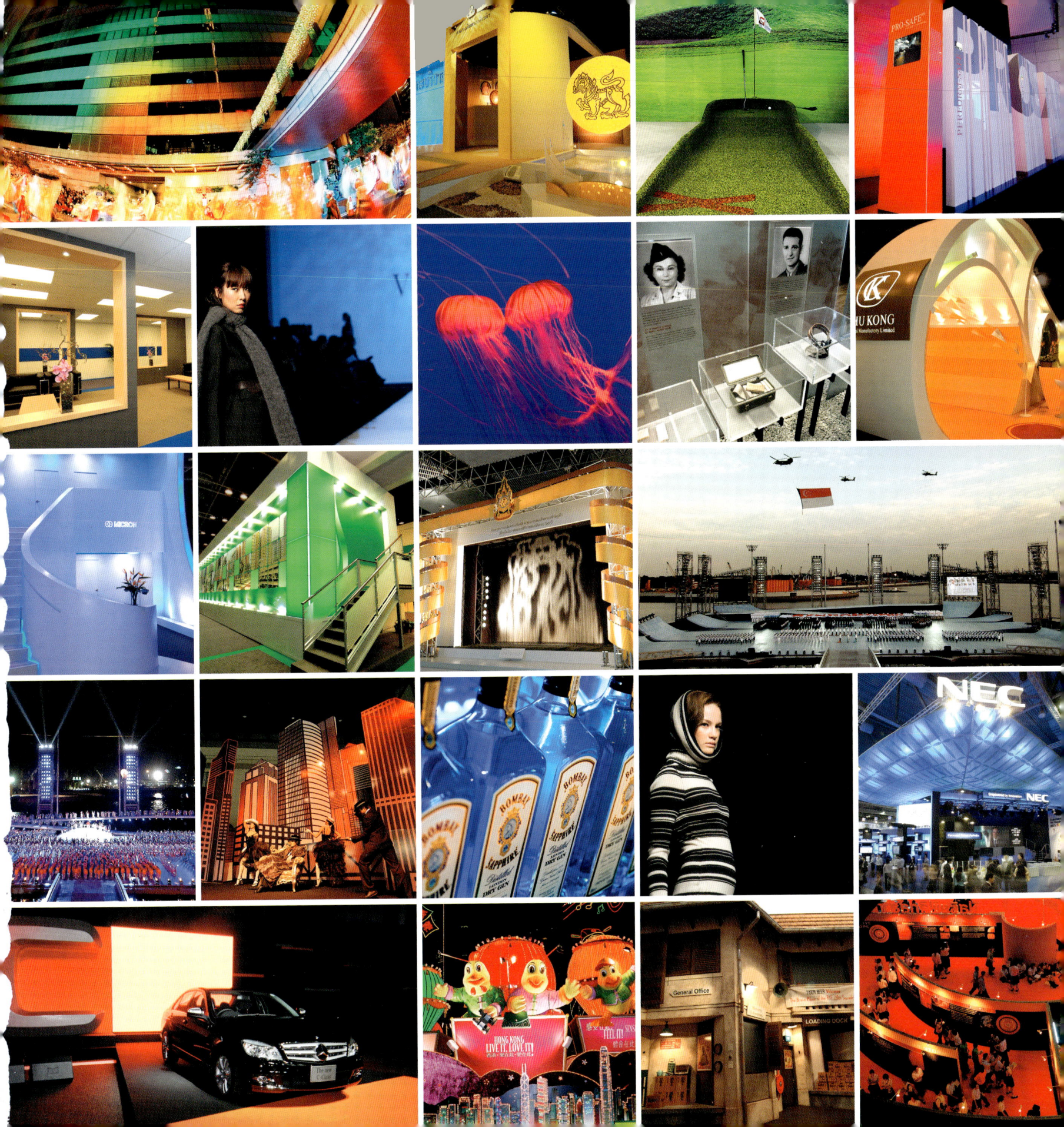

Copyright © 2008 by Pico Global Services Limited (www.pico.com)

All rights reserved. No part of this book may be reproduced in any form or by any electronic or mechanical means, including information storage and retrieval systems, without permission in writing from the publisher.
Library of Congress Cataloging in Publication Data:
Excellence in Exhibit & Event Design
ISBN: 978-1-58471-121-6   ISBN: 1-58471-121-3

Distributors to the trade in the United States and Canada
Watson-Guptill
770 Broadway Avenue
New York, NY 10003
Distributors outside the United States and Canada
HarperCollins International
10 East 53rd Street
New York, NY 10022-5299

Exclusive distributor in China
Beijing Designerbooks Co., Ltd.
Building No.2, No.3, Babukou, Gulouxidajie,
Xicheng District, Beijing 100009, P.R. China
Tel: 0086(010)6406-7653 Fax: 0086(010)6406-0931
E-mail: info@designerbooks.net   www.designerbooks.net

Printed and bound in China

excellence in
exhibit + event
design

Visual Reference Publications Inc., New York

10 The 60th Anniversary of His Majesty's Accession to the Throne
16 MasterCard Luxury Week Hong Kong
20 Mercedes-Benz C-Class Launch
22 Singapore National Day Parade
26 IMF and World Bank Group Annual Meetings
28 Caritas Bianchi Fashion Show
30 Chinese New Year Parade
34 GE Money at Money Fair

38 National Science and Technology Fair
44 NEC at ITU Telecom World
48 Motorola at ITU Telecom World
52 Chevrolet at the 28th Bangkok International Motor Show
58 Micron at the Hong Kong Optical Fair
62 Kohler at China Building & Construction Trade Fair
66 LANXESS at ChinaPlas
70 Mercedes-Benz at the 28th Bangkok International Motor Show
76 Mercedes-Benz at Taipei Auto Show
78 The Daodejing: Its Editions and Versions
80 Chu Kong at the Hong Kong Optical Fair
84 Mizuno at the 5th International Golf Trade Fair
88 Peugeot at Auto Shanghai
92 Raytheon at the 47th International Paris Air Show
98 Toshiba Private Show

{content}

102	Bombay Sapphire Martini Glass Exhibition Display
108	JetQuay - CIP Terminal
112	OSIM ChairSpa
118	Leica Flagship Shop
122	Mercedes-Benz Accessories Shop
124	Qingdao CNC Centre
126	Motorola Facilities Branding Projects
128	Siemens Automation Showroom
130	Siemens Visitor Centre
134	Cellnet Executive Briefing Centre

138	Ocean Park Hong Kong
142	Hua Song Museum
148	Ngong Ping Theme Village
152	Cathay Pacific Experience
158	Kiang Saket Energy Centre
162	APB TigerLIVE Gallery
166	Malaysia Export Exhibition Centre
168	Normandy American Cemetery Visitor Centre

174 *acknowledgements*

176 *index*

interior

themed

:// foreword

People expect to be entertained, amused, surprised and stimulated. It doesn't matter if it's at a retail store, a restaurant, a museum, a trade show or corporate headquarters – people today, expect "eye-candy;" showmanship and active participation. "Spectacle" just isn't big enough anymore and "spectacular" is only good for a moment or two before something even more arresting shows up. With all the advances in the last two decades in electronics, lighting effects and assorted media techniques, it takes master designers and craftspeople to devise new ways to amuse and retain the viewer's attention. The Pico Group is a team of these master talents.

The Pico organisation consists of a multinational and culturally diverse group of some 3,000 talented versatile people who are in the business of creating exhibitions, events, signage, themed environments and exhibition hall management. Pico originates concepts and designs, plans, manages, produces and installs as well as dismantles. All this is accomplished with the company's commitment to excellence and service.

I first became aware of the Pico Group and its unique talents when I was assembling a book on outstanding international trade show stands and exhibitions. The size and scope of the company's work was immediately apparent as material came pouring in from Singapore, Malaysia, Thailand, Japan, China and Hong Kong. Of course, I was only too pleased to be able to include several of the diverse and attractive projects that showcased Pico's ability in that book. There are other companies around the world that design and construct exhibits, but I know of no other company that does it so successfully, thoroughly, and crosses more international borders than Pico. Since it's an idea driven company with a network of partners, it can and does provide high quality creative services literally around the world with offices in five continents. Pico's multinational staff have knowledge of local customs, cultures and business practice. A client anywhere in the world can rely on Pico to create and deliver the client's message in the context appropriate for the target audience.

This book showcases some of Pico's many capabilities in the following four sections. This review begins with "Event" – anything from sporting events and big parades to anniversary celebrations, corporate meetings and product launches then proceeds to "Exhibition." This section includes trade show set-ups and more. "Interior" showcases corporate offices, showrooms and retail stores. The final section is devoted to museums and themed attractions. What the book cannot show but we note here is Pico's stature in the industry as specialists in hall and facilities management in many of the top-of-the-line exhibition and convention centres. The company currently operates facilities in Colombo, Ho Chi Minh City and Xian. Professional teams create and manage conferences as well as numerous incentive meetings and events for its corporate clients. Though not shown here, Pico has also been involved in the set-up for the Olympic Games in Athens and Torino, and will be involved in the 2008 Beijing Olympics.

Pico considers itself "the guardian of the client's brand" and whether it's an exhibit, a trade show, a retail showroom or corporate office, Pico works at understanding, interpreting and presenting the client's brand image throughout the process.

"We help to transform the client's needs into amazing yet, cost-effective realities. We deliver on the promise with single or multi-storey exhibition stands, country pavilions and world expositions that are seen by millions of people worldwide."

I am pleased and proud to present to you the many talents and capabilities of the Pico Group and to open up its world for your perusal.

Martin M. Pegler

The dictionary defines an "event" as an occurrence or a happening – a social gathering or activity. It can be that or so much more when Pico's design team turns an "event" into a "happening." In today's sense of the word a "happening" is something unique, one-of-a-kind, a sensory and sensual experience filled with drama, lighting and lots of action.

Pico has conceptualised, constructed and managed many national day parades, festive celebrations, international staged events that have been broadcast to hundreds of millions of people around the world, and mammoth entertainment launches. On a smaller scale there are product launches, sales promotions, brand campaigns, road shows and opening ceremonies. To each of these events or happenings, Pico brings its core value of "Excellence."

To create the desired high pitch of excitement, Pico delivers these super spectacular extravaganzas through the use of state-of-the-art interactive computer programming and the latest in electronics and lighting techniques. Pico is also responsible for designing and producing complete theatrical productions inclusive of visuals, original musical compositions and lyrics, staging, choreography, costuming and special effects.

The gigantic 140,000 sq. m. exhibition celebrating the King of Thailand's 60th anniversary accession to the throne included a theatre and a musical presentation of over 350 performances, and 500 sq. m. living rice field. In 45 days Pico set up 1,032 double-storey office suites to accommodate the annual meetings of the IMF and World Bank Group in Singapore. For Luxury Week, the company managed and produced the set-up for an upscale fashion festival while the Singapore National Day parade required building a large stage on a floating platform with towers of over 25 metres, an orchestra pit, lighting and audio towers – and all within three weeks.

Where other design and construction companies may see "problems," Pico sees "challenges." Where others rely on "tried and true" solutions, Pico sees opportunities to explore new and different approaches.

Martin M. Pegler

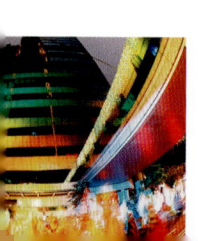

event.

The 60th Anniversary of His Majesty's Accession to the Throne

where Bangkok, Thailand

To commemorate the King of Thailand's 60th anniversary of accession to the throne, a 140,000 sq. m. exhibit space was constructed at the IMPACT Convention Centre in Bangkok, Thailand. History came to life through a multimedia live musical infused with music and lyrics. Displays such as the "Commemorative Pavilion," the "Water of Life," the "Royal Descents," and the "Sufficiency Economy" added depth and perspective to the space.

A spectacular graphic waterfall highlighted the King of Thailand's contributions to the development of water resources. For this, the designers imported a new technology, combining water pressure and gravity that orchestrated the water into a series of forms and shapes. For the "Royal Descents" area, a display of traditional Thai architecture was fused with special sounds and effects to engage the guests and generate an overall atmosphere of reverence.

The designer's intent was to promote and enhance people's understanding and appreciation of the King's Sufficiency Economy Theory. For this, the space was divided in two sections: Live Exhibition and Musical Stage Performance, which immersed the visitors in a dynamic atmosphere. This concept was promoted through a seven-minute stage musical. Over 350 shows were performed for audiences totalling more than 800,000. A living rice field of about 500 sq. m. was created to represent a model of a sufficiency farming.

This event was so popular that at least five million Thais came to honour their Monarch. After the event, a VCD and a book of this successful exhibition were sold for charity.

event. exhibit. interior. themed.

ศาลาเฉลิมพระเกียรติฯ

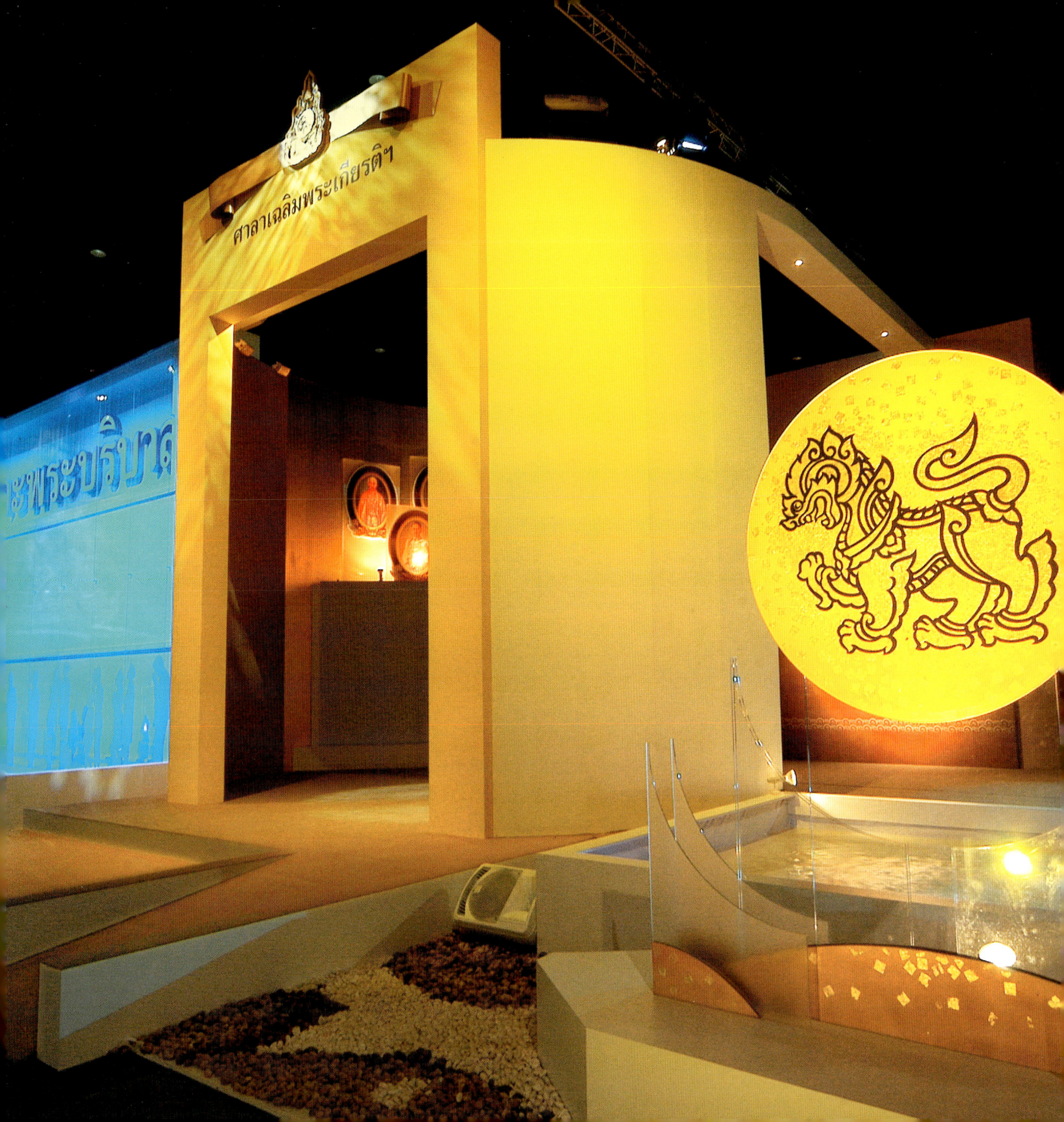

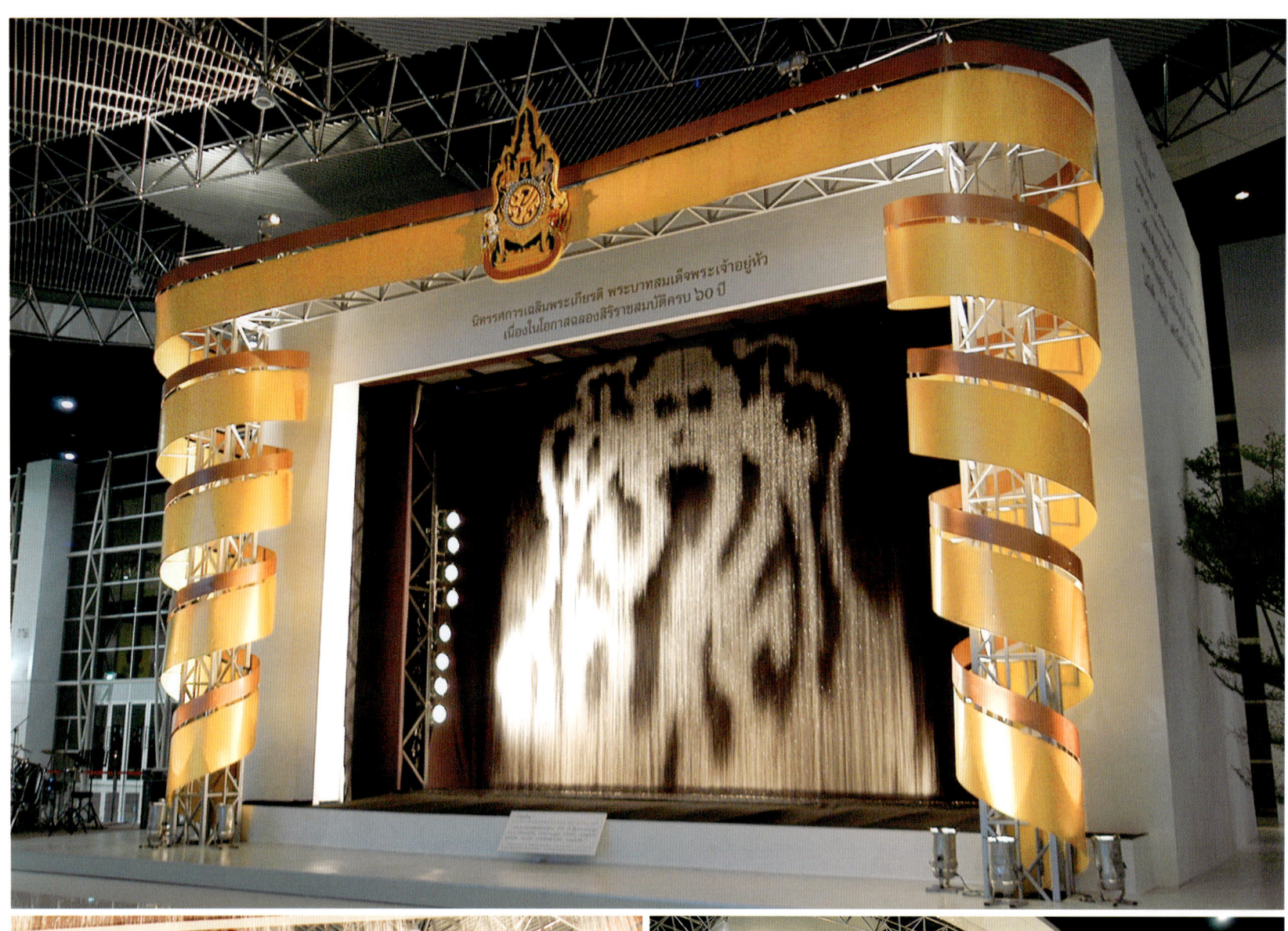

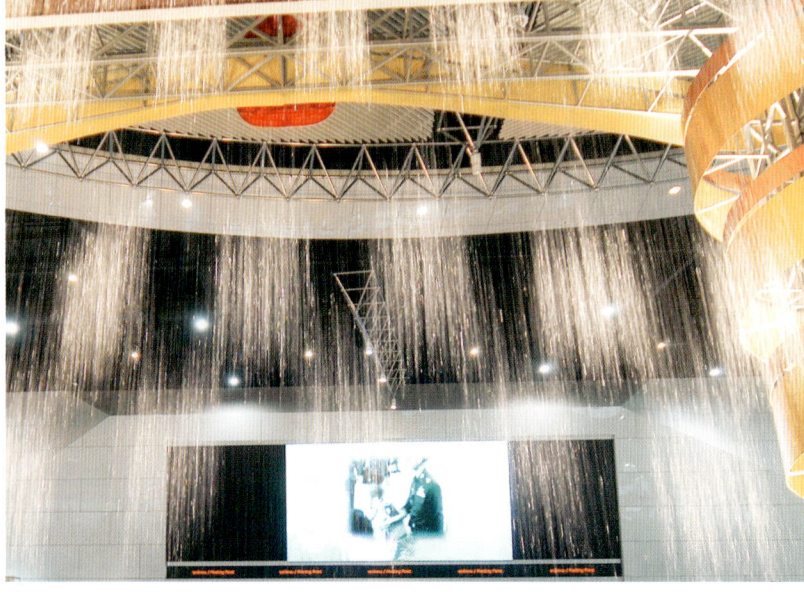

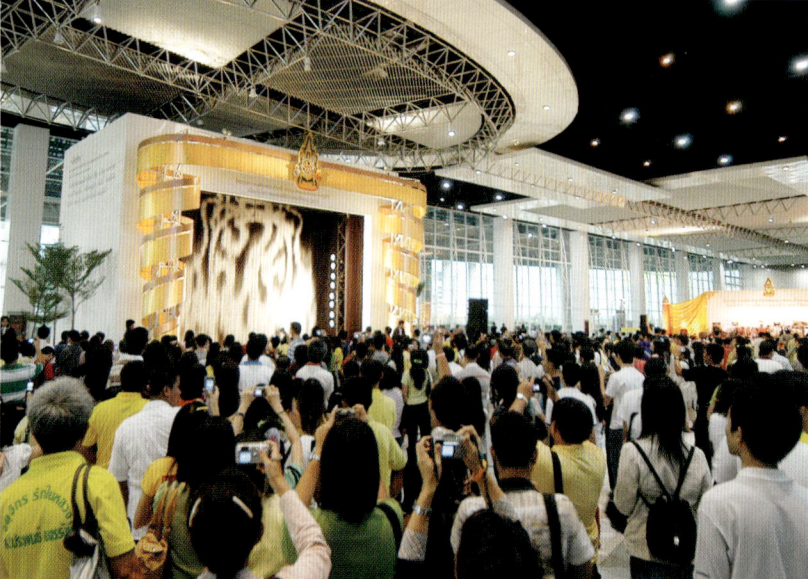

นิทรรศการเฉลิมพระเกียรติ พระบาทสมเด็จพระเจ้าอยู่หัว
เนื่องในโอกาสฉลองสิริราชสมบัติครบ ๖๐ ปี

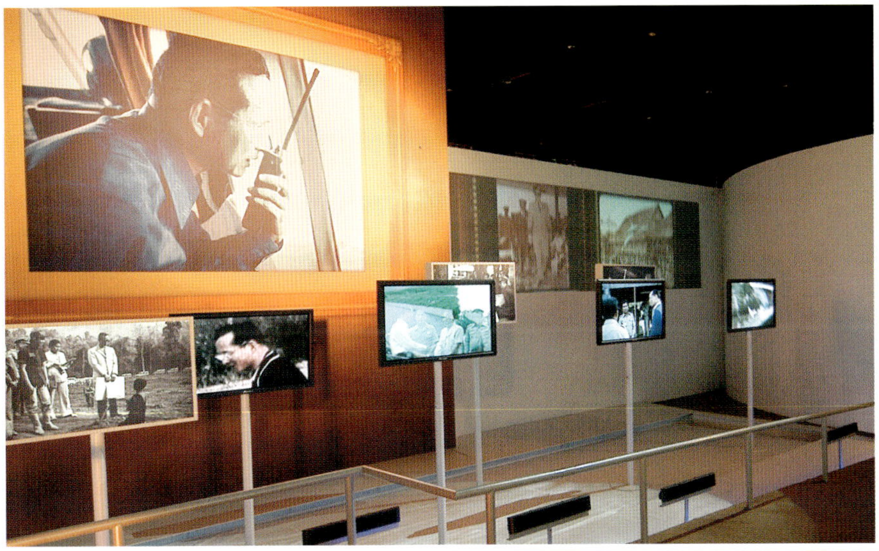

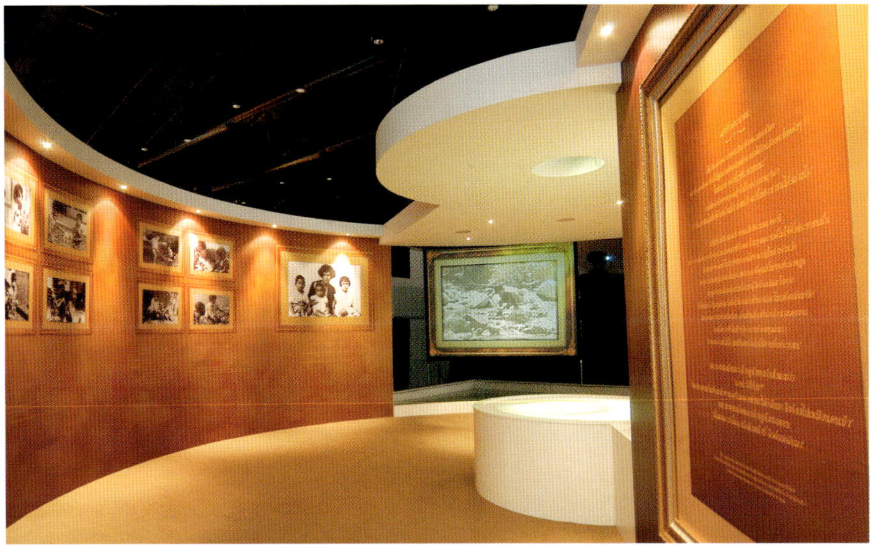

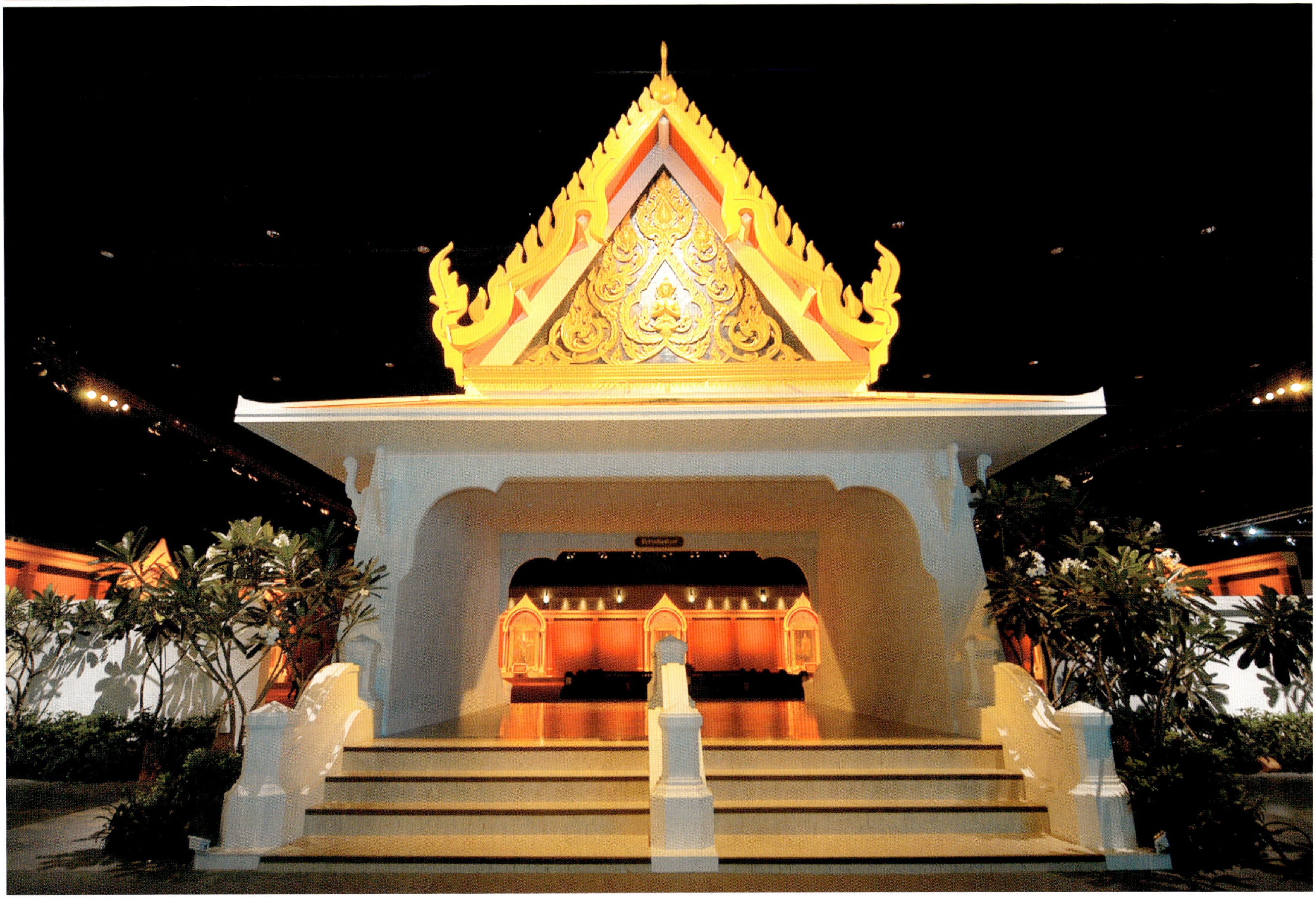

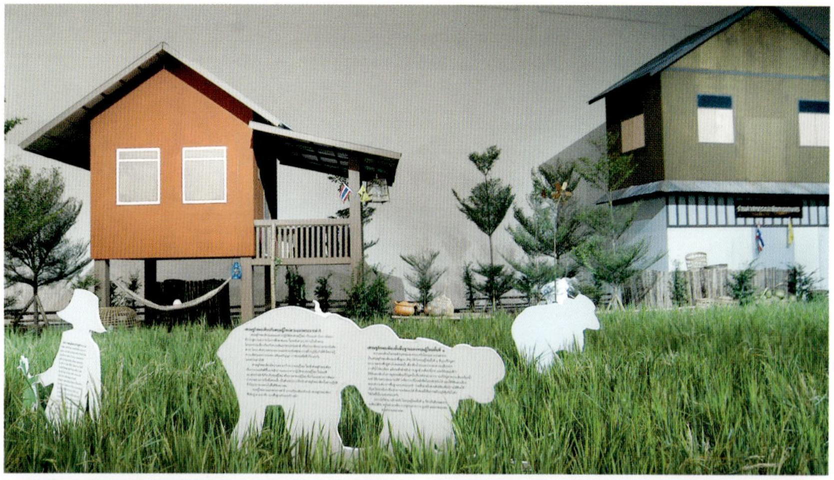

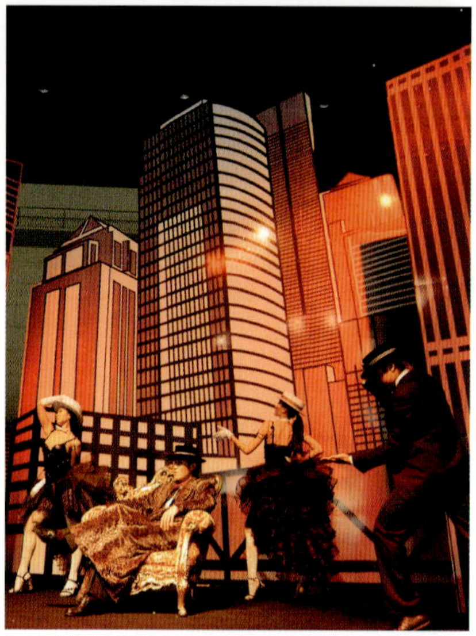

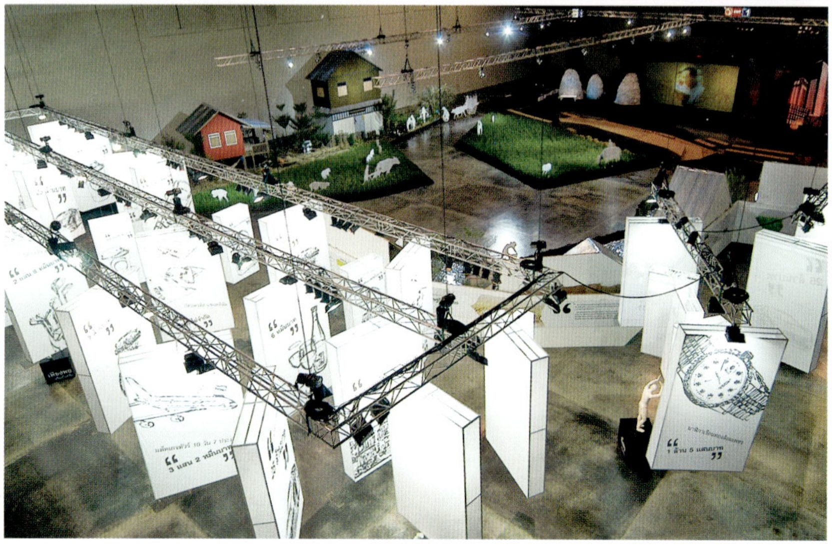

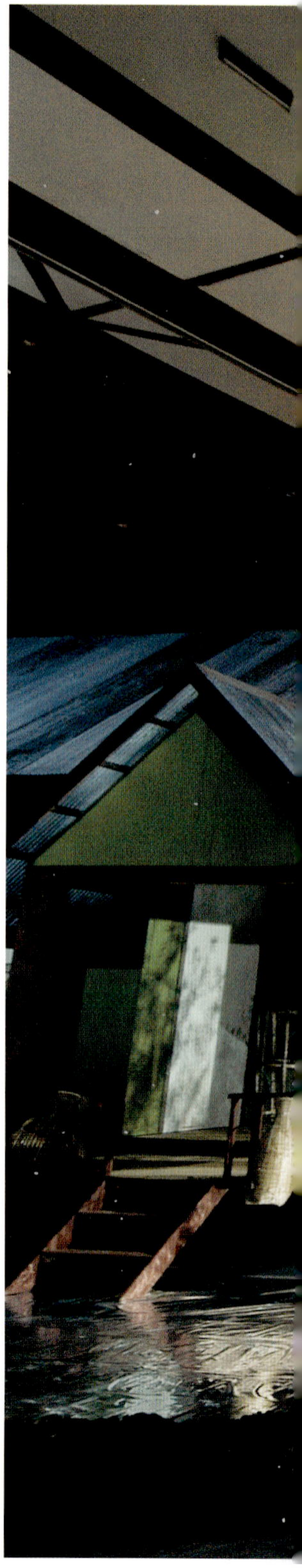

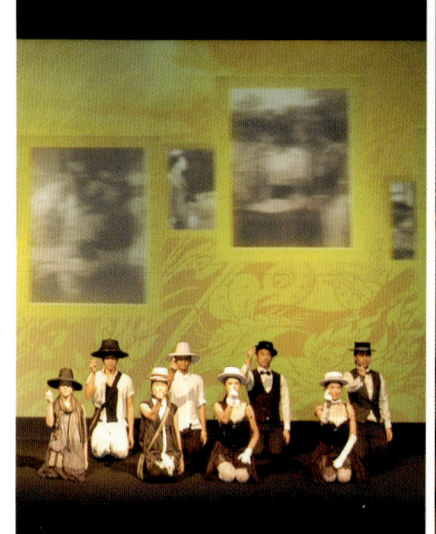

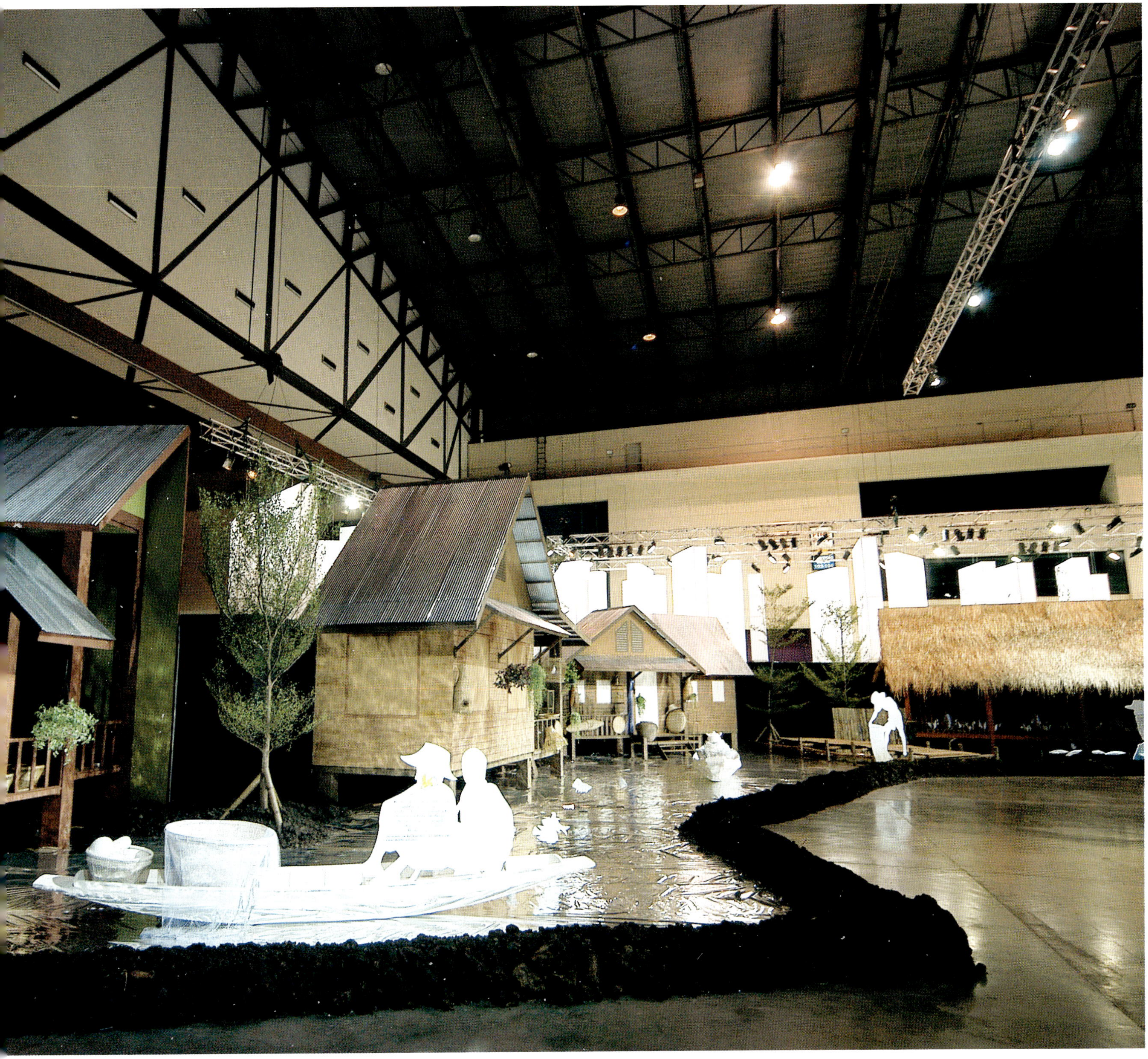

MasterCard Luxury Week Hong Kong

where Hong Kong SAR, China

MasterCard Luxury Week was held in Chater Garden in Hong Kong's central business district. The outdoor venue occupied approximately 1,000 sq. m. which included a mezzanine floor.

The event was Hong Kong's premier consumer-focused luxury fashion event which profiled various luxurious consumables from high-end apparel and exquisite accessories, to opulent automobiles and champagne. Organised by the world's leading fashion event specialist, IMG, the event generated quite a buzz over the 10-day period.

MasterCard Luxury Week created a direct connection between luxury fashion and the premium consumer market. The organiser expects it to potentially be the number one event for premium brands to showcase their products in the expanding Asia market.

The event included an exclusive schedule of catwalk shows which featured the work of leading fashion designers from around the globe. This was the first time that many of the brands had presented their collections in this thriving Asian metropolis.

To accomodate the many collection shows, catwalks, celebrities and supermodels, an outdoor venue was created with various zones – back stage, runway, car display, hospitality and catering. All space was carefully planned to accommodate users' different requirements.

A multimedia system with video and interactive fixtures brought to life the fashion shows and performances. The space was awash with logos of prominent fashion designers.

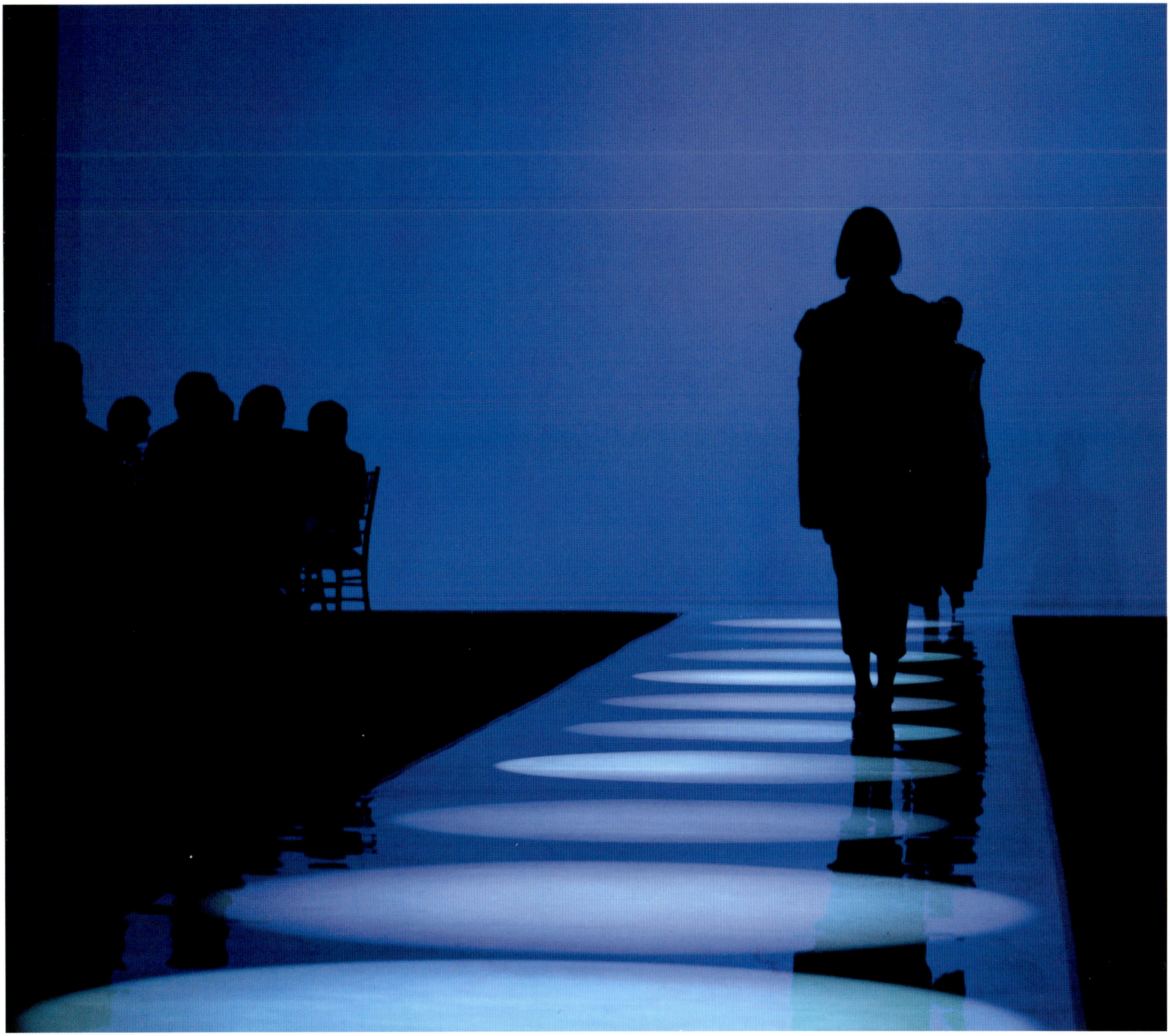

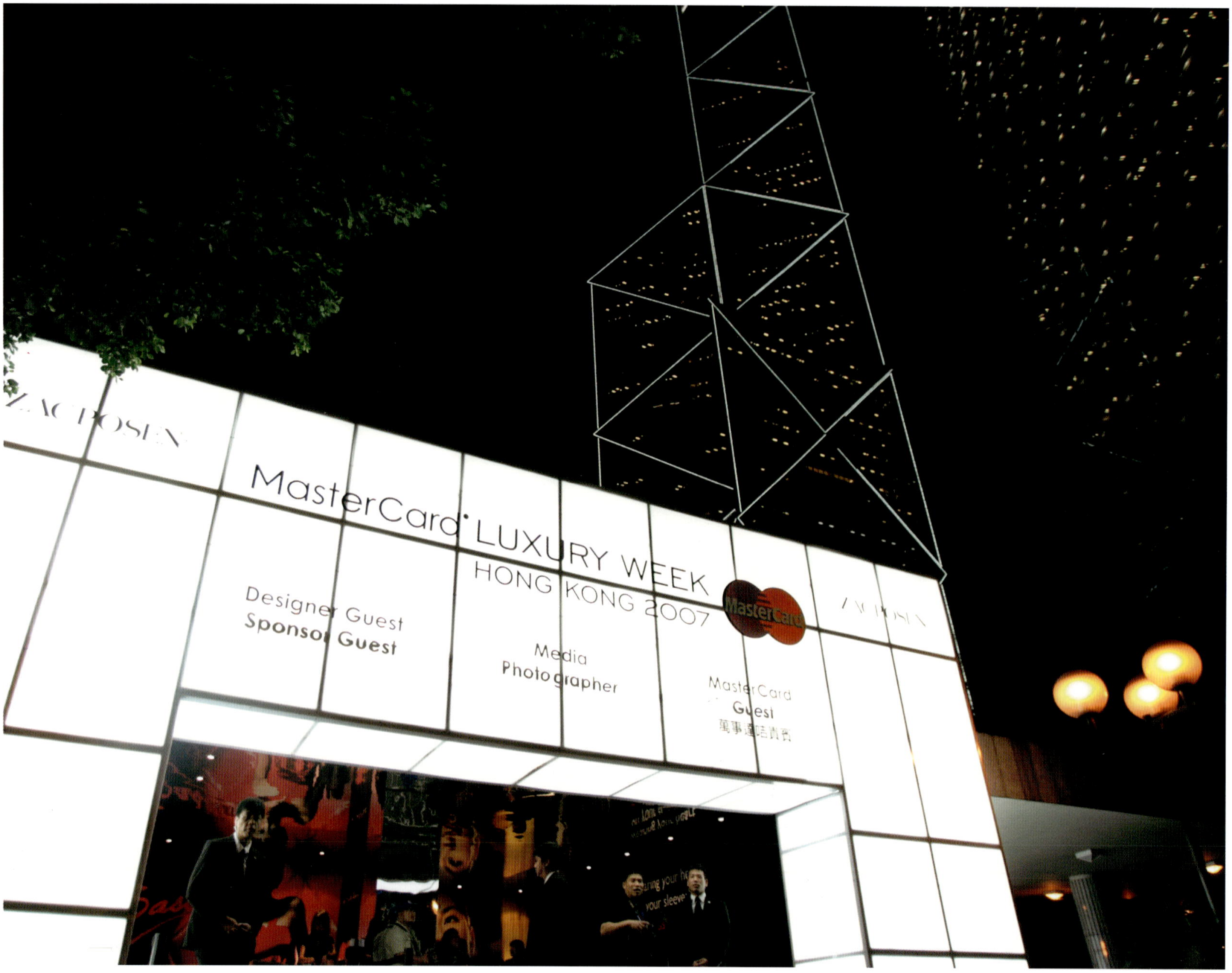
MasterCard® LUXURY WEEK
HONG KONG 2007
Designer Guest
Sponsor Guest
Media
Photographer
MasterCard
Guest

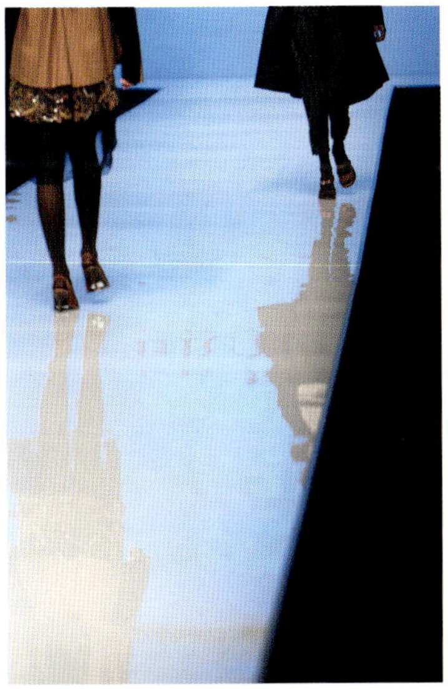

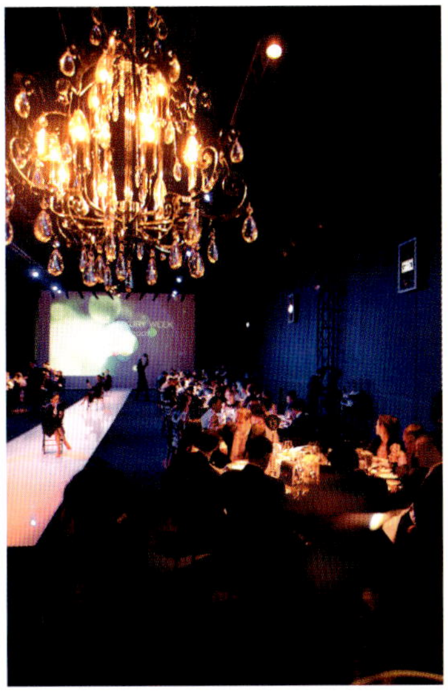

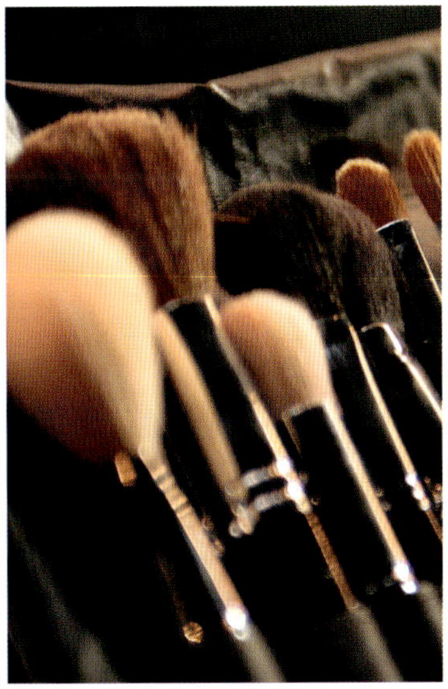

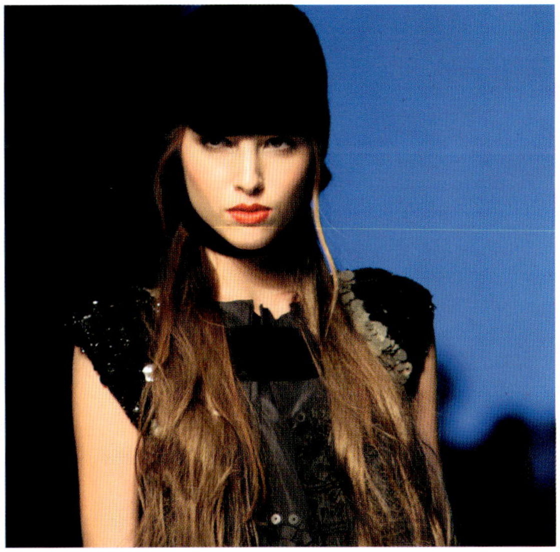

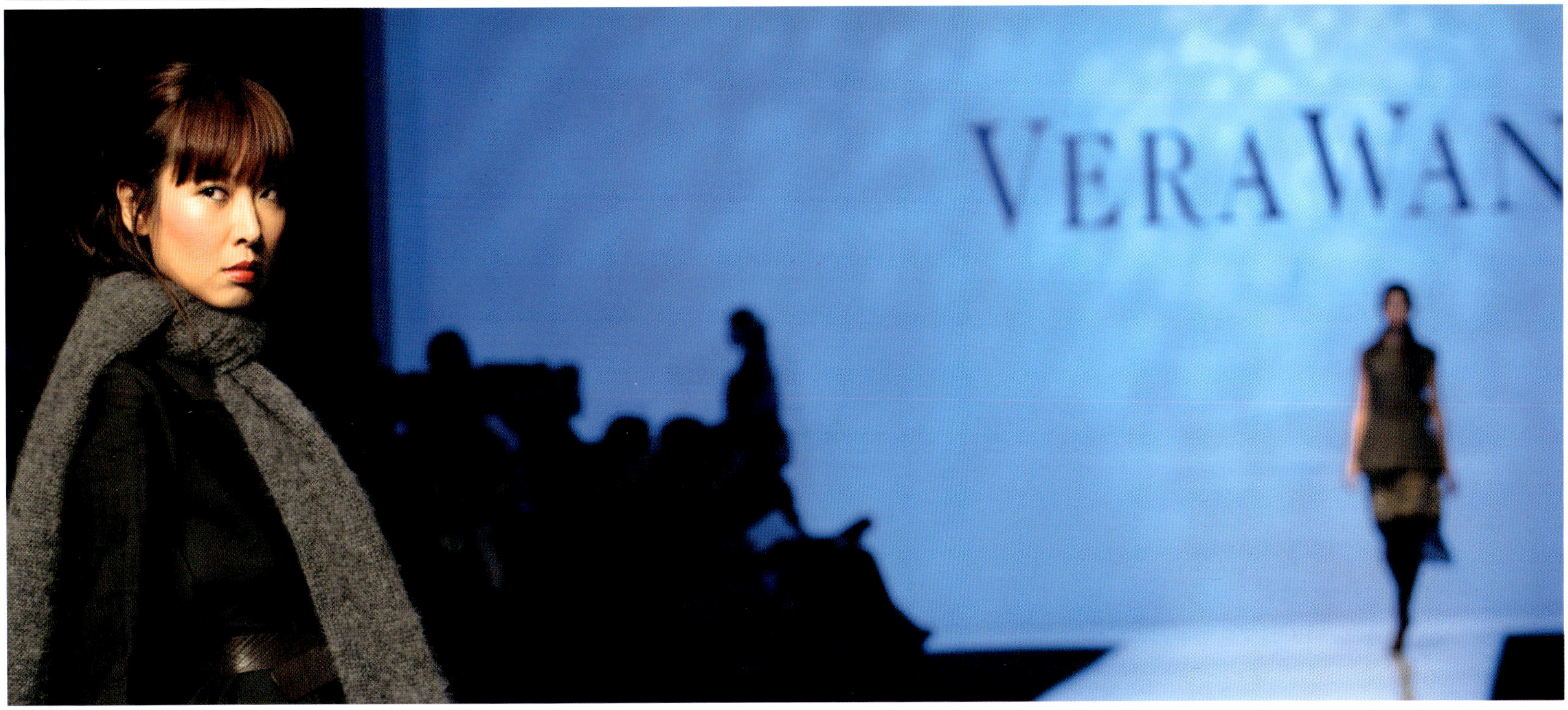
VERAWAN

Mercedes-Benz C-Class Launch

where Bangkok, Thailand

The introduction of the new Mercedes-Benz C-Class in Thailand was held at a prestigious hotel in Bangkok with an exhibition space of 1,985 sq. m.

The design theme was "Agility at Your Command." One of the main features was the enlarged letter "C" in huge light boxes which complemented both the elegantly finished fixtures and the automobiles on display. "C for Yourself" was the campaign slogan. Orange, white and black were used in combination with a striking lighting design to create a draw around the new models.

LED images and a special interactive video system showed the story behind the development of the C-Class and displayed the launch advertisements of the new cars.

A tactical website was created to complement the launch event, www.cforyourself.in.th, which served as a virtual showcase for the new C-Class and achieved excellent exposure.

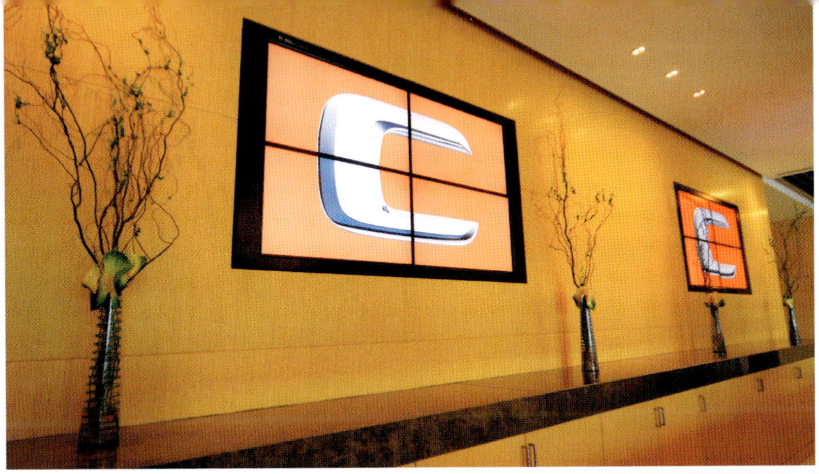

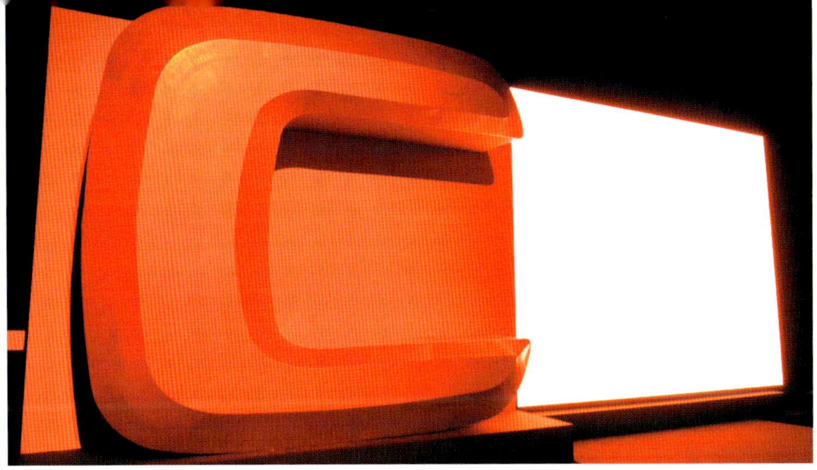

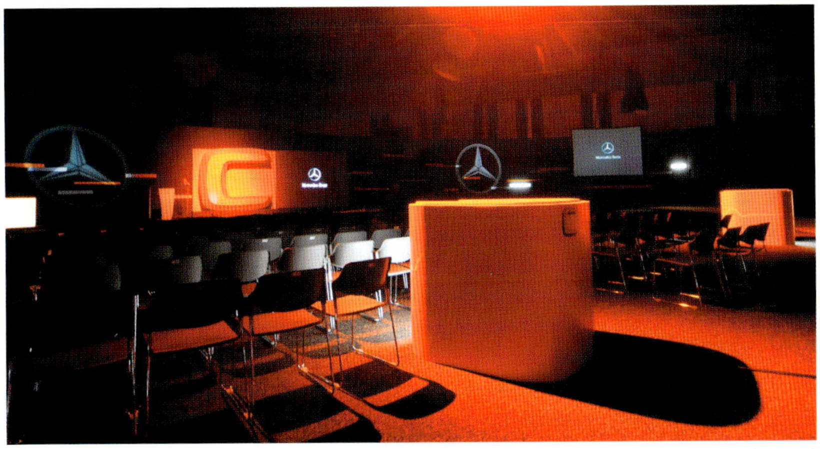

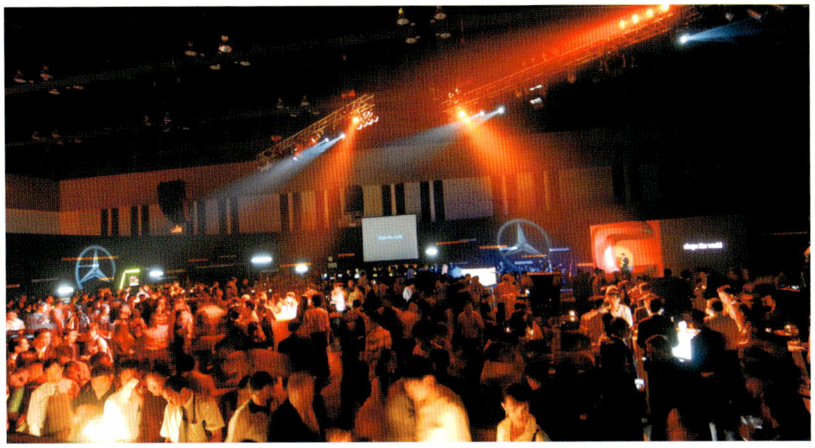

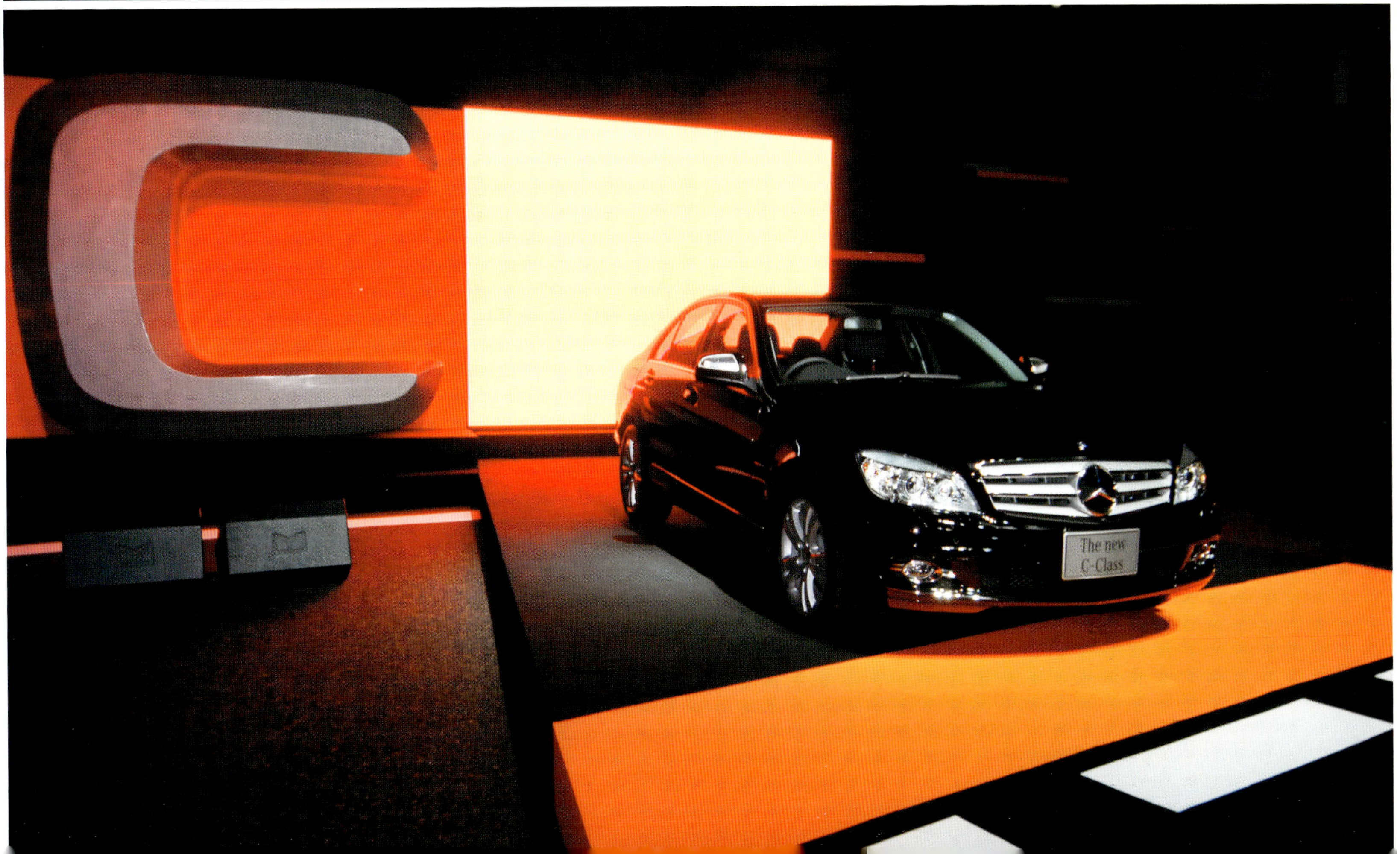
The new
C-Class

Singapore National Day Parade

where Singapore

To celebrate Singapore's 42nd birthday, a parade themed "City of Possibilities" was held in Marina Bay for the first time. The stage set was situated on the largest floating platform in the world. It transformed the new downtown into a bay of celebrations where people watched the parade from various vantage points along the waterfront.

The project team fabricated the orchestra pit, Presidential Dias, lighting towers and audio towers, and provided temporary seating and jetty complete with specialised painting and finished works. Many challenges were overcome. Taking into account the changing tide conditions, all aspects of safety were carefully considered. The massive stage, supporting 25m high towers on a floating platform, was built with dedicated efforts.

The parade retained the traditional parade favourites to entertain spectators. It also featured fresh performances that made use of waters in the bay and skies above as an extension of the stage. The Singapore skyline served as a dramatically lit giant backdrop.

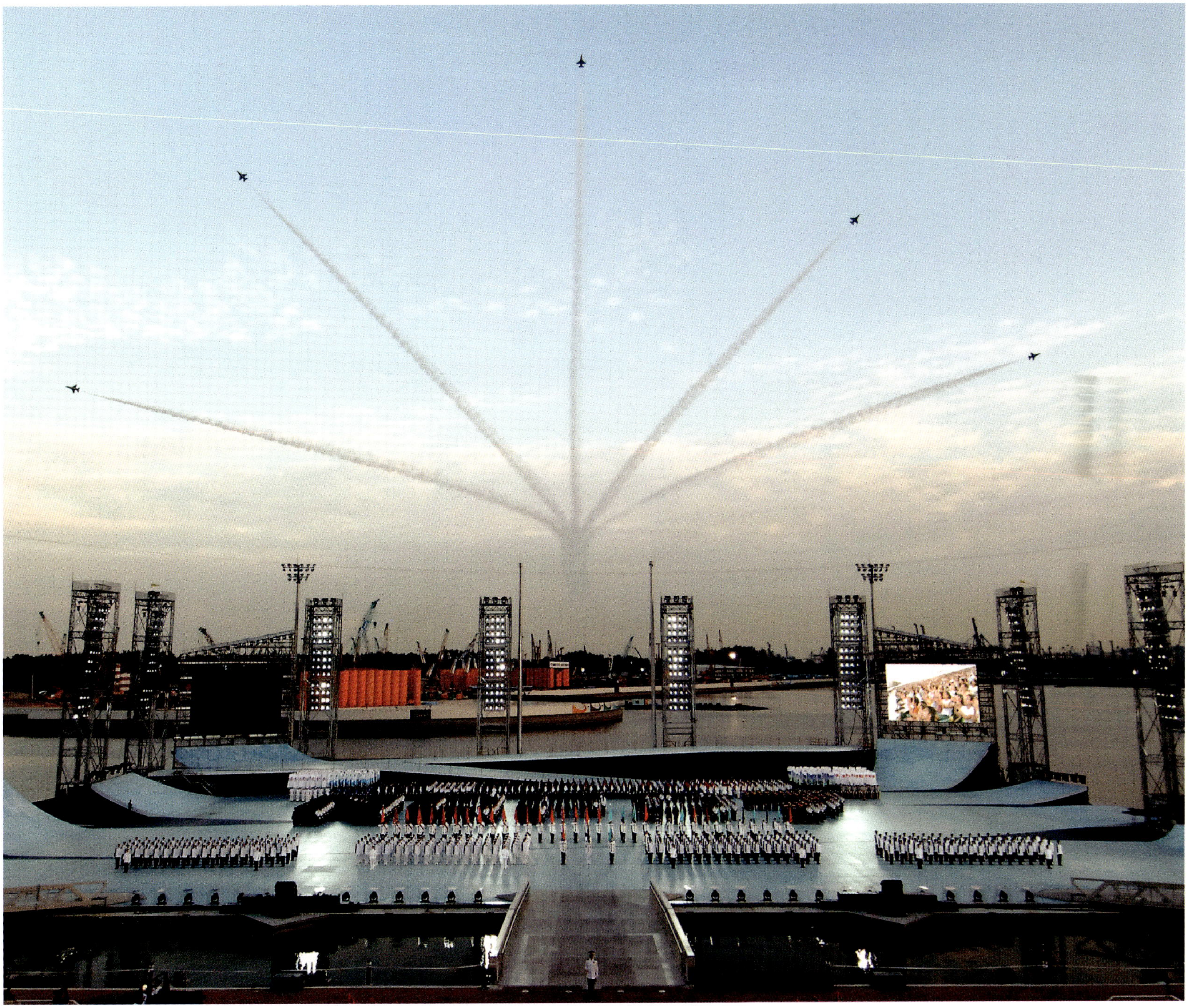

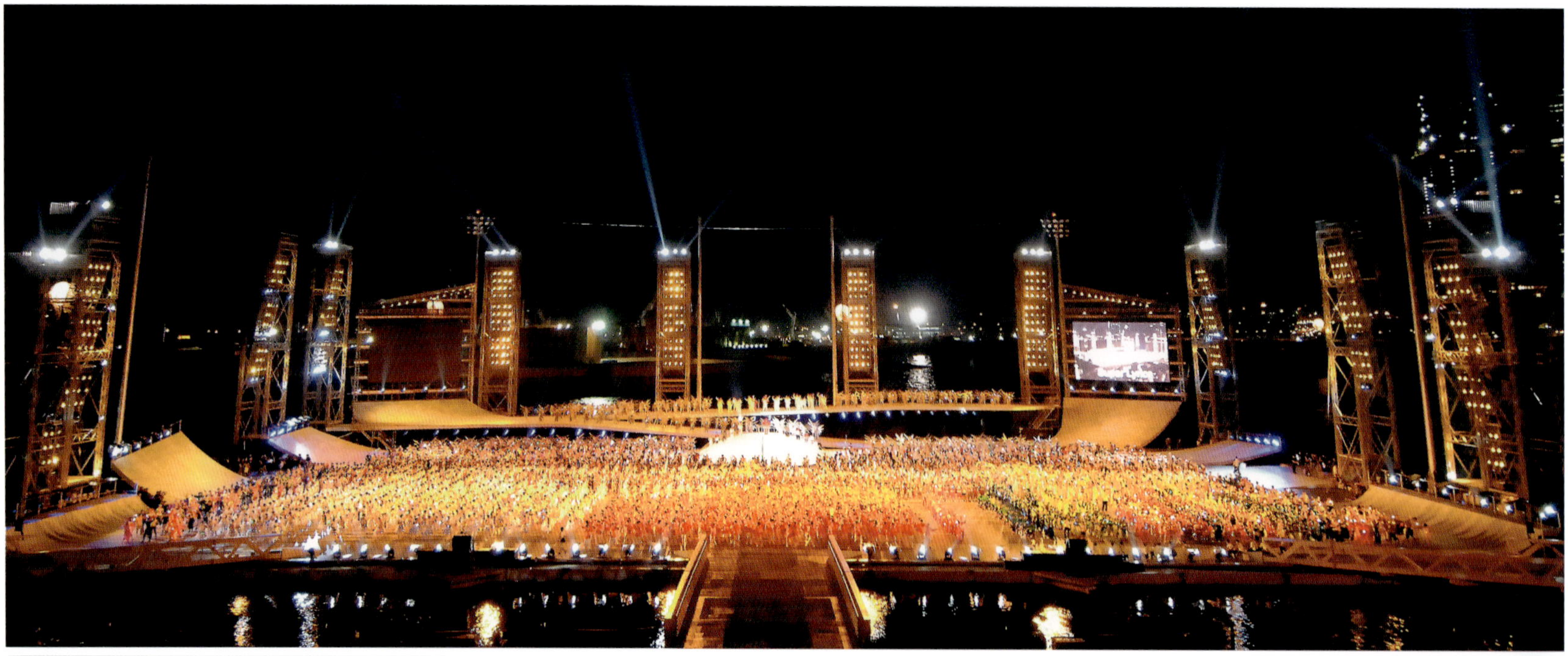

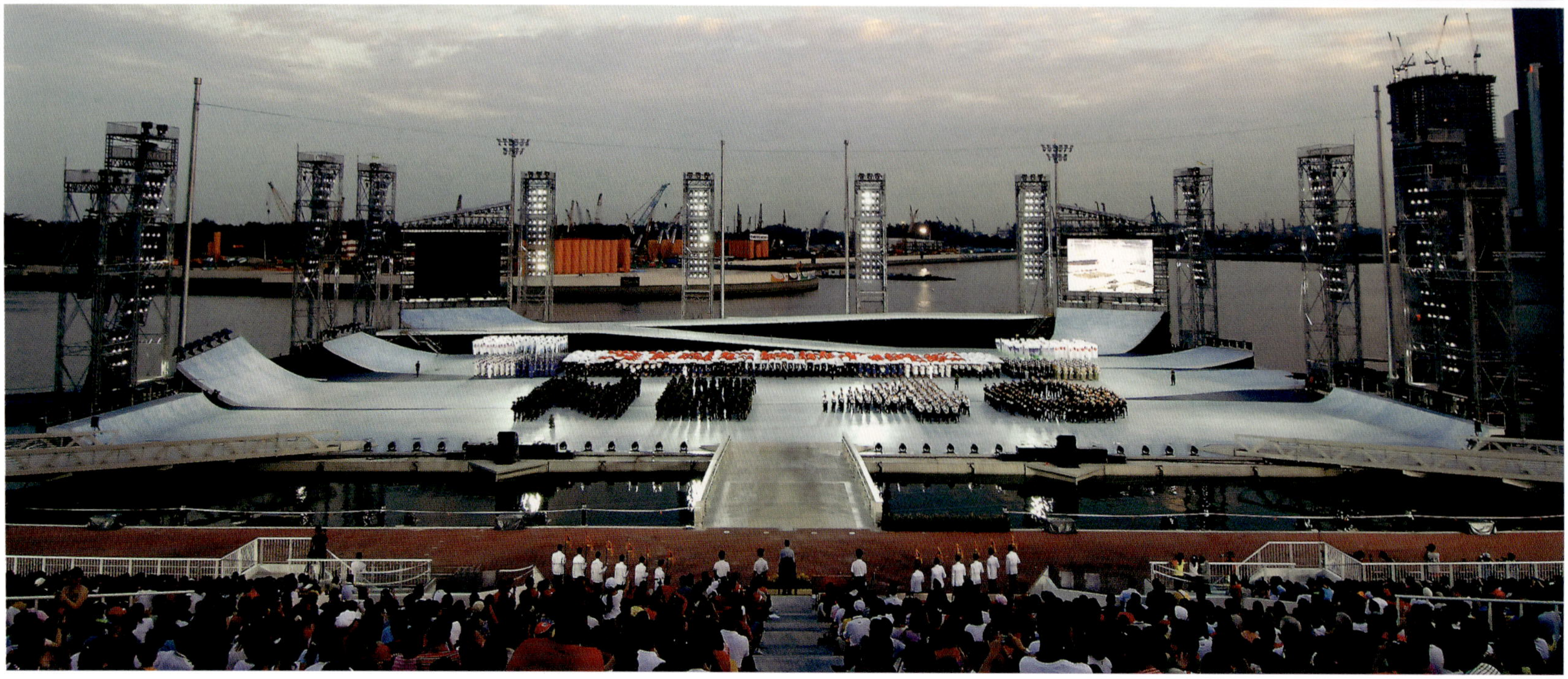

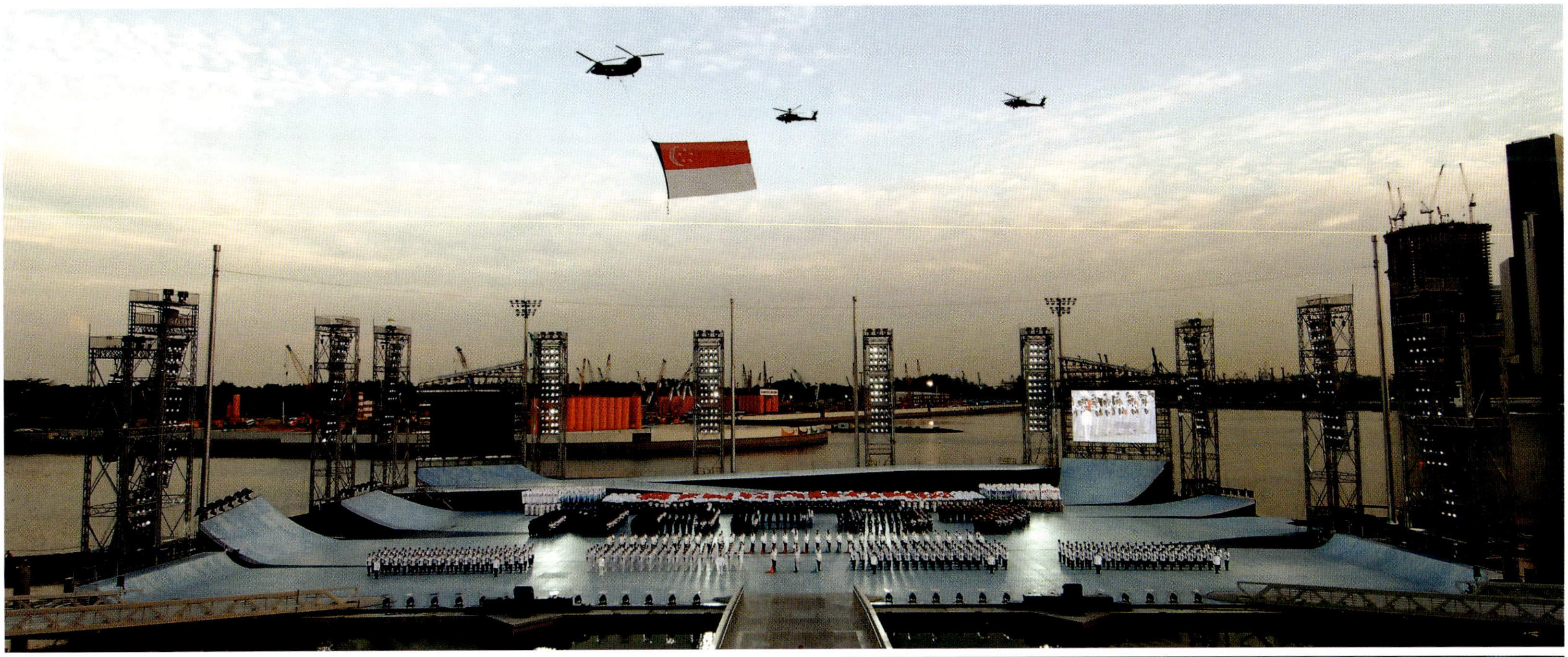

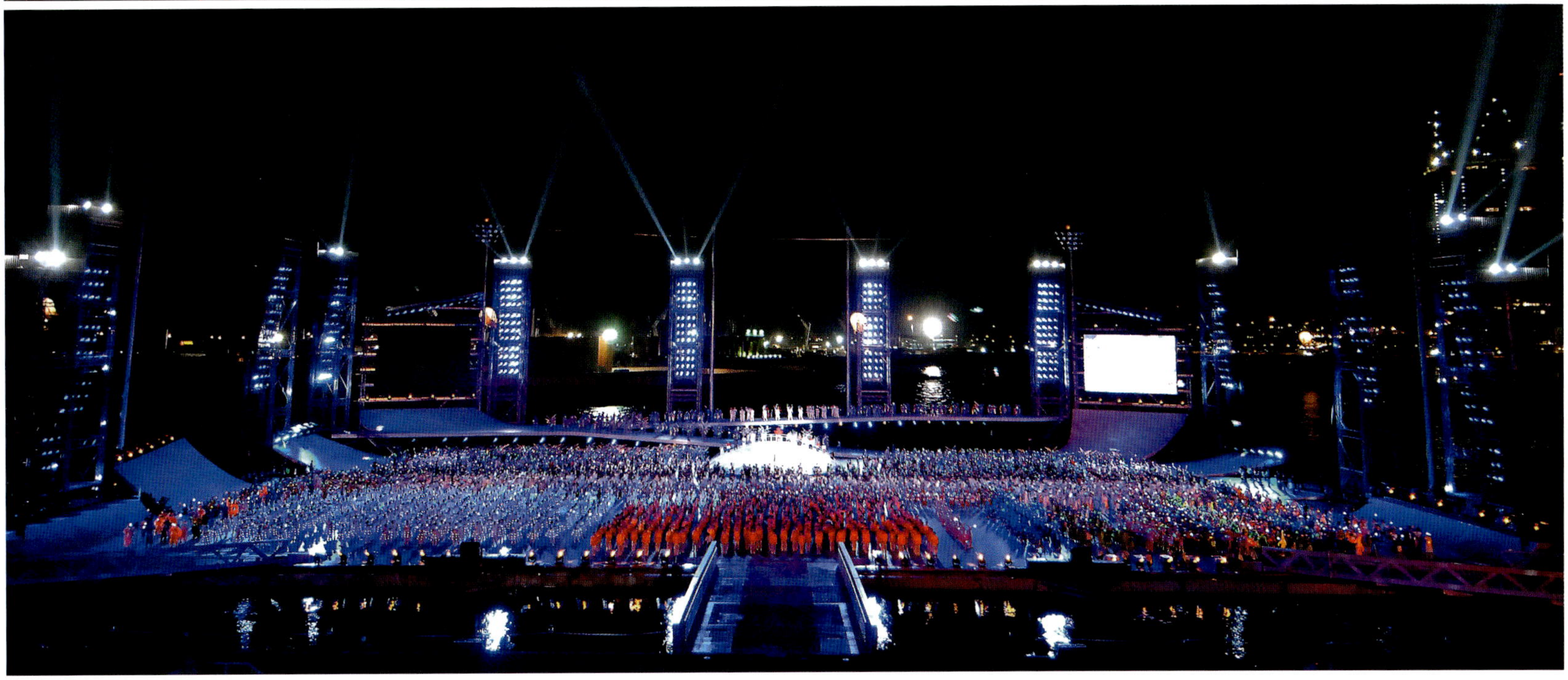

IMF and World Bank Group Annual Meetings

where Singapore

The International Monetary Fund and World Bank Boards of Governors Annual Meetings are traditionally the largest and most comprehensive gathering of financial decision makers in the world. An impressive venue was paramount.

The project team provided logistic and infrastructural support, which included the provision of 1,032 double-storey office suites, complete with interior design fitting, air-conditioning, lighting, electricity, and telephony for the 16,000 delegates attending the conference. This was the first time that the creative concept of two-storey offices were designed and adopted. The concept used to develop the construction of the offices was a Modular Unit System, utilising pre-fabricated panels and lightweight steel structures.

An additional 25 facilities were delivered which included the plenary stage, press centre, registration hall, security command, provision of large format banners and posters, signage works, temporary hoarding, furniture, equipment and supplies, landscaping, key installation and power supply.

The installation work was impressively completed in 45 days. Pico's effort was subsequently rewarded with a Bronze Award in the "Interior Builder" category from the Singapore Furniture Industries Council in recognition of excellence and contributions to interior design.

event. exhibit. interior. themed.

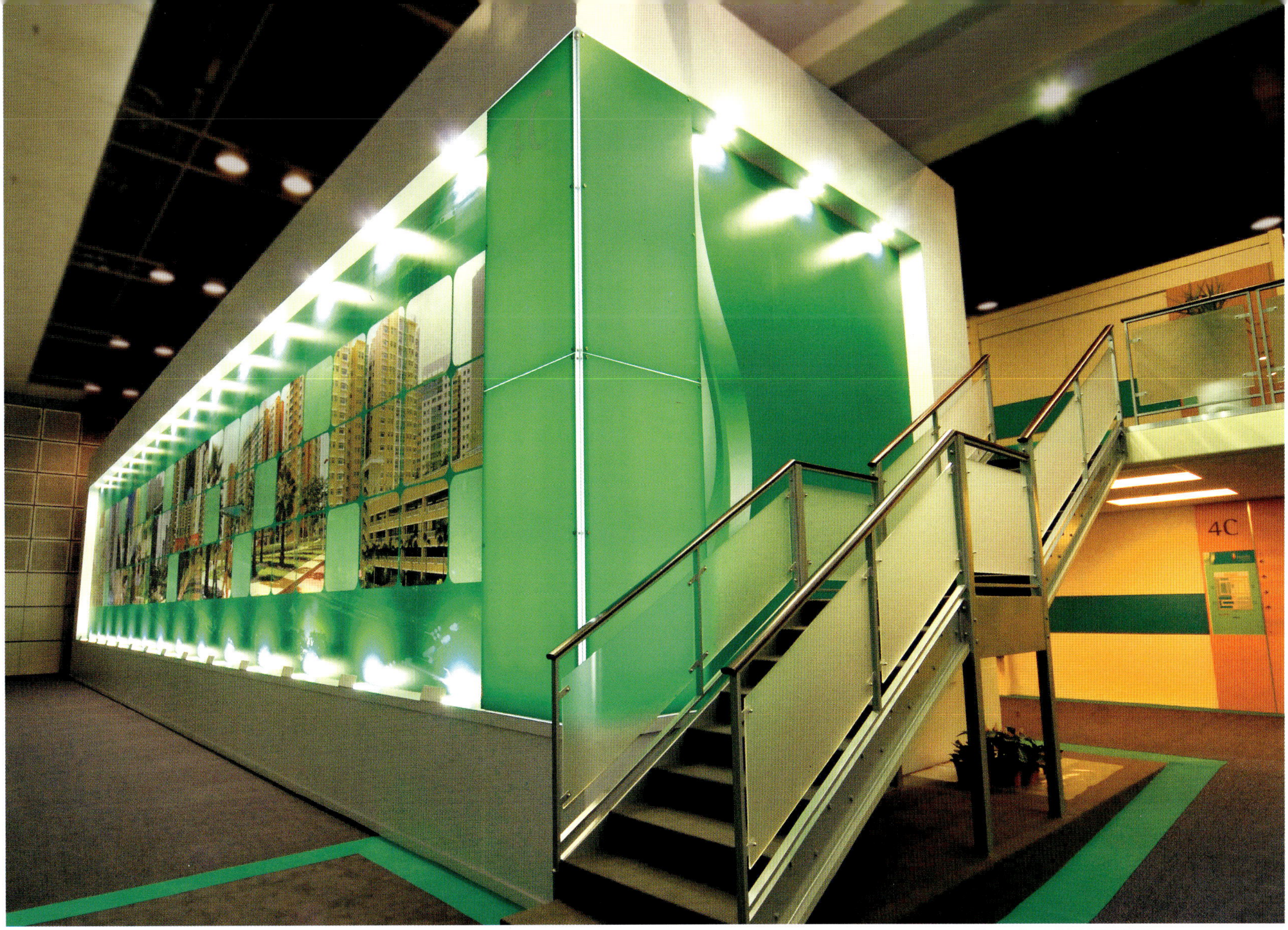
4C

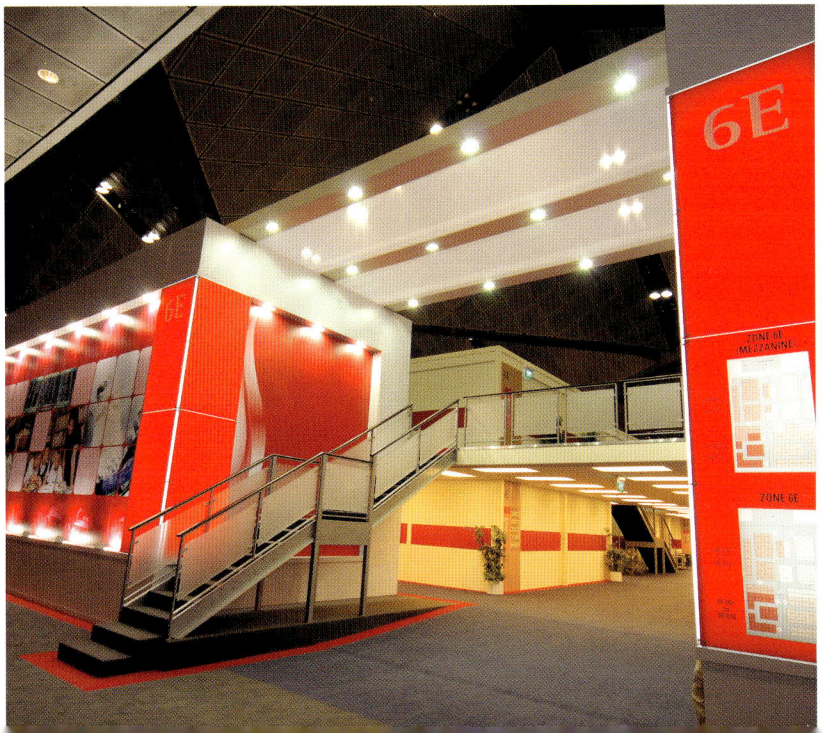
6E

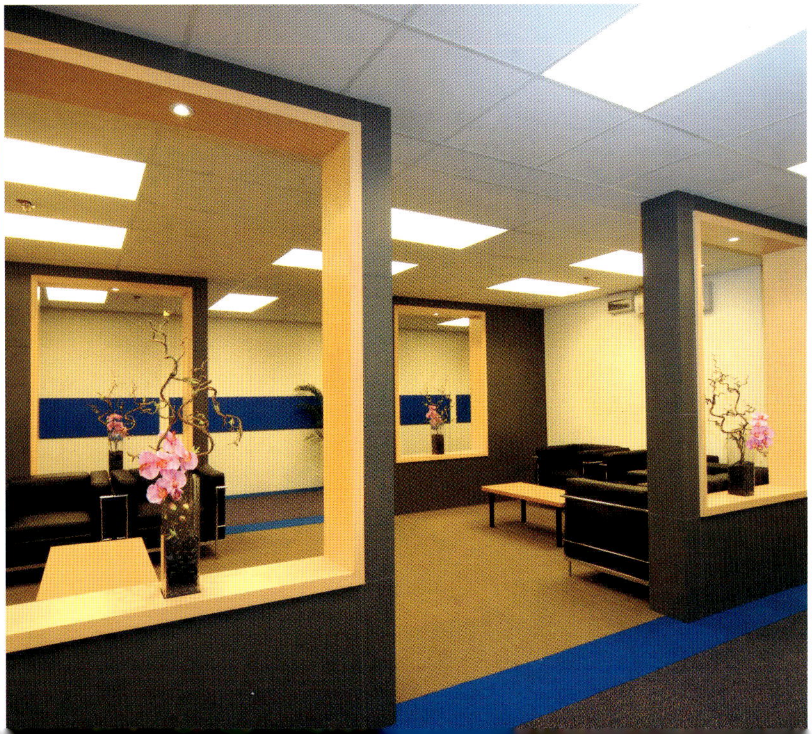

Caritas Bianchi Fashion Show

where Hong Kong SAR, China

Caritas Bianchi College of Careers targeted both students and the public to promote their graduate student work to the local business community.

"Bonz Simple" was the theme of the 2,500 sq. m. space in the Hong Kong Convention and Exhibition Centre. This was a tribute to Bonz, the chief designer for this project. His symbolic trademark is based on the philosophy of simplicity is always the best way to design. Creation of a space always starts from a simple idea.

Paper, cut with irregular and geometric dots, lines and faces, was the visual thread throughout the space. Within a single white atmosphere with spotlights, the pieces of paper were positioned on the wall. The paper also served as a foil to project students' creative ideas. To highlight the outstanding designs, a combination of conventional and unconventional materials was employed.

The space included an exhibition booth, a central area dedicated to displays and a stage for fashion shows. The creative use of lighting and imaginative graphics resulted in a tight design that carried the flair of the fashion event.

FASHION <
< INTERIOR
GRAPHIC >

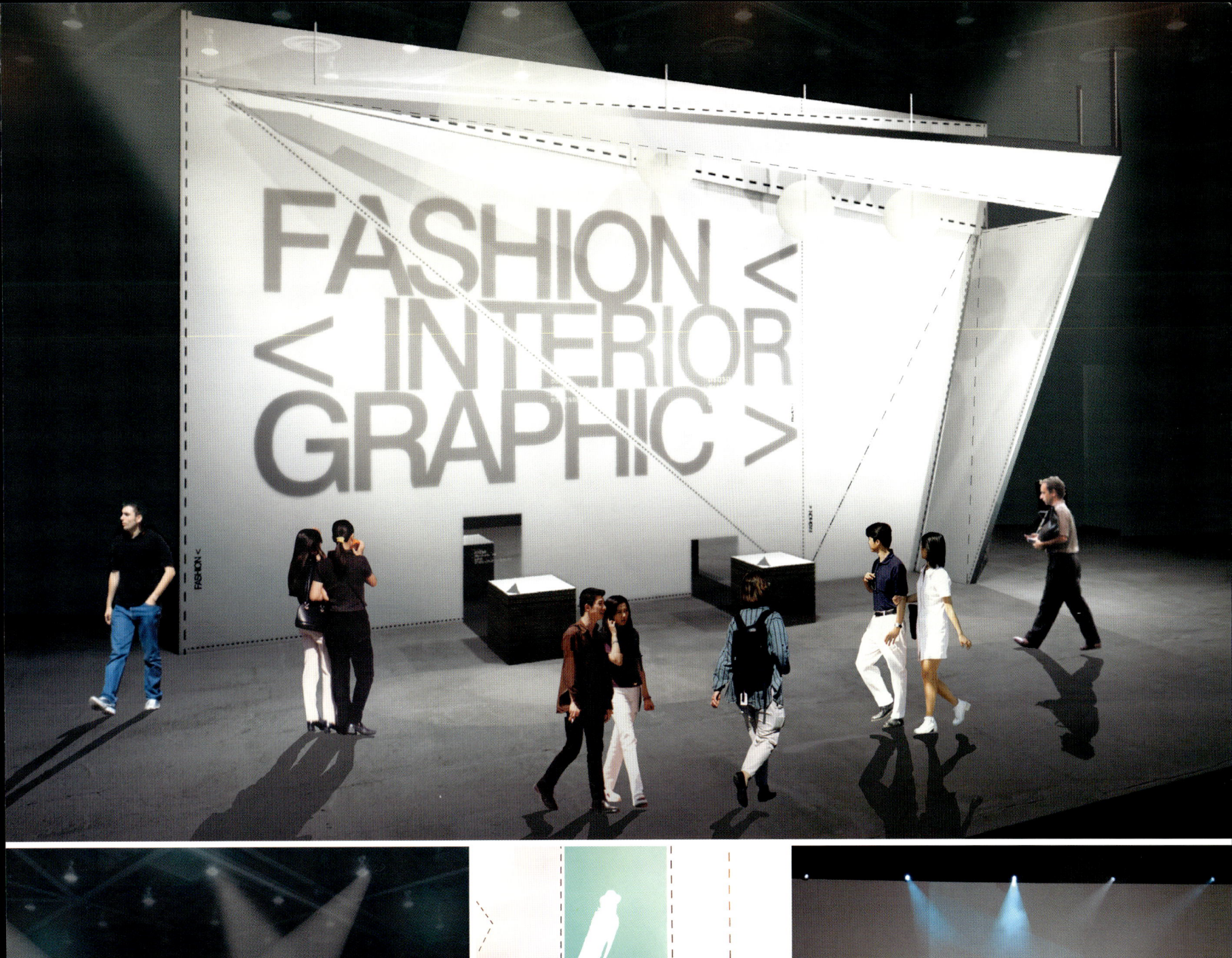

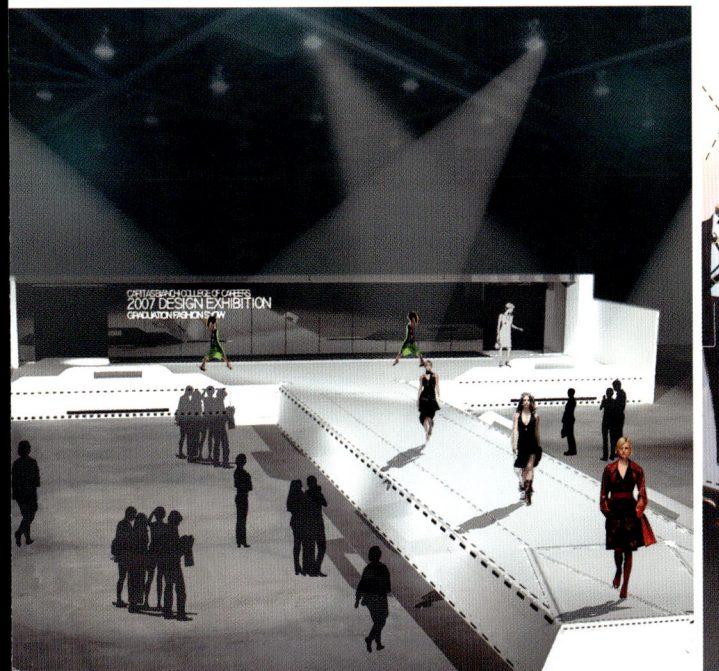

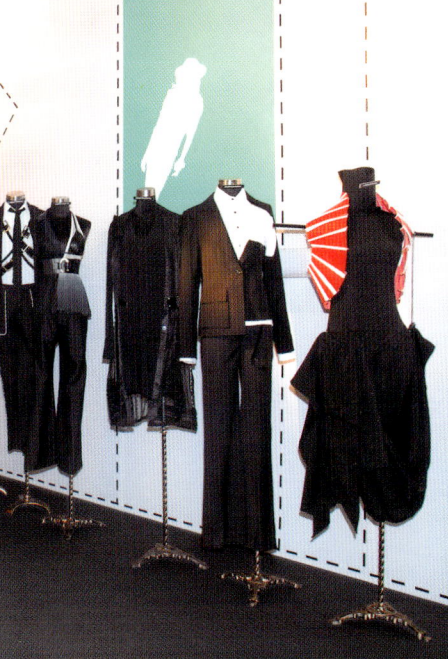

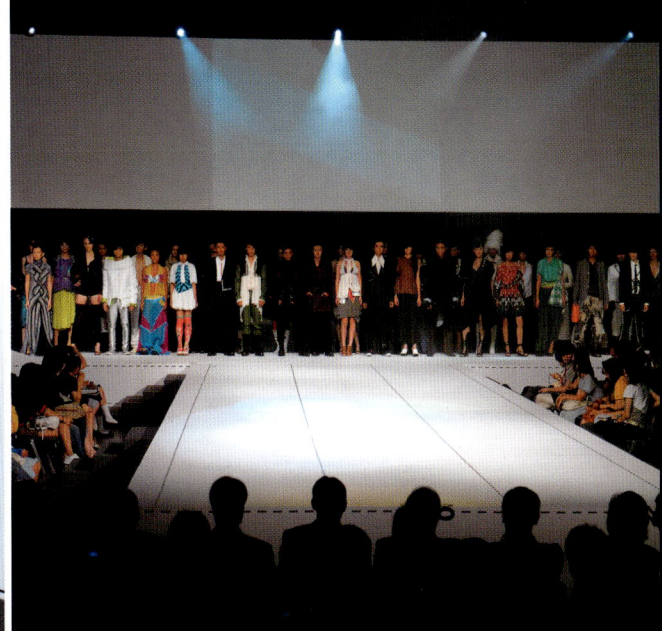

Chinese New Year Parade

where Hong Kong SAR, China

The annual Chinese New Year Parade is organised by the Hong Kong Tourism Board. In the past ten years, it has become one of the city's most important attractions for visitors from around the world and is broadcast in many countries. Pico has been the official event manager for many years.

The event management team was required to coordinate numerous government departments and external suppliers, managing the creation of special effects, decorations and other detailed logistics. The work was done in conjunction with production coordinators, design specialists and lighting consultants, which included projections, videos, and a special lighting system for a choreographed lighting show.

Special attention was paid to the parade route, divided into seven zones characterised by special colours and creative designs. The parade was organised with the participation of sponsors' floats. "Discover Sparkling Hong Kong," "Cherry Blossom Symbolises Springtime in Japan" and "Streamlined Bullet Parade Float" were brought to life through the lights and performers. Sparkling colours, musical fanfares, festive costumes and live performances created a memorable celebration for spectators and TV audiences.

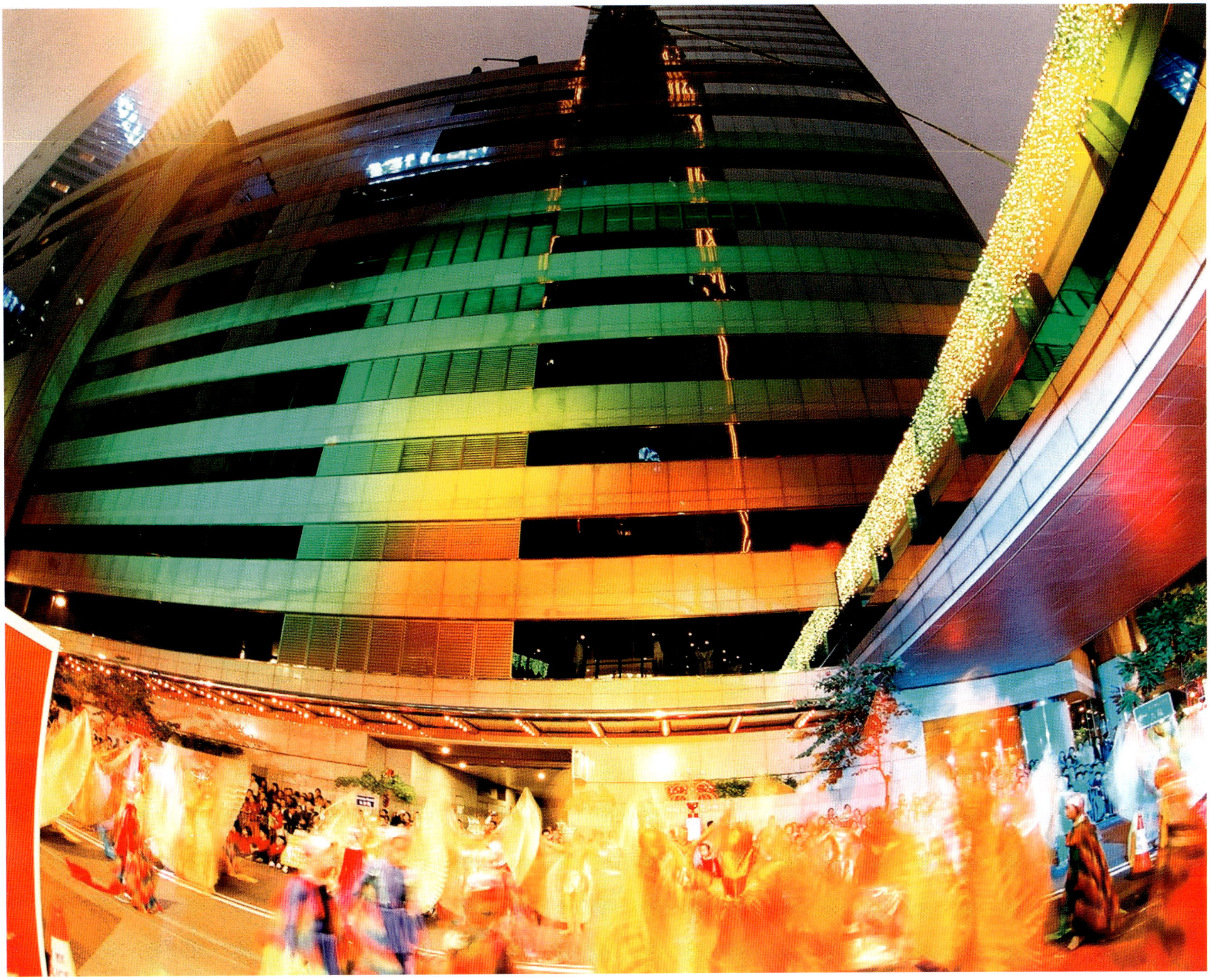

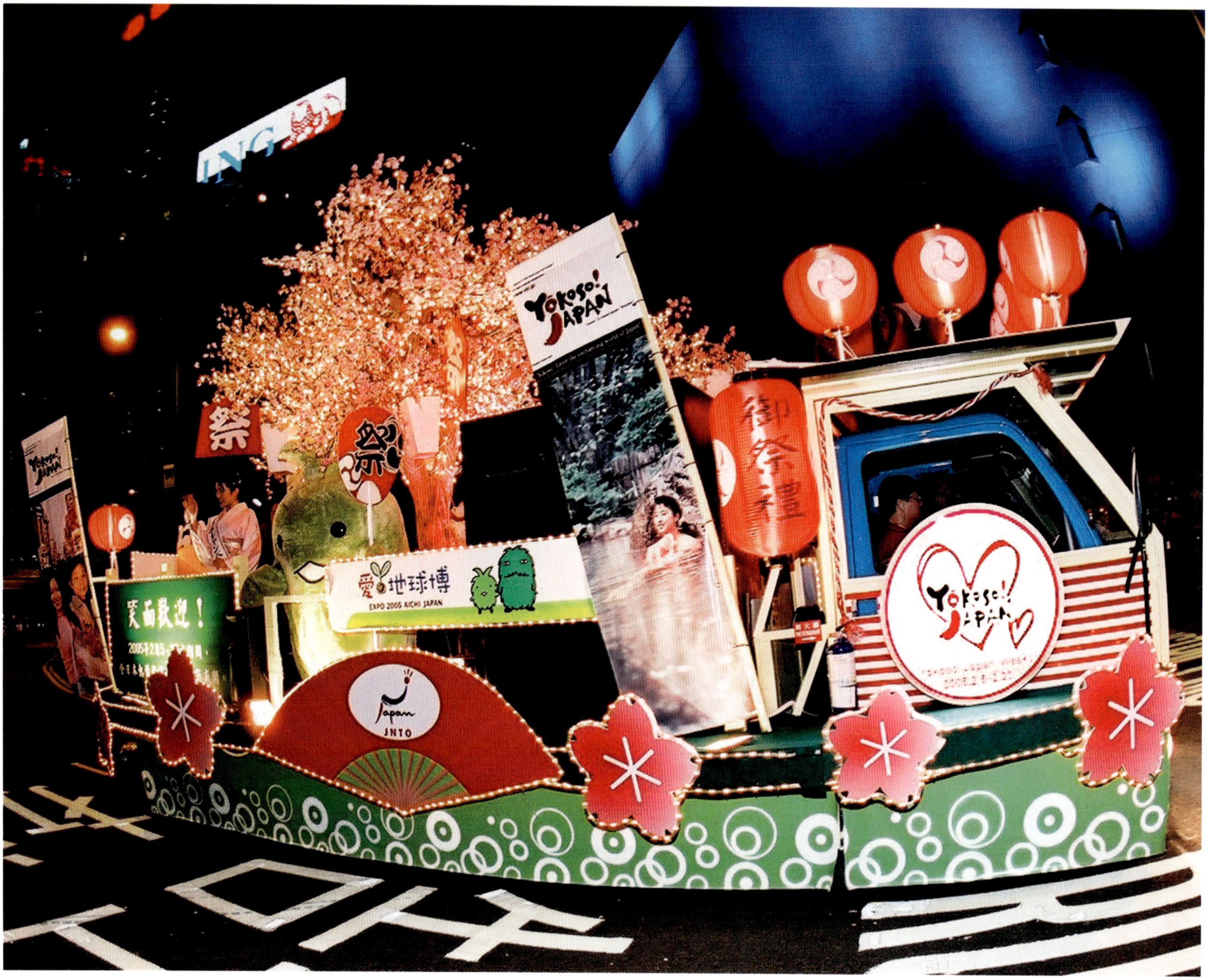
ING
Yokoso! JAPAN
祭
御祭禮
笑面歡迎！
愛地球博
EXPO 2005 AICHI JAPAN
Japan
JNTO

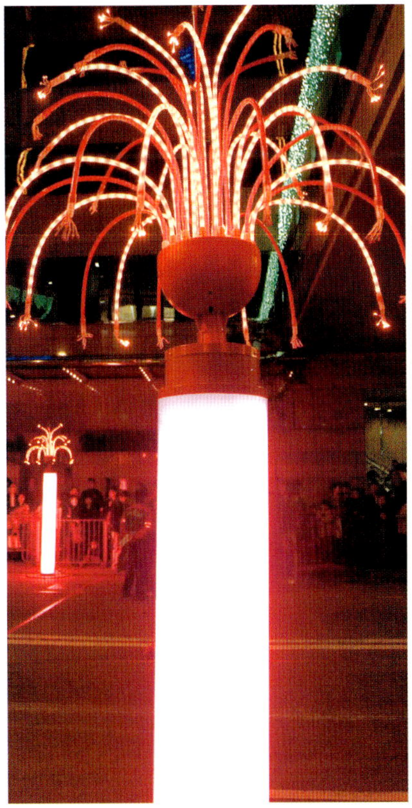

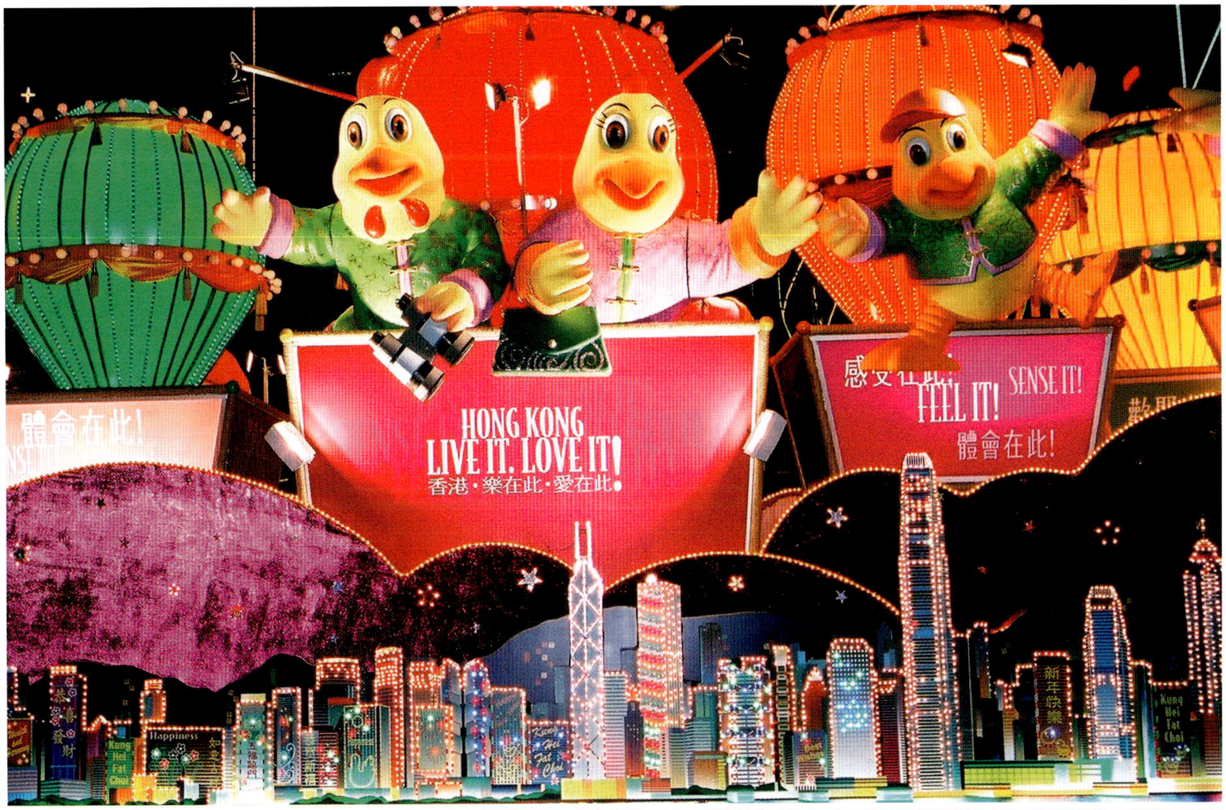
HONG KONG
LIVE IT. LOVE IT!
香港・樂在此・愛在此!
FEEL IT!
SENSE IT!
體會在此!
體會在此!
Happiness
Kung Hei Fat Choi

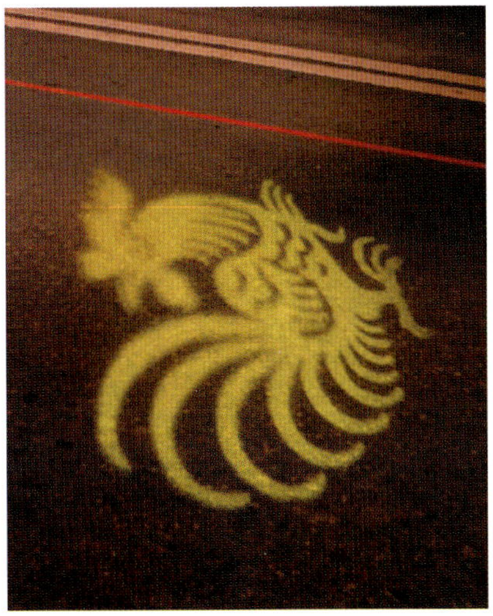

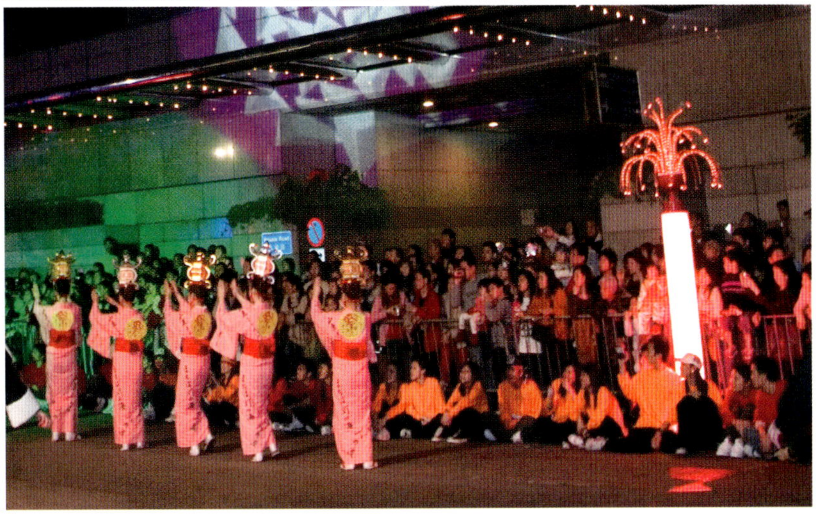

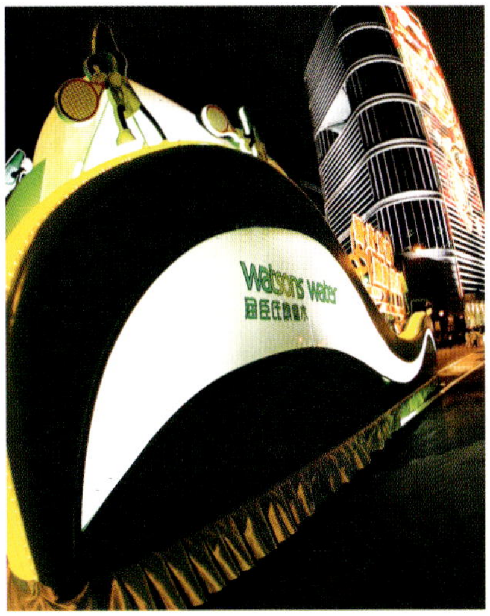
watsons water

GE Money at Money Fair

where Bangkok, Thailand

In a space of 150 sq. m. at the Money Expo, GE Money held a successful event that achieved its marketing objectives as well as demonstrated its unmatched position in the investment industry.

To generate interest and foot traffic, the design was skilfully arranged in a cleverly distinctive structure with mirror laminates. This created an eye-appealing reflective effect in white and blue. The booth was illuminated with a system of lanterns, which enhanced the onlookers' experience at the shows and performances taking place in the exhibit.

A comprehensive line-up of performances entertained and engaged visitors. The restricted and small space available for the exhibit showcased not only the client's products but also the designer's ability and competence. The design team won the "Money and Banking Magazine" prize for the best designed area.

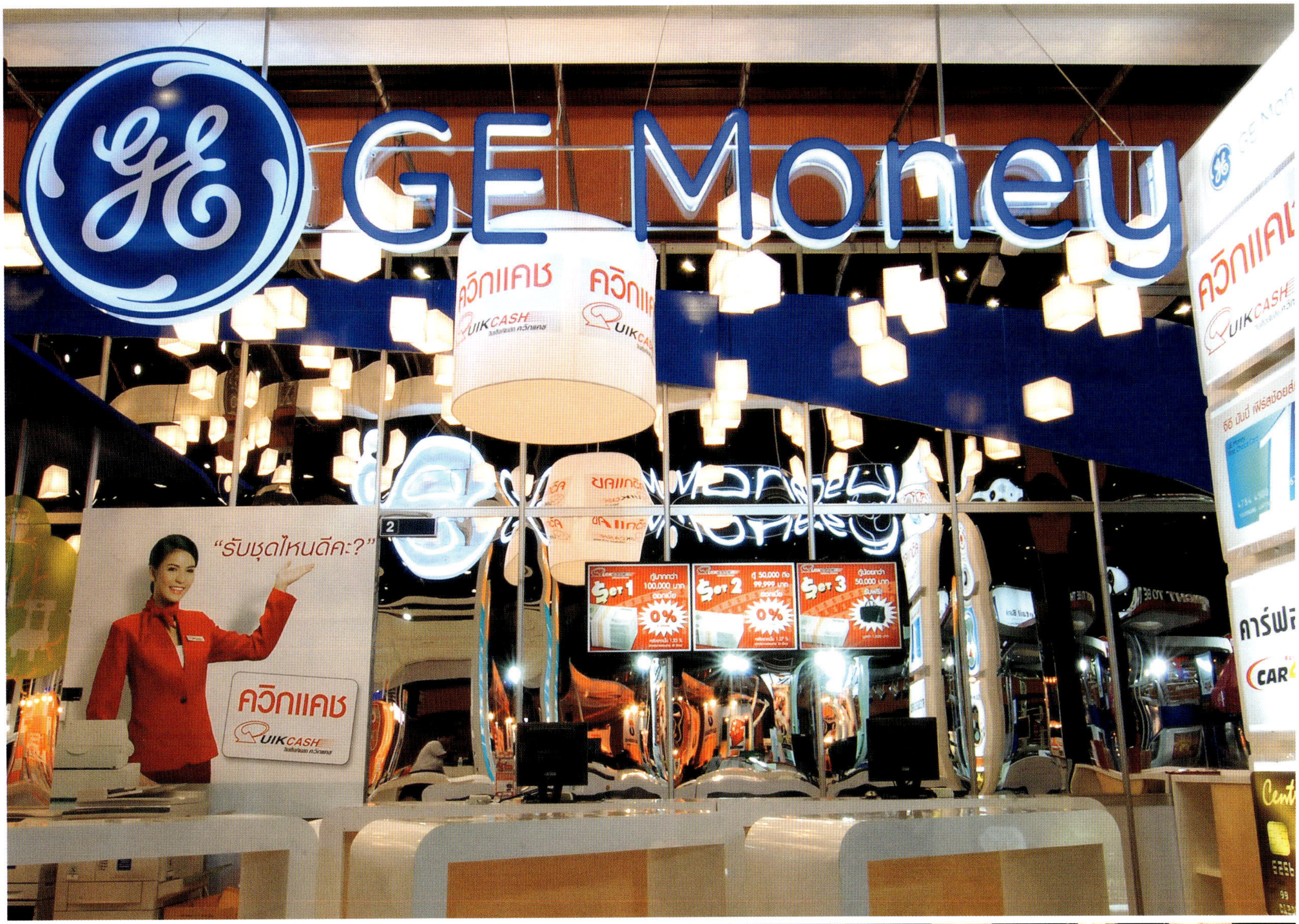
GE Money
ควิกแคช
QUIKCASH
“รับชุดไหนดีคะ?”
ควิกแคช
QUIKCASH

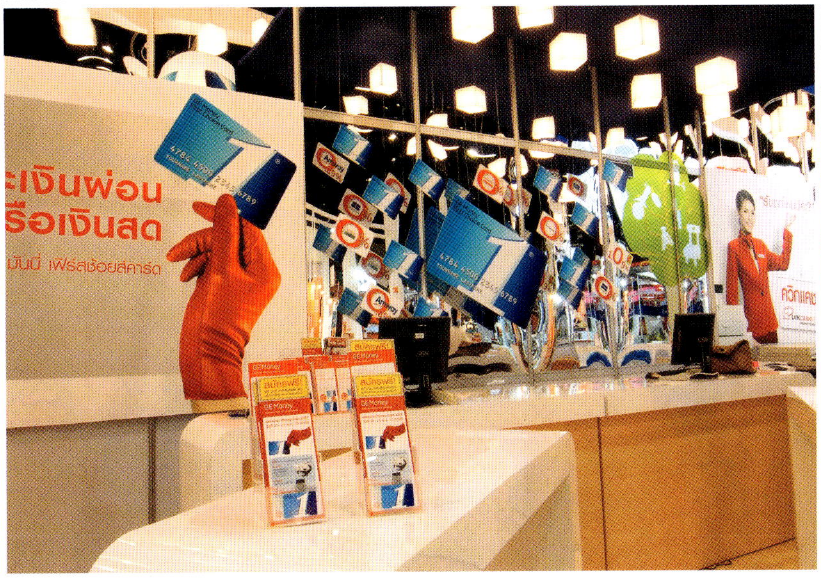

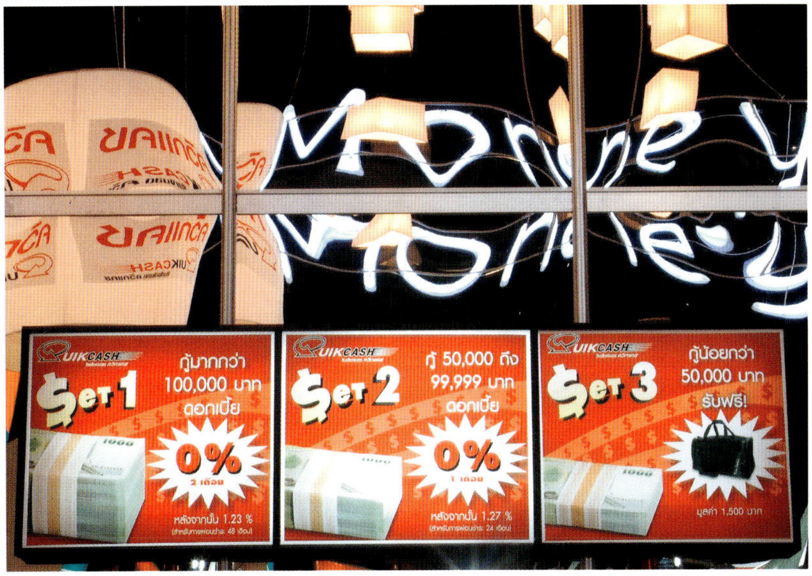
QUIKCASH
Set 1
กู้มากกว่า 100,000 บาท ดอกเบี้ย
0%
2 เดือน
หลังจากนั้น 1.23 %
(สำหรับการผ่อนชำระ 48 เดือน)
QUIKCASH
Set 2
กู้ 50,000 ถึง 99,999 บาท ดอกเบี้ย
0%
1 เดือน
หลังจากนั้น 1.27 %
(สำหรับการผ่อนชำระ 24 เดือน)
QUIKCASH
Set 3
กู้น้อยกว่า 50,000 บาท รับฟรี!
มูลค่า 1,500 บาท

Trade shows have not only grown in importance and in size, but they are now an international phenomenon. No longer is it only the U.S. and Germany and a few other countries that dominate the world's trade show scene, it is happening in India, China, Singapore, Japan and the entire Pacific Rim. The main purpose of a trade show exhibit is to present and promote the brand in a face-to-face setting. Even when there is no product / service presented, the exhibition promotes the ideas and values of the sponsor such as the case for The Daodejing for the Hong Kong Taoist Association.

The design of an exhibition stand is in some ways similar to the design of a retail store; a blend of style, function and showmanship. The graphics, signage, and exterior of the booth are similar to a store's facade with a giant display window giving glimpse to what lies inside. It's the first impression and introduction to the brand and image. Just as the designer of a retail store must consider traffic patterns, special layout, fixtures and furnishings, colours, textures and lighting, an exhibit designer must also combine these elements into a suitable setting for the client. It means understanding the client's needs for both private and public spaces, an area for self-discovery or for entertaining, food and drink and important conversations. All this has to be accomplished within the confines of the rigid regulations of the industry, the convention centre or even the local government.

Seventy sq. m. or 2,600 sq. m. – single storey or multi-storey – Pico does them all and with the same devotion to detail, graphics, lighting and special effects. Whether it's creating unique fixtures and props to create interaction, or a live theatre for presentations, or relaxed ambiance for high level conferencing, Pico's talented group is up to the challenge. Pico executed a gigantic, three-dimensional ceiling wrapped in Warlon sheeting over the NEC booth requiring special analysis and engineering to construct. In order to display 20 autos in the two-storey, 1,584 sq. m. Chevrolet booth, special raised platforms were constructed and various lighting techniques were used to heighten the effect of the presentation. This exhibit won a Best Stand Design award for Pico as did the 72 sq. m. booth for Micron Eyewear and the double-storey exhibit with soaring ceiling designed for Mercedes-Benz.

The clients vary, the subject matter and the products and services are all different, but Pico's clients all come to a trade show or exhibition hall to make a statement. Pico helps them deliver their messages and along the way garners more and more design awards.

Martin M. Pegler

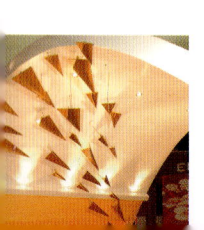

exhibit.

National Science and Technology Fair

where Bangkok, Thailand

For the National Science and Technology Fair 2007 in Bangkok, the Ministry of Science and Technology required the design and construction of a 40,000 sq. m. exhibition. The event hosted a total of 1.2 million visitors, including a large number of students and educators.

The space was divided into four main highlight areas: the Royal Pavilions for King Rama IV and King Rama IX, the Global Warming Pavilion and the Sustainable Energy Pavilion.

The King Rama IV area was approximately 800 sq. m. In a darkened and luminous golden atmosphere, a half-sphere shaped planetarium projected the King's biography in VDO. At the King Rama IX area of 1,700 sq. m., white and gold dominated the space. The multimedia and interactive presentations educated and entertained visitors.

The Global Warming Pavilion was 2,500 sq. m. in size. A 4-D theatre was created with special effects which included real floods, heat waves and smoke.

The Sustainable Energy Pavilion, measuring 1,800 sq. m., was designed in red, white and black. A pathway leading through the area featured displays that heightened awareness of the world's energy crisis and alternative energy sources.

The effective and exciting multimedia was easy to understand for children as well as adults, creating a unique educational experience for visitors of all ages.

event. exhibit. interior. themed.

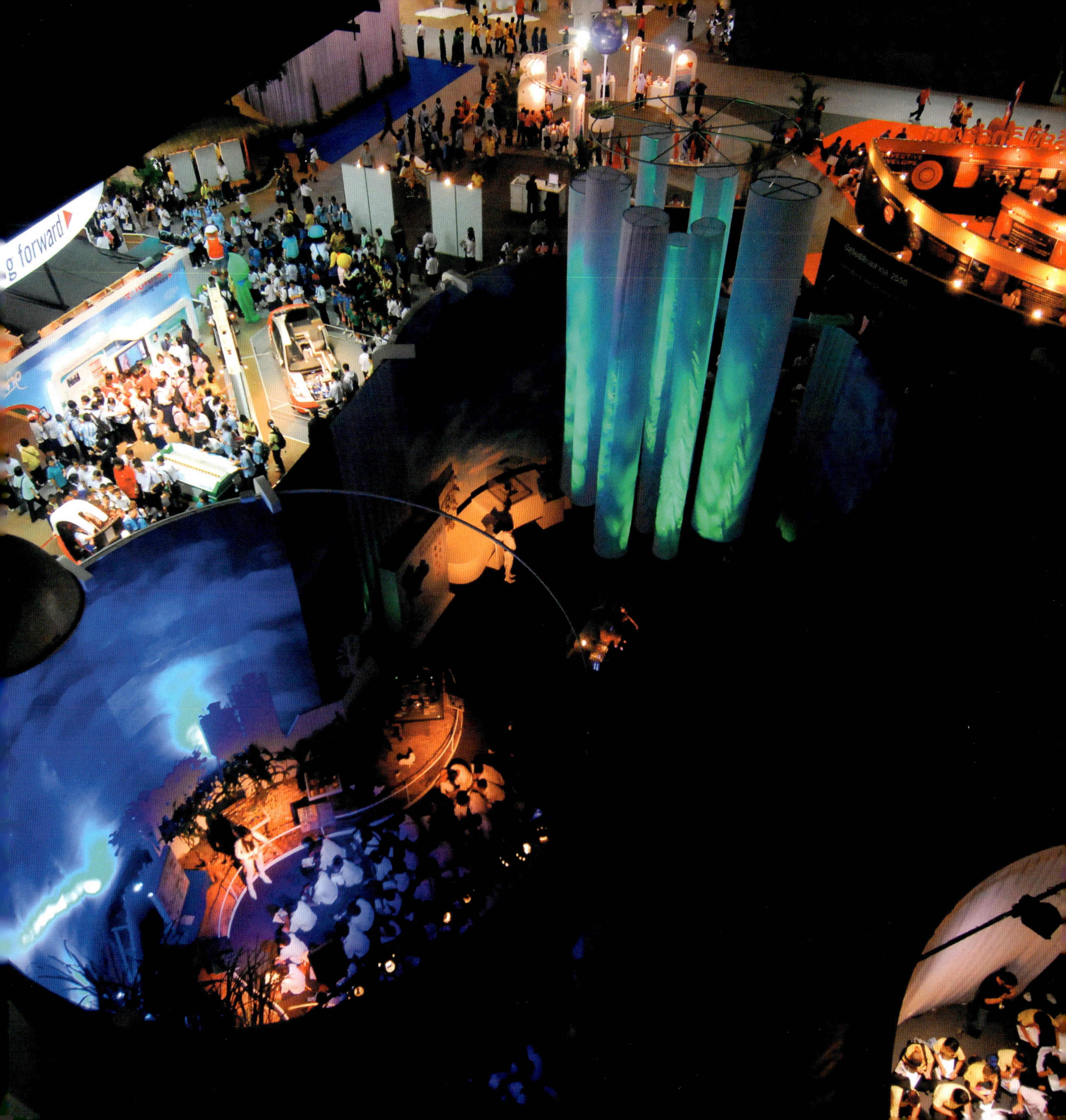
g forward

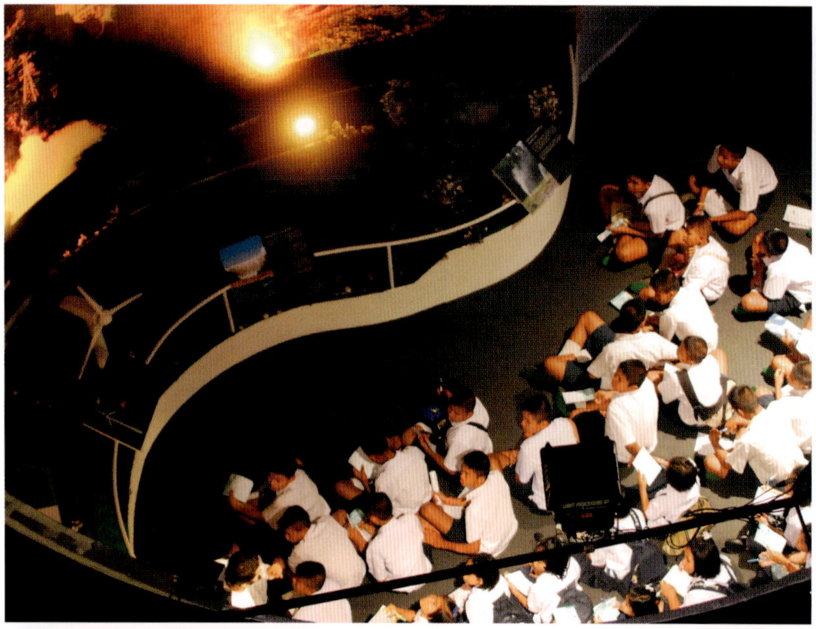

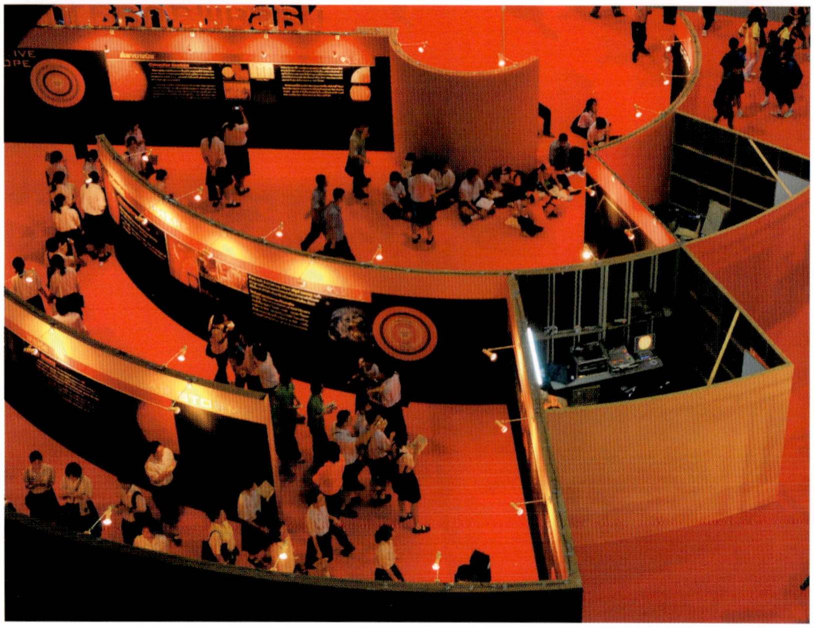

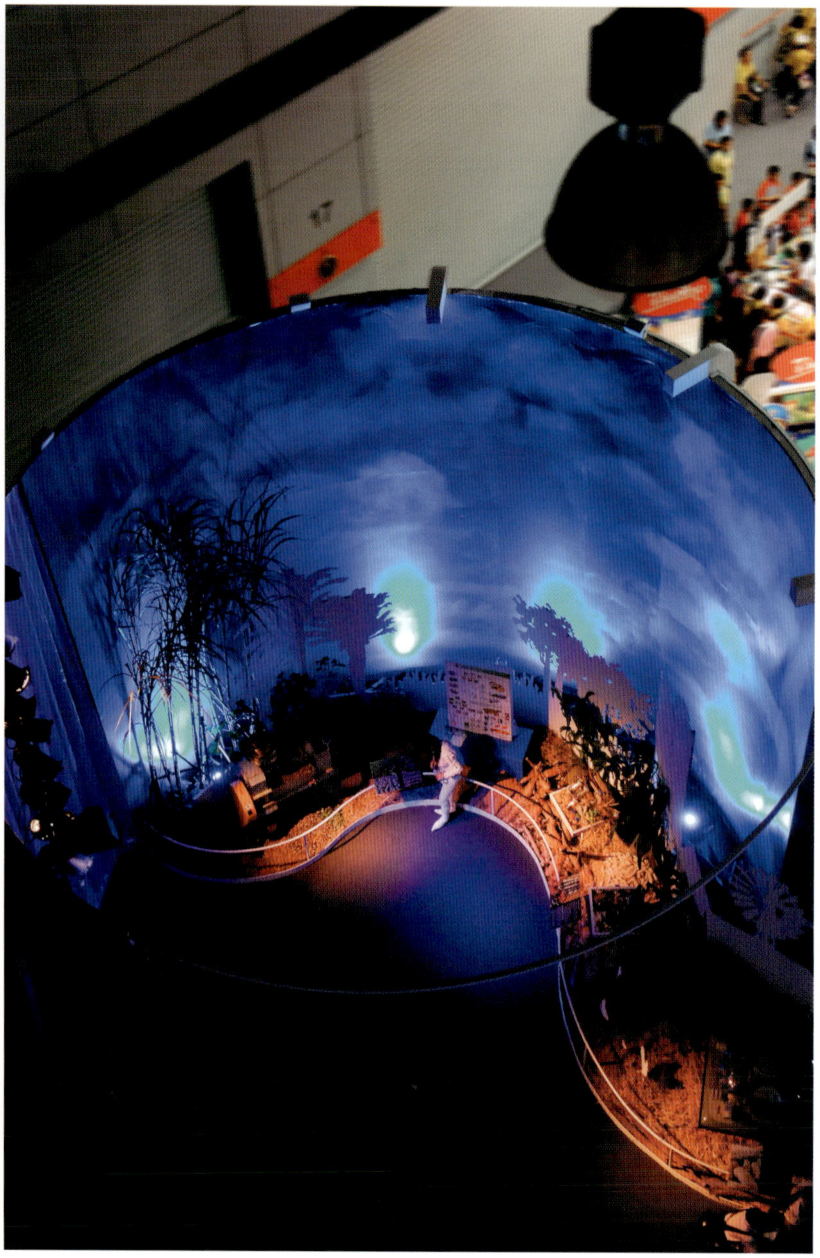

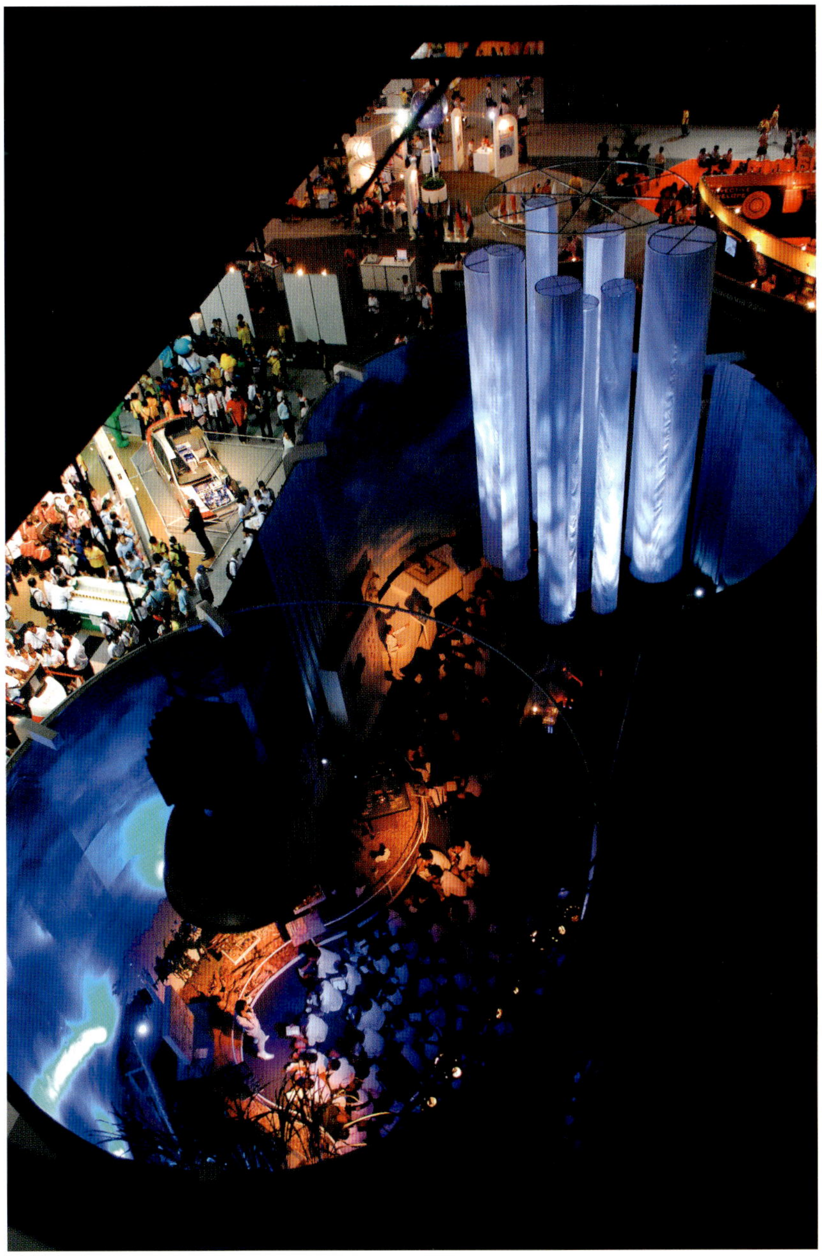
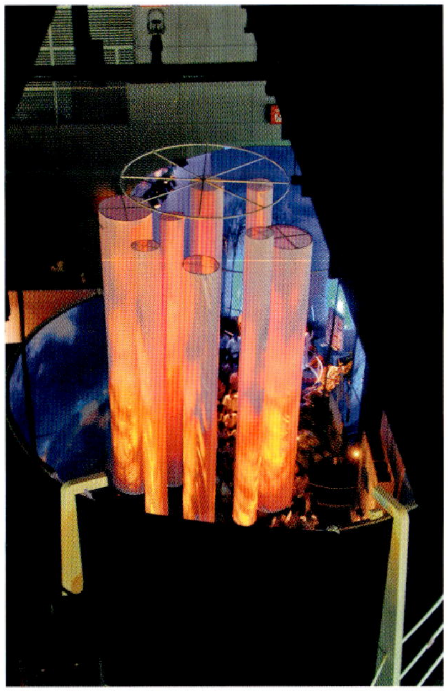
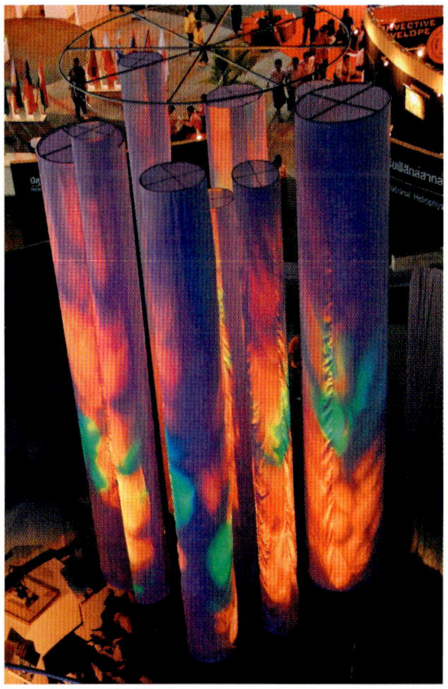
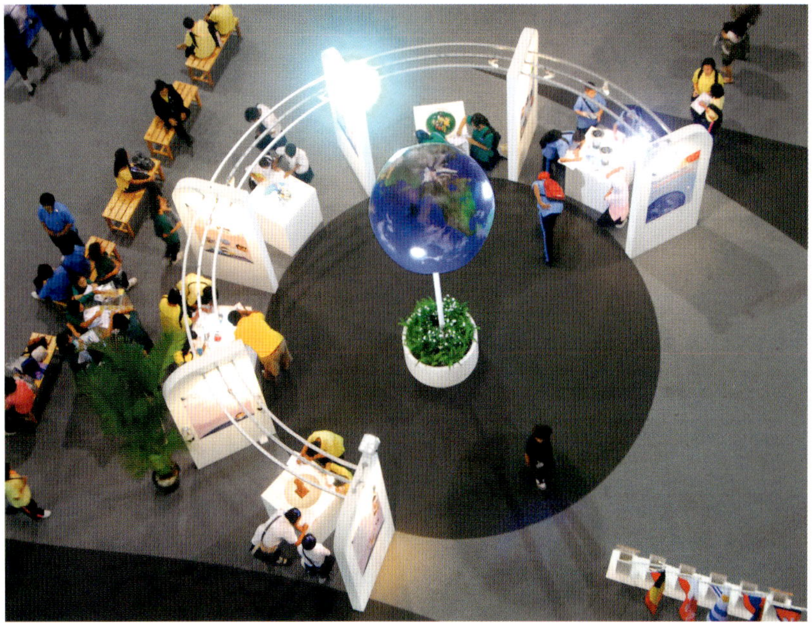

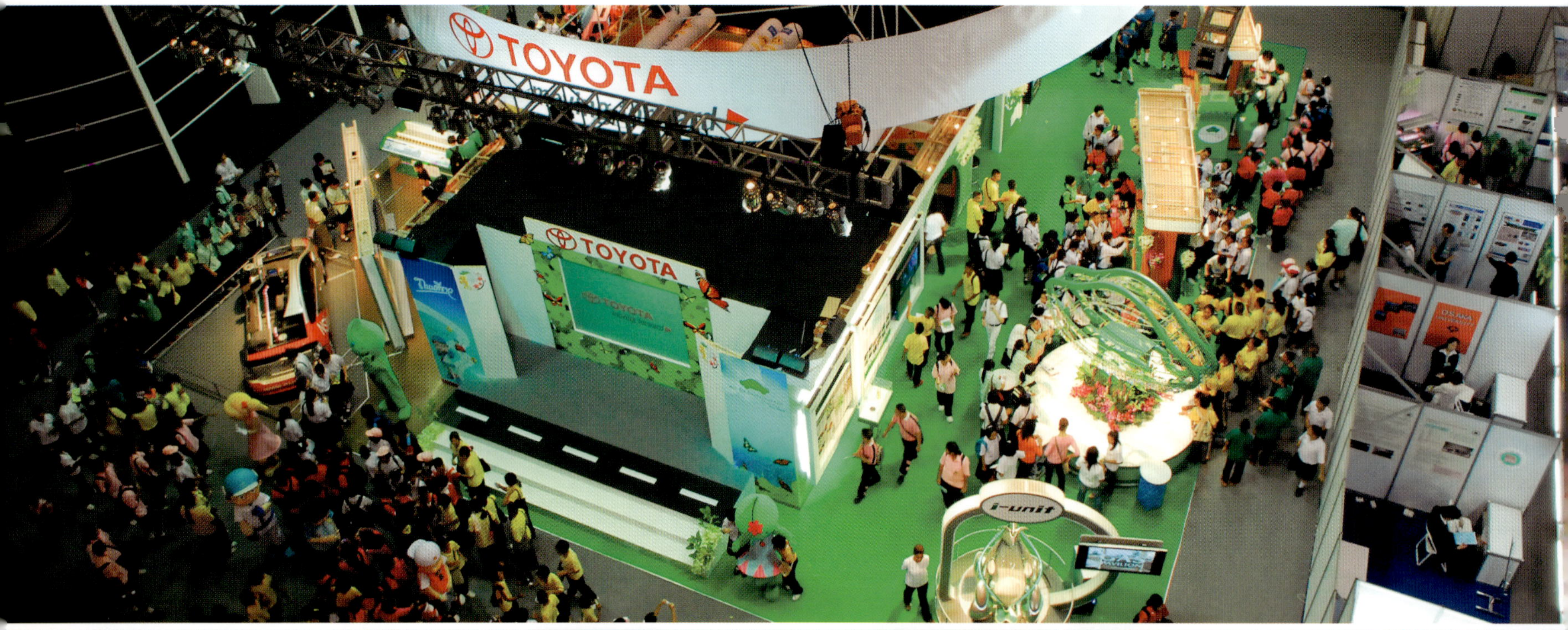
TOYOTA
TOYOTA
i-unit
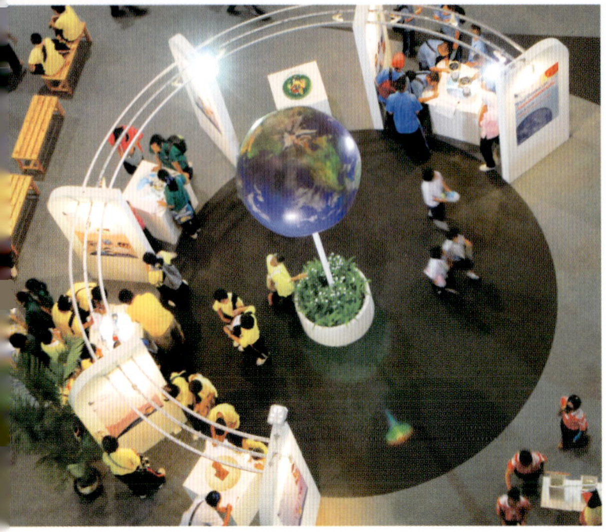
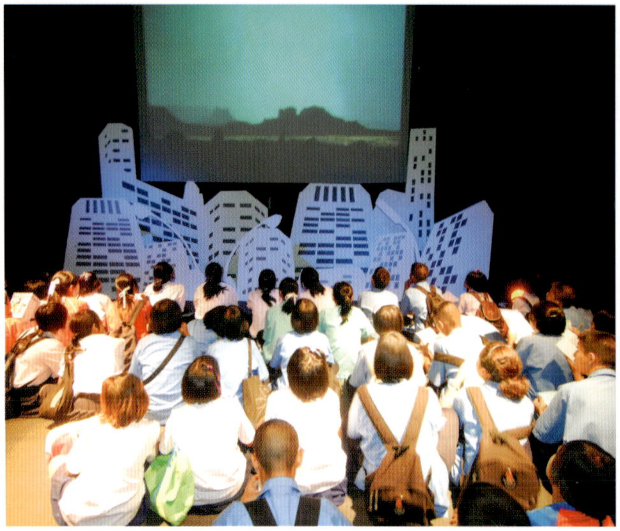
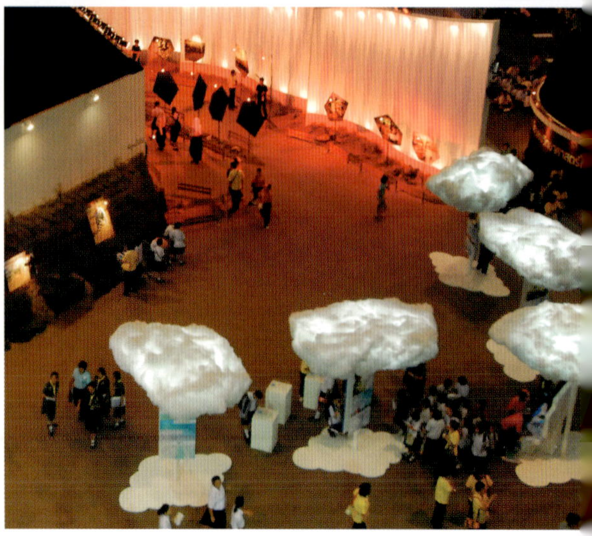

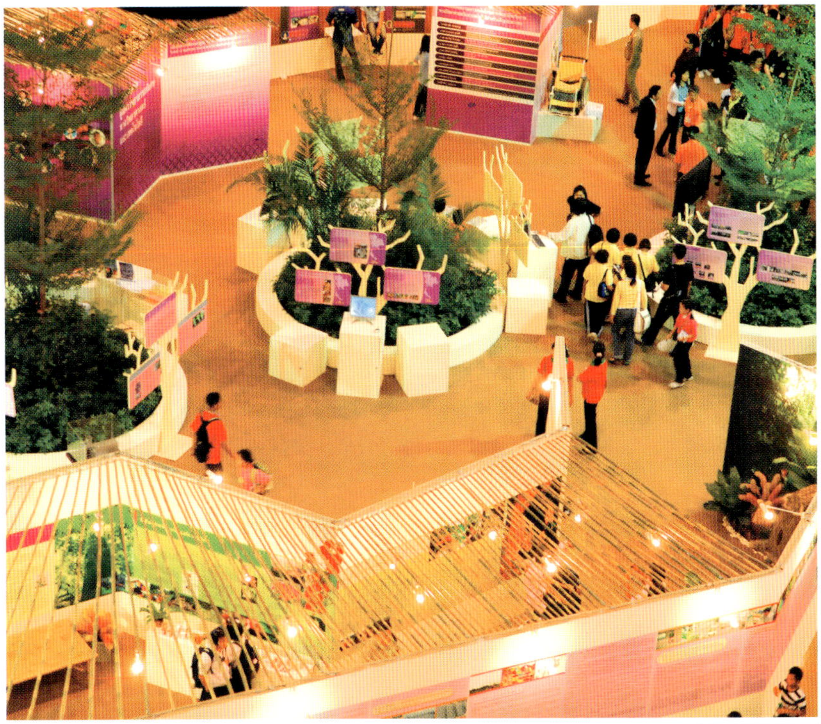

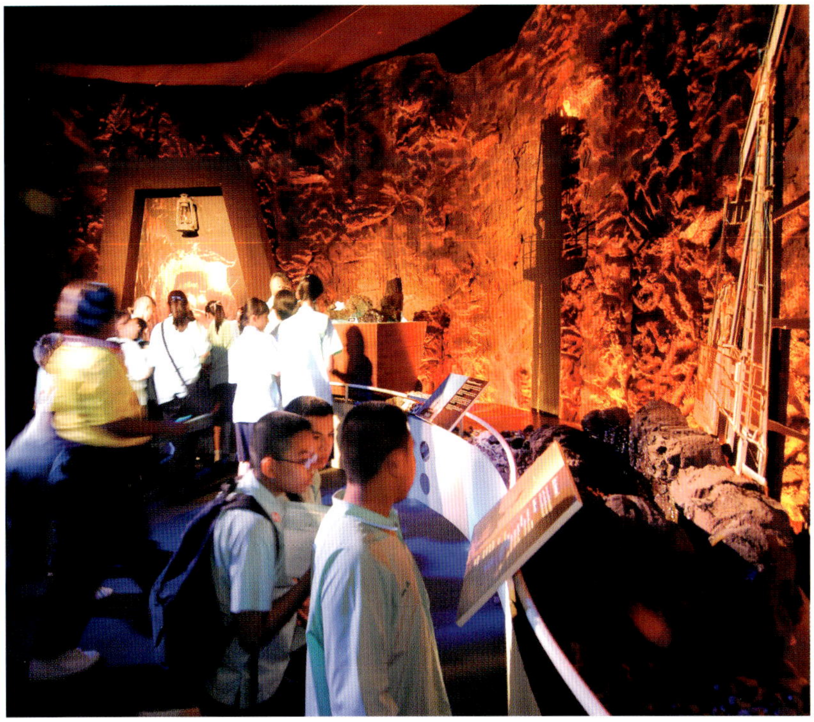

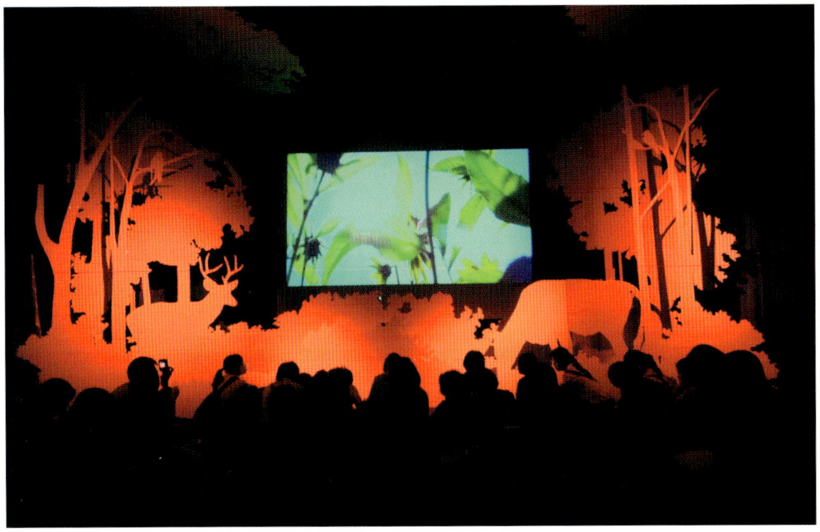

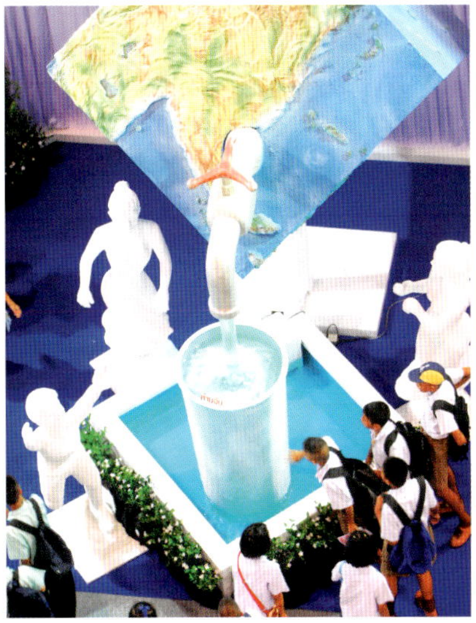

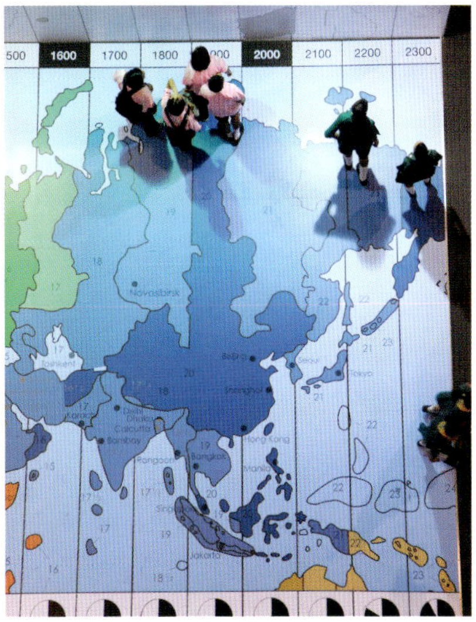
1600
1700
1800
2000
2100
2200
2300

NEC at ITU Telecom World

where Hong Kong SAR, China

The NEC booth employed different zones to convey a variety of messages. Visitors could find Seamless Community, Triple Play, Service Delivery Network, Heterogeneous Access, Secure Networking, Broadband Access, Mobile Network Application and Enterprise FMC Solution amongst others. At the themed stage area, a cinema screen inside a multimedia zone and live performance area were created to entertain and inform visitors.

The gigantic three-dimensional ceiling wrapped in a Warlon sheet presented the greatest challenge for the project team. The 3-D curved ceiling appeared to be free-falling from its own weight which created many technical difficulties. The futuristic design by NEC's agency was ultimately achieved after much careful analysis, research and engineering.

event. exhibit. interior. themed.

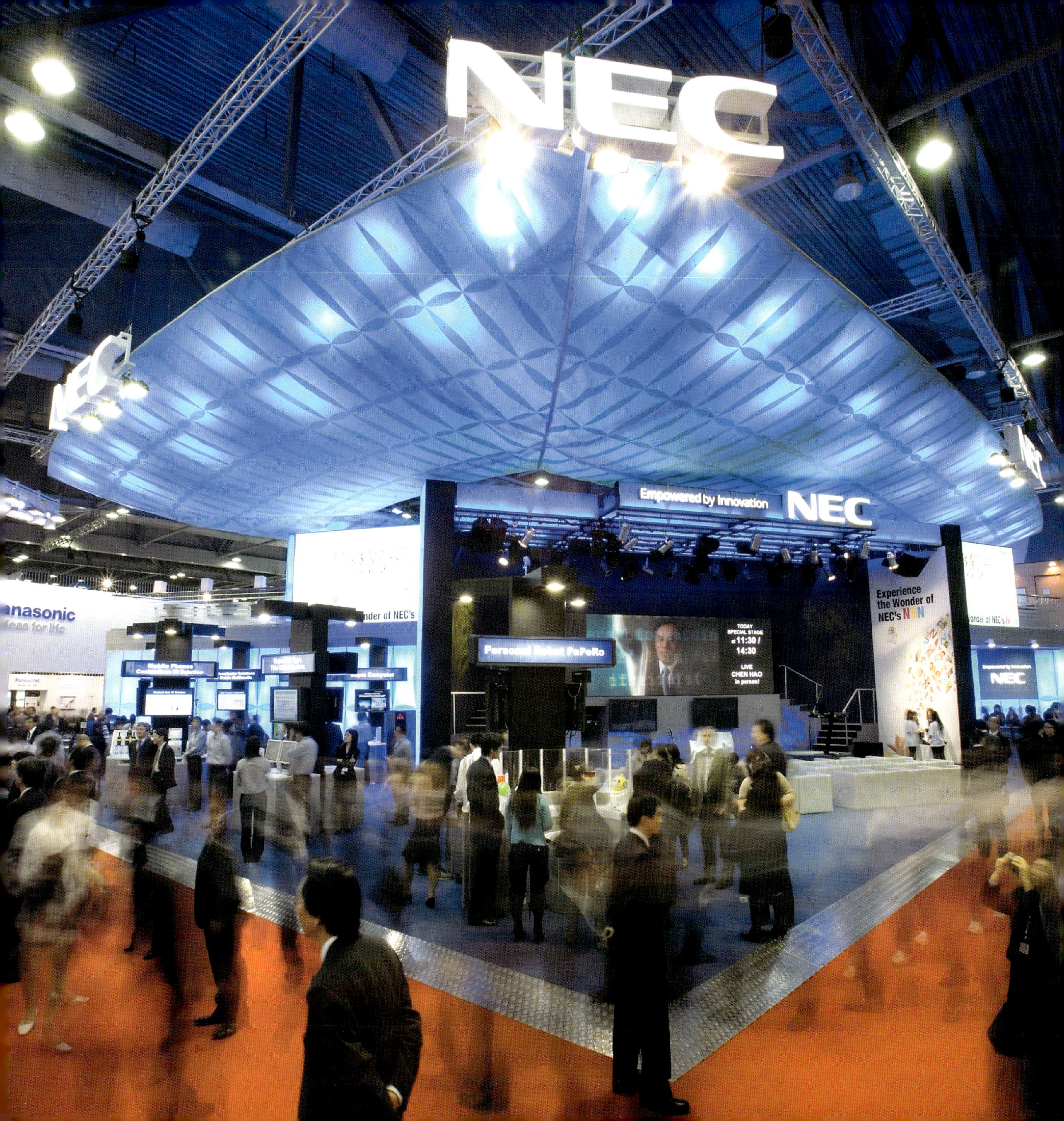
NEC
Empowered by Innovation
Experience the Wonder of NEC's
Personal Robot PaPeRo
TODAY SPECIAL STAGE at 11:30 / 14:30
LIVE CHEN HAO in person!
Panasonic
ideas for life

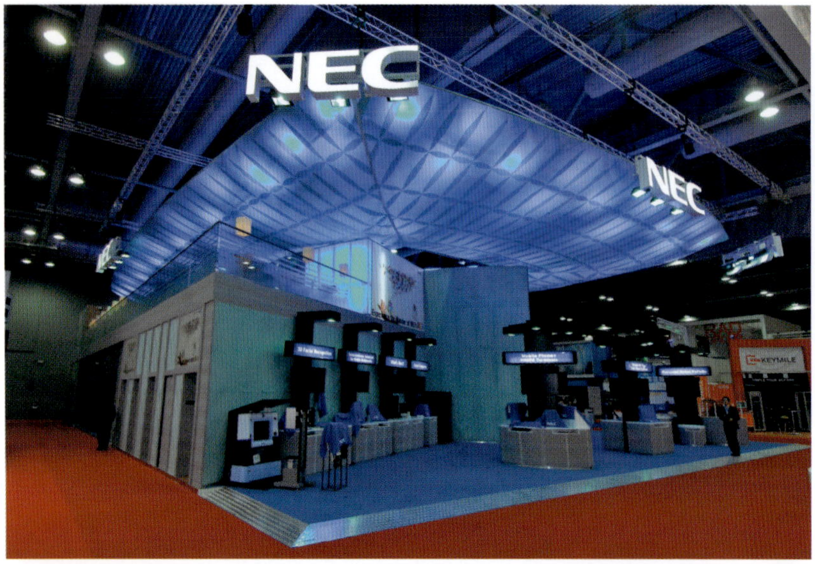
NEC
NEC

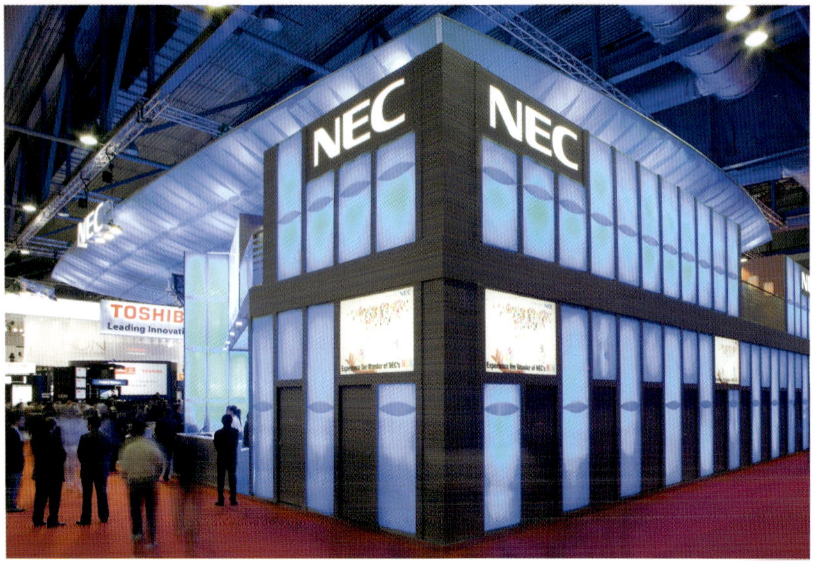
NEC
NEC

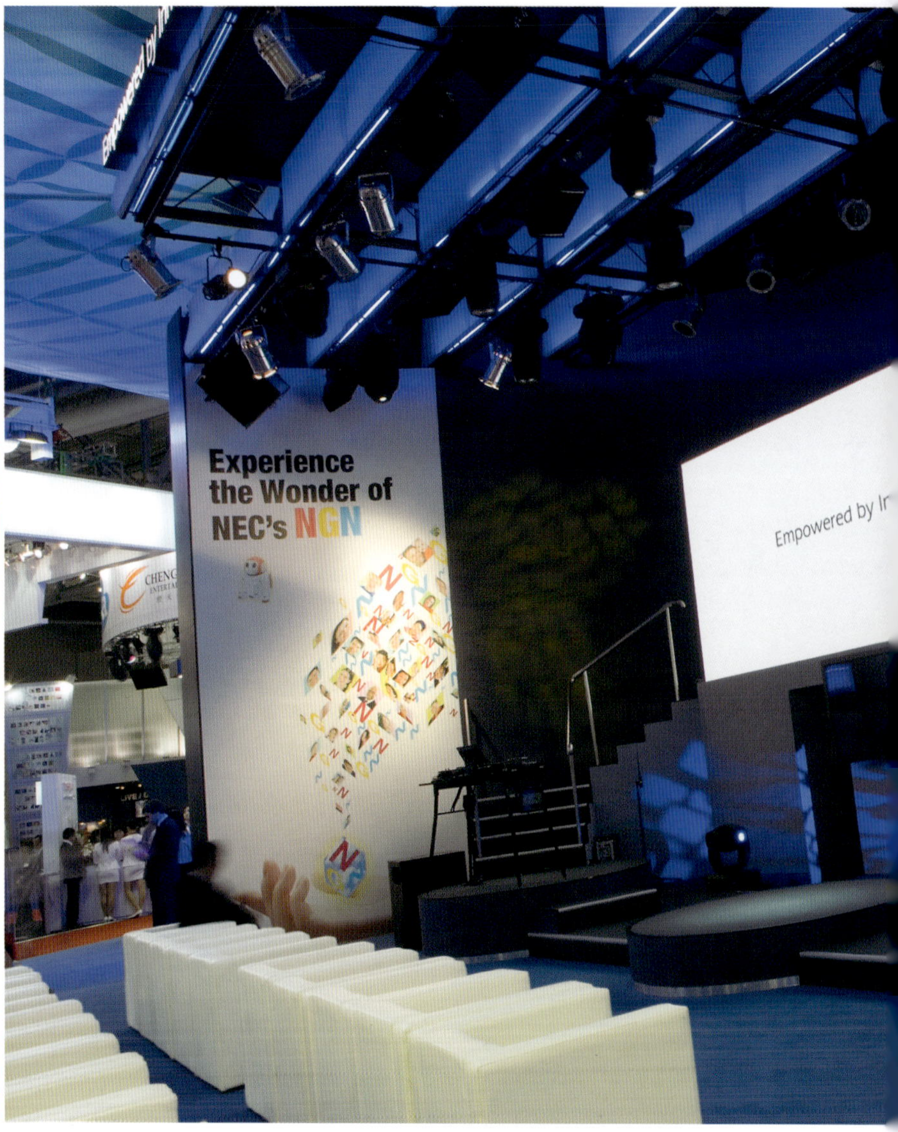
Experience
the Wonder of
NEC's NGN

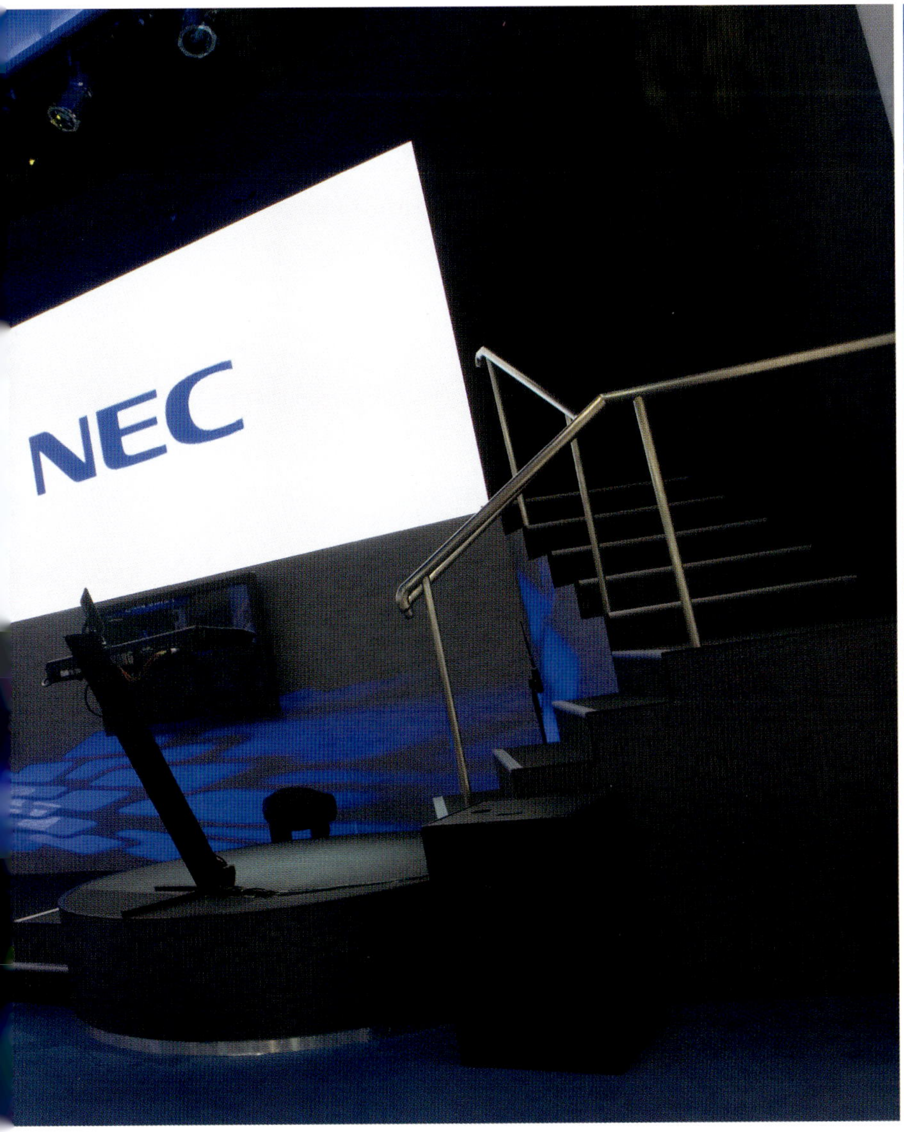
NEC

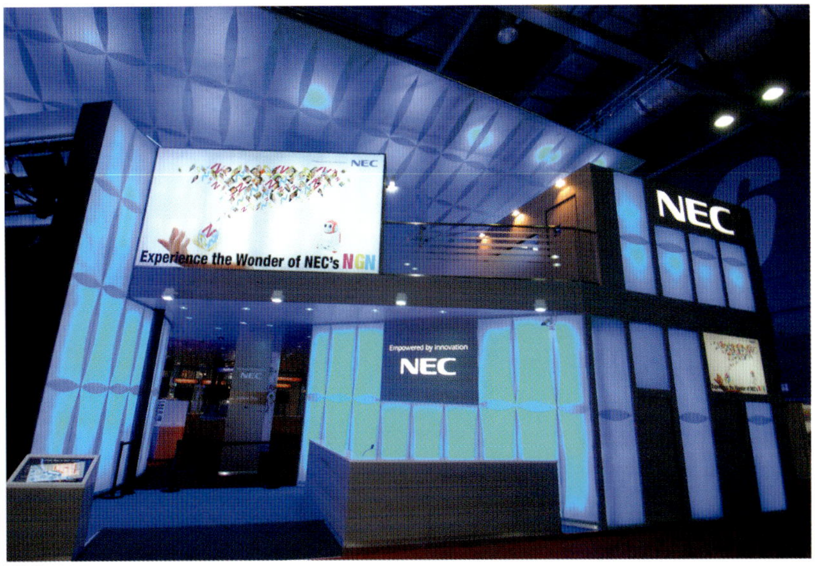
NEC
Experience the Wonder of NEC's NGN
NEC
Empowered by Innovation
NEC

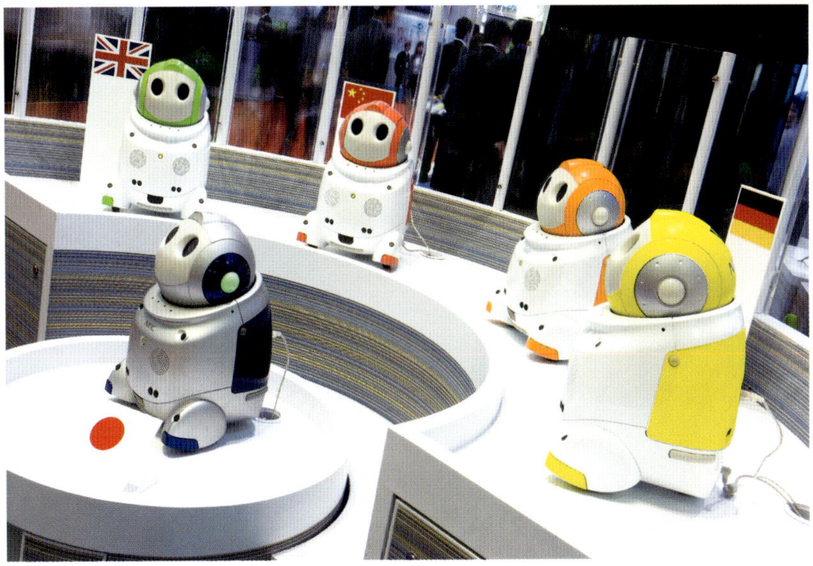

Motorola at ITU Telecom World

where Hong Kong SAR, China

Motorola is one of the world's telecom giants who exhibited at the ITU Telecom World. ITU Telecom World, a triennial event traditionally held in Geneva, Switzerland was held in Hong Kong for the first time. The event is strategically important to global telecom players for strengthening worldwide business networks with an emphasis on the China market. Visitors numbered 43,846 from 141 different countries.

Motorola's 660 sq. m. featured different themed pods to display Motorola network solutions for different market segments – office, home, foyer, park, university, sales office, MTR setting and gaming areas. To reinforce the thematic effect, Motorola's handsets were showcased dramatically in one line. Larger than life images of Motorola's brand ambassadors, David Beckham and Jay Chou, were featured throughout the space.

event. exhibit. interior. themed.

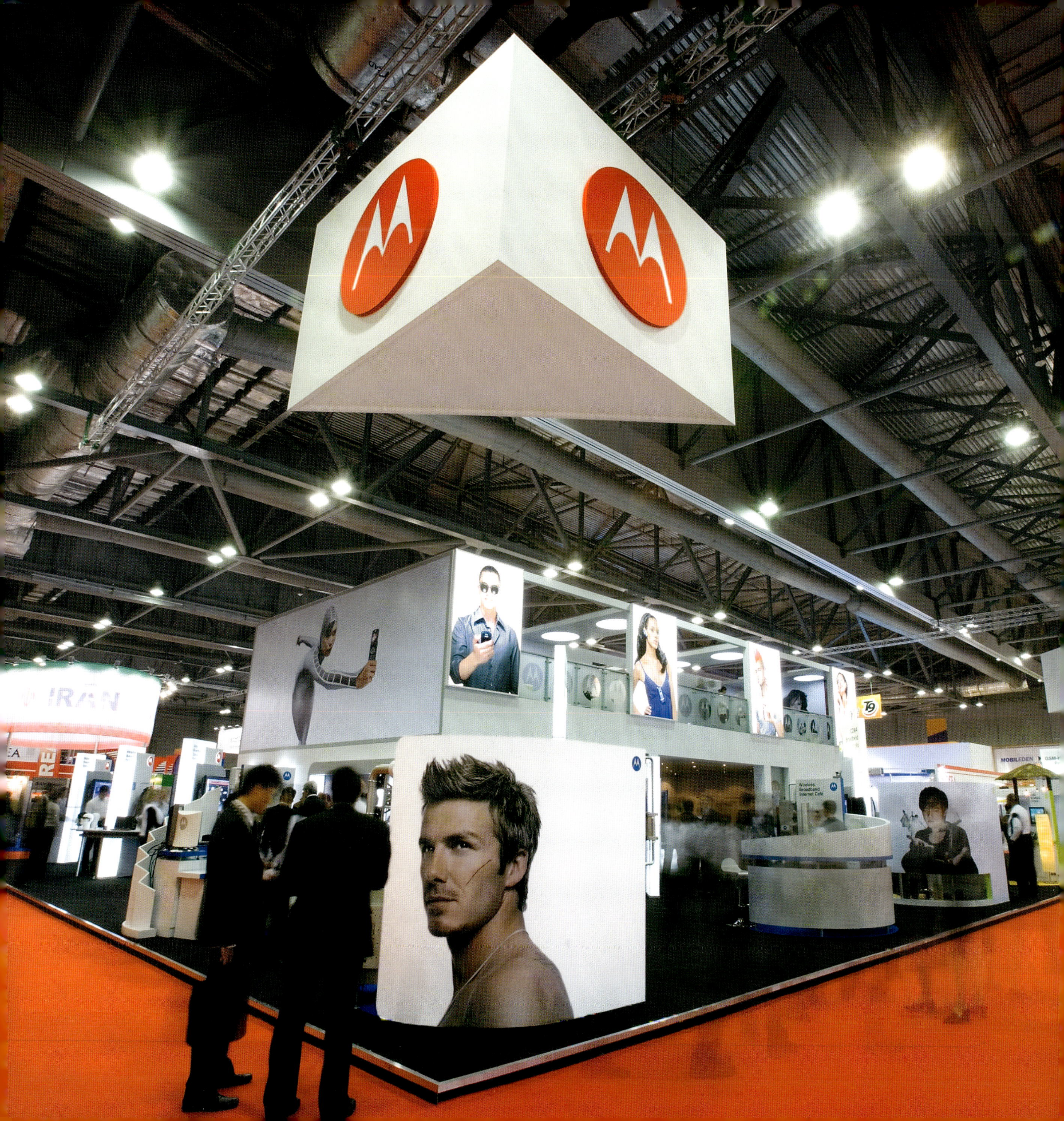
IRAN
T9
MOBILEDEN
Wireless Broadband Internet Cafe

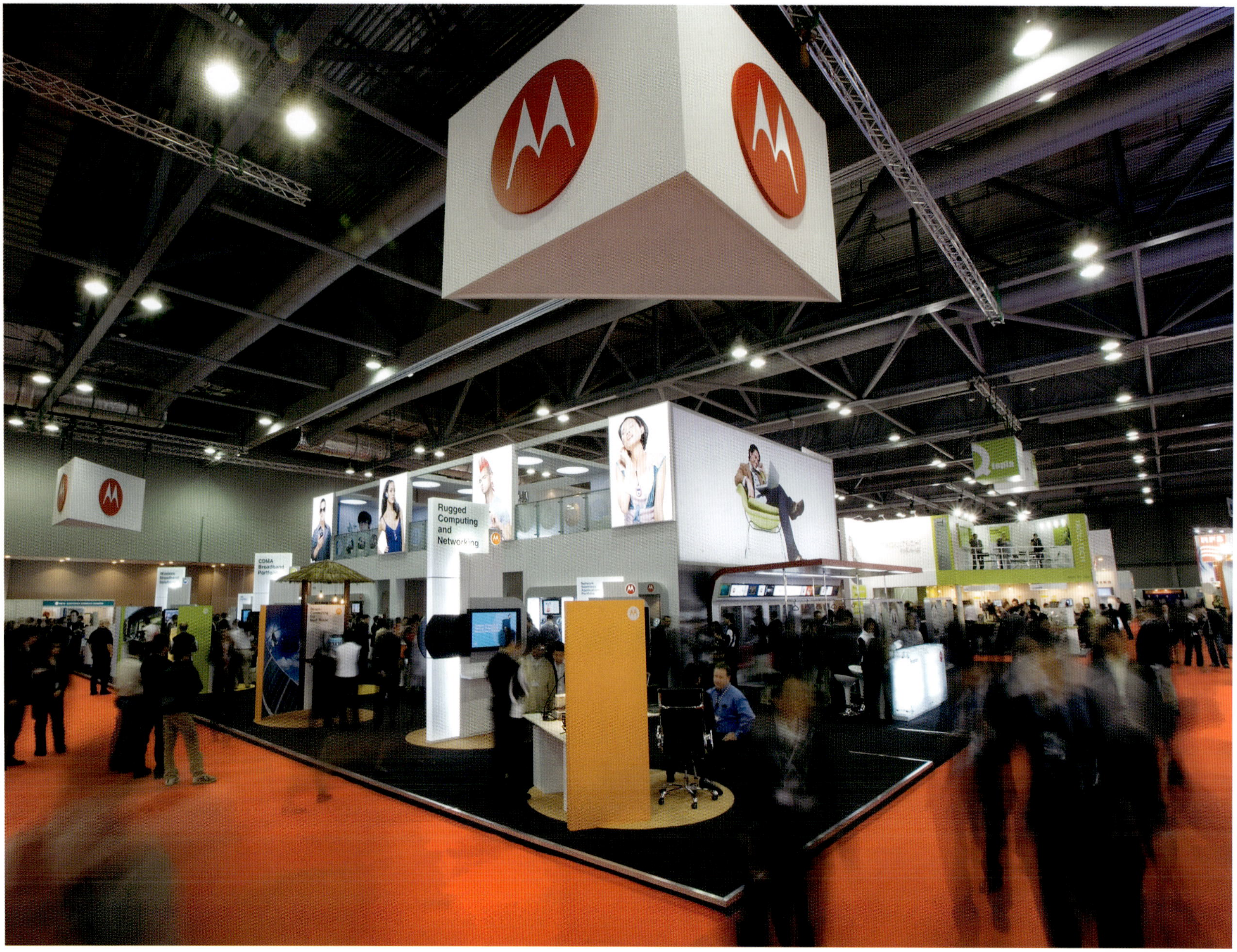
Rugged
Computing
and
Networking

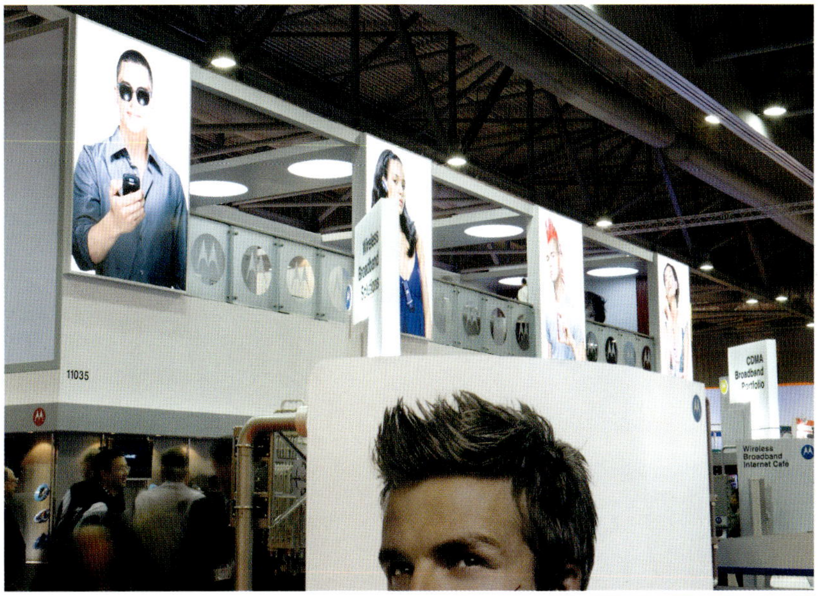
11035
CDMA
Broadband
Portfolio
Wireless
Broadband
Internet Cafe

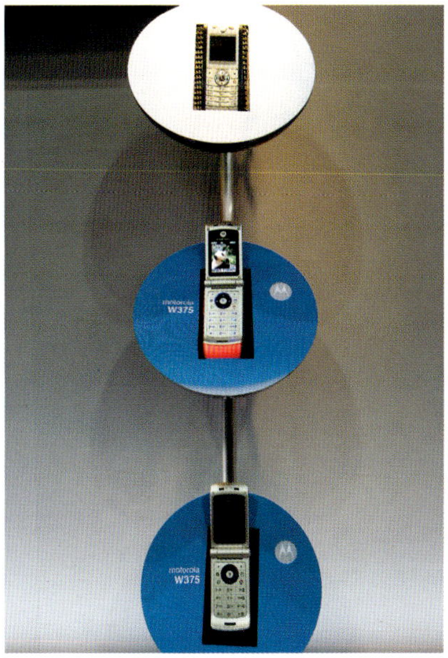
motorola
W375
motorola
W375

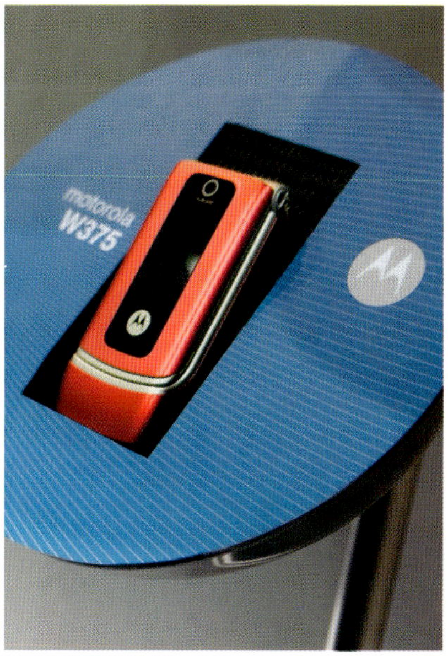
motorola
W375

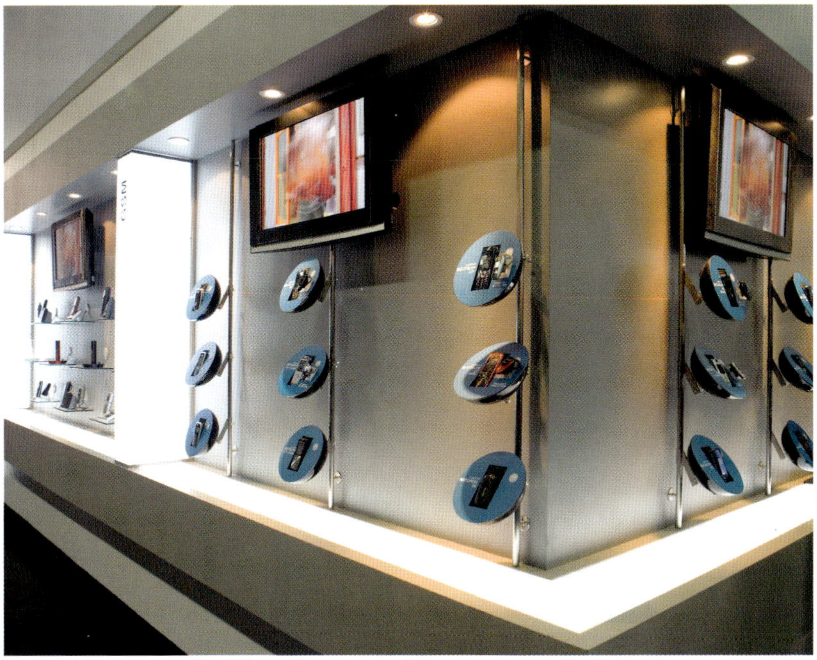

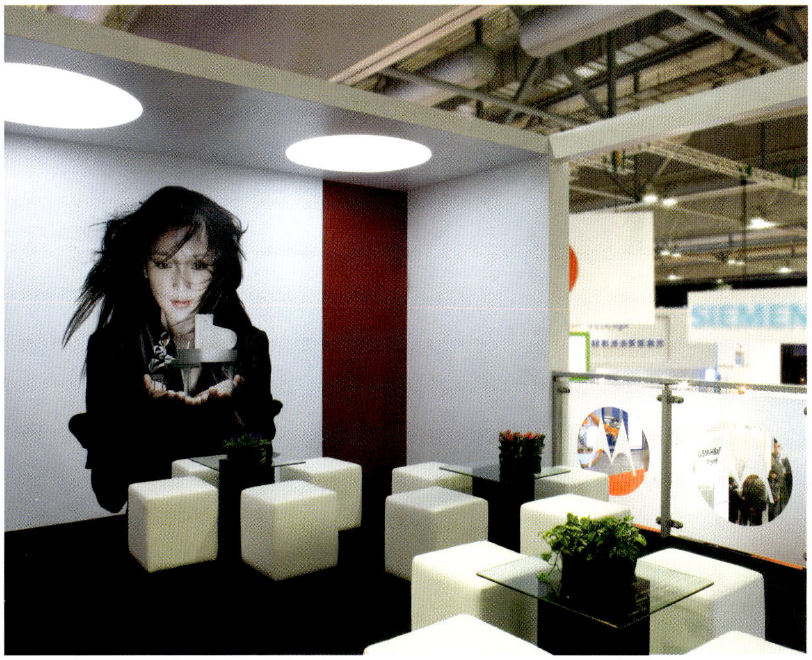

Chevrolet at the 28th Bangkok International Motor Show

where Bangkok, Thailand

The Bangkok International Motor Show is considered to be one of the primary automotive expositions in the world and is held at the Bangkok International Trade and Exhibition Centre in Thailand. This show was so successful that 130 world-renowned auto manufacturers from 11 countries were represented. The visitor count reached two million during the ten-day event.

Chevrolet has repeatedly participated in this glamorous show with a unique theme every year. This year's theme "Enlightening Your Life" was conveyed through a bold colour palette, beautiful finishes and dynamic, synchronised, live graphics. A sweeping black lacquered two-storey structure created the focal point. Pink and black glass accents complemented the centrepiece. Floor finishes of wood and polished white platforms defined the different zones. Additional features that enhanced the product line-up such as the brightly illuminated "Chevrolet Service Centre" and "Chevrolet Proshop," were situated at the ground level.

A special "Best Design" Award was presented to Chevrolet as a result of the excellent design and fabrication of this exhibit.

event. exhibit. interior. themed.

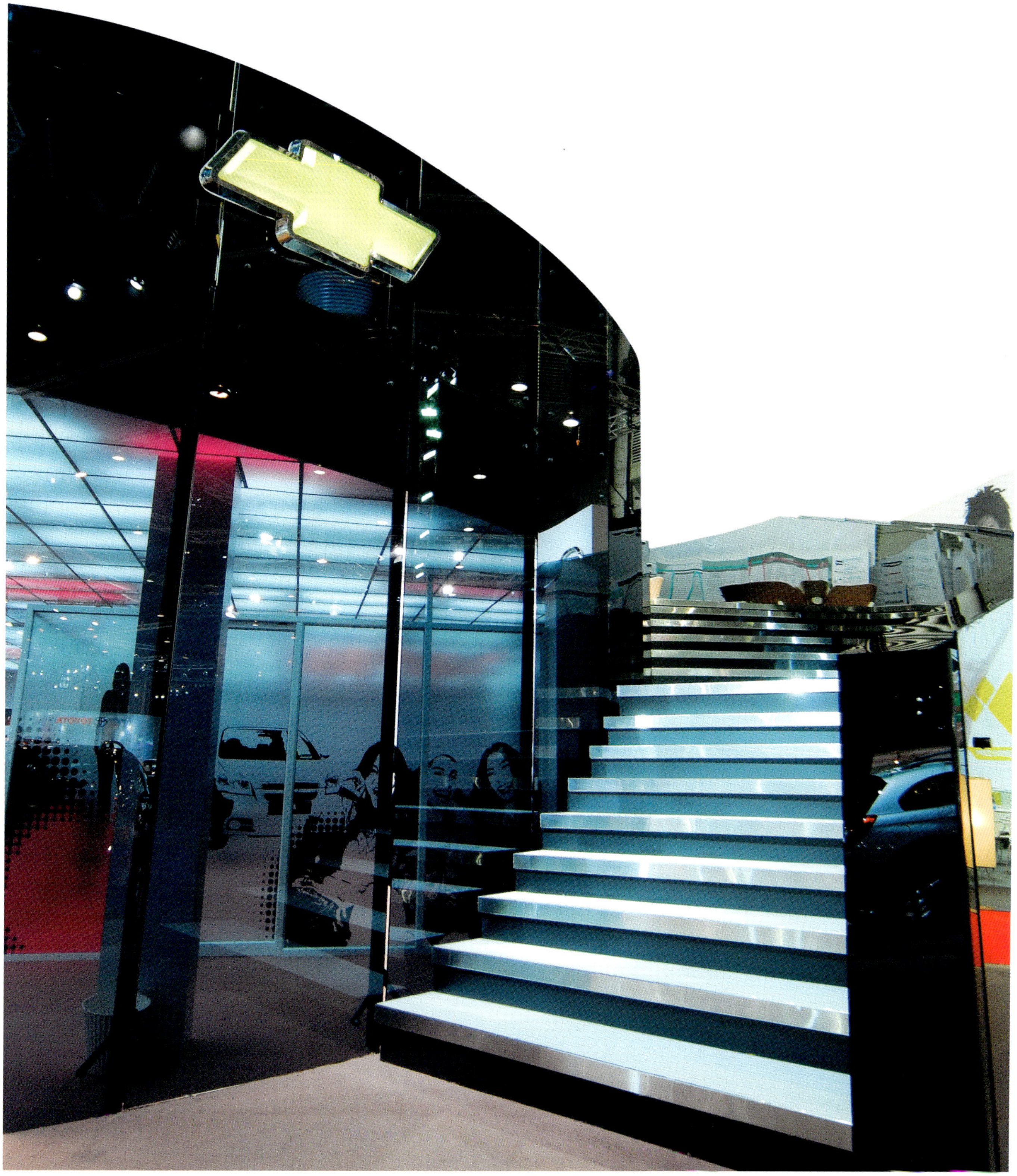

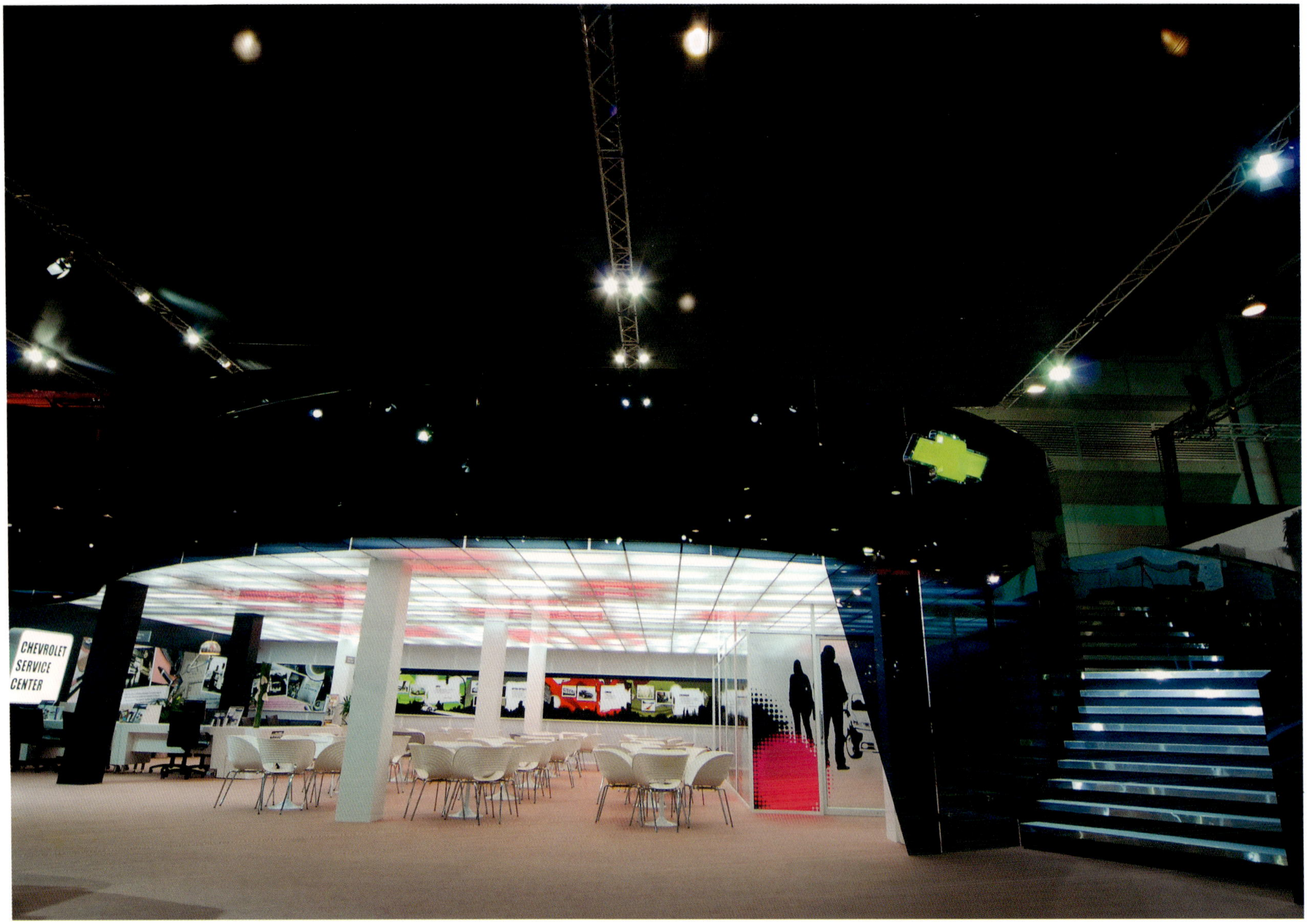
CHEVROLET
SERVICE
CENTER

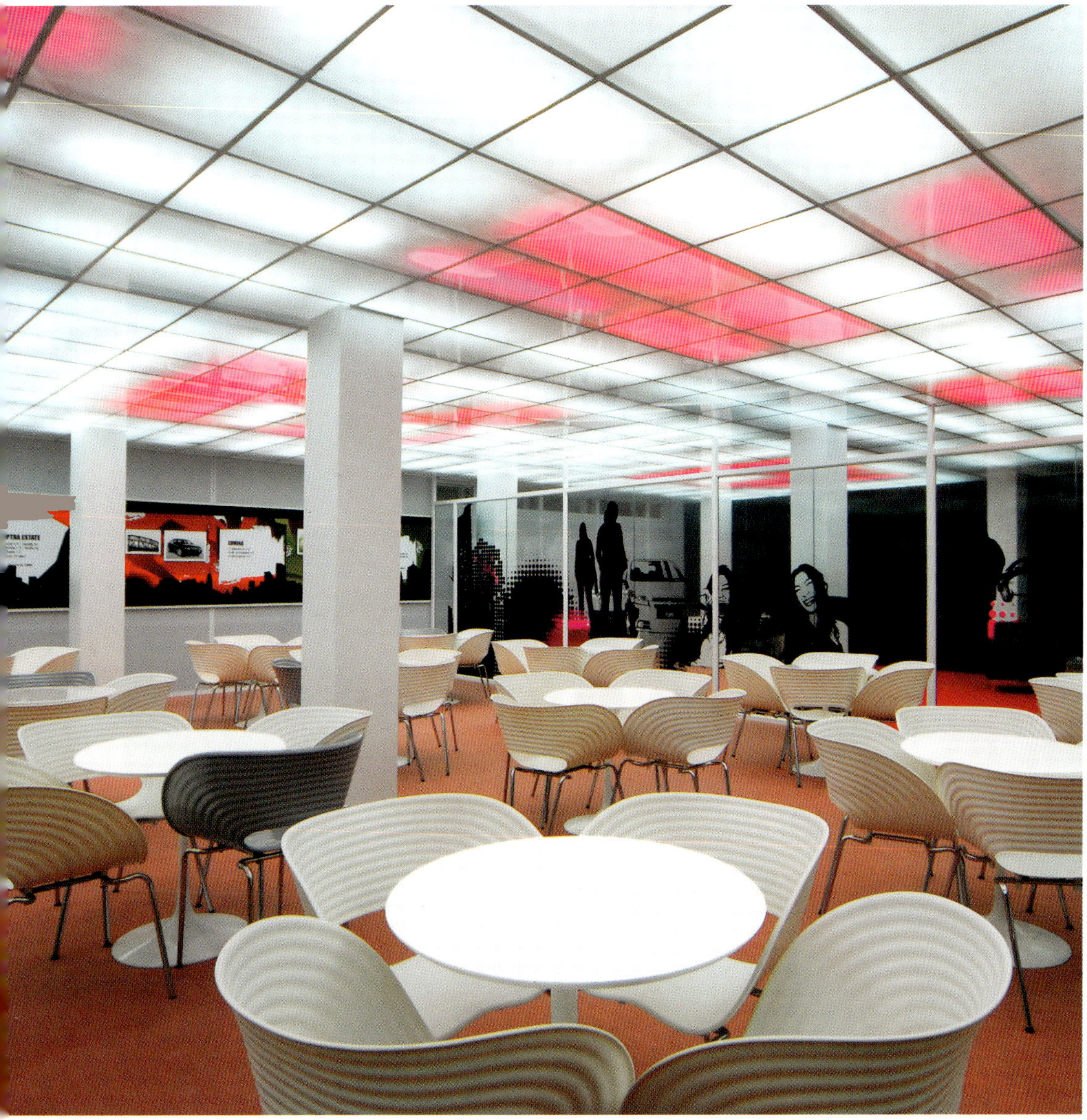

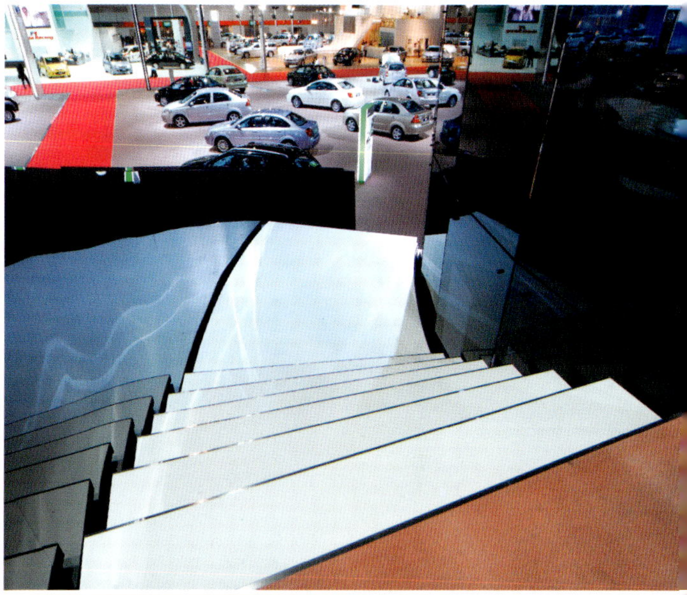

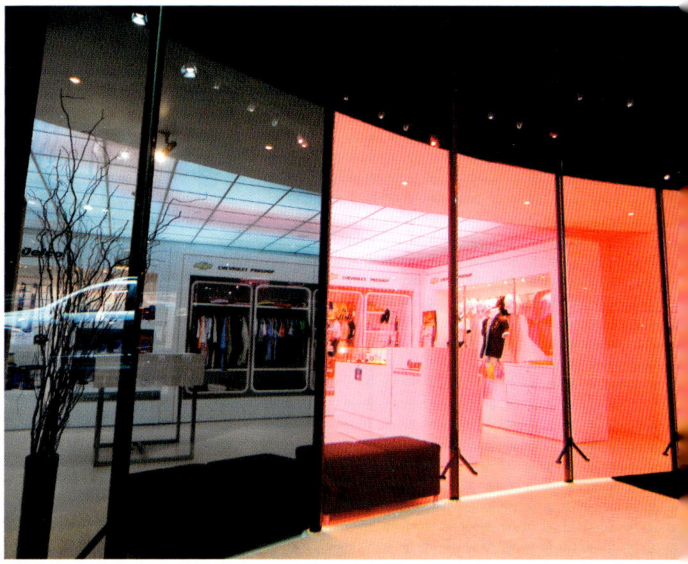

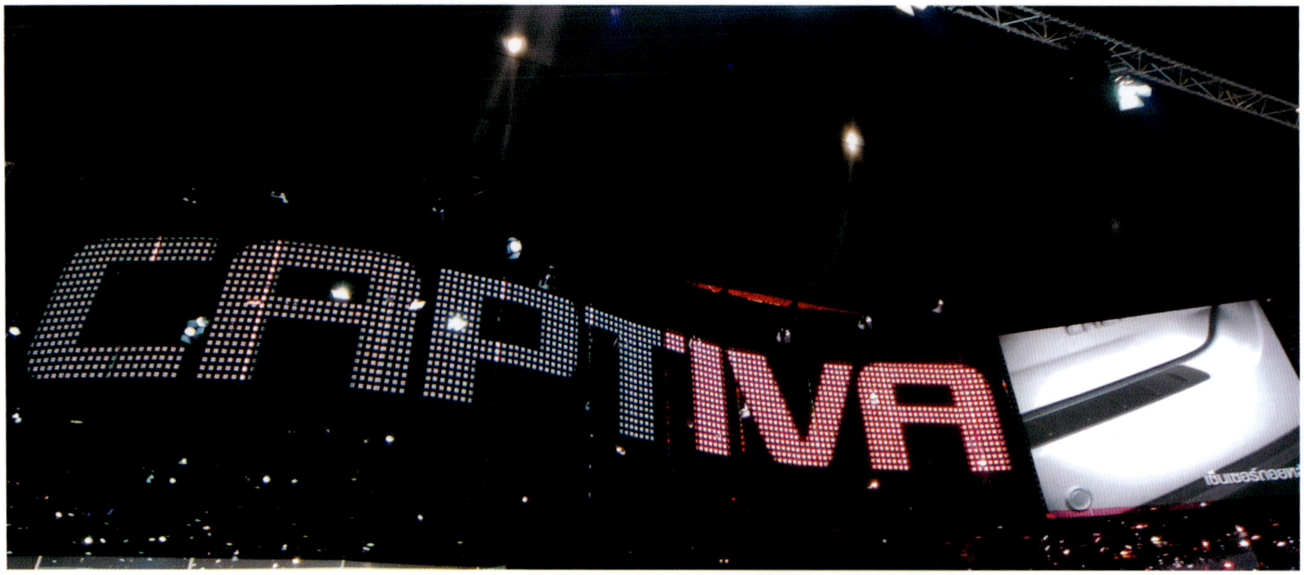
CAPTIVA

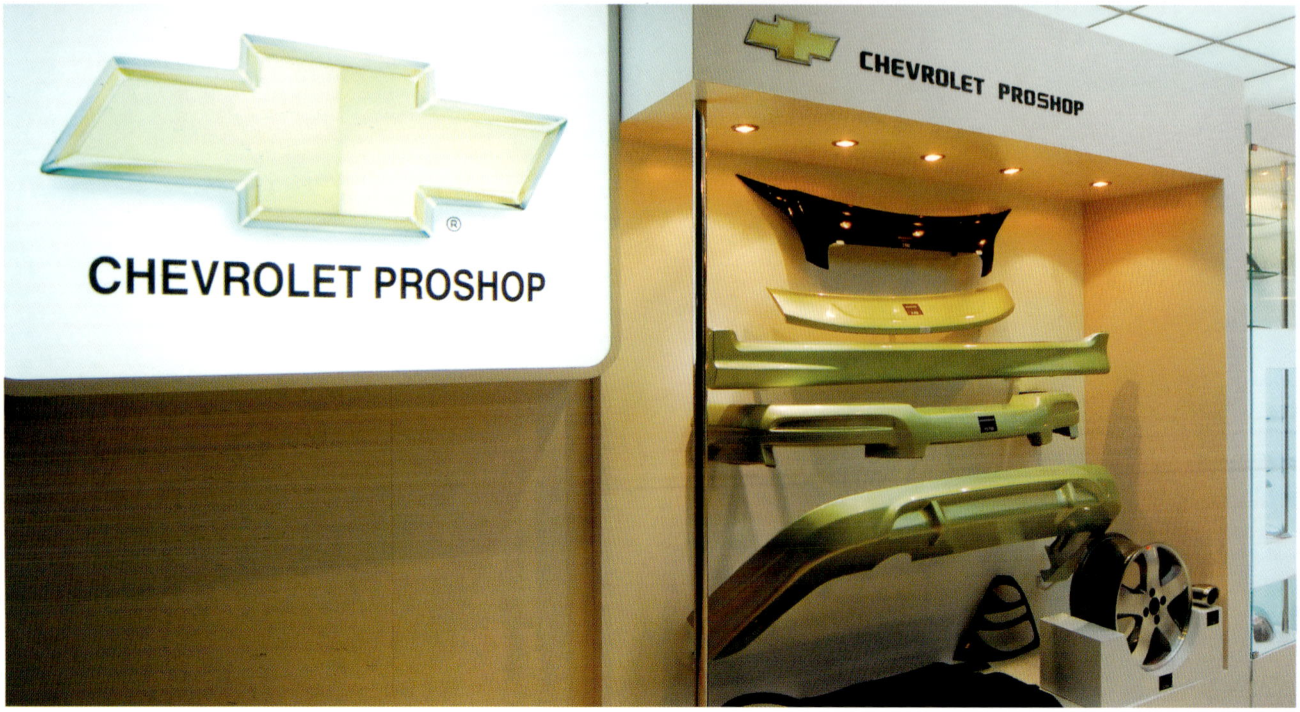
CHEVROLET PROSHOP
CHEVROLET PROSHOP

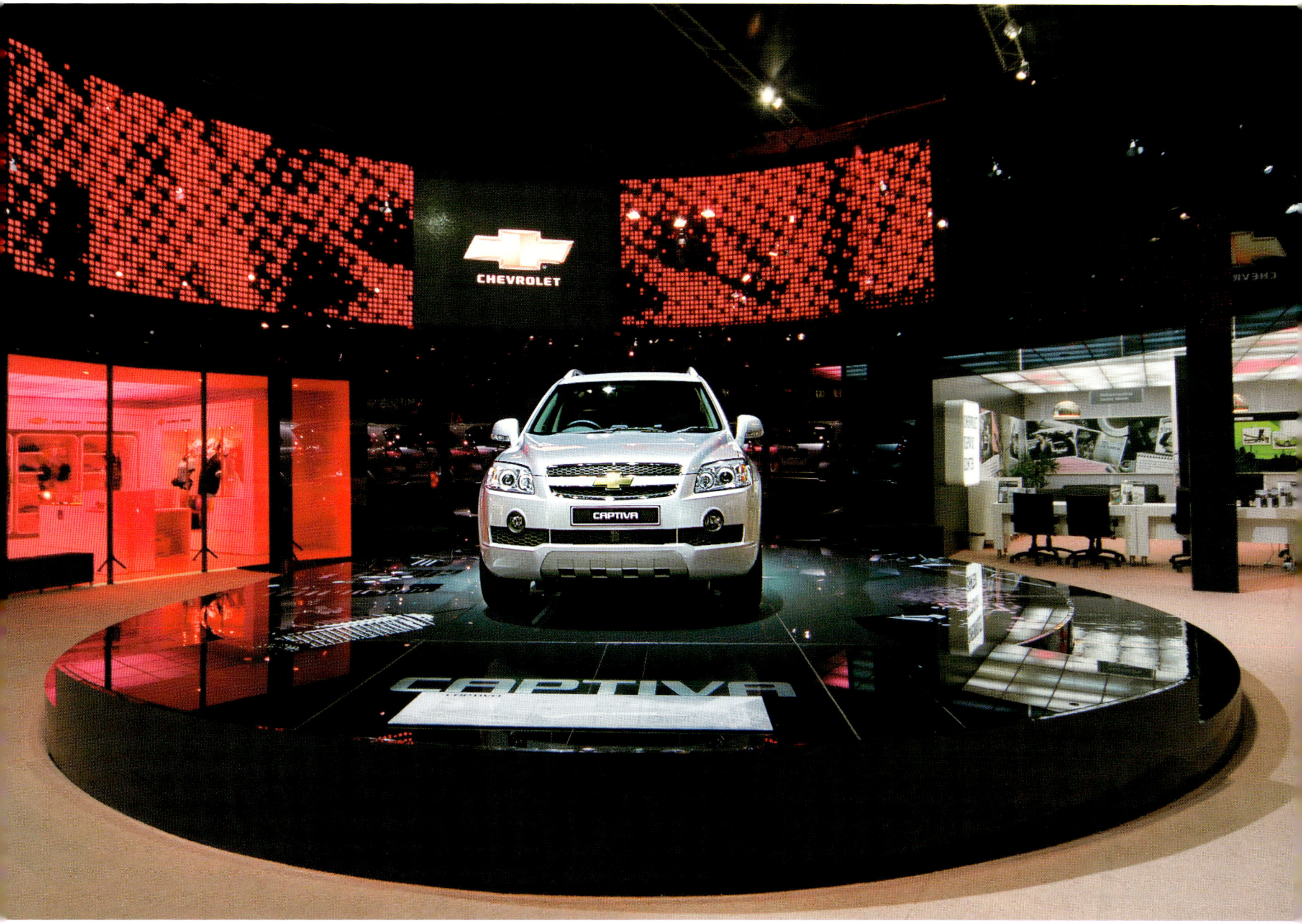
CHEVROLET
CAPTIVA
CAPTIVA

Micron at the Hong Kong Optical Fair

where Hong Kong SAR, China

In a space of just 48 sq. m., Micron Eyewear created a total brand experience for the Optical Fair 2006 at the Hong Kong Convention and Exhibition Centre.

The thematic design was an eye-shaped booth which offered a glimpse of the centrepiece staircase within. Simultaneously from within the exhibition space, the eye-shaped design functioned as a "window" to events outside.

The eye-catching and inviting design elements were brought together through innovative lighting effects and the contrasting colours, white and blue. For a degree of privacy, the meeting rooms were located on the upper level.

This unique structure was simple yet striking and effective. It was voted the winner of the Booth Design Award for the show.

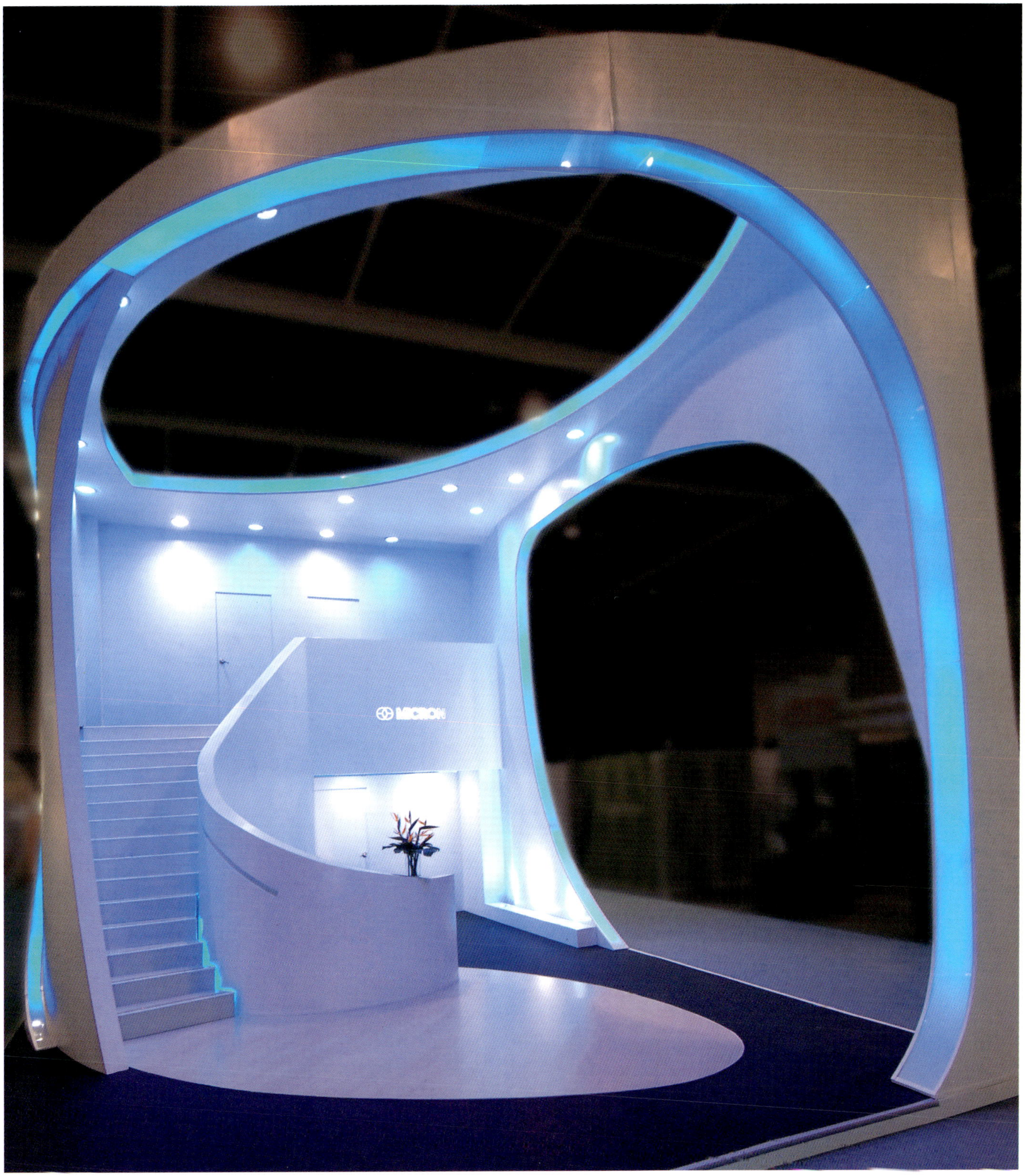
MICRON

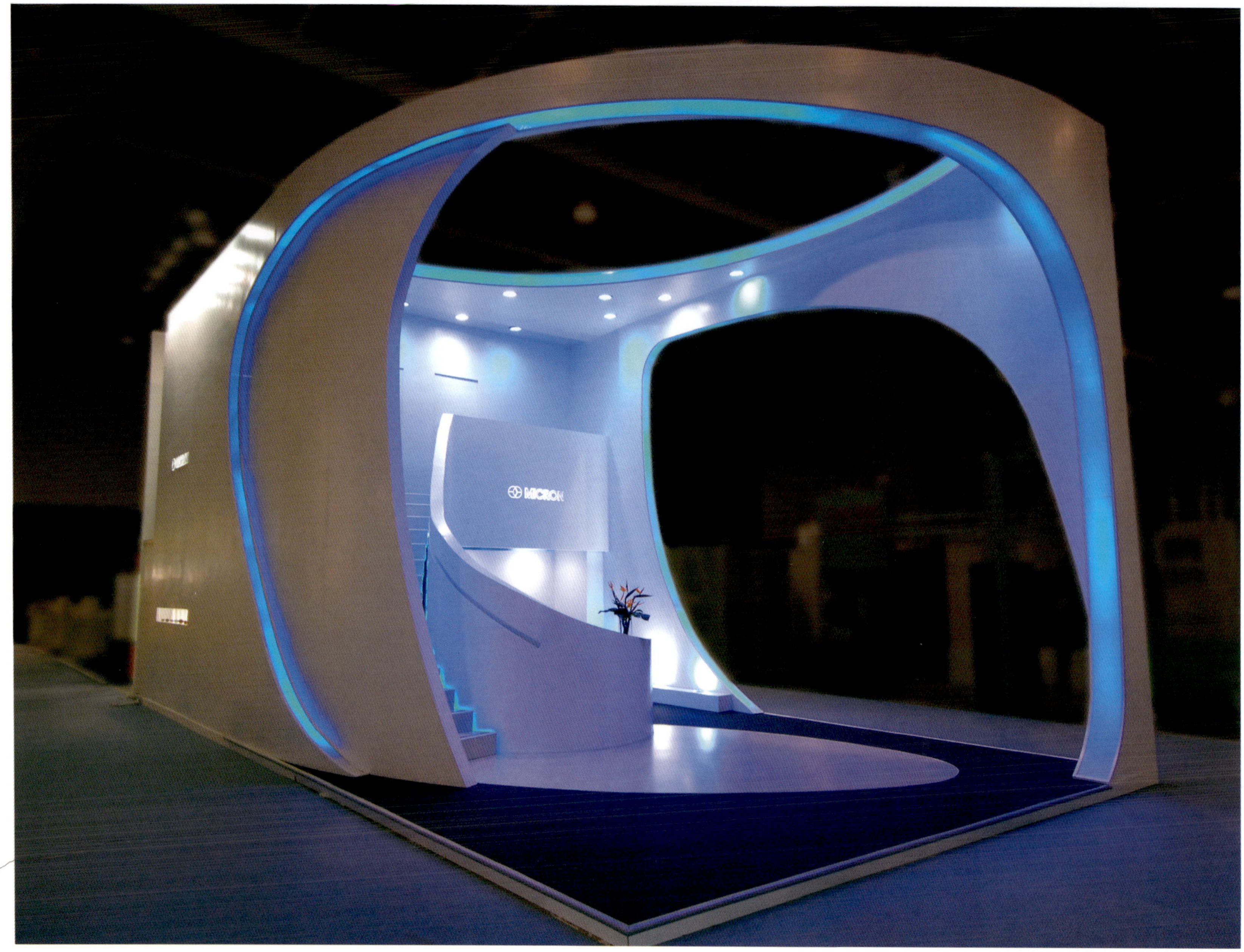
MICRON

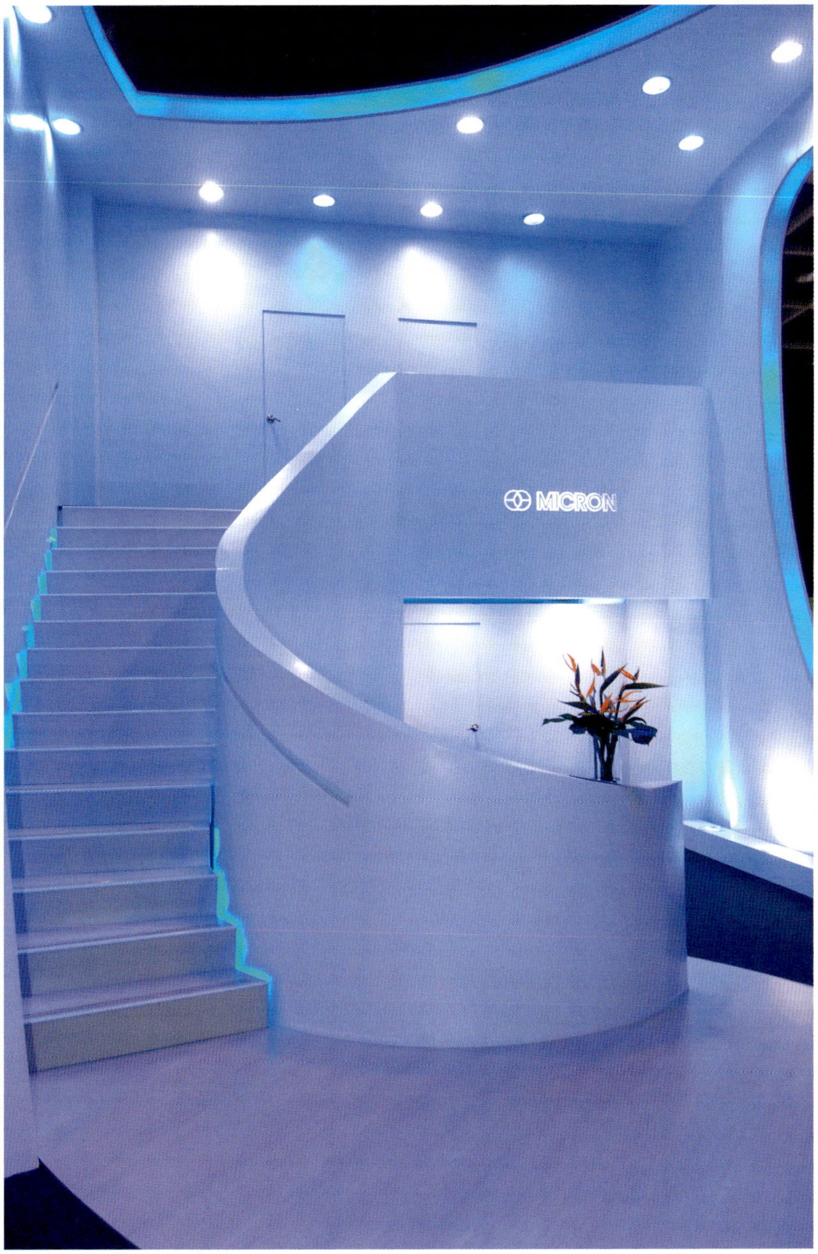
MICRON

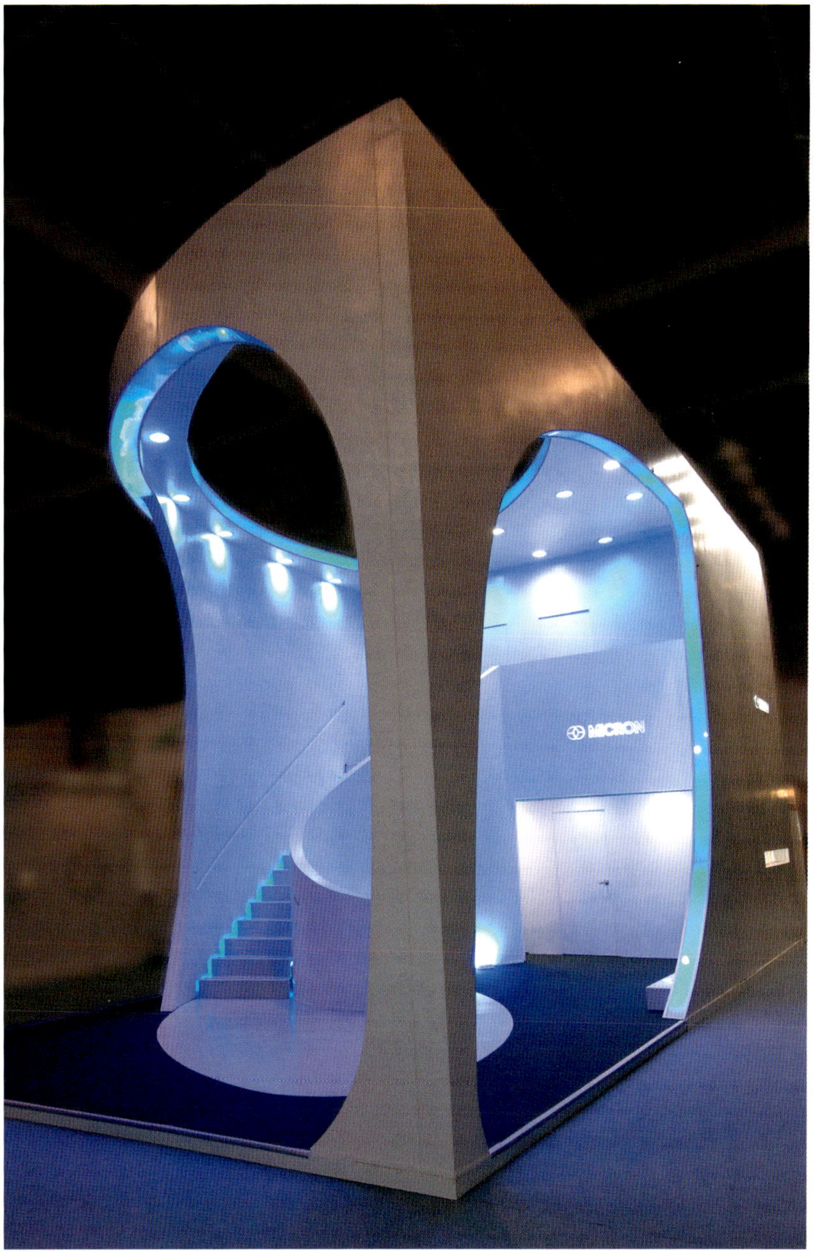
MICRON

Kohler at China Building & Construction Trade Fair

where Shanghai, China

The China Building Construction Trade Fair attracts more than 100,000 sponsors and visitors from China and Asia each year. Kohler's stand at the Shanghai New International Expo Centre occupied a space of 483 sq. m. and a height of six metres.

Kohler's aim is to contribute to gracious living for those who are touched by their products. They believe that gracious living is attributed to qualities of charm, good taste and generosity of spirit. This message was conveyed by Kohler's products and exhibition design.

The designers used a series of water images to dramatise and illustrate the many water-saving benefits for commercial and residential users gained through the innovative Kohler products. The simple, yet elegant design with sweeping arches and curves and predominantly white colour palette conveyed a fresh clean image. The overall result was an elegant Kohler space.

event. exhibit. interior. themed.

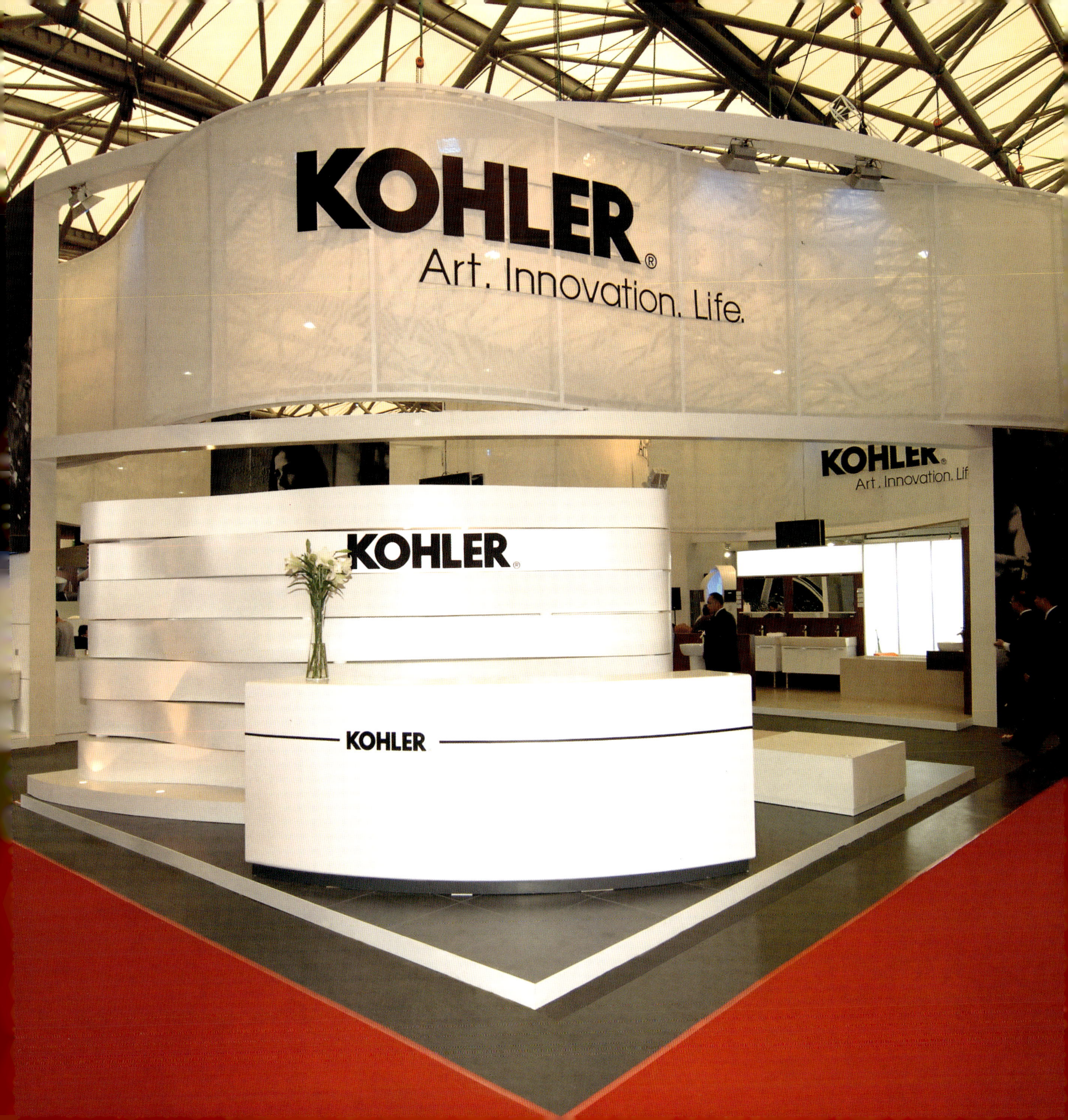
KOHLER®
Art. Innovation. Life.
KOHLER®
KOHLER
KOHLER®
Art. Innovation. Lif

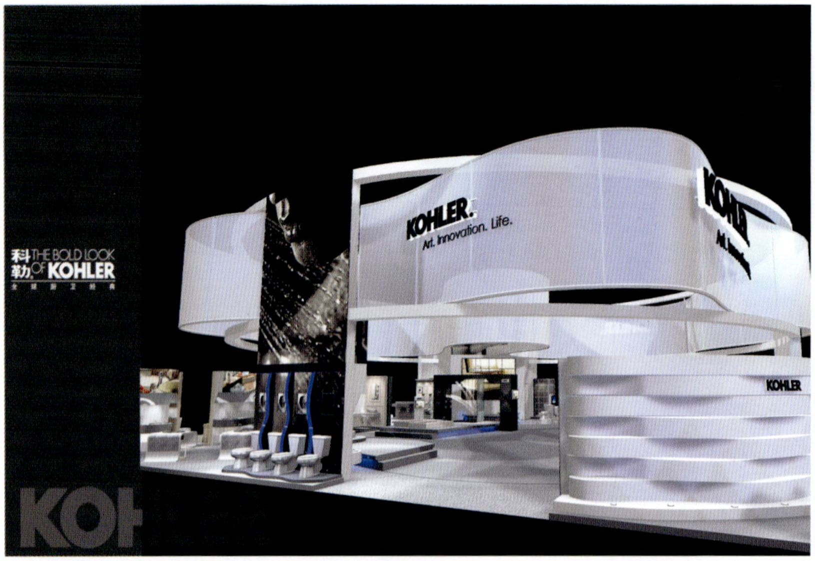
科勒 THE BOLD LOOK OF KOHLER
KOHLER.
Art. Innovation. Life.
KOHLER

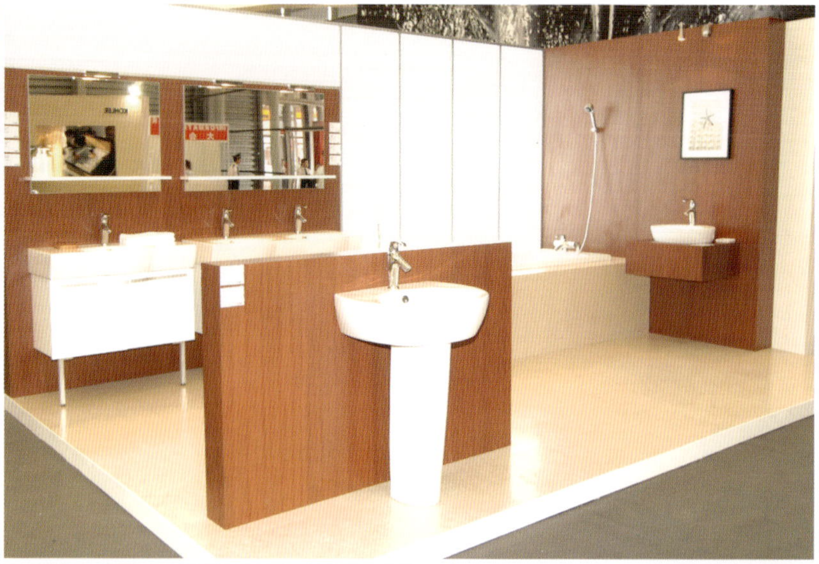

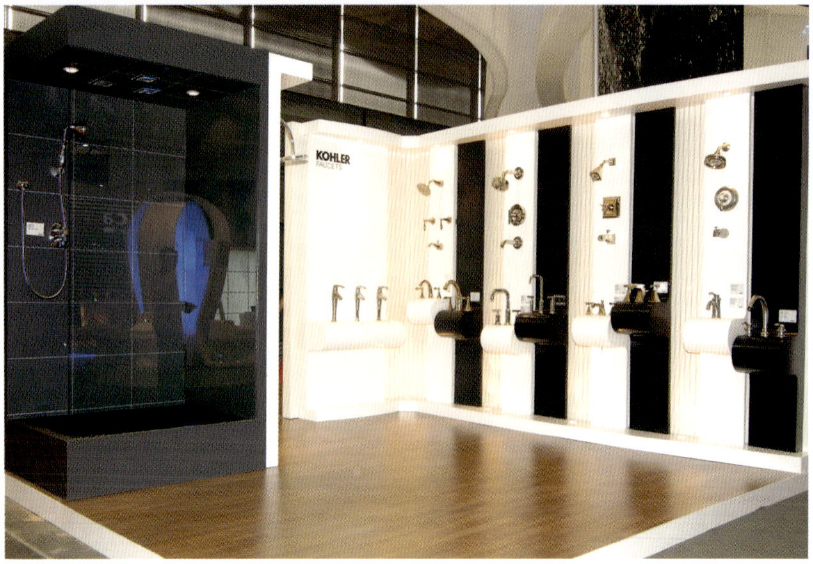
KOHLER

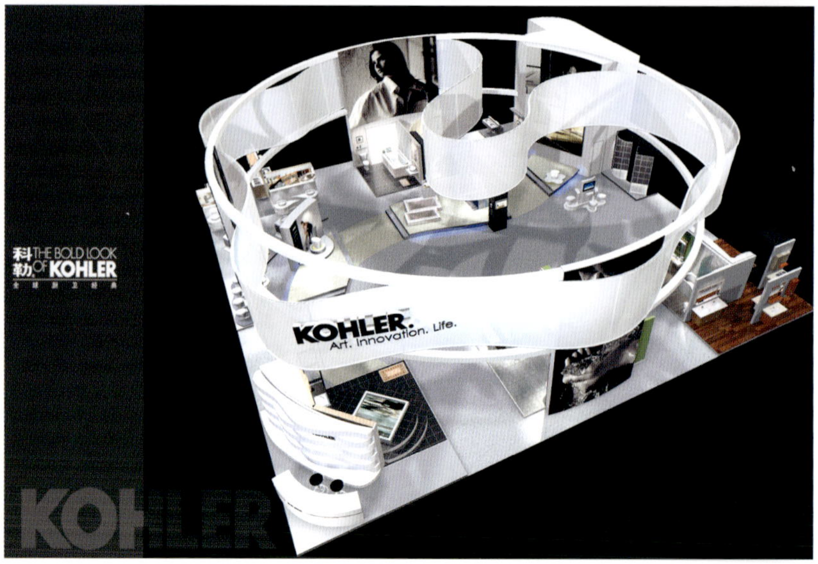
科勒 THE BOLD LOOK OF KOHLER
KOHLER.
Art. Innovation. Life.
KOHLER

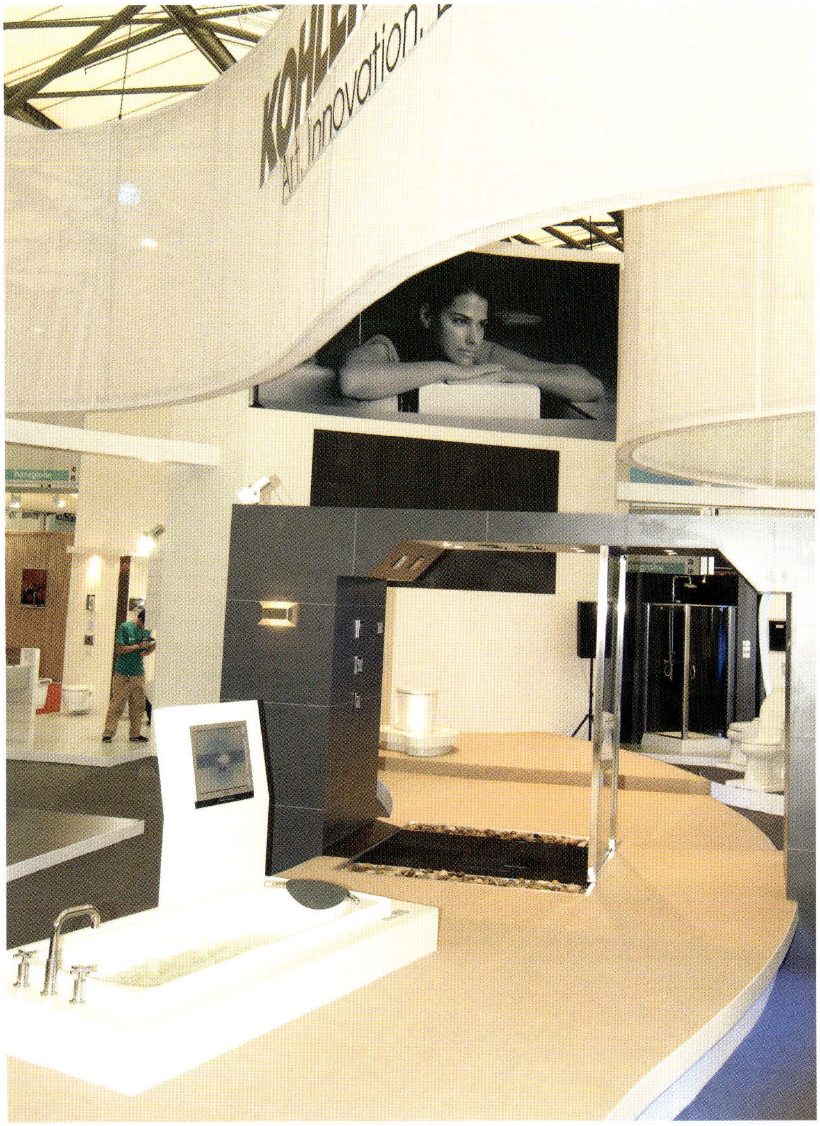
Art. Innovation.

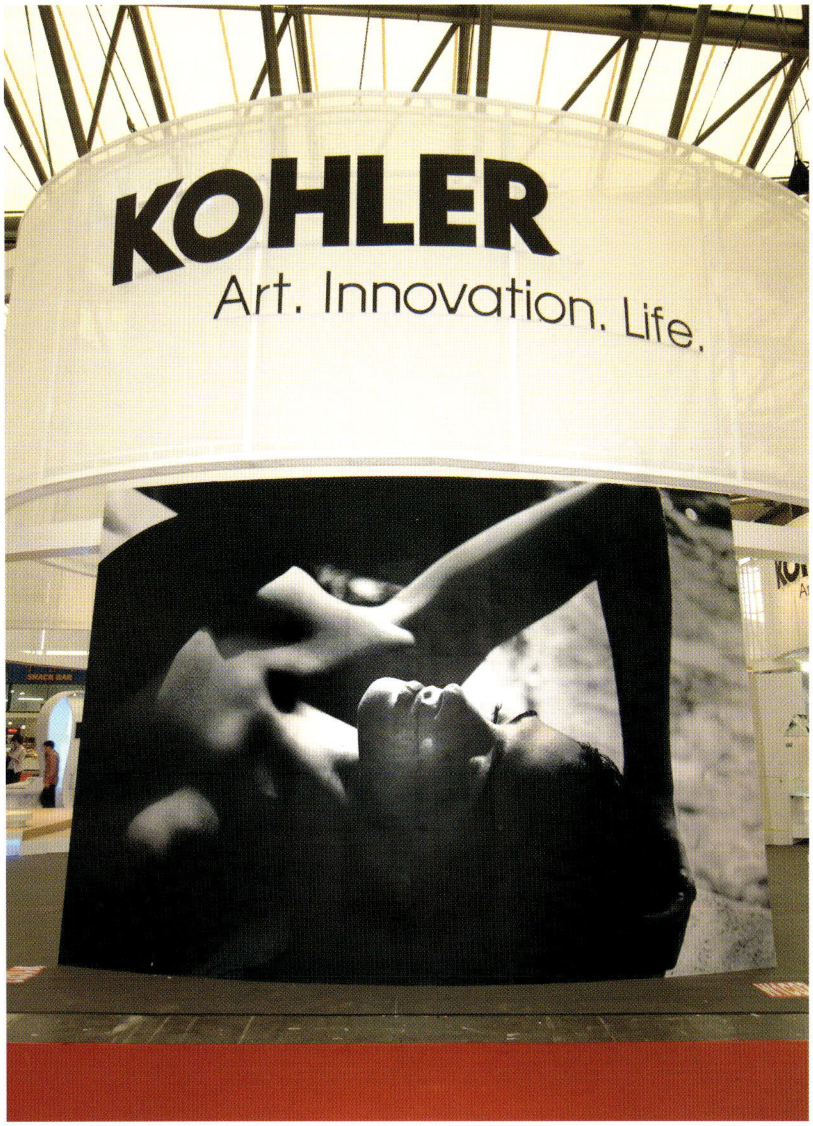
KOHLER
Art. Innovation. Life.

LANXESS at ChinaPlas

where Guangzhou, China

The LANXESS booth occupied 232 sq. m. at the Guangzhou International Convention & Exhibition Centre for ChinaPlas, the largest plastic and rubber trade show in Asia. A colour palette utilising black and red as primary colours was created by the designers, in order to differentiate the booth from previous exhibitions. The bold colours also served to distinguish it from surrounding stands.

The giant "X" was positioned to create a draw while the ceiling was raised to varying levels and heights according to the various zones.

The new hybrid technology for the automotive industry pioneered by LANXESS was demonstrated amidst an exhibition featuring different plastics applications. Large-scale images also gave the space a look and feel that was both unique and spectacular. The exhibition fulfilled the client's desire to project an innovative and progressive image for the brand.

event. exhibit. interior. themed.

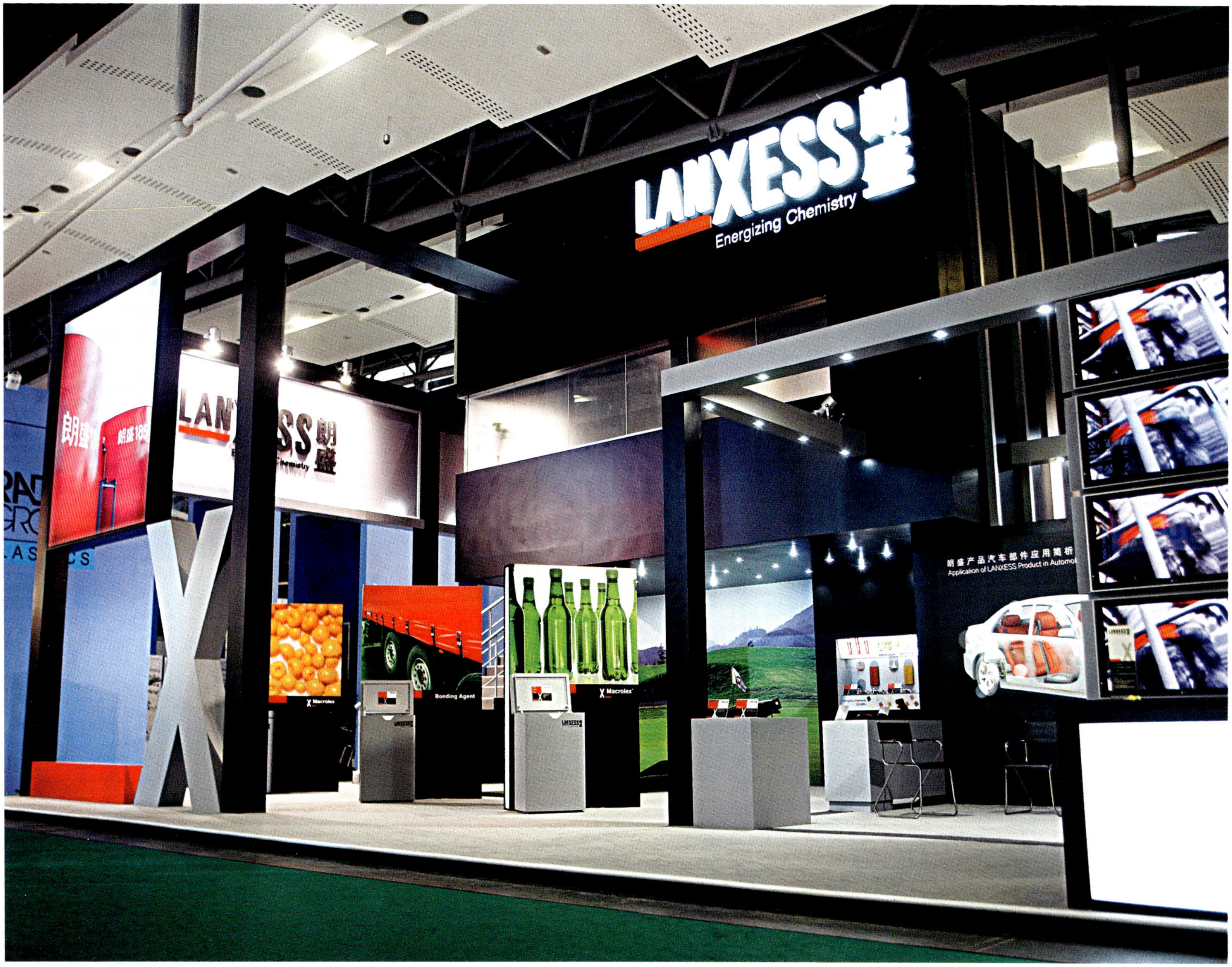
LANXESS 朗盛
Energizing Chemistry
Bonding Agent
Macrolex
朗盛产品汽车部件应用简析
Application of LANXESS Product in Automo

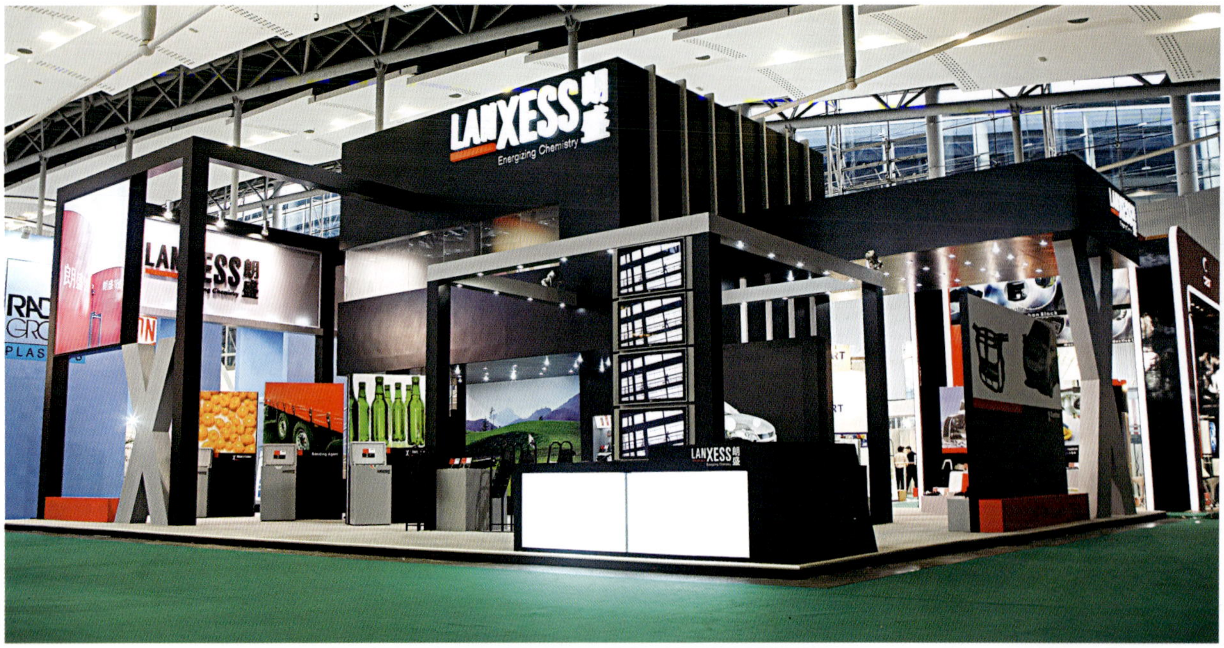
LANXESS 朗盛
Energizing Chemistry

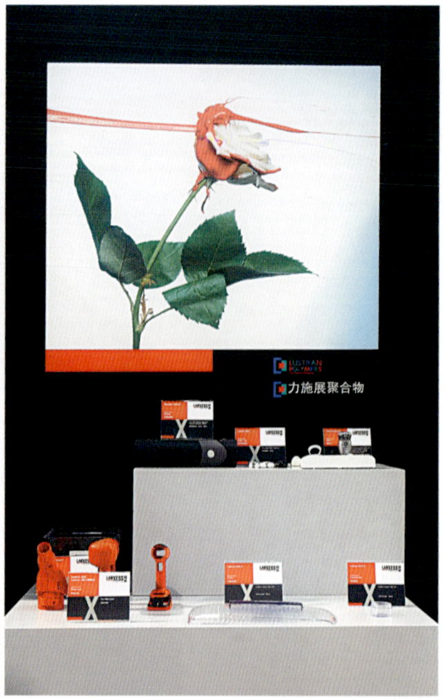
力施展聚合物

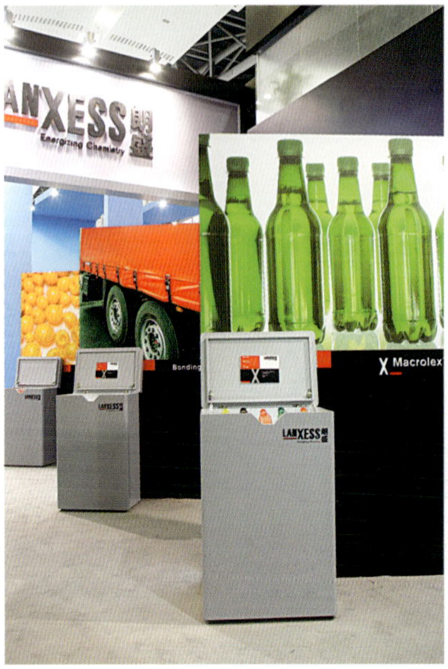
Macrolex

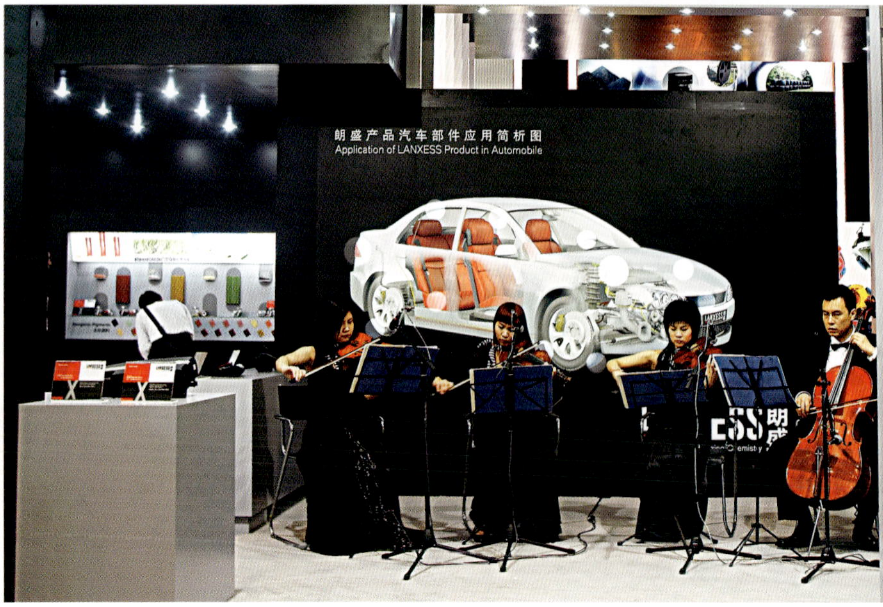
朗盛产品汽车部件应用简析图
Application of LANXESS Product in Automobile

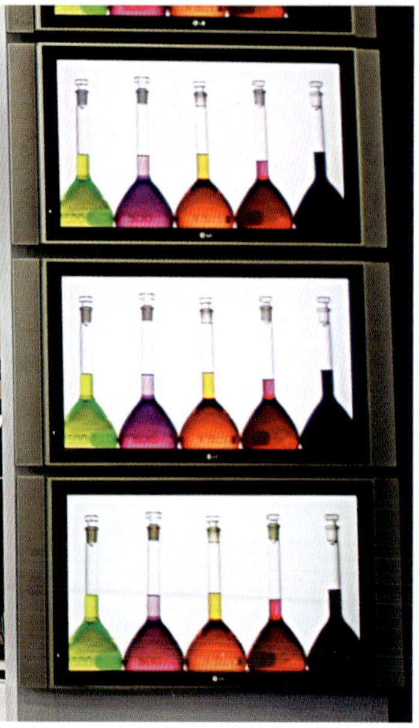

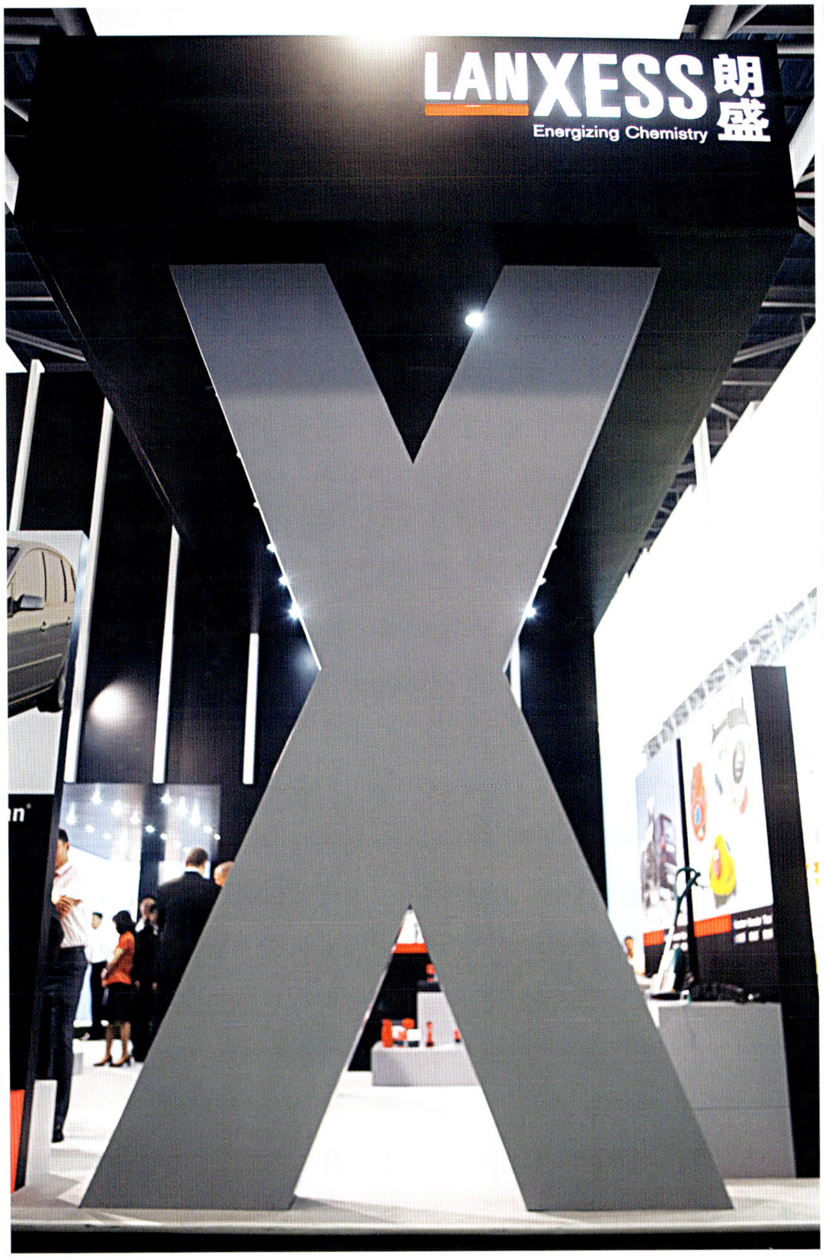
LANXESS 朗盛
Energizing Chemistry

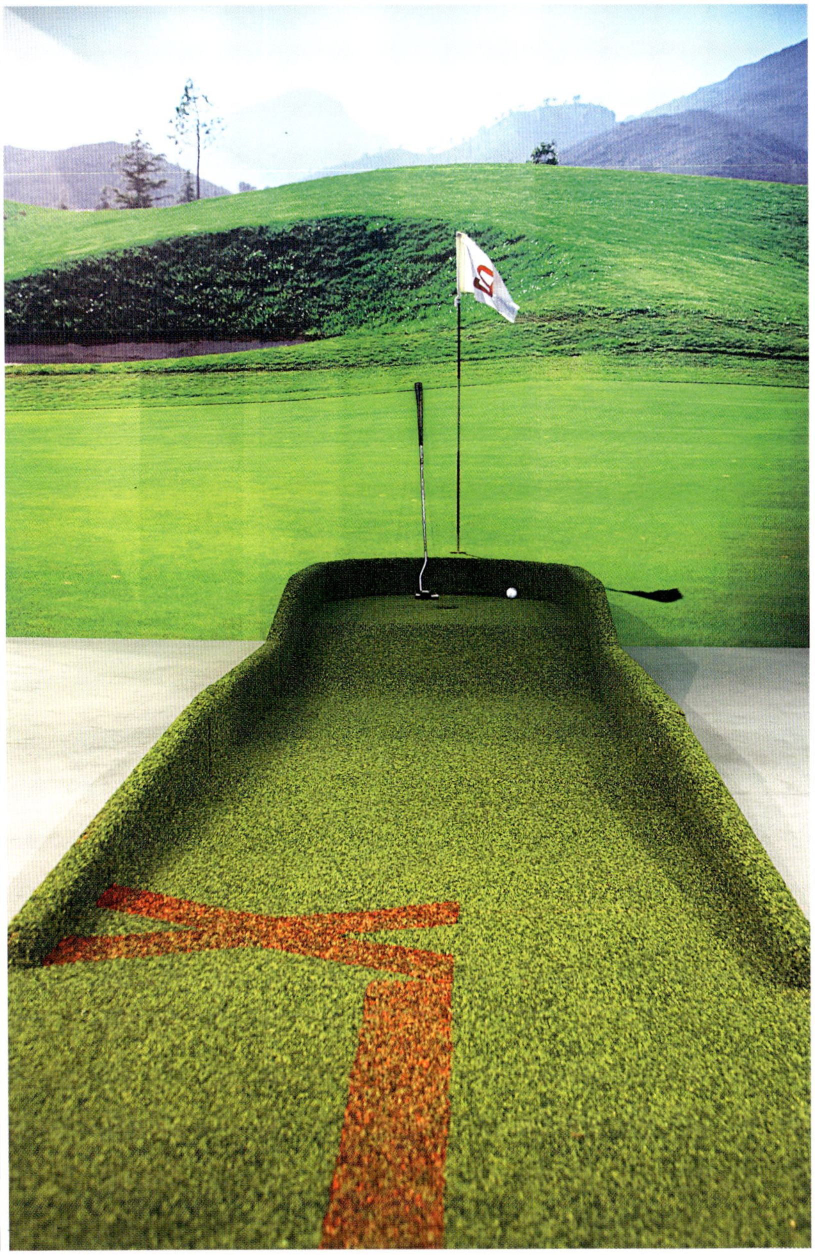

Mercedes-Benz at the 28th Bangkok International Motor Show

where Bangkok, Thailand

DaimlerChrysler (Thailand) Limited occupied this booth of 1,620 sq. m. in the Bangkok International Trade and Exhibition Centre at the 28th Bangkok International Motor Show. This event was one of the world's foremost automobile expositions attracting 130 automaker brands from 11 countries.

The booth was organised in a manner that showcased a large number of products, including the new CL, the latest luxury S300, and a line-up of the new generation E-Class automobiles. There were multiple levels: the first floor consisted of the display area, where the latest models were set on a wood-finished floor with matte black surface. The second floor was arranged as a hospitality zone for the guests, where white furniture contrasted with the illuminated sweeping wooden arch.

The booth also served as a venue for highlighting new Mercedes-Benz technology and innovation, effectively utilising LED screens and graphic waterfall techniques to introduce Mercedes-Benz's new comprehensive safety PRO-SAFE™.

The popularity of the event is reflected in the number of attendees, in excess of 1.9 million. The designer's work and the team effort received acknowledgment by winning a "Best Design Award" for Mercedes-Benz.

event. **exhibit.** interior. themed.

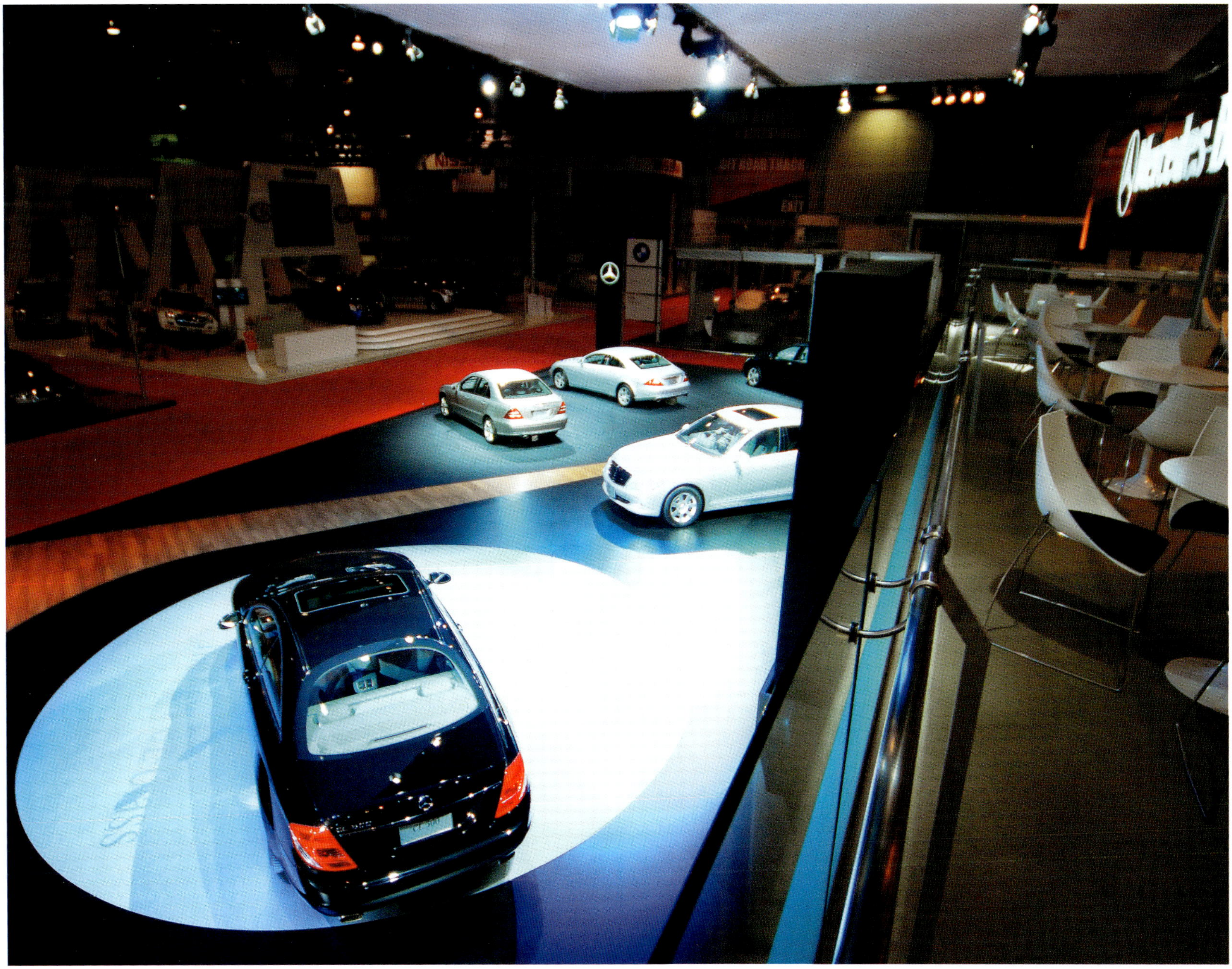

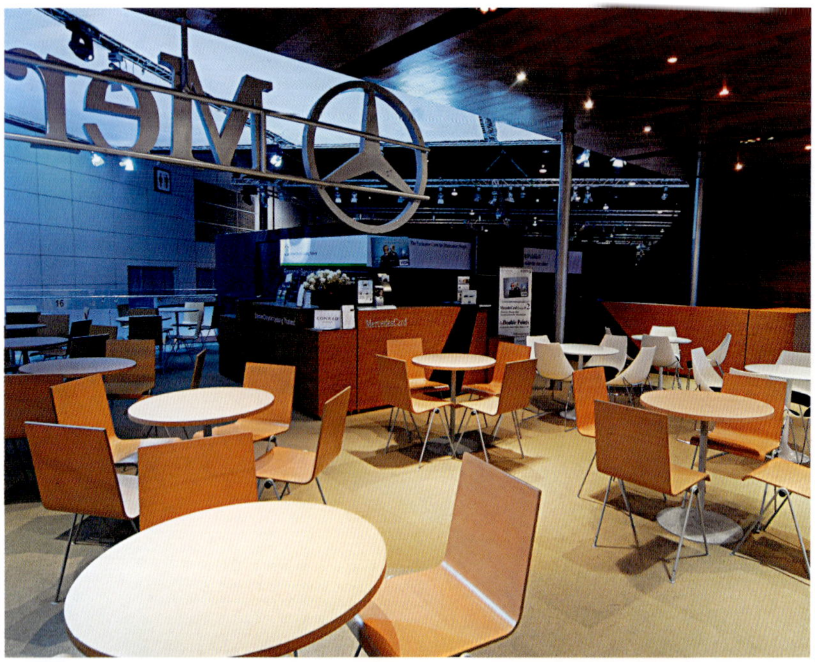

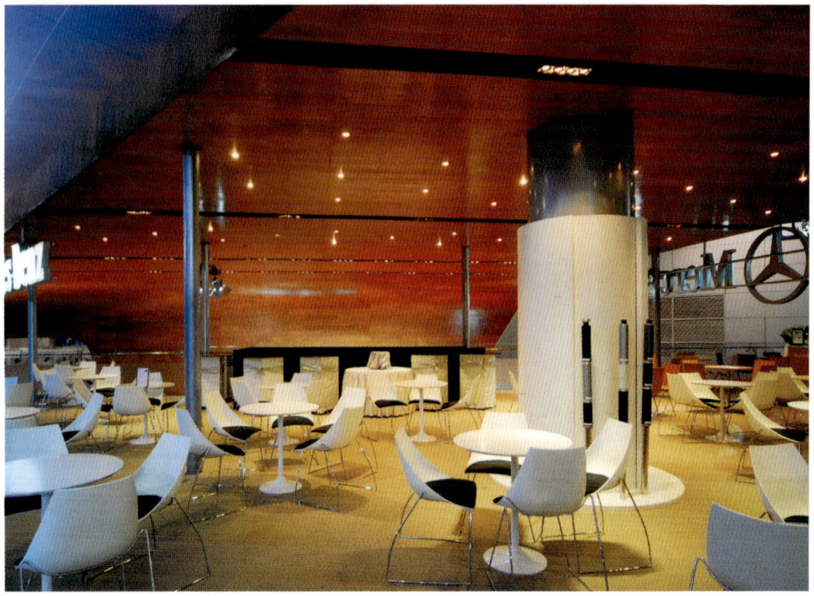

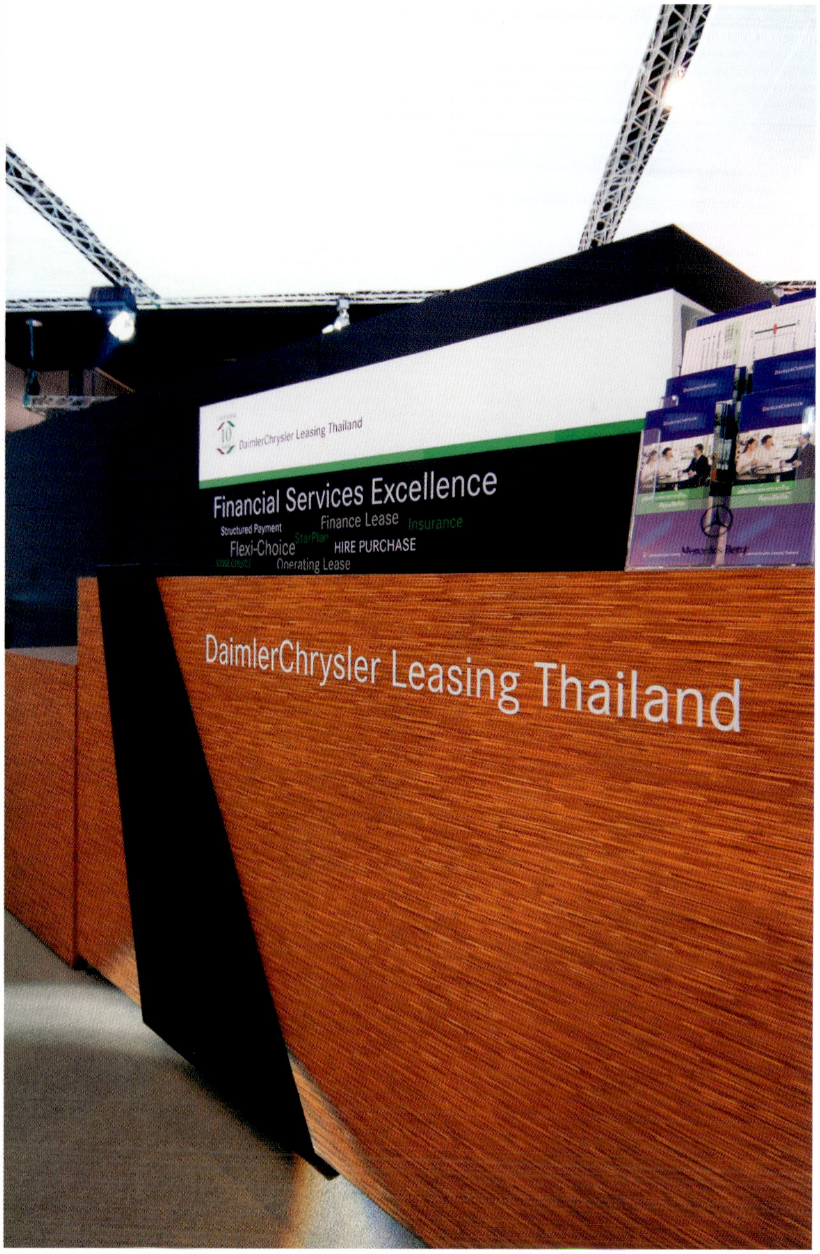
DaimlerChrysler Leasing Thailand
Financial Services Excellence
Structured Payment
Finance Lease
Insurance
Flexi-Choice
HIRE PURCHASE
Operating Lease
DaimlerChrysler Leasing Thailand

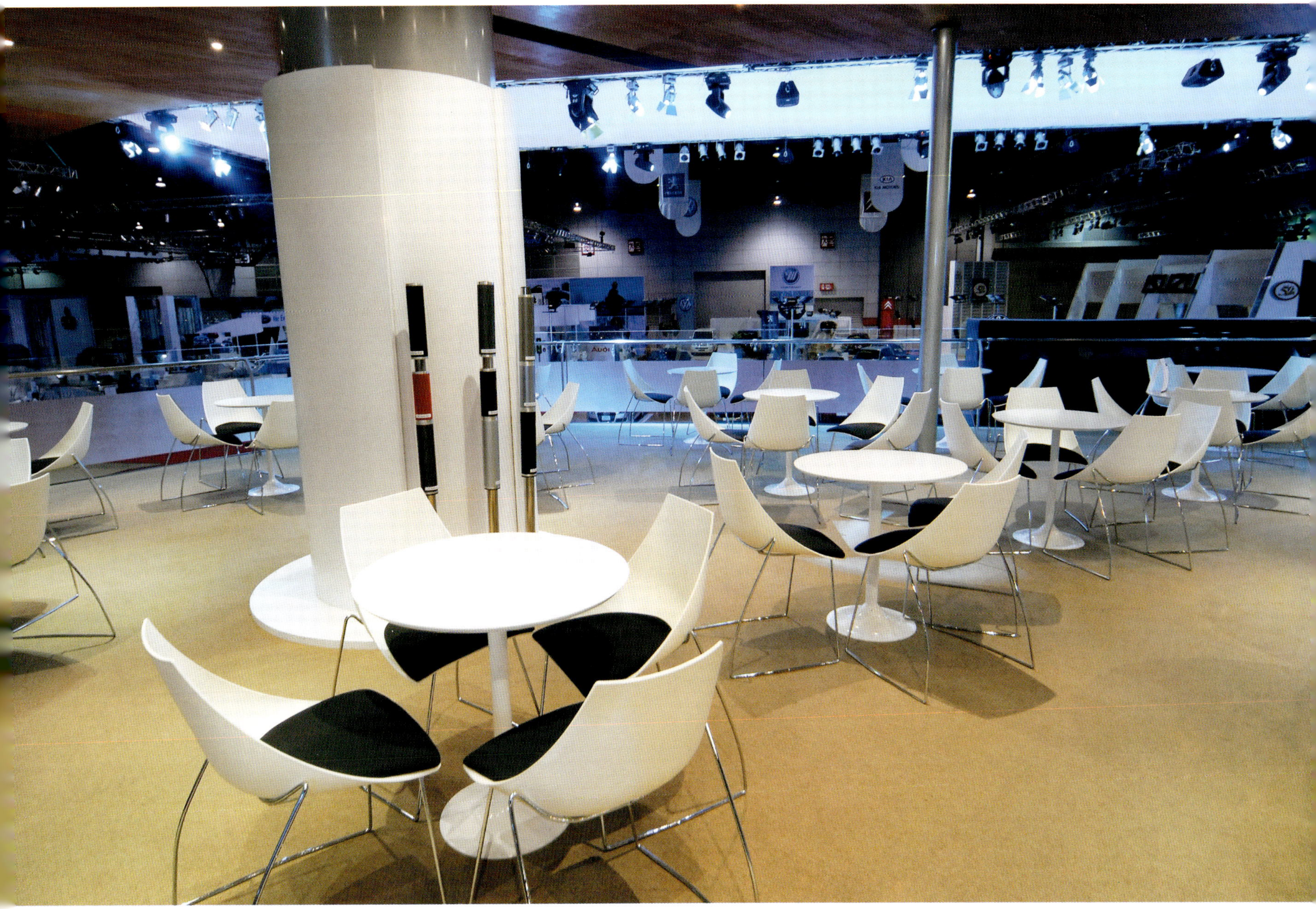

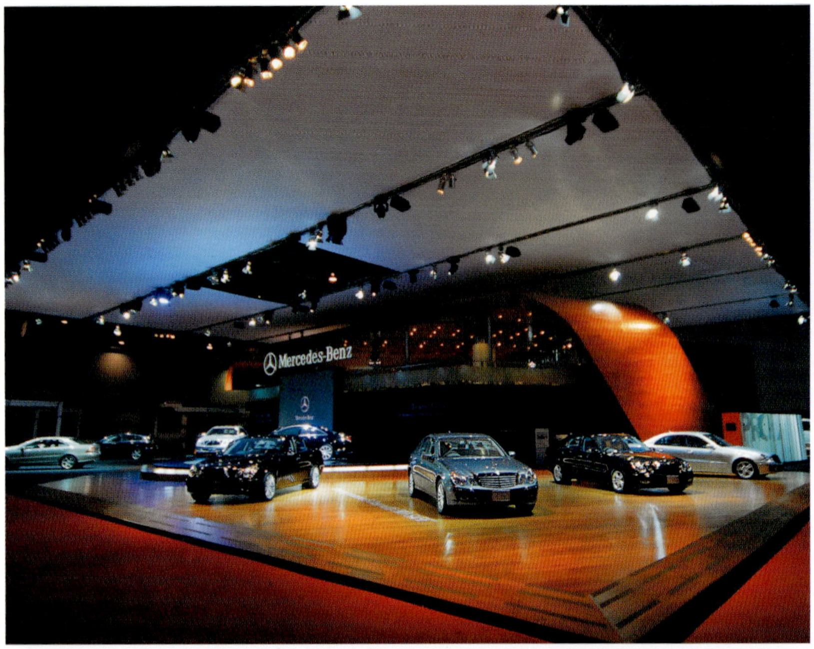
Mercedes-Benz

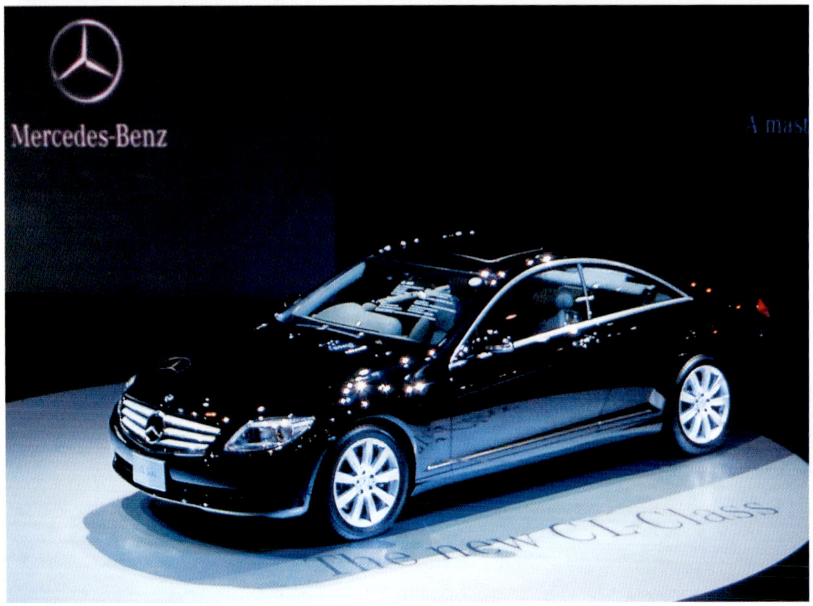
Mercedes-Benz
The new CL-Class

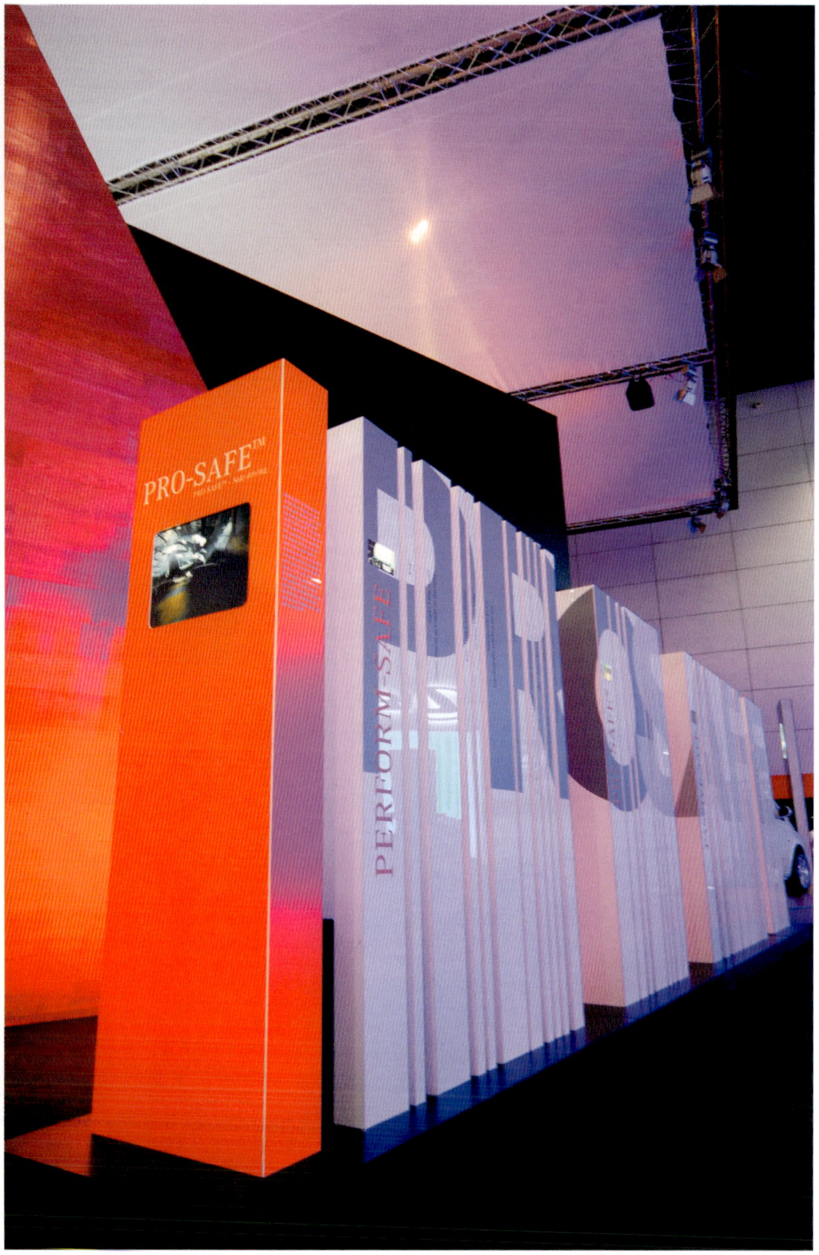
PRO-SAFE™
PERFORM-SAFE

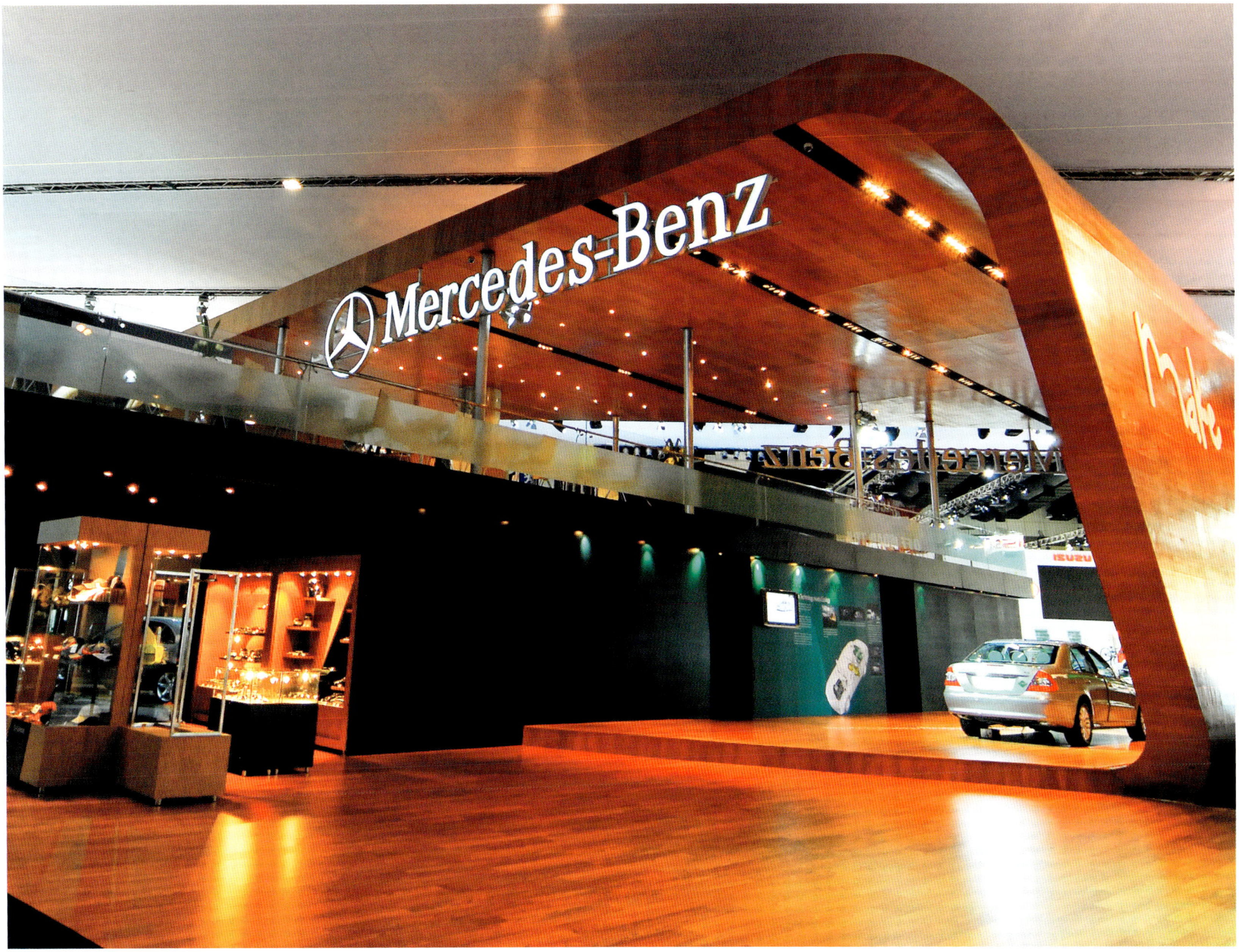
Mercedes-Benz

Mercedes-Benz at Taipei Auto Show

where Taipei, Taiwan

Mercedes-Benz wanted to design an exhibition space for one of the largest automobile events of the year, the Taiwan Auto Show.

The design concept was the evolution of the Mercedes-Benz product. This idea was brought to life by creating an S-shaped race track to effectively display the progressive design changes and improvements through the company's history.

Materials such as glass, decorative "light penetrating" canvas and maple wood floorings were utilised. Glass floorings and light boxes gave the space a sense of bold elegance.

What made this space unique was the creative use of lighting which attracted visitors to the Mercedes-Benz booth.

Mercedes-Benz was pleased with both the ingenious design of the race track concept and the overall outcome of the entire presentation.

event. exhibit. interior. themed.

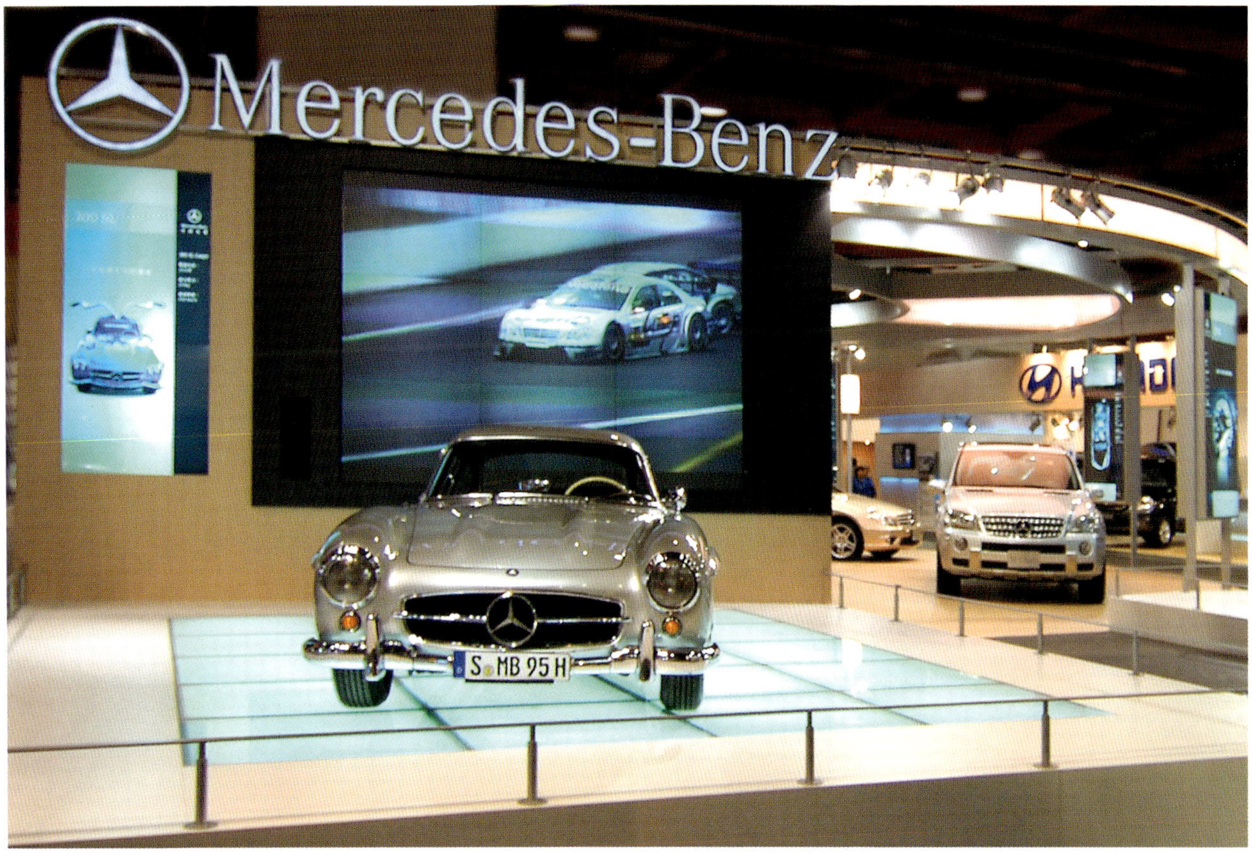
Mercedes-Benz
S MB 95 H

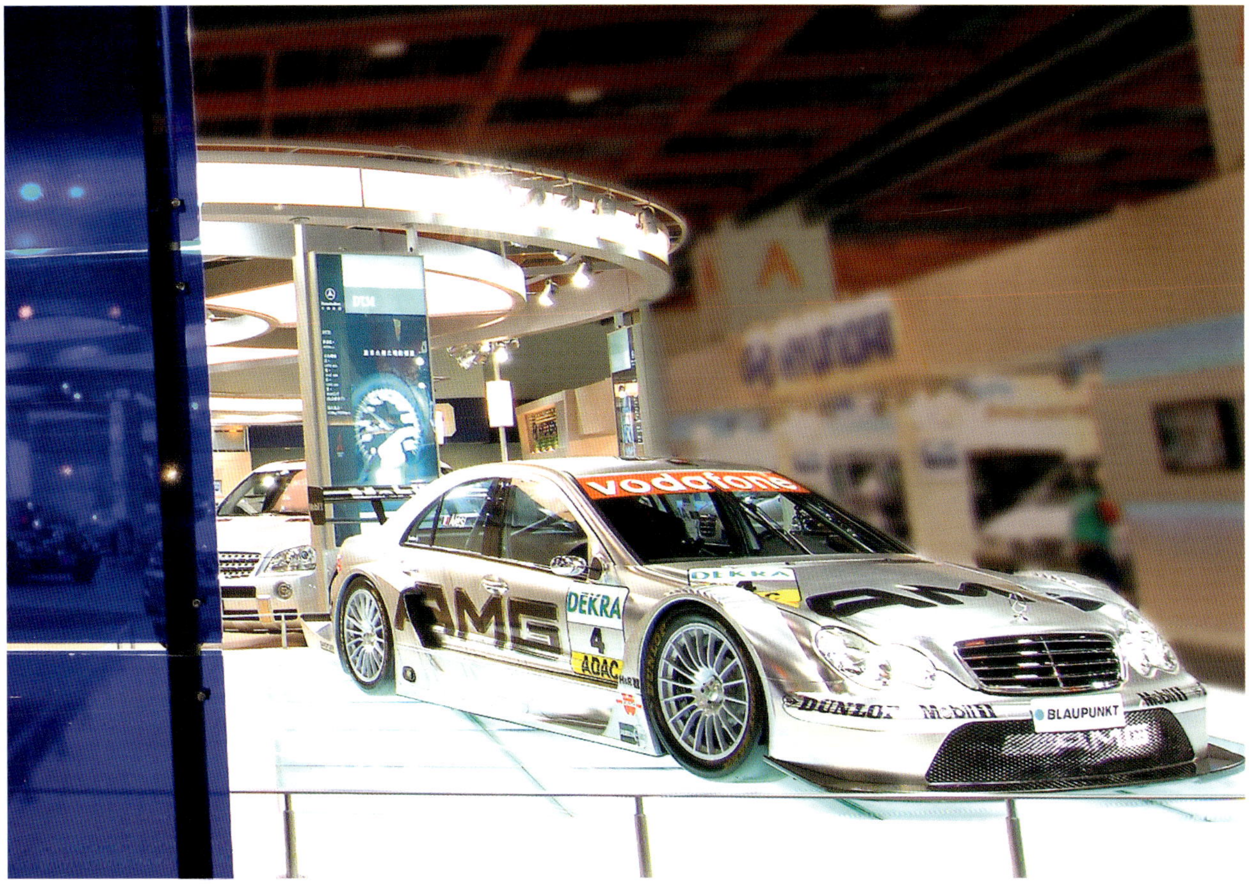
vodafone
AMG
DEKRA
4
ADAC
BLAUPUNKT

The Daodejing: Its Editions and Versions

where Hong Kong SAR, China

This exhibition, part of The International Forum on Daodejing, was sponsored by the China Religious Culture Communication Association and the China Taoist Association. The Hong Kong History Museum recommended Pico to be the exhibition's designers.

Cultural relics including a "bamboo slip" Daodejing from the Warring States period (the earliest version discovered in archaeological finds), various editions, textual commentaries, modern Chinese language editions and multiple foreign language translations were exhibited. This was the largest Daodejing exhibition ever held.

The total area dedicated to the project was approximately 12,000 sq. ft., with interactives providing more detailed information about Daodejing. The space was a minimalist white with appropriate design features which communicated the essence of Daodejing. The case designs fulfilled the stringent requirements of displaying national treasures in a temporary exhibition setting.

The exhibition was also featured on the National Library of China's website, drawing many positive comments which far exceeded expectations.

event. exhibit. interior. themed.

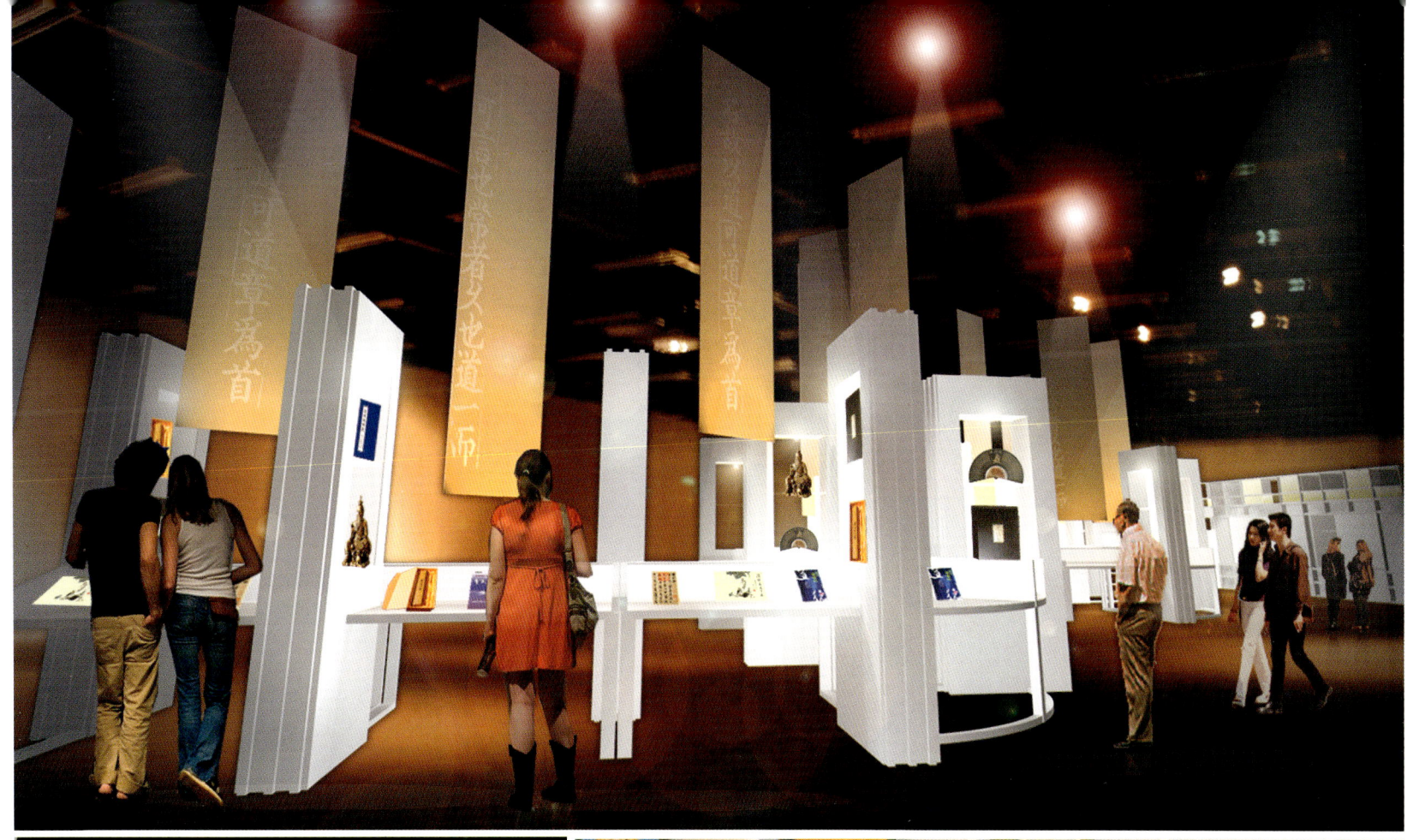

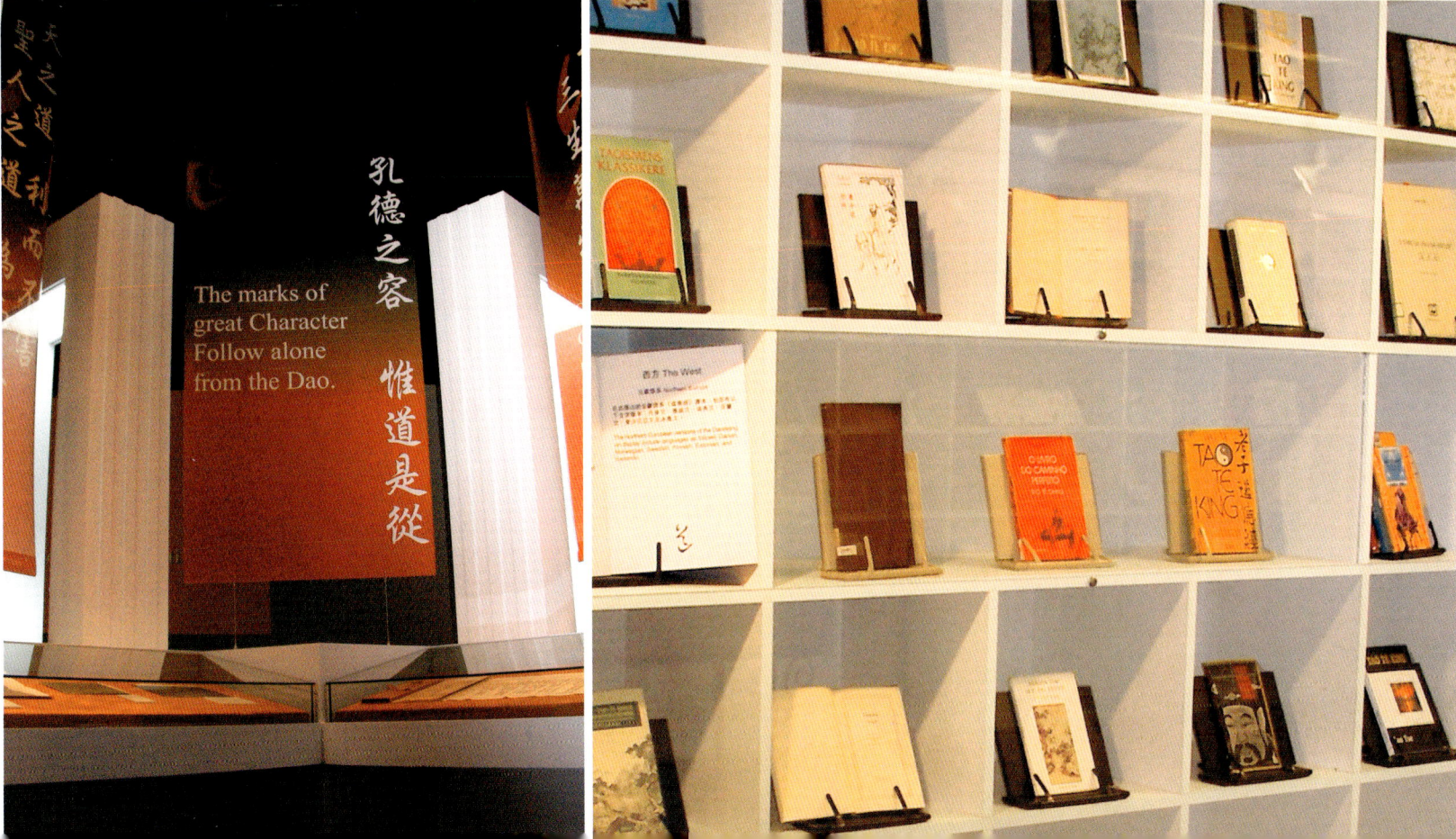

The marks of great Character Follow alone from the Dao. 孔德之容 惟道是從

Chu Kong at the Hong Kong Optical Fair

where Hong Kong SAR, China

Chu Kong Optical participated in the Hong Kong Optical Fair with an exhibition stand to build their brand awareness.

The design was simple and dynamic with sweeping curved lines and irregular forms, creating a welcoming space for visitors to enter. The white, orange and yellow of the booth were complemented with lighting that projected a tasteful, classy atmosphere. A flurry of golden "planes" accentuated the form and drew visitors into the booth. The diagonal layout created a spacious open atmosphere.

The layout and unique quality of the space impressed both judges and visitors, and won the second runner-up Booth Design Award at the show.

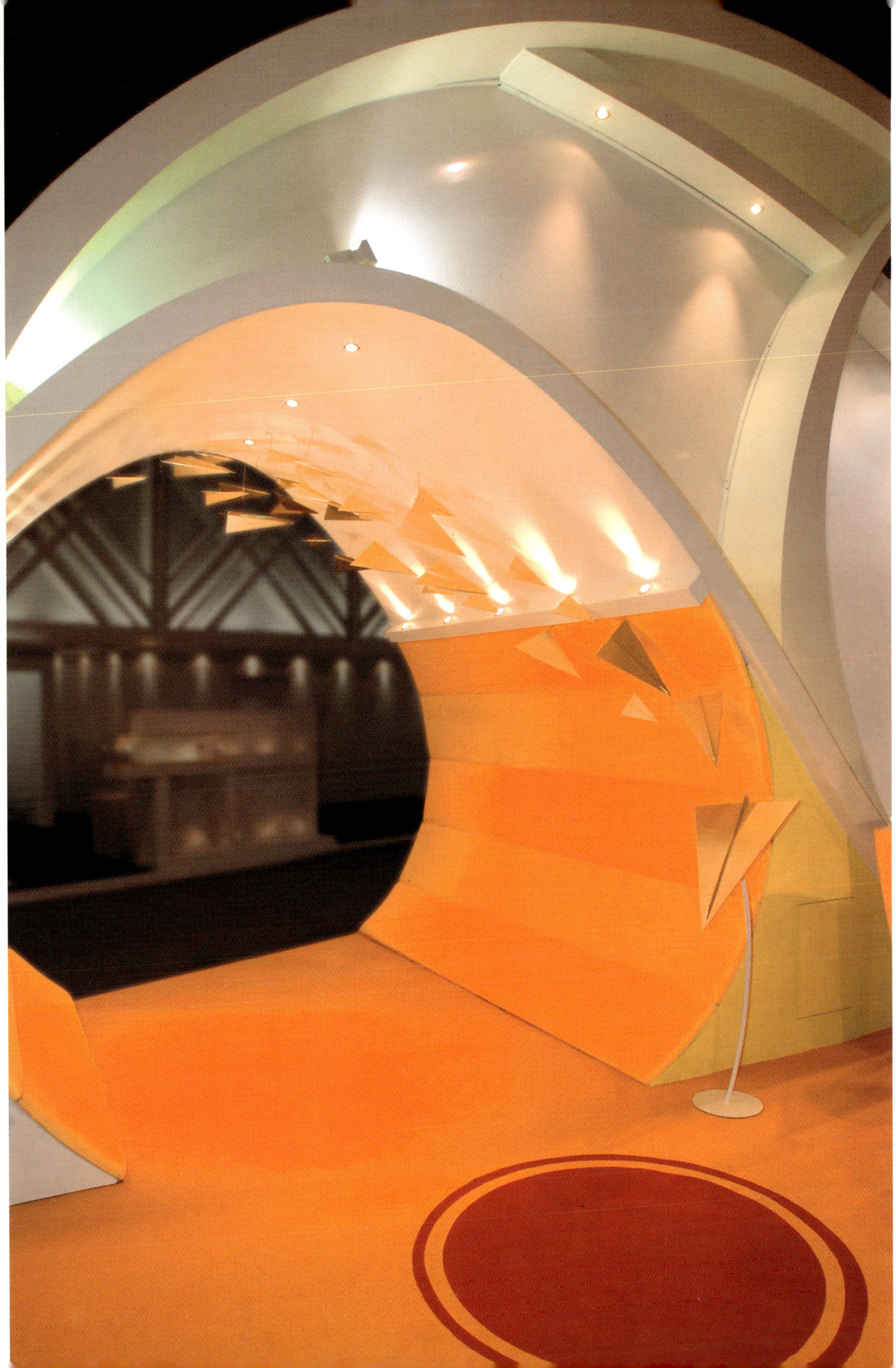

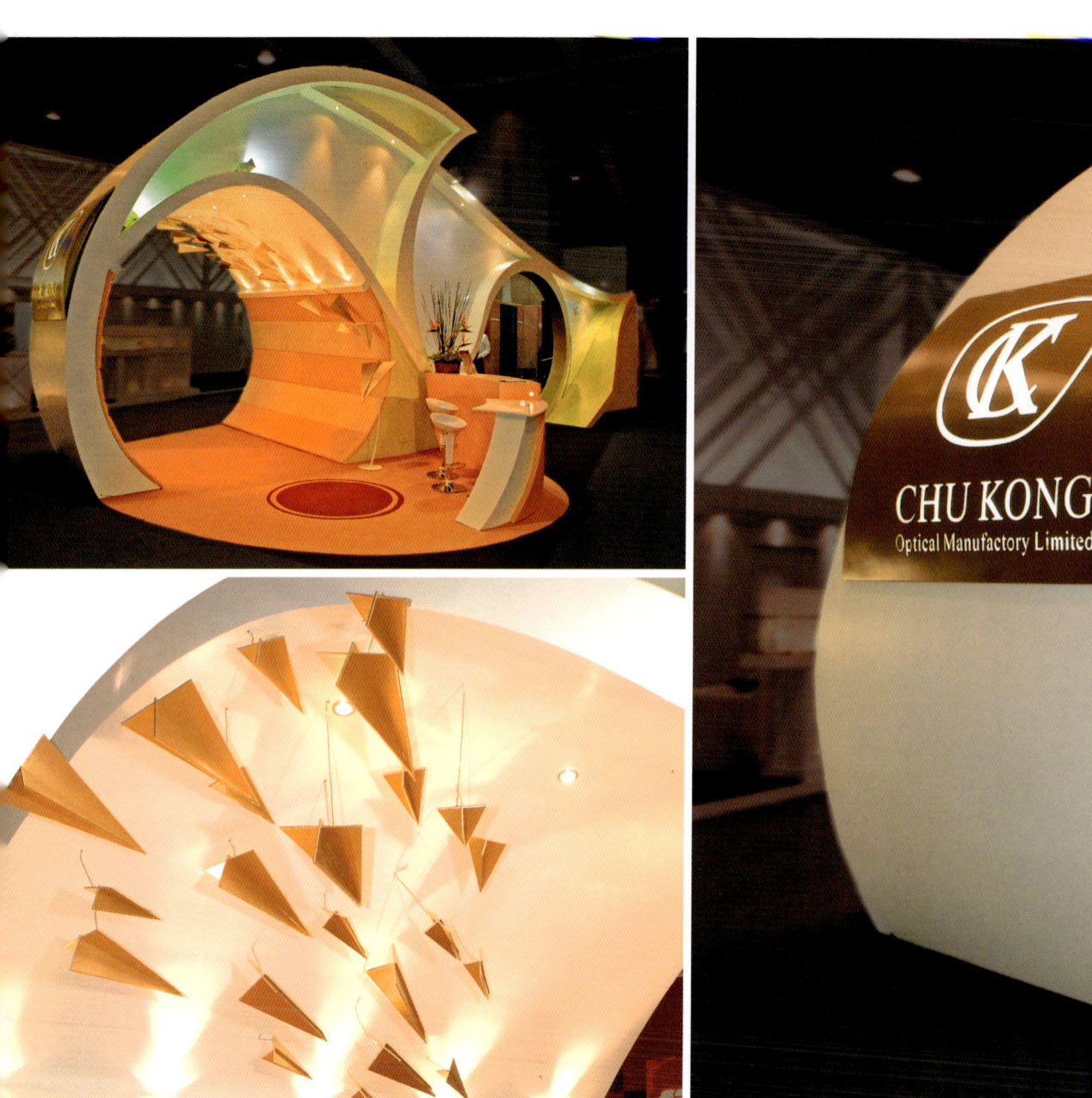

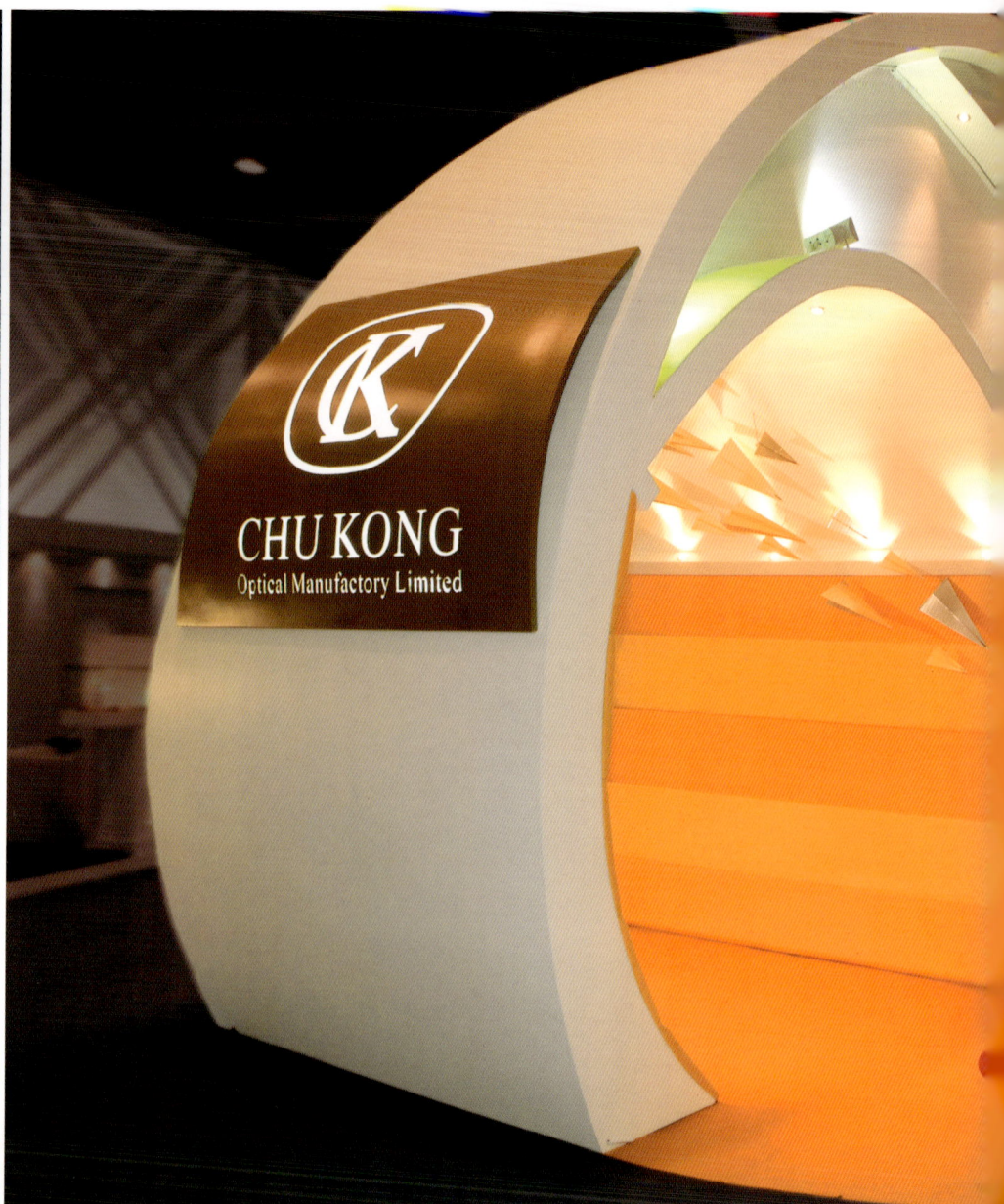

CHU KONG
Optical Manufactory Limited

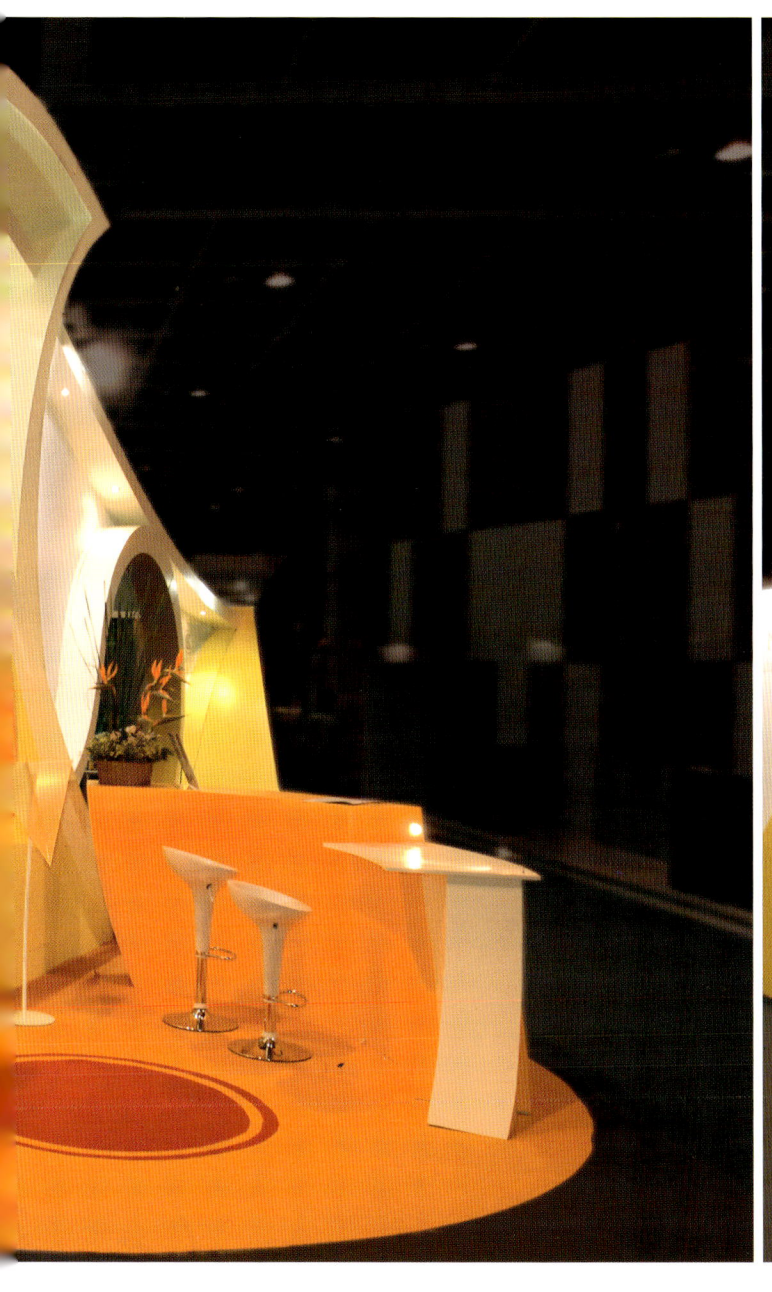

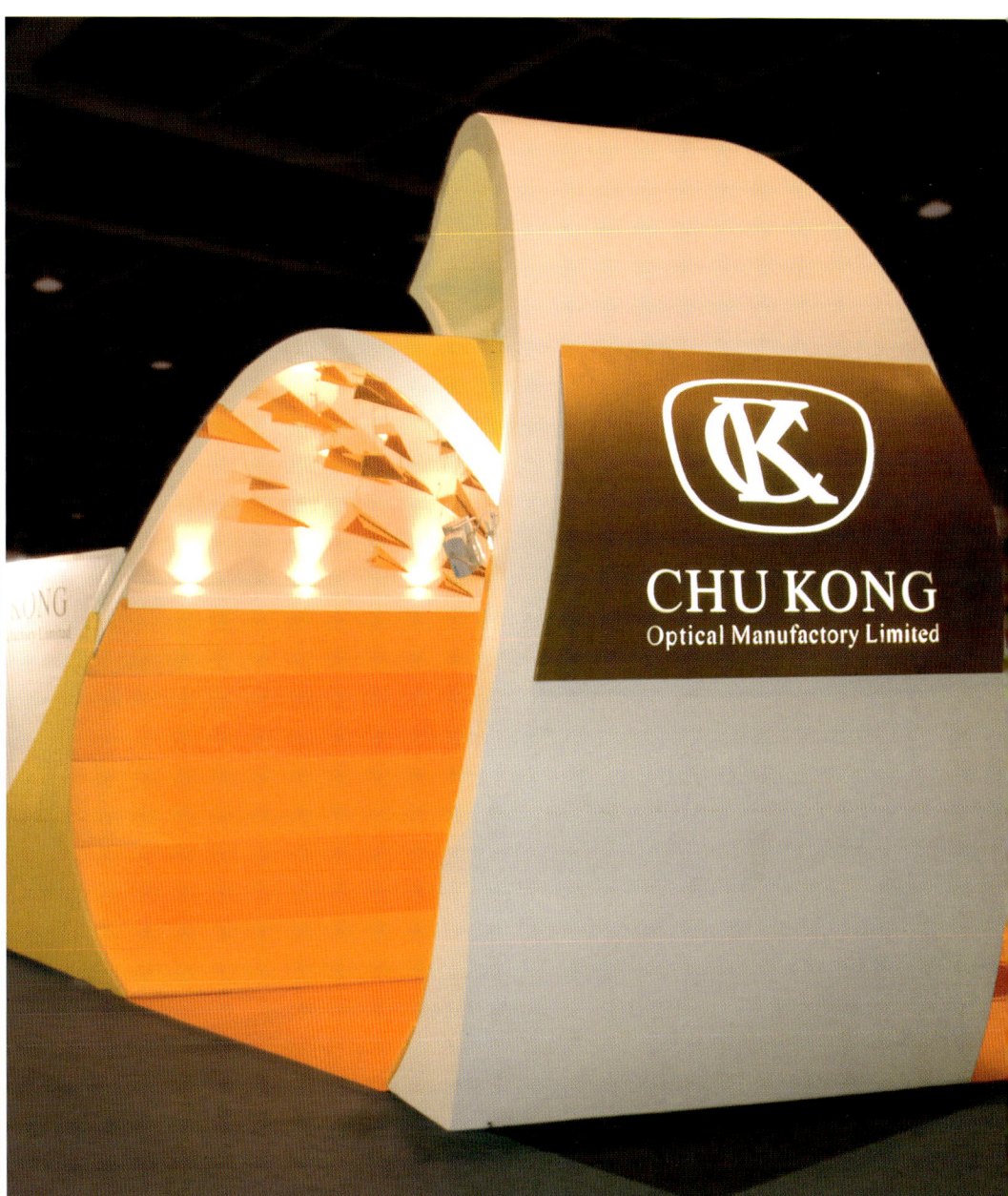

CHU KONG
Optical Manufactory Limited

Mizuno at the 5th International Golf Trade Fair

where Beijing, China

The Mizuno exhibit space at the National Agriculture Exhibition Centre, Beijing, was designed and constructed for one of Asia's largest golf exhibitions, the 5th China (Beijing) International Golf Trade Fair. Both the booth and golf trade fair provided a perfect platform for Mizuno to promote its products and brand image.

The team created a structure incorporating two giant "golf ball" sections, effectively integrating Mizuno's "X8" golf balls into the design. Passersby were instantly attracted to the streamlined structure by the arc-shaped construction which effectively displayed their products within. The overall colour scheme was dominated by eye-catching reds and blues.

event. exhibit. interior. themed.

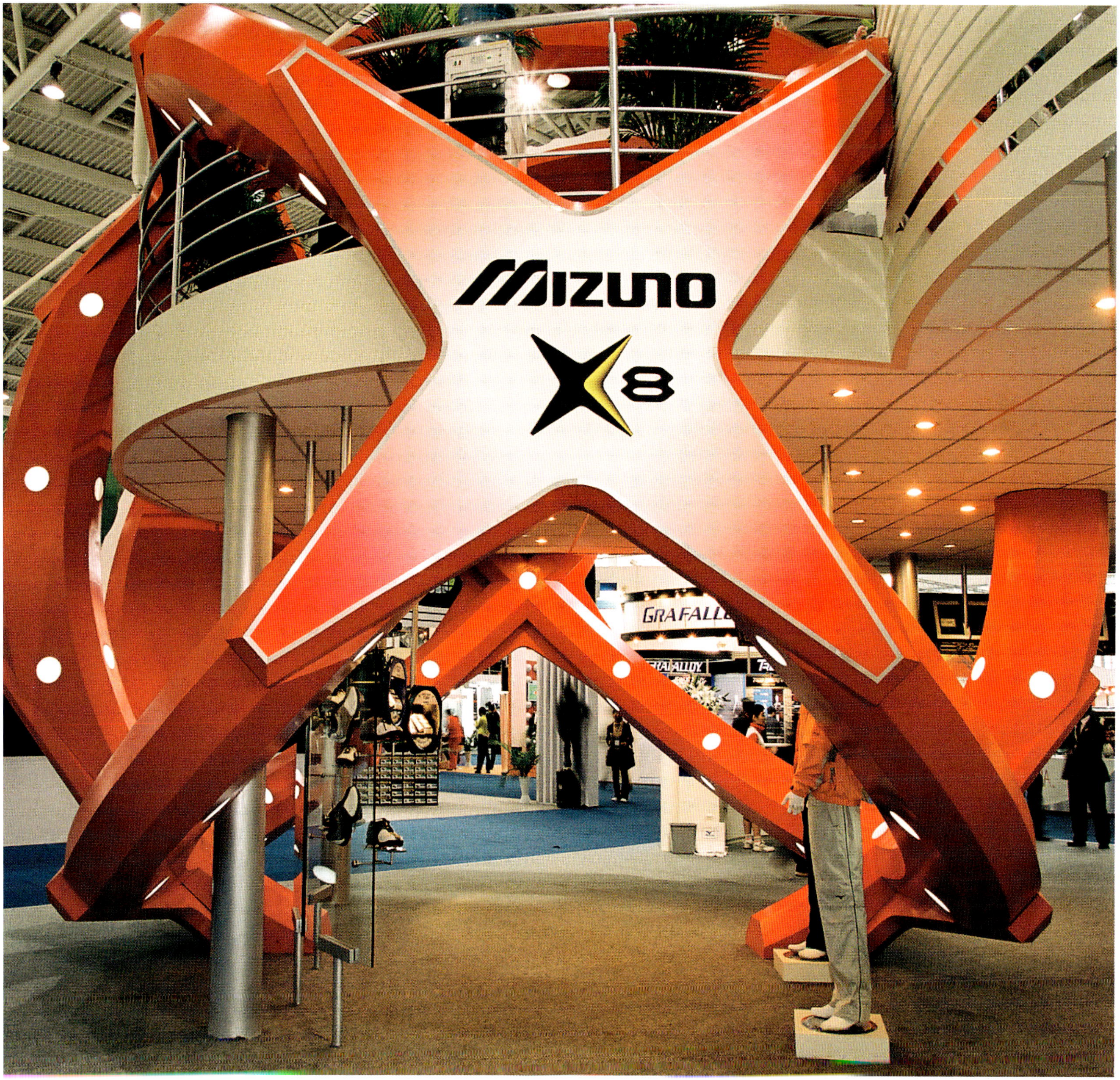
MIZUNO
X8

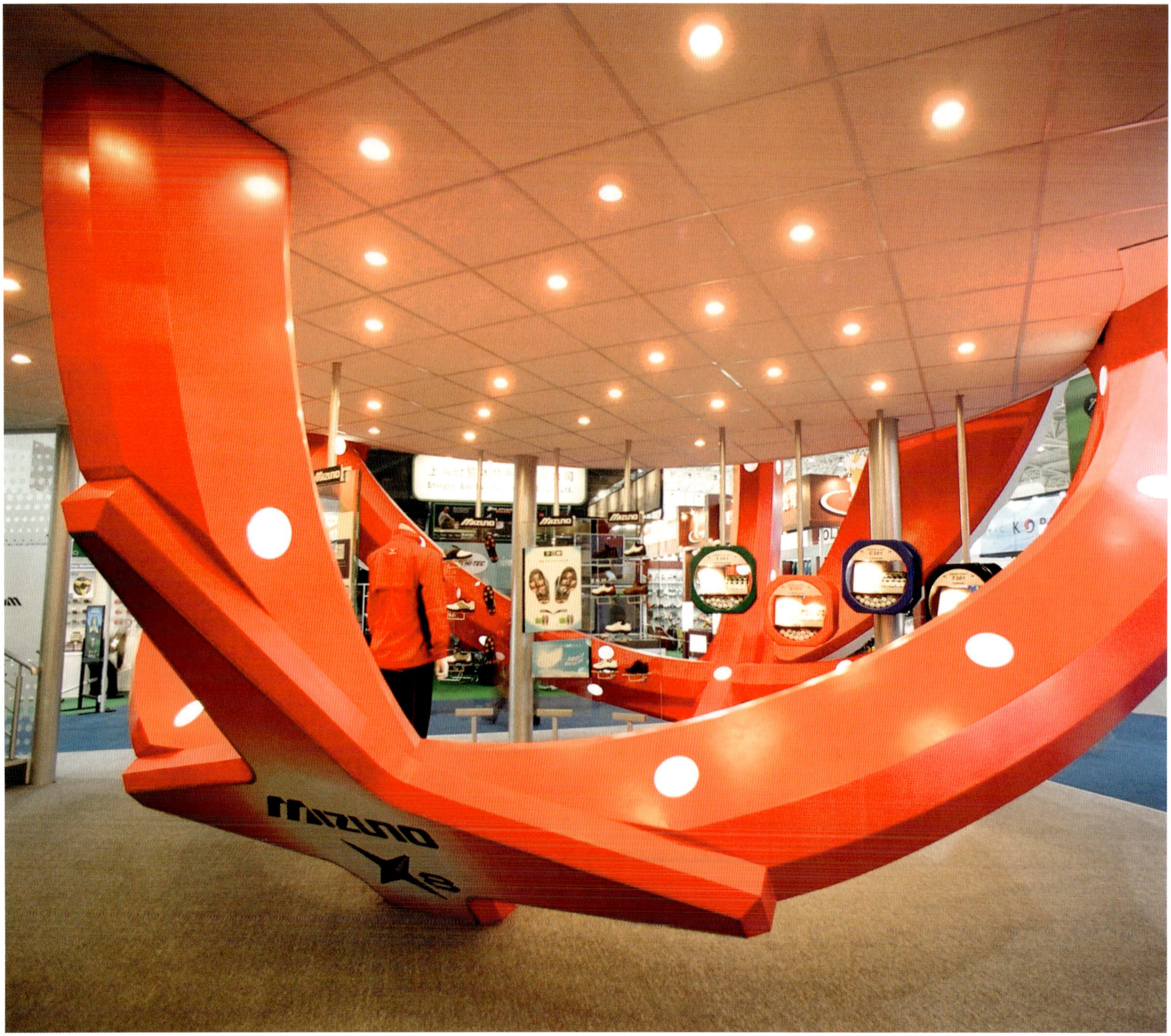

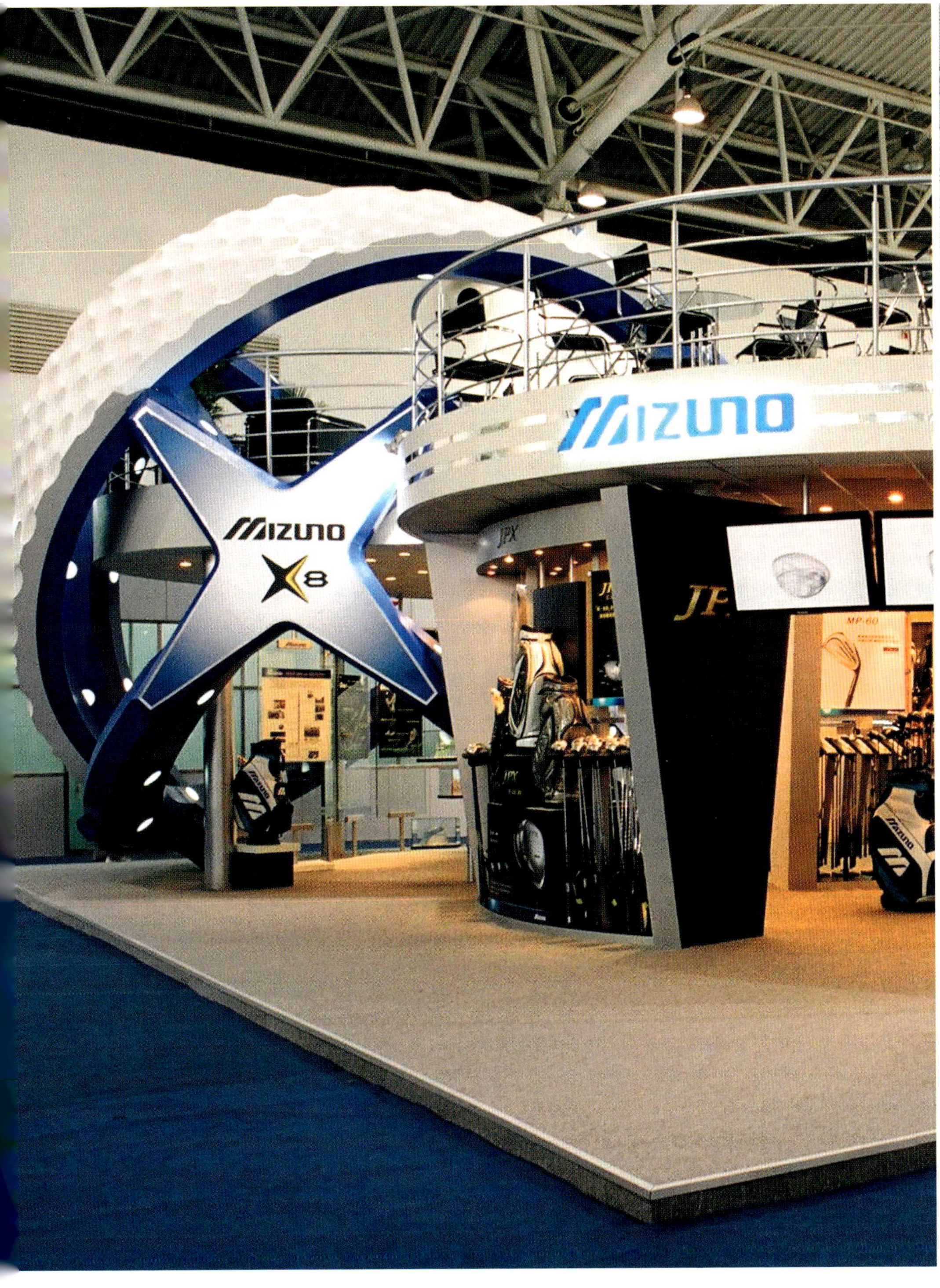
MIZUNO
MIZUNO
X8
JPX
JPX
MP-60

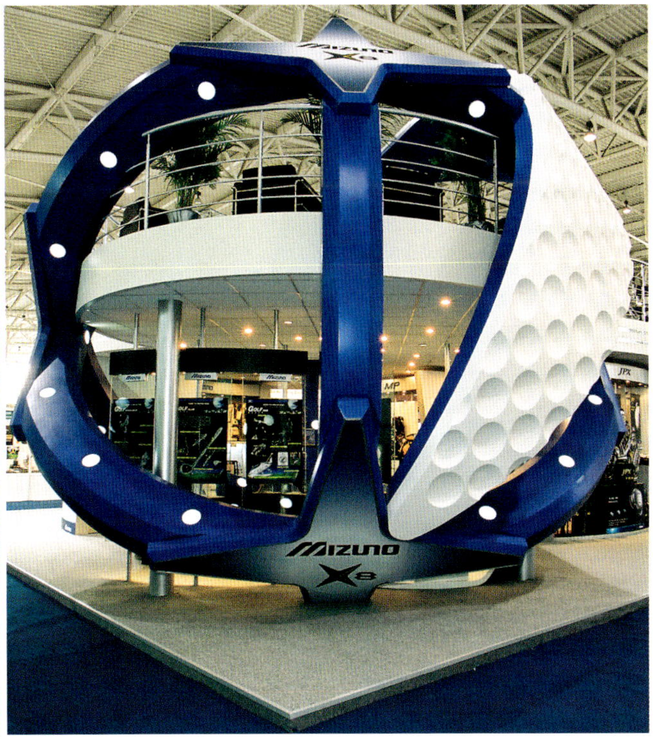
MIZUNO
X8
MIZUNO
X8
JPX
MP

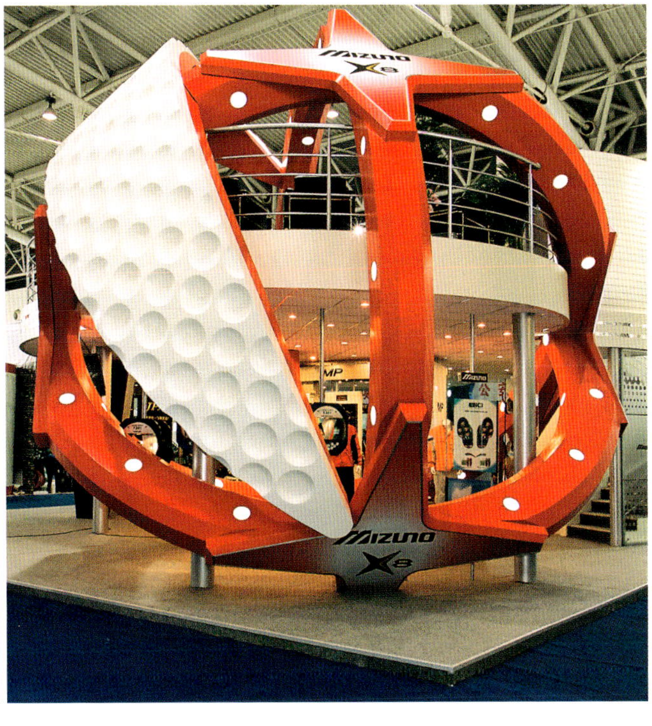
MIZUNO
X8
MIZUNO
X8
MP

Peugeot at Auto Shanghai

where Shanghai, China

The bi-annual Auto Shanghai is a landmark event on the automotive industry's global calendar. Sprawling over 140,000 sq. m. and attracting more than 500,000 visitors from 108 countries, Auto Shanghai 2007 was the biggest and best show yet.

The theme for the exhibition, the twelfth in the series, was "Technology and Nature in Harmony." Peugeot, among other international automotive manufacturers, wanted to dramatise and emphasise this theme by creating high-tech launch displays to introduce alternative and fuel-efficient cars to the world.

The stand was designed and fabricated with a special space on the mezzanine floor dedicated to conferences and events. At both sides of the stand, two blue panels with Peugeot's logo were erected. Large-scale images of Peugeot cars were framed by "lion's eyes" viewable from the entire exhibition hall, to focus the attention of the visitor on the vast, colourful space and the featured vehicles.

The designers also created three platforms as exposition support for the cars, with a concealed lighting system to create a sense of excitement and emphasise the modern design of the product.

event. exhibit. interior. themed.

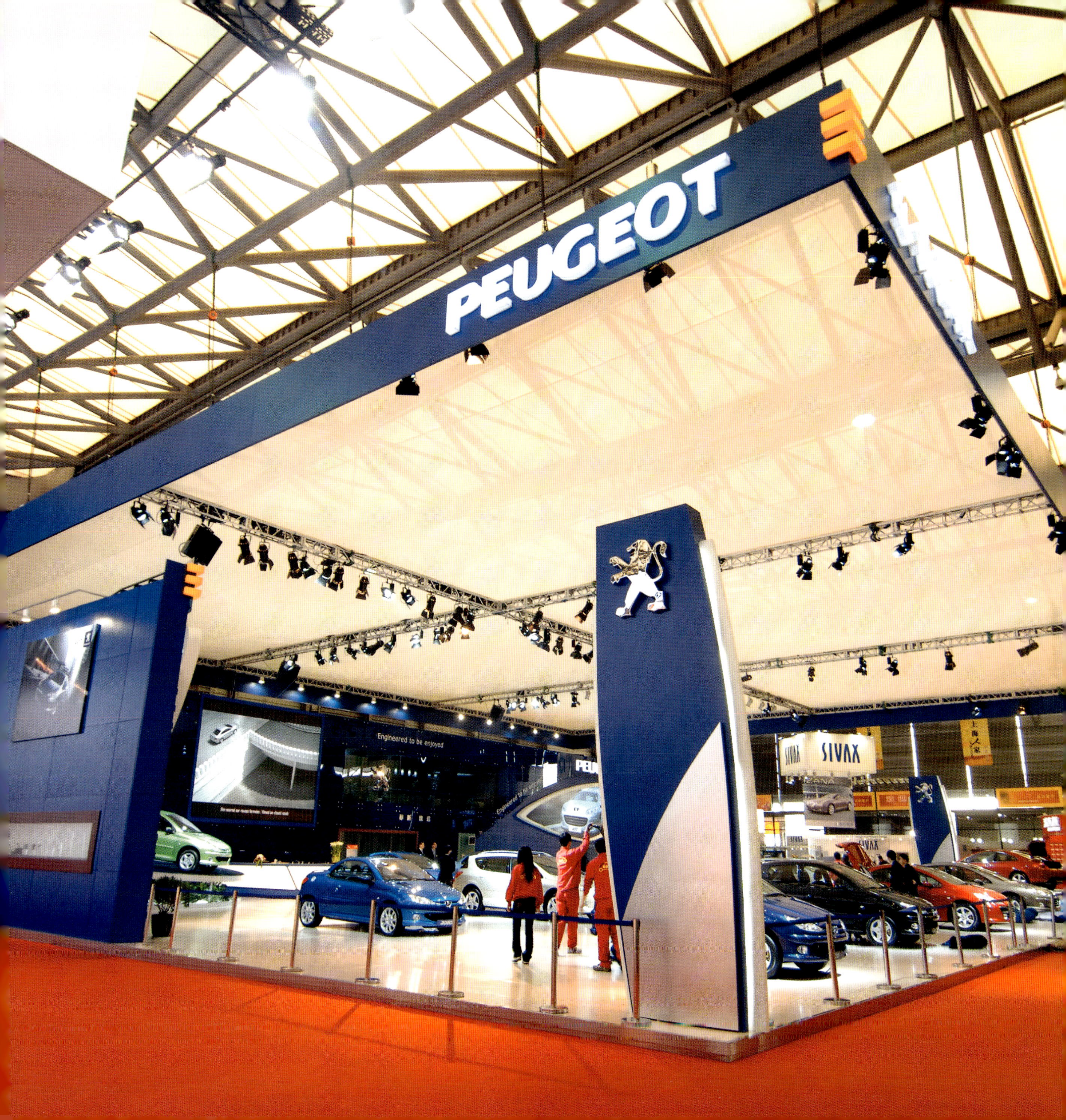
PEUGEOT
Engineered to be enjoyed
SIVAX

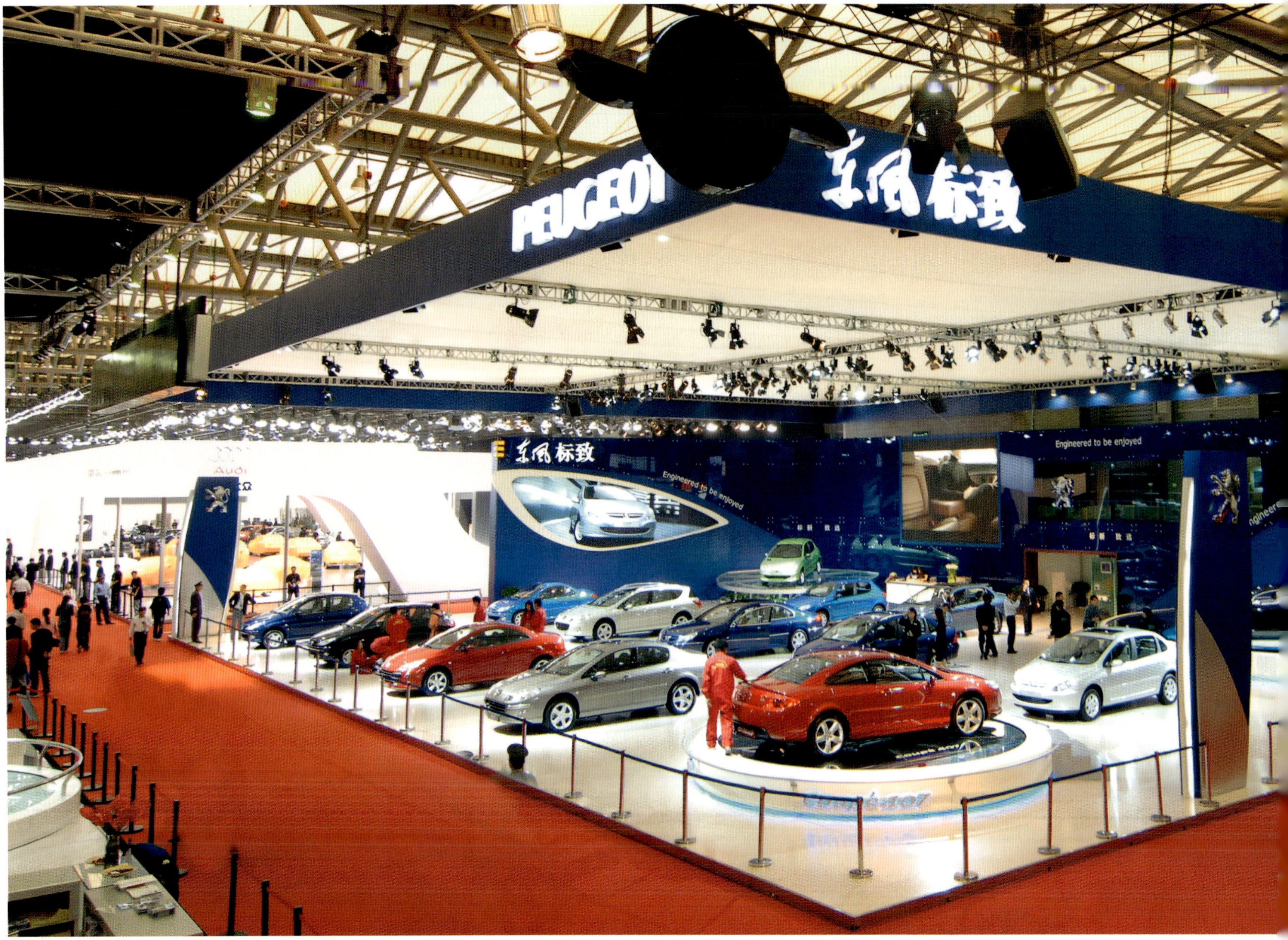

PEUGEOT
东风标致
Engineered to be enjoyed

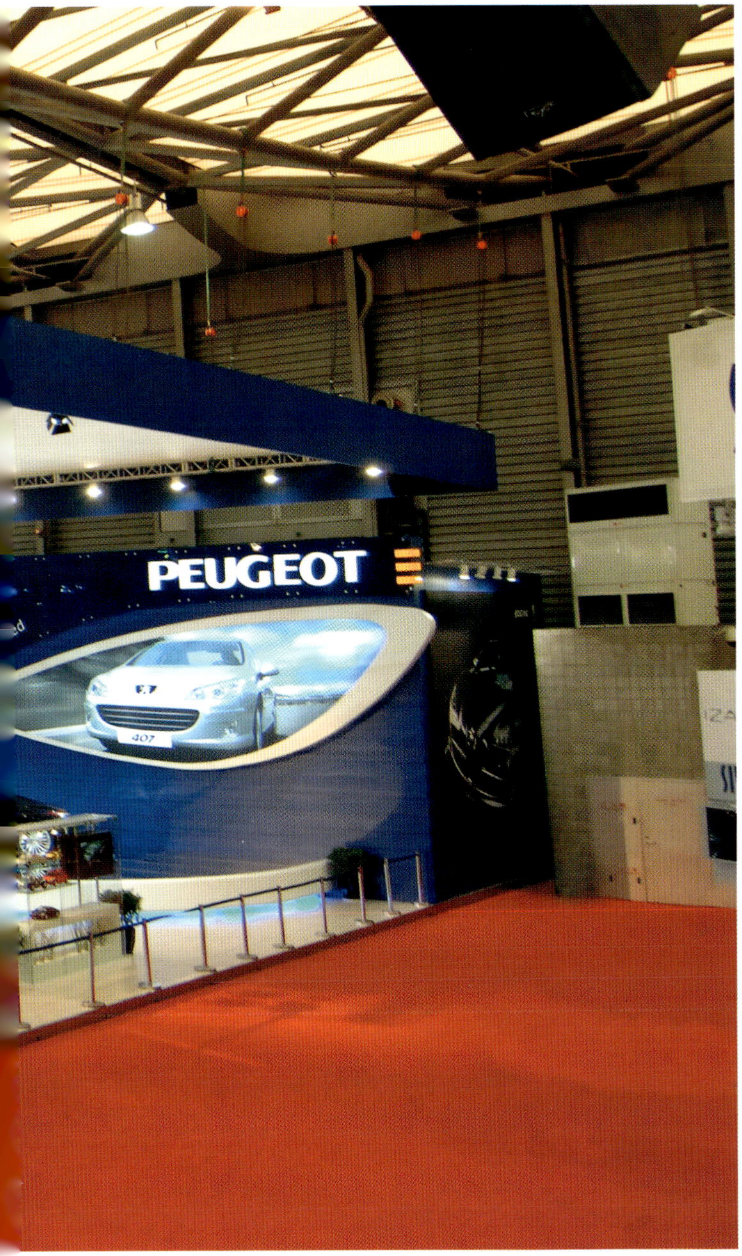
PEUGEOT

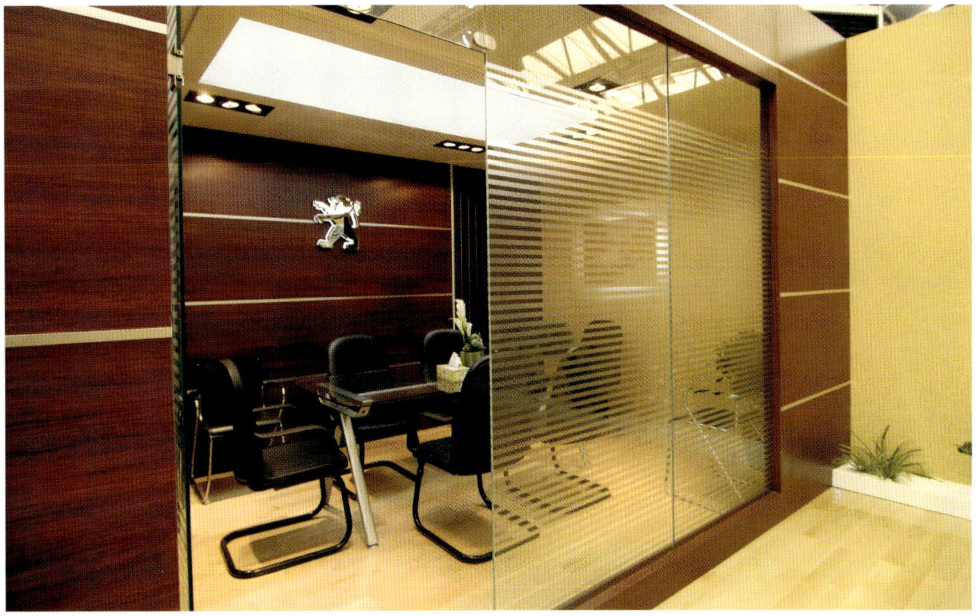

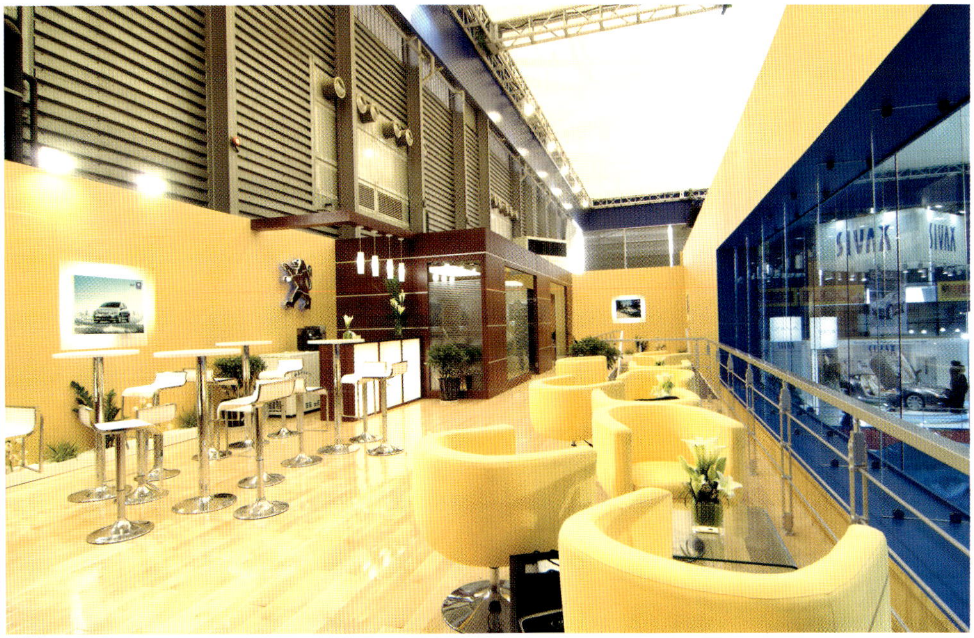

Raytheon at the 47th International Paris Air Show

where Le Bourget Airport, France

A hospitality chalet and an exhibition pavilion were designed and built for Raytheon at Le Bourget Airport, France. The concept was to provide a space for Raytheon to showcase their latest product lines, and create a place for business. Pico offices in the U.S. and Singapore collaborated in the design and build, resulting in a contemporary and functional design with a distinctly European flair.

The entire space was arranged with a minimalist approach, on the use of imagery and customised lighting fixtures. Convertible conference rooms and fully functional kitchens were constructed on both levels.

The result was a blend of colours and high-quality materials, posh white walls, grey brushed-aluminium panels, textured wallpapers, glazed mirrors, custom light fixtures and multi-tone floors. The hospitality chalet consisted of a five-unit, two-storey structure with an inviting reception area, meeting rooms and an open brasserie for informal and self-service dining on the ground floor. The second floor was dedicated to more private spaces – the CEO meeting room with three additional secured VIP areas, an executive staff support space and food / beverage stations. The exhibition pavilion showcased the core businesses of Raytheon: Sensing, C3I, Sensors and Mission Support. A 3-way rotating billboard welcomed customers and guests to the hospitality chalet.

The air-conditioned space provided a comfortable venue for patrons to visit the featured models, detailed products, interactive demo stations and displays.

The show, the Raytheon exhibition, and the designer's innovative concepts were very successful and much appreciated by the Raytheon staff.

event. exhibit. interior. themed.

Raytheon
Customer Success Is Our Mission

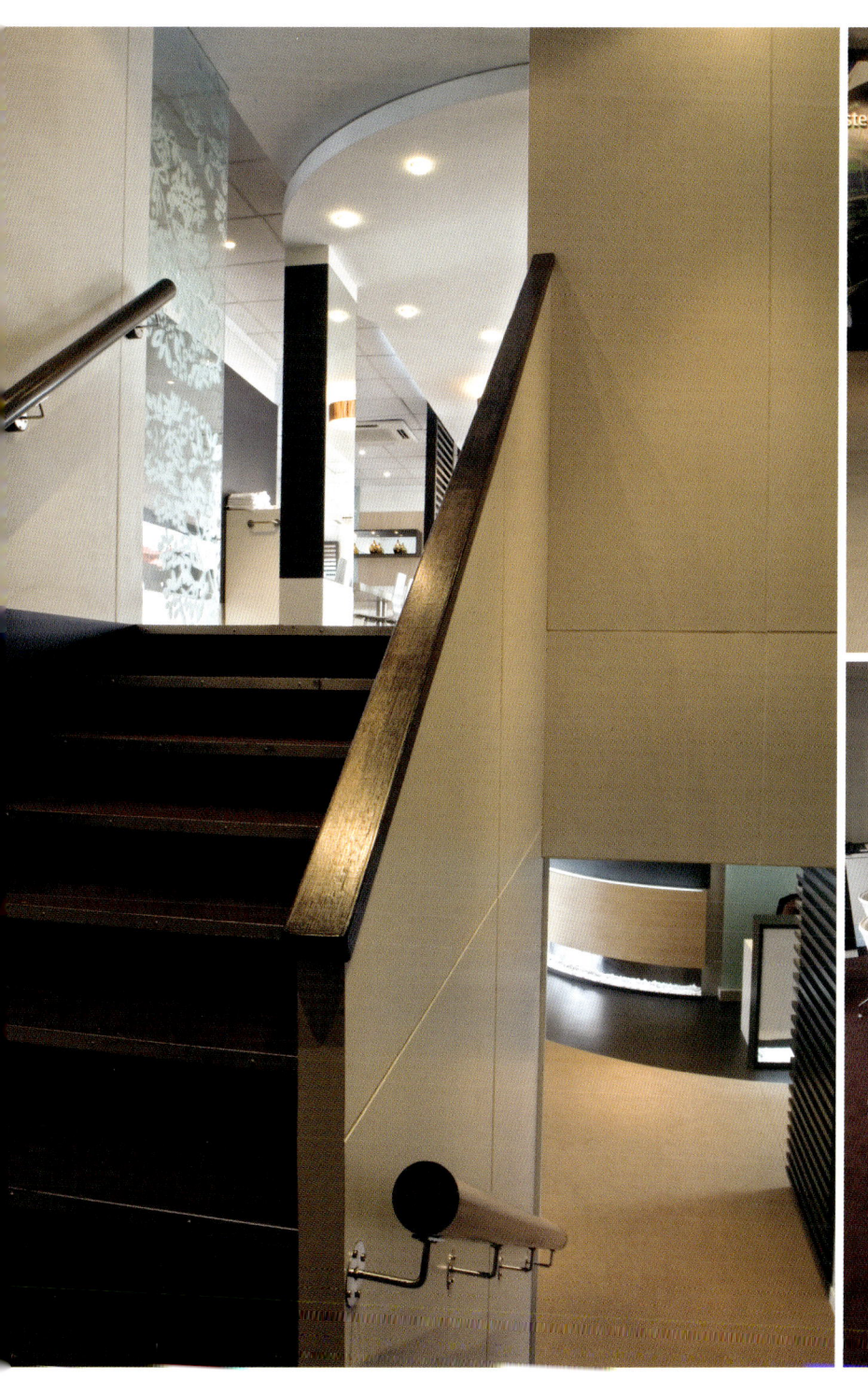

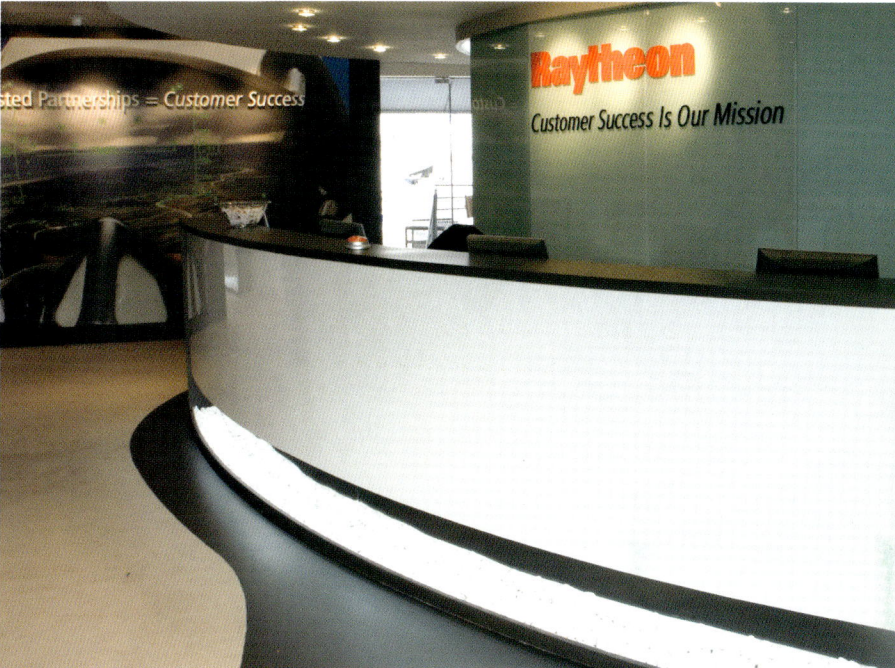

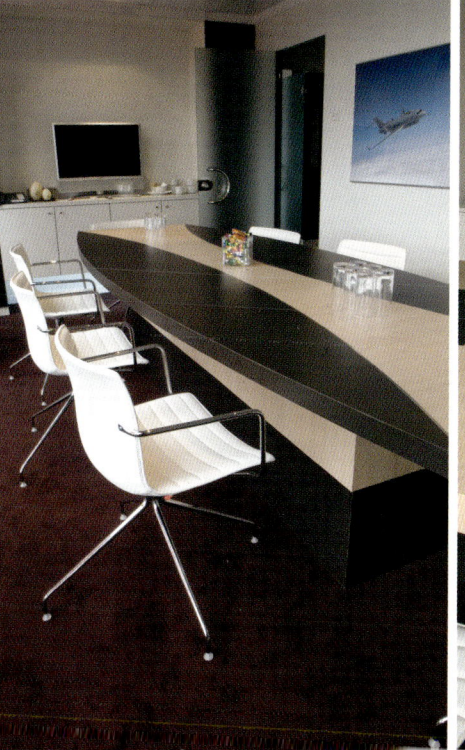

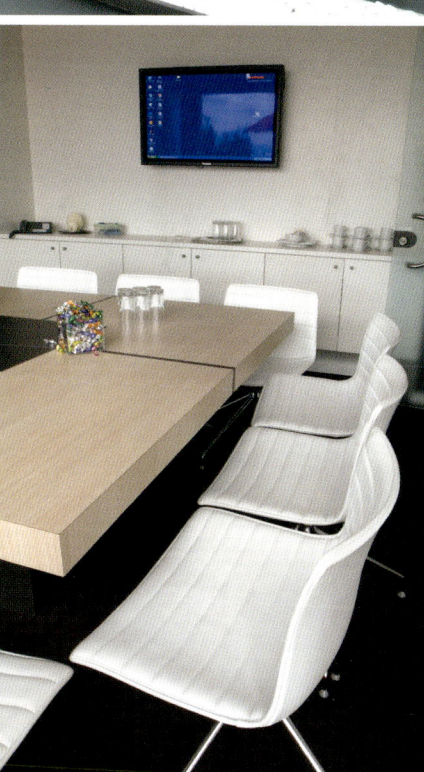

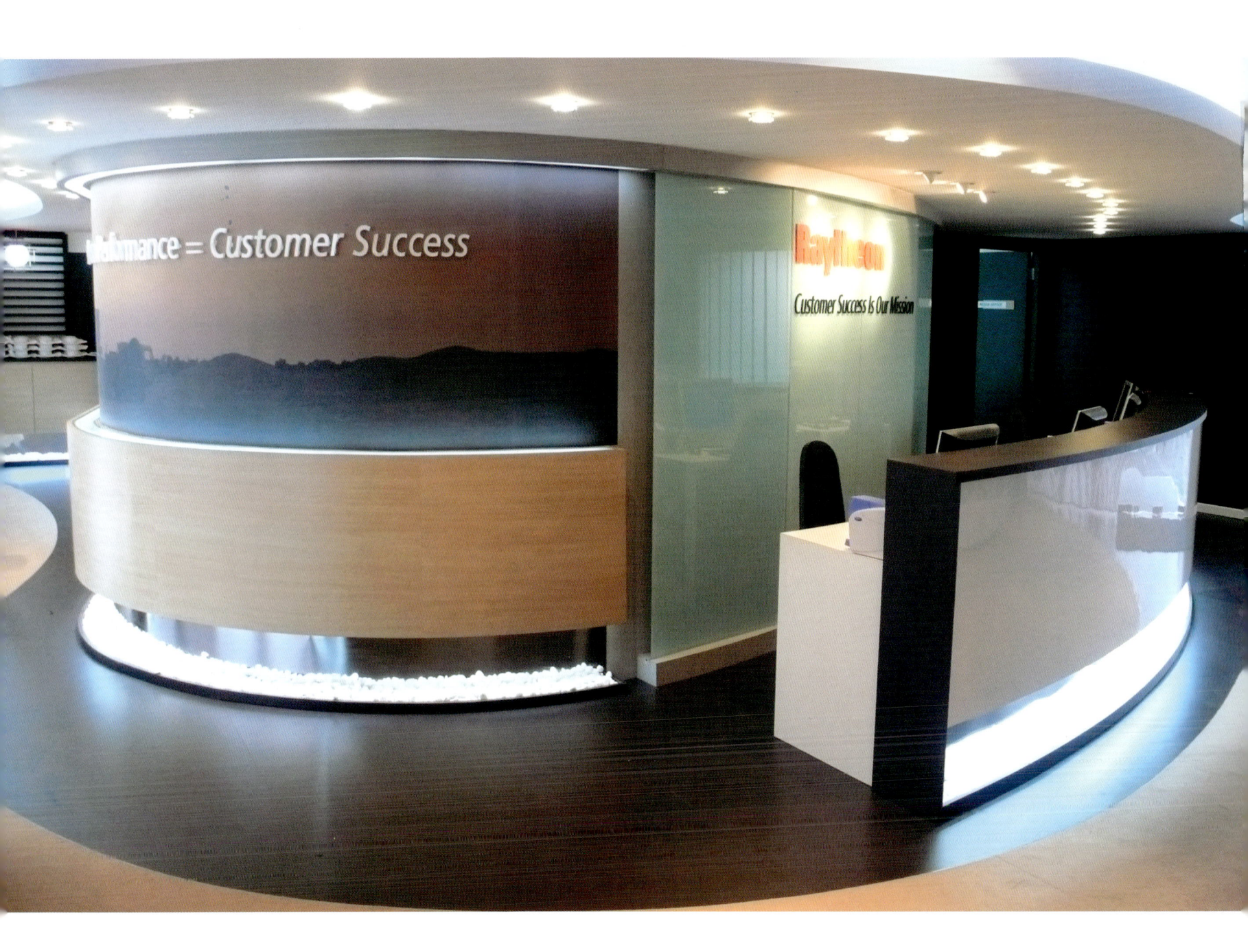

rformance = Customer Success

Raytheon
Customer Success Is Our Mission

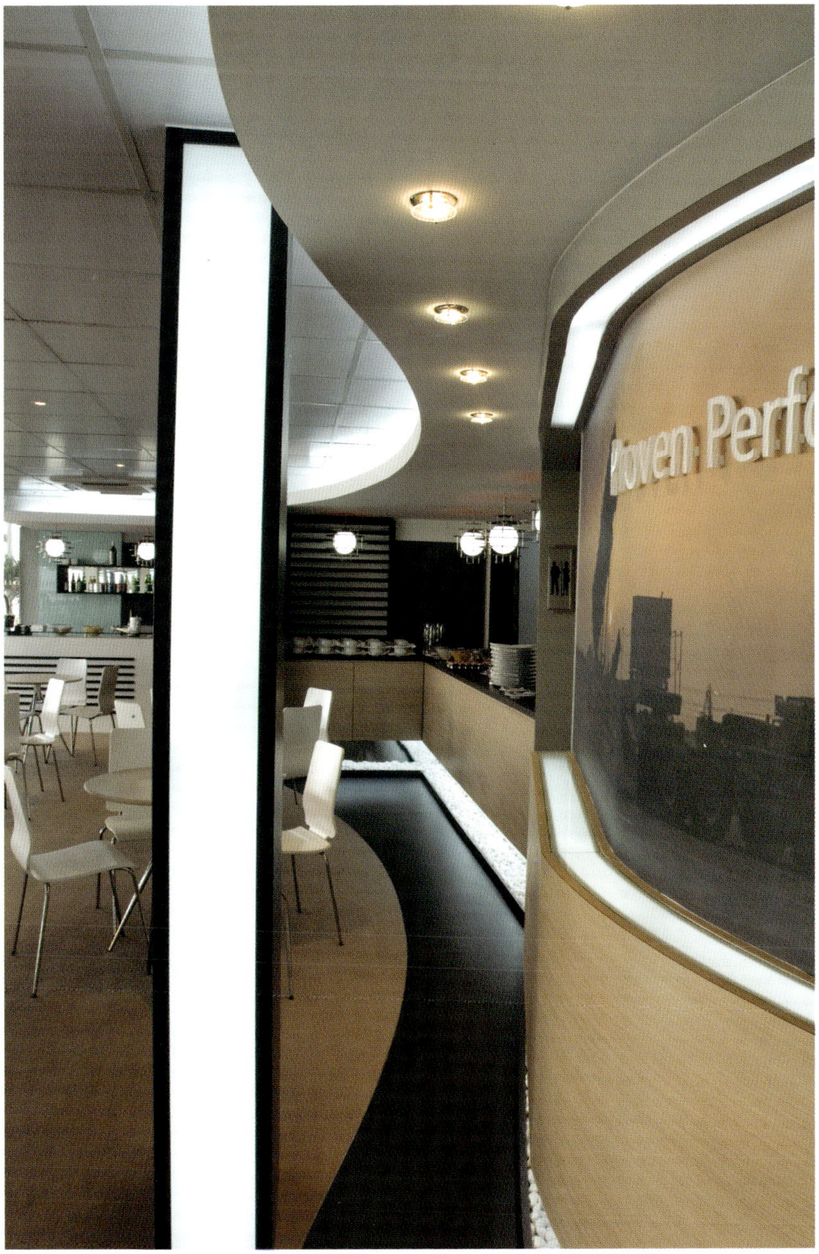

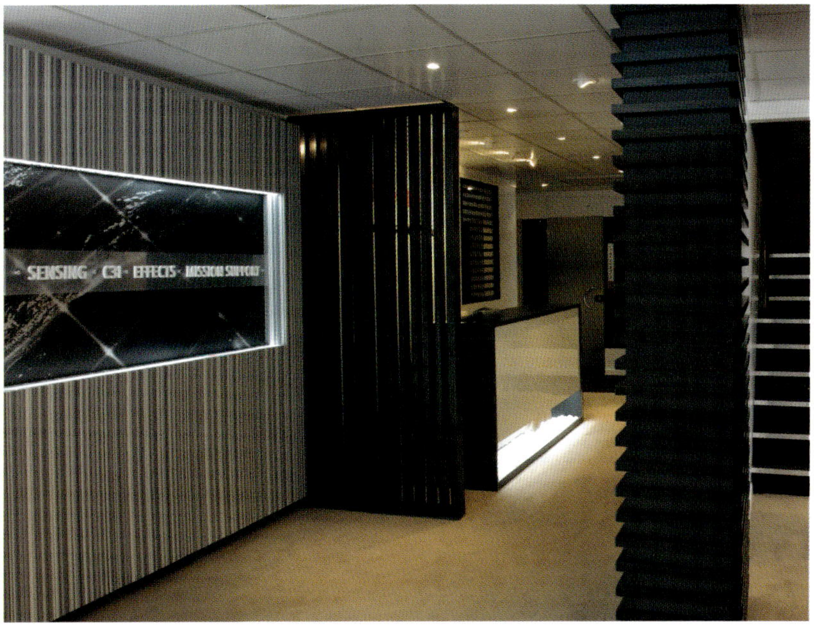
SENSING

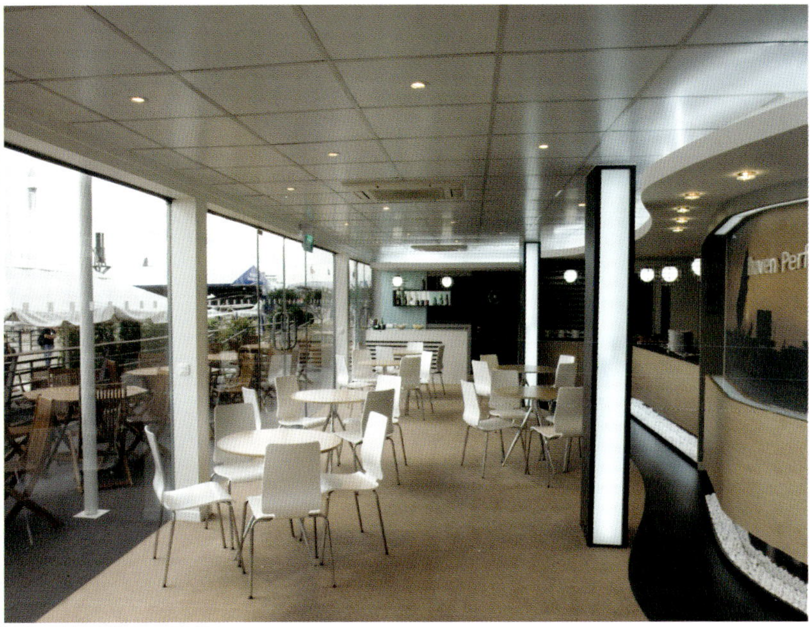

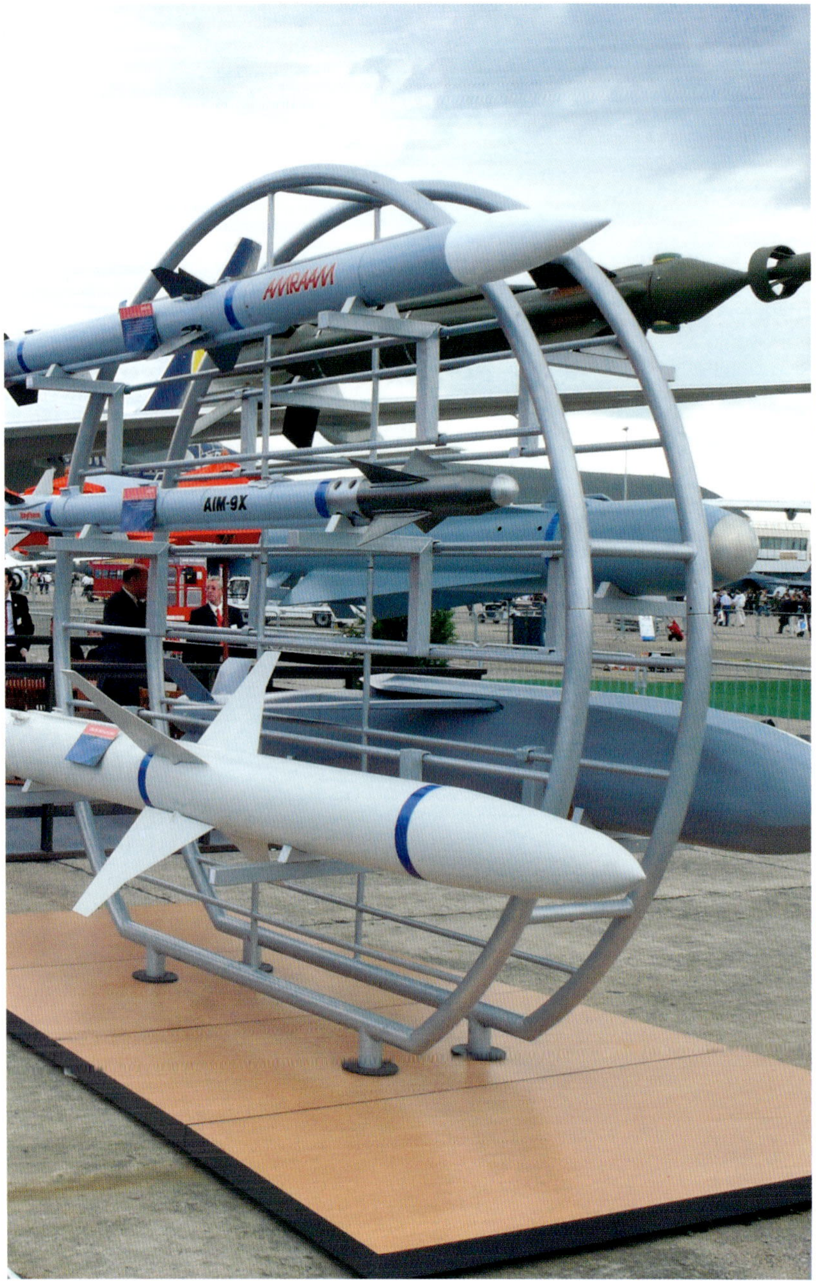
AMRAAM
AIM-9X

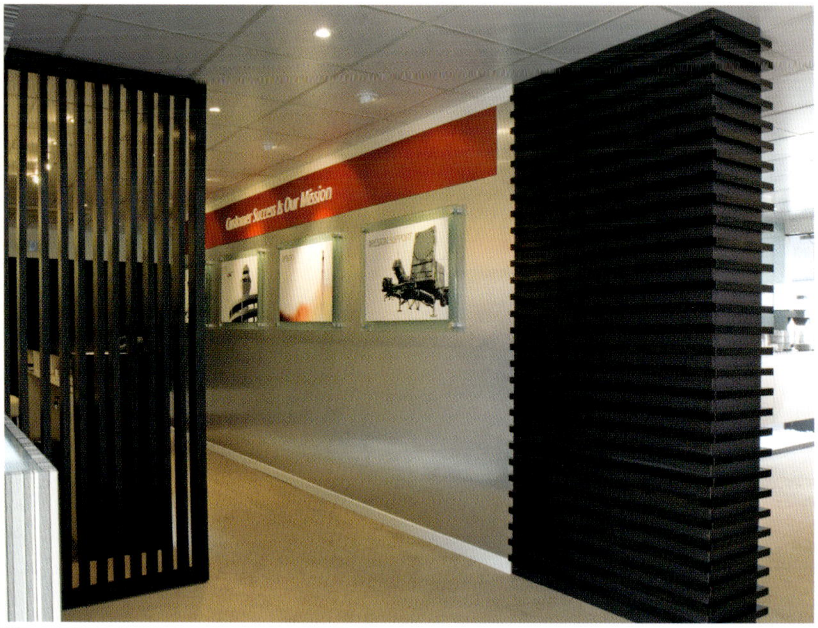
Customer Success Is Our Mission

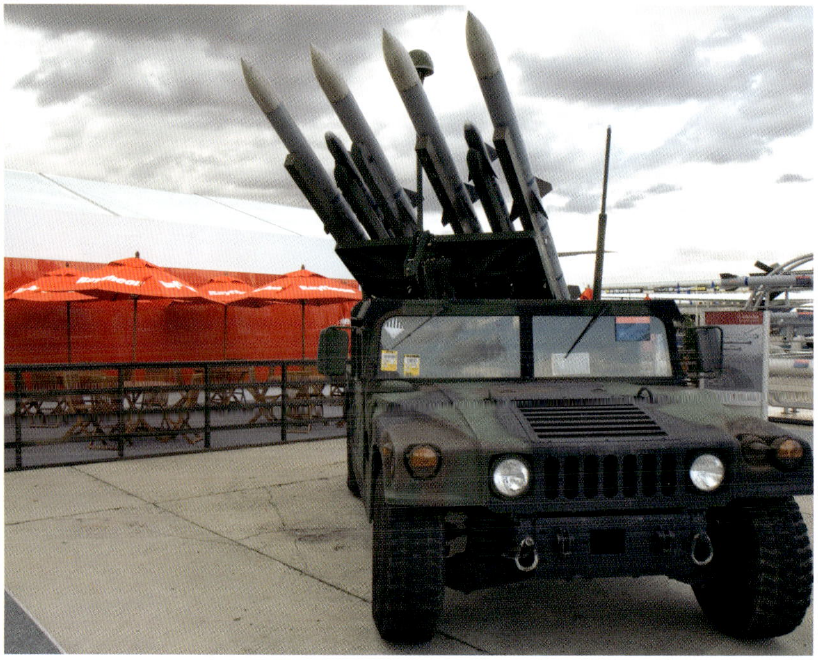

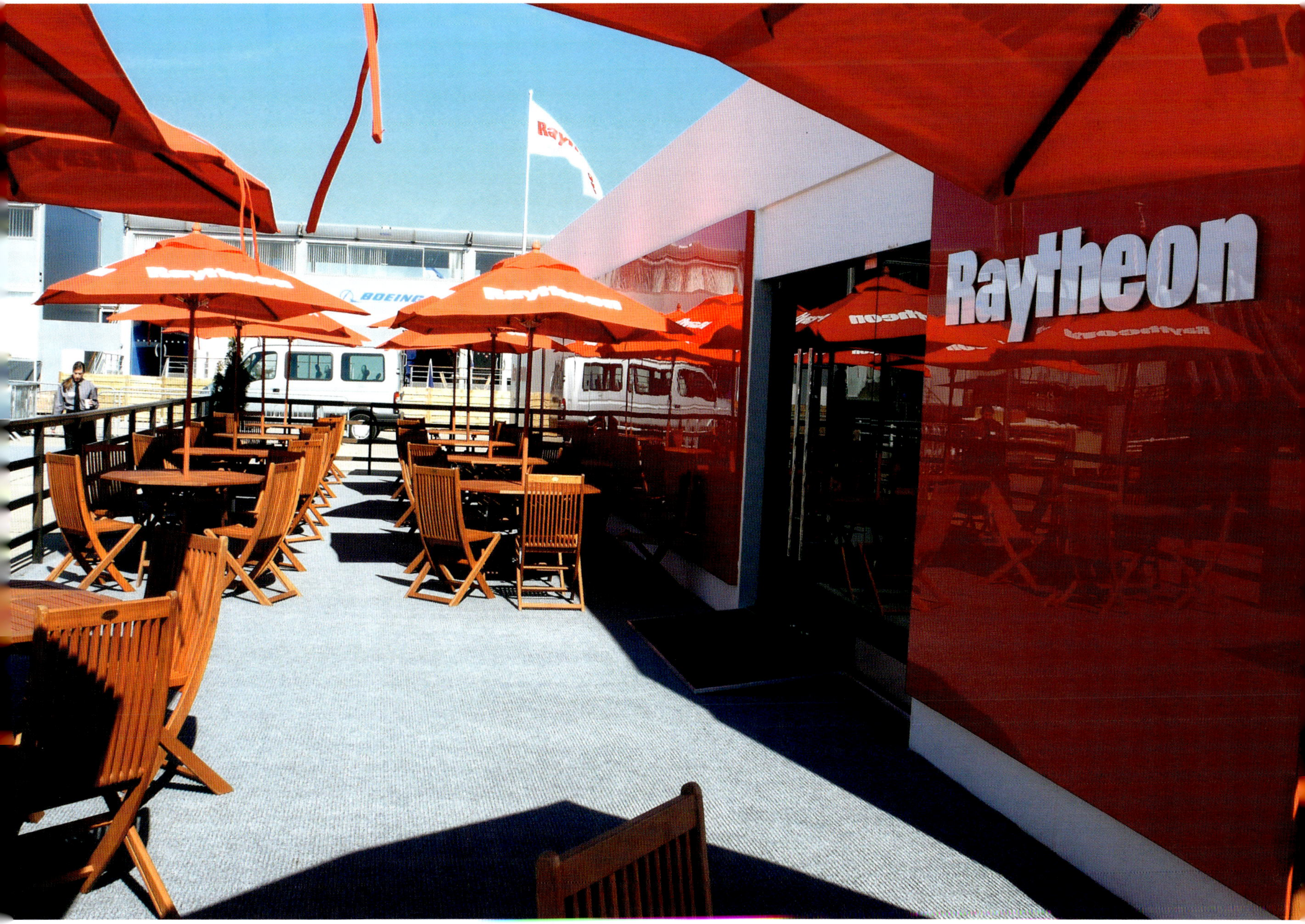
Raytheon
Raytheon
Raytheon
BOEING

Toshiba Private Show

where various cities in China

With a strong presence in China for some 20 years, Toshiba's management decided to organise a Toshiba Private Show in Beijing and then extend the show to Shanghai and Guangzhou. The premier booth occupied 2,000 sq. m. at the China Hotel in Beijing. Following suit, seventy-five Chinese subsidiaries of Toshiba also participated in the event. Toshiba's booth was designed and fabricated with special consideration for reuse at exhibitions in Shanghai and Guangzhou.

The colours blue and red were used to distinguish between different product zones. Several circular constructions and a canopy with vivid lettering extending over the booth gave it a unique appearance. Bars of lighting changed from blue to red, illuminating the booth space and the canopies above.

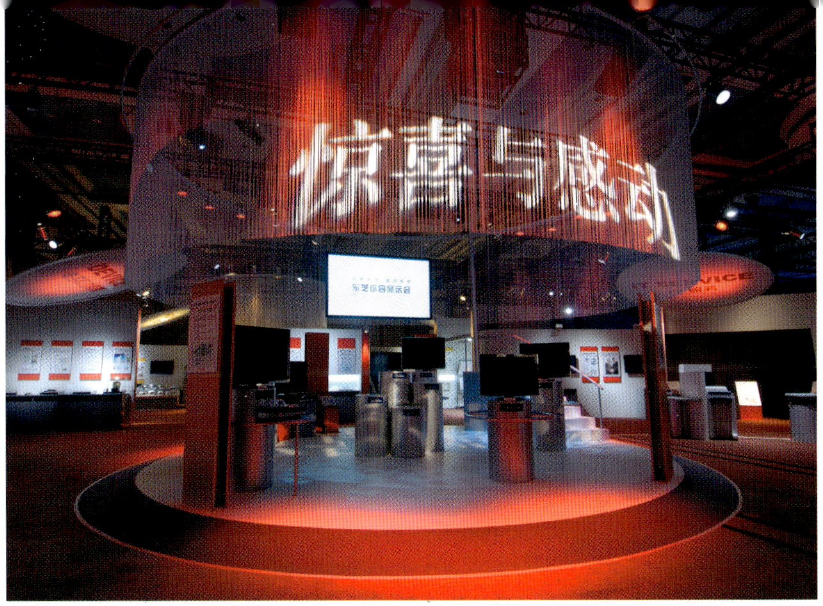
惊喜与感动

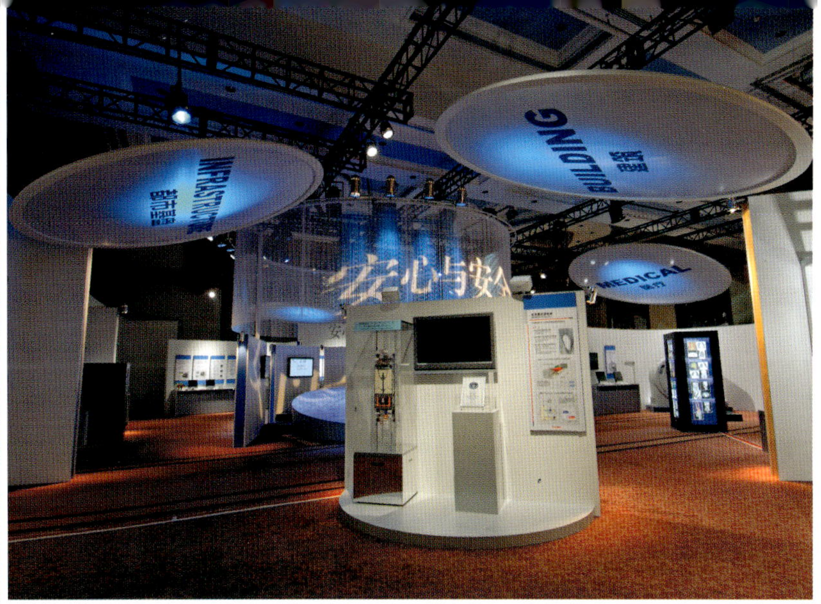
BUILDING
MEDICAL

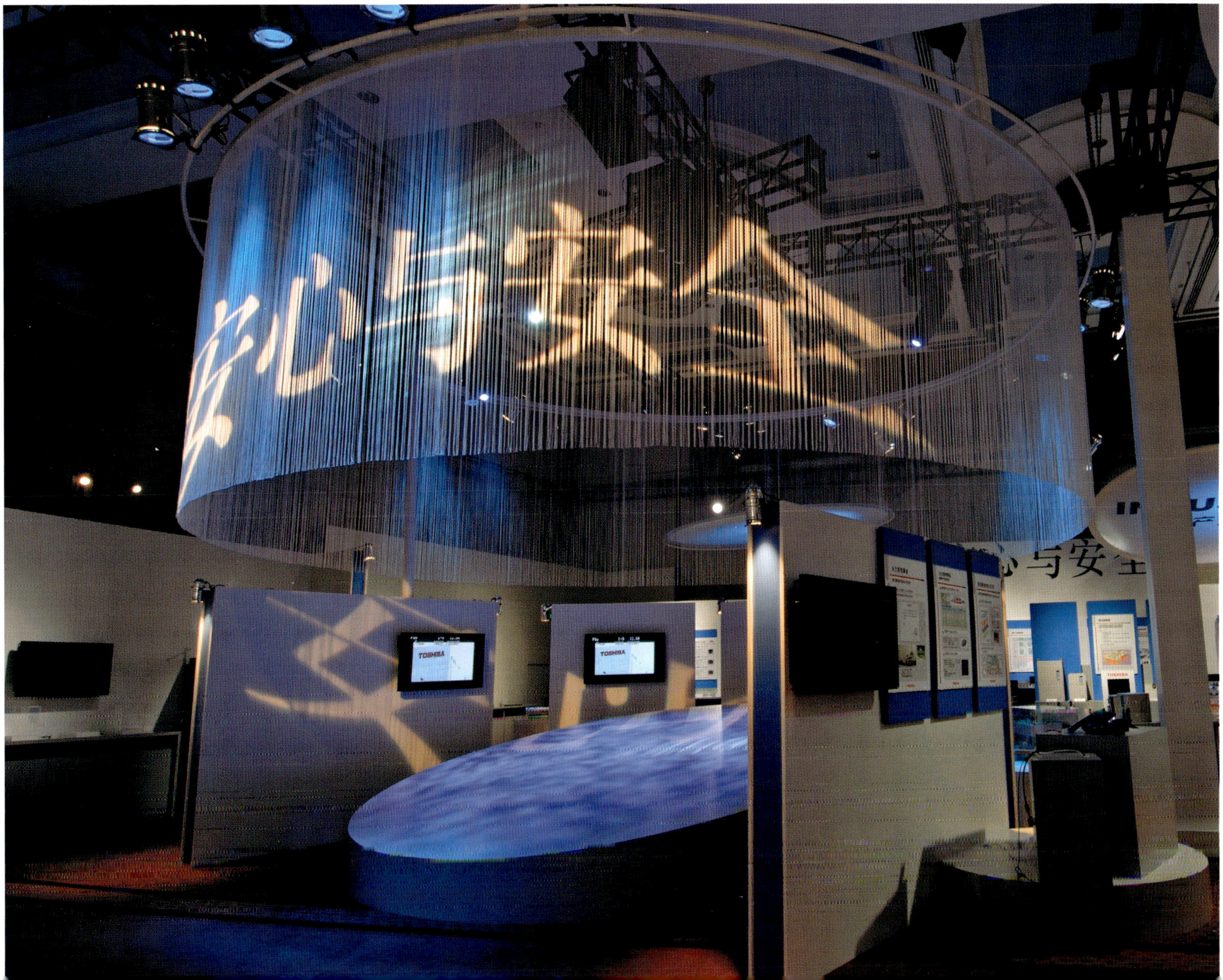
TOSHIBA

Whether it's a suite of offices, a shop or a roll-out for a chain of stores, Pico's designers understand that an attractive presentation plays a key role in successful marketing. Pico builds functional interiors that can and do make strong signature statements.

Here, too, the overall corporate brand image becomes the main focus. Using corporate colours and signature elements, Pico creates environments that not only function but add new dimensions to the corporate or retail image.

No space is too small or too large for Pico. It can be a precious mirror and glass illusion created for the Bombay Sapphire Martini Glass in the Hong Kong Airport or the two-level, 2,000 sq. m. open and gracious JetQuay VIP Lounge in Changi Airport in Singapore.

The 300 sq. m. Leica shop in Taiwan stands out from the surrounding camera shops. The interior is contemporary with smart and stylish shelving and cabinetry. Some of the upper floors of the building are finished as photo galleries where the patrons' photos are displayed.

The 73 sq. m. Mercedes-Benz accessories shop in Korea makes each product appear almost jewel-like and the custom lighting design underscores and highlights each presentation.

Branding was important for Motorola when they asked Pico to create a uniform corporate environment that could be adapted as needed by different locations. Giant graphics, internally illuminated logo "lollipops" with changing colours and coffee tables, inset with 42" flat screen monitors, create a unique design and help promote the Motorola brand. Cellnet also wanted their brand and services promoted when they challenged Pico to design the 1,728 sq. m. briefing centre in the company's headquarters in Georgia. The modular concept and design keep this area always fresh, always current and always all about Cellnet.

Creative backed with strong production, Pico delivers branded interiors with flair and on schedule.

Martin M. Pegler

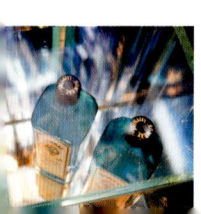

interior.

Bombay Sapphire Martini Glass Exhibition Display

where Hong Kong SAR, China

Bacardi Global has a total of four locations at the Hong Kong International Airport. Shown here are the designs for the promotion at some of the HKIA Sky Connection Shops.

To reflect the premium and creative image of one of Bacardi brands, Bombay Sapphire Gin, the Bacardi design team furnished the space utilising high quality materials such as mirrors, glass and silk-screening. The cool, blue colour scheme was created by adopting the Bombay Sapphire "blue" as the primary colour of the area.

Bacardi Global Conference, which was held in Hong Kong this year, coincided with this airport promotion. The senior management team took the opportunity to view and appreciate the work created by the Bacardi Global Travel Retail team. Bacardi management was greatly appreciative of Pico's efforts to work within an extremely tight timeframe, from the initial design concept development to the actual realisation.

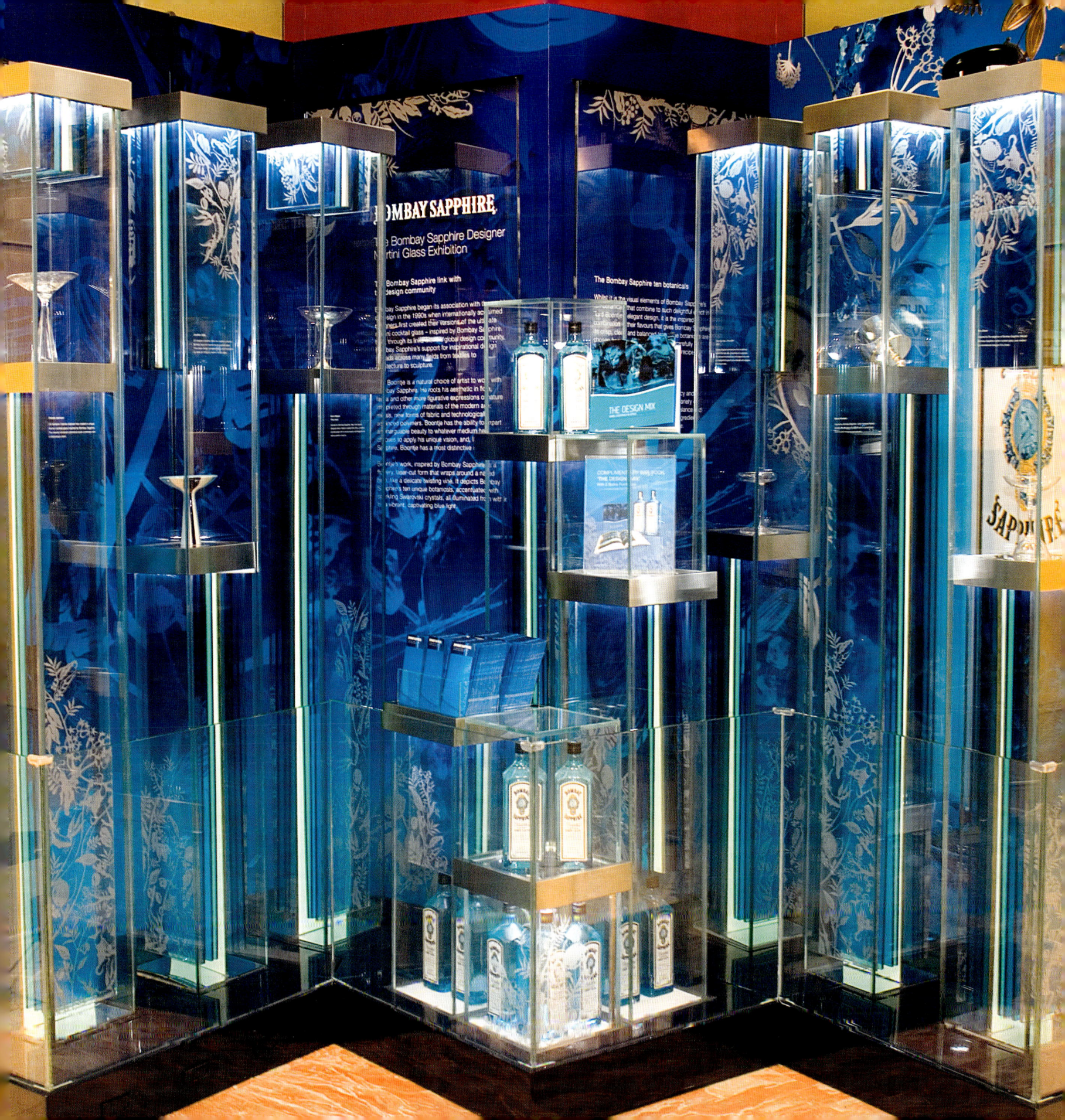

BOMBAY SAPPHIRE

The Bombay Sapphire Designer
Martini Glass Exhibition

The Bombay Sapphire link with the design community

Bombay Sapphire began its association with the design in the 1990s when internationally acclaimed designers first created their versions of the ultimate martini cocktail glass – inspired by Bombay Sapphire. Through its innovative global design community, Bombay Sapphire's support for inspirational design extends across many fields from textiles to architecture to sculpture.

Boontje is a natural choice of artist to work with Bombay Sapphire. He roots his aesthetic in flora, and other more figurative expressions of nature interpreted through materials of the modern and new forms of fabric and technological advanced polymers. Boontje has the ability to impart unique beauty to whatever medium he chooses to apply his unique vision, and, like Sapphire, Boontje has a most distinctive

Boontje's work, inspired by Bombay Sapphire is a delicate laser-cut form that wraps around a needle like a delicate twisting vine. It depicts Bombay Sapphire's ten unique botanicals, accentuated with sparkling Swarovski crystals, all illuminated from with a vibrant, captivating blue light.

The Bombay Sapphire ten botanicals

Whilst it is the visual elements of Bombay Sapphire's elegant design, it is the inspired combination of flavours that gives Bombay Sapphire its crisp, clean and balanced taste. Ten botanicals are carefully chosen

THE DESIGN MIX

COMPLIMENTARY BOOK
"THE DESIGN MIX"

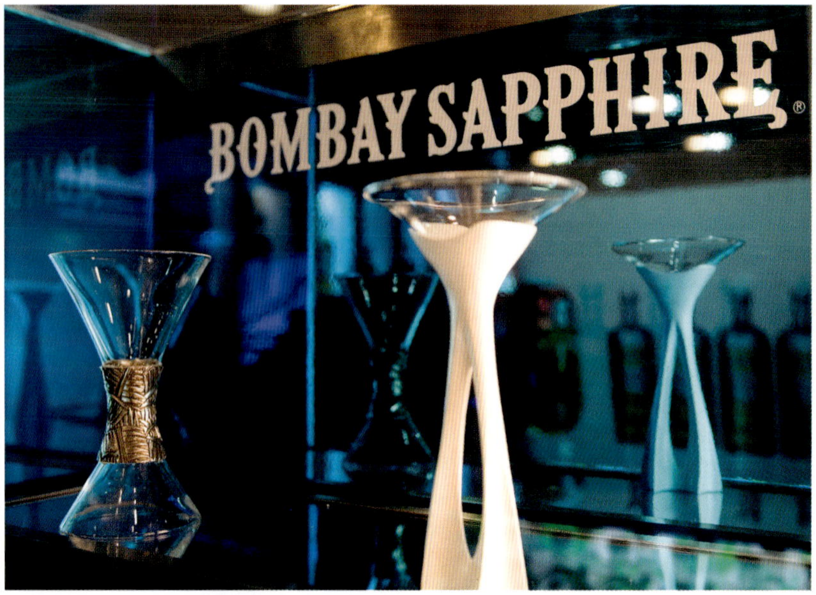
BOMBAY SAPPHIRE

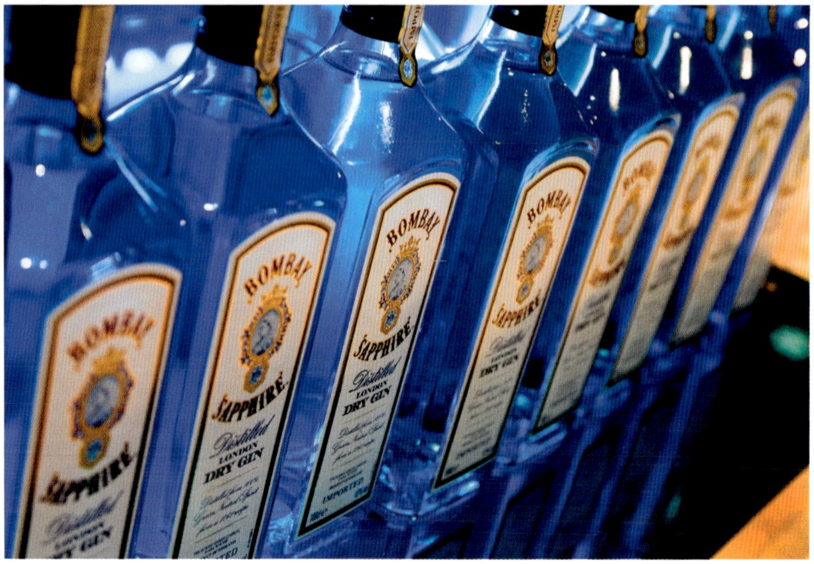
BOMBAY
SAPPHIRE
Distilled
LONDON
DRY GIN

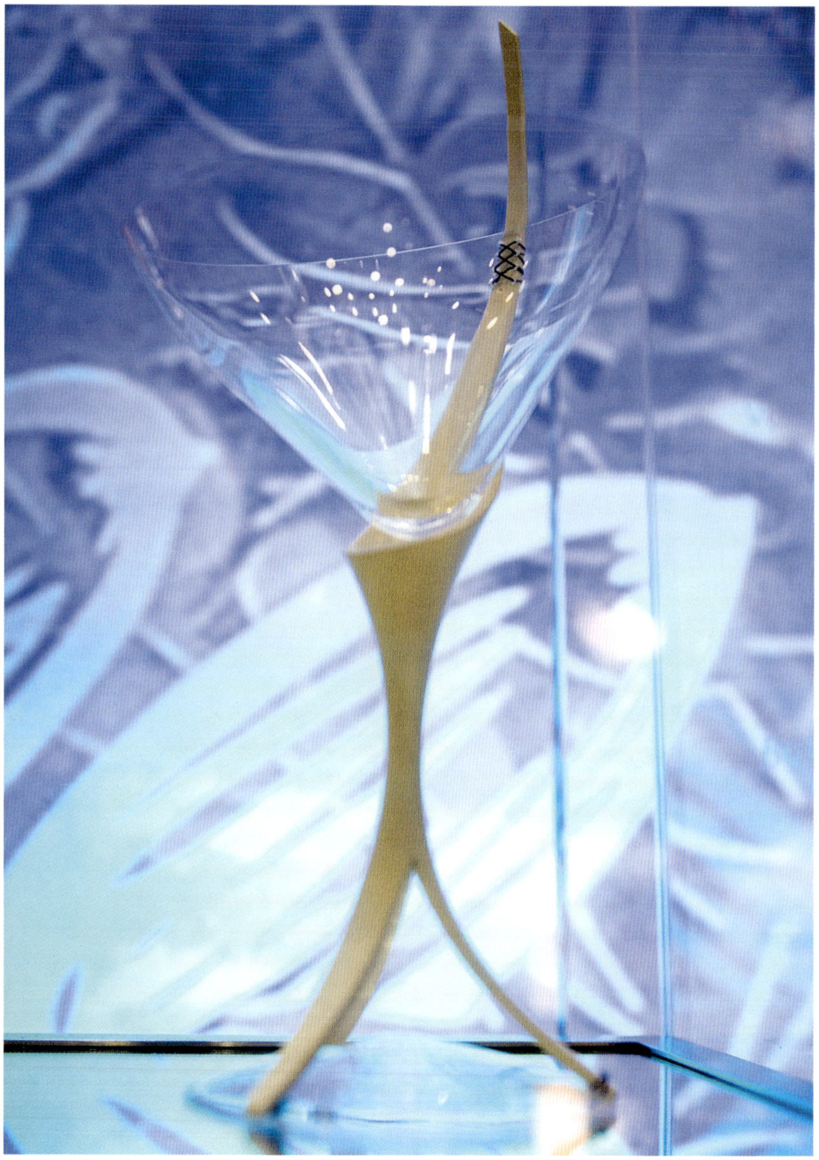

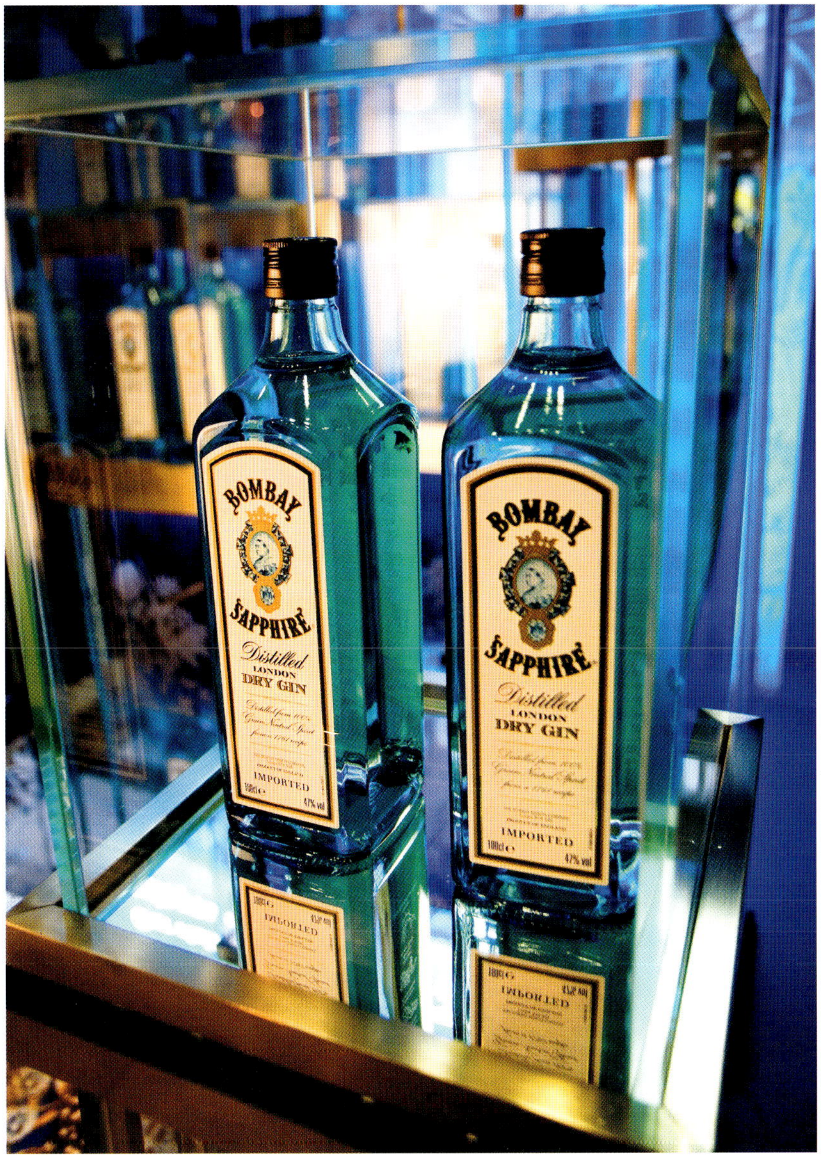
BOMBAY
SAPPHIRE
Distilled
LONDON
DRY GIN
IMPORTED

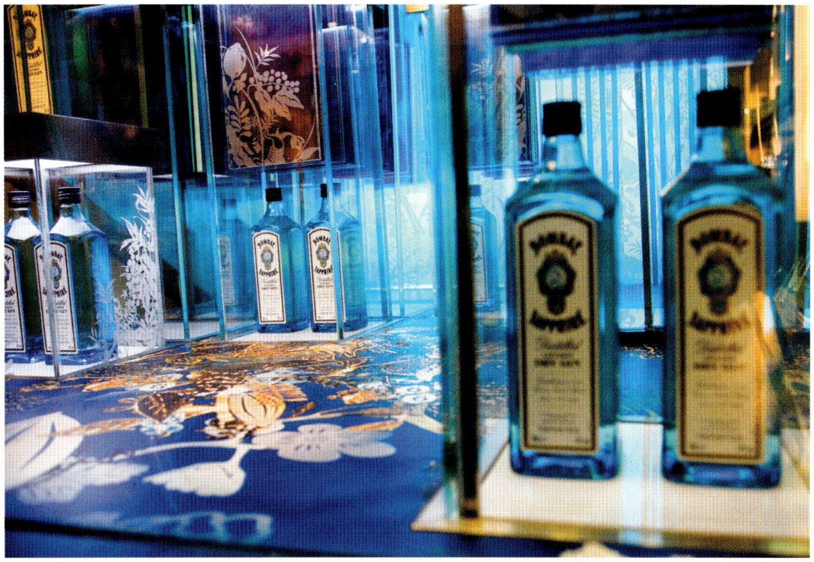

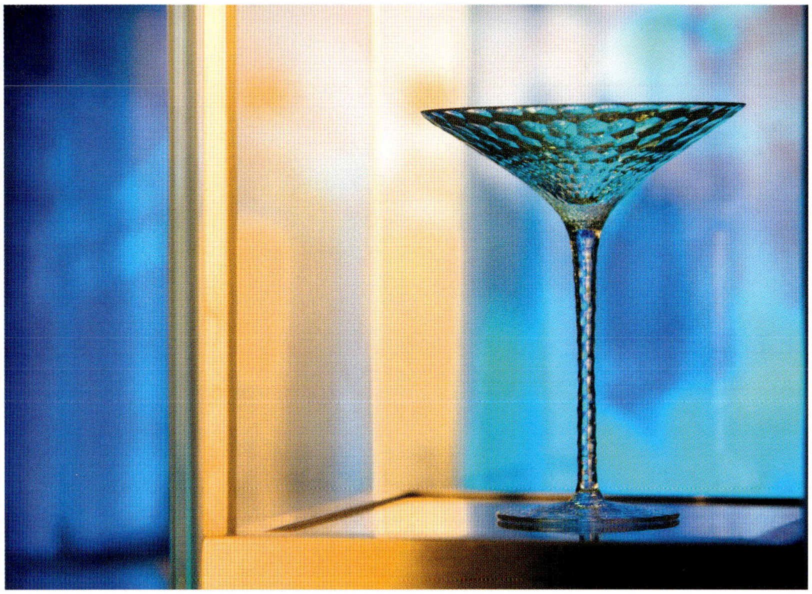

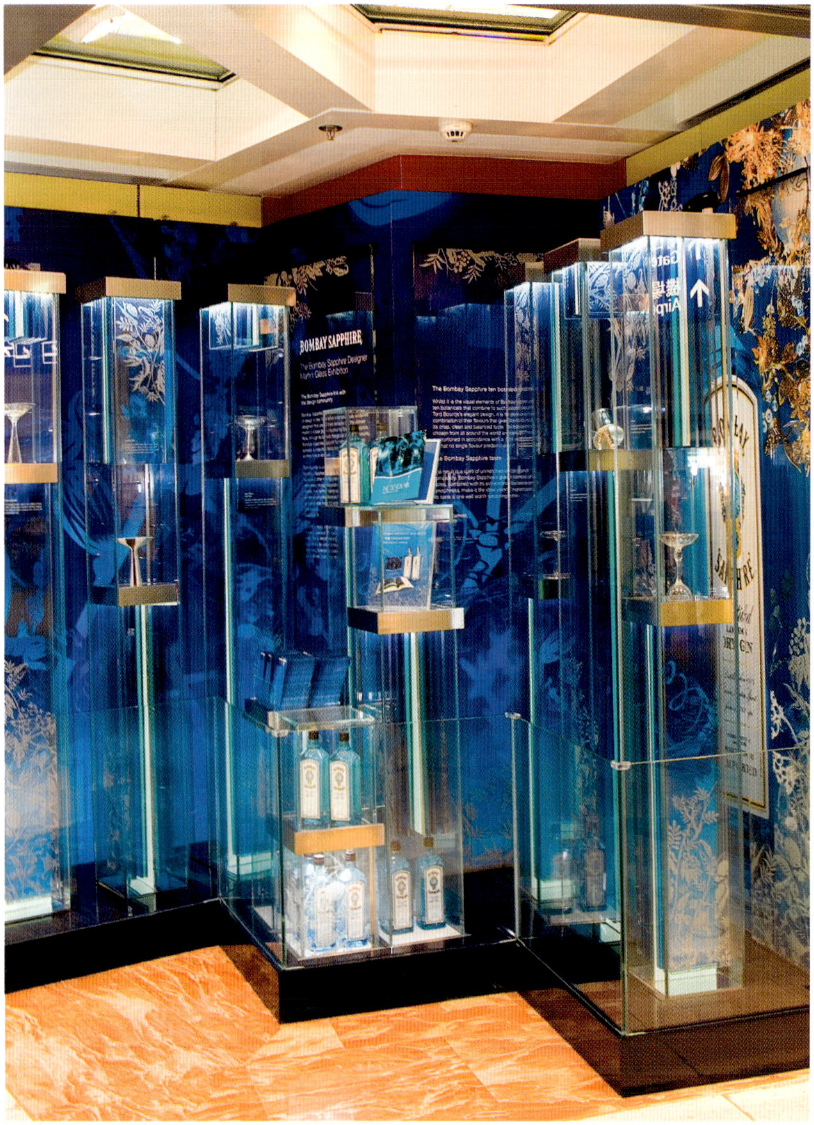
BOMBAY SAPPHIRE

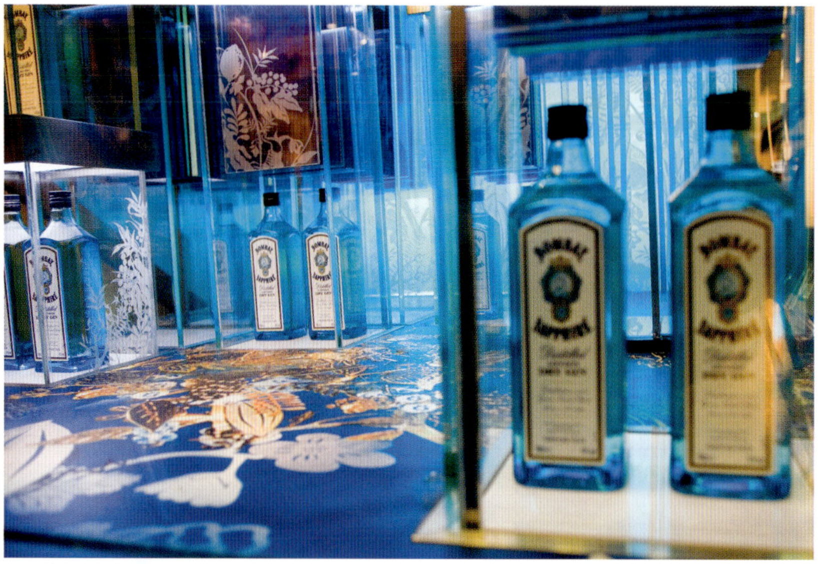

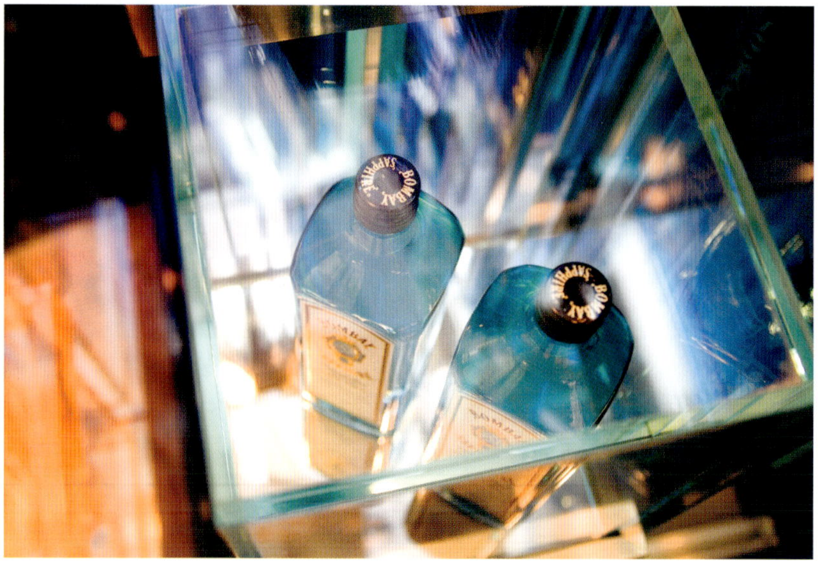

Marcel Wanders

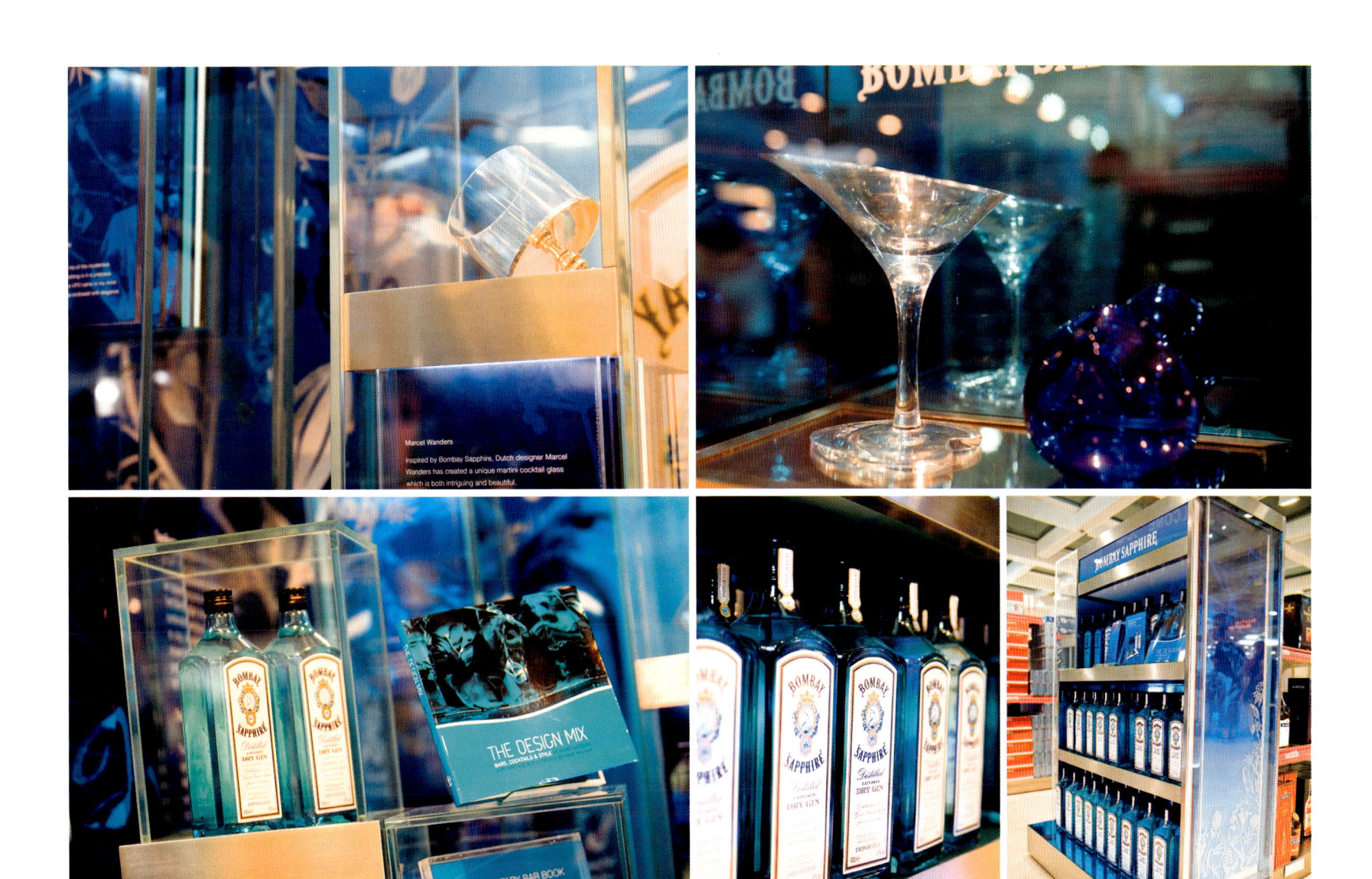

Inspired by Bombay Sapphire, Dutch designer Marcel Wanders has created a unique martini cocktail glass which is both intriguing and beautiful.

THE DESIGN MIX

COMPLIMENTARY BAR BOOK
'THE DESIGN MIX'
With 2 Bottle Purchase

JetQuay – CIP Terminal

where Changi Airport, Singapore

JetQuay Pte Ltd. required the design, development, and furnishing of the Commercially Important People (CIP) luxury terminal, which daily services 50 passengers, flying on commercial and private jets.

The designer's task was to provide a highly exclusive environment with upscale interior finishes, utilising quality materials and refined details. The two-storey building covers an area of 2,000 sq. m. and includes a state-of-the-art lounge, VIP rooms, mini gym, sauna, nap room, restaurant, private rooms for night stays and a business centre complete with conference and meeting rooms.

The lounge features simple and elegant, snow-white furniture which adds to the upscale ambiance of the lounge. The business centre features maple wood flooring that gives a sense of splendor and richness while the built-in table-top PCs allow Wi-Fi access for easy internet connectivity.

The design firm was able to successfully complete the entire project in three months meeting JetQuay's accelerated deadline.

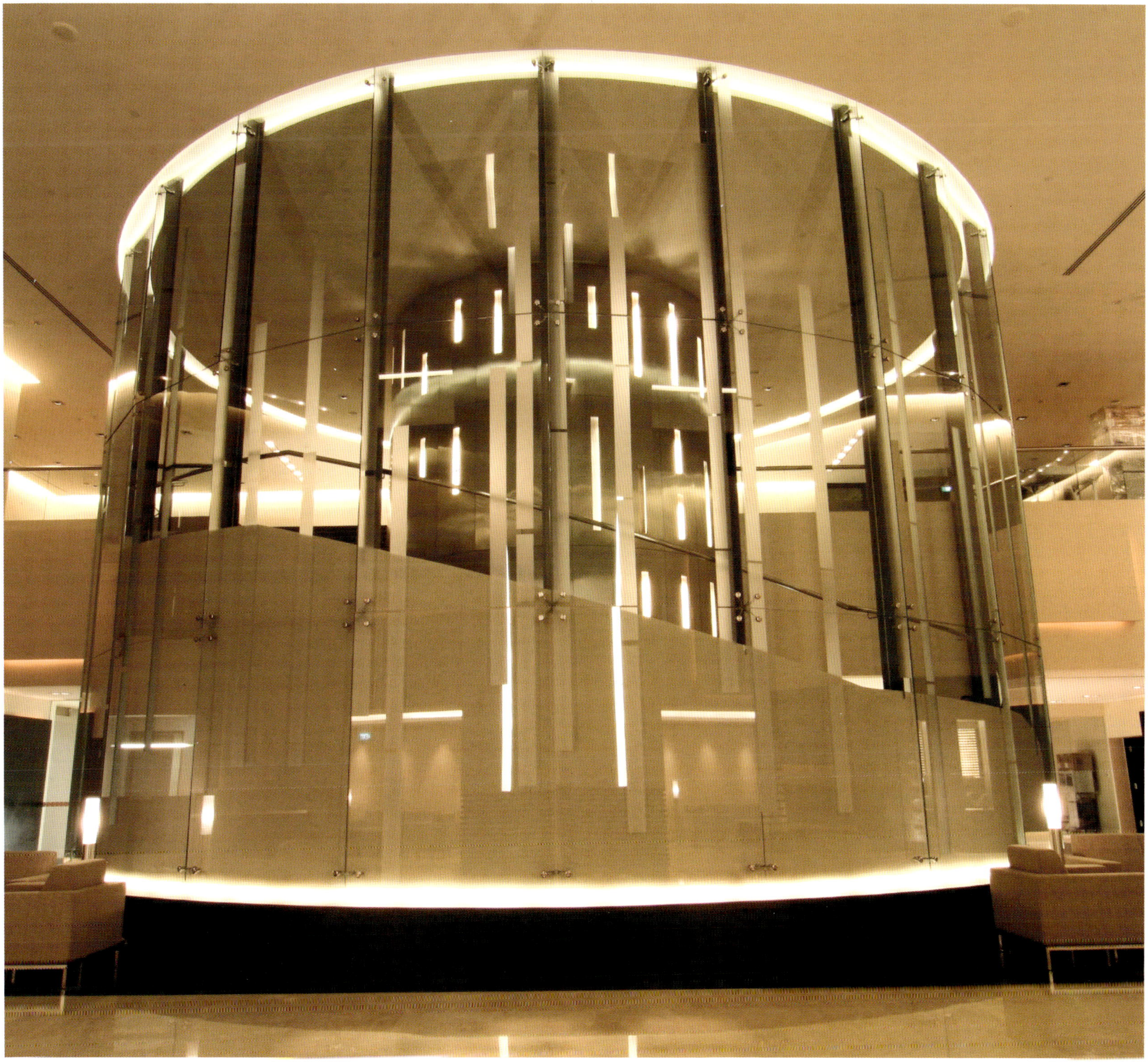

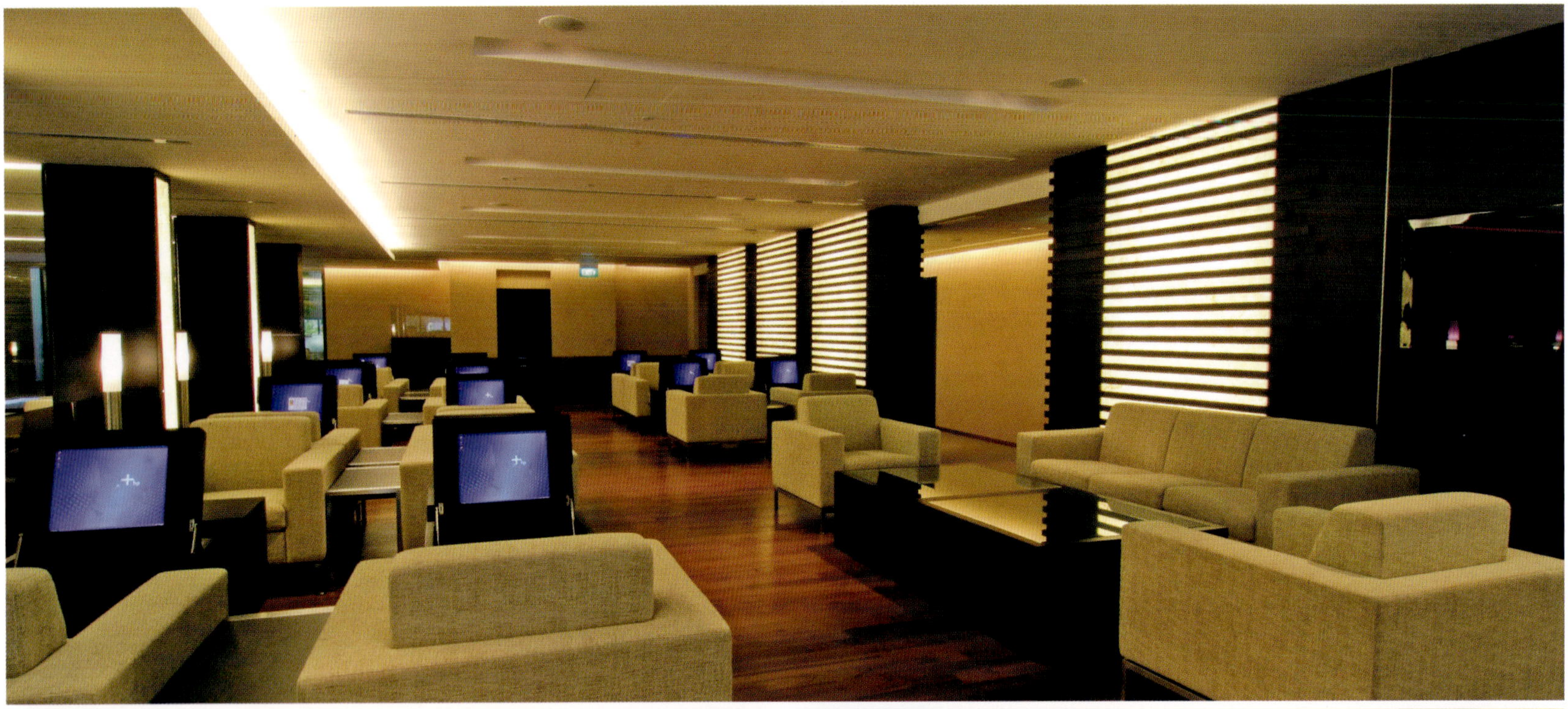
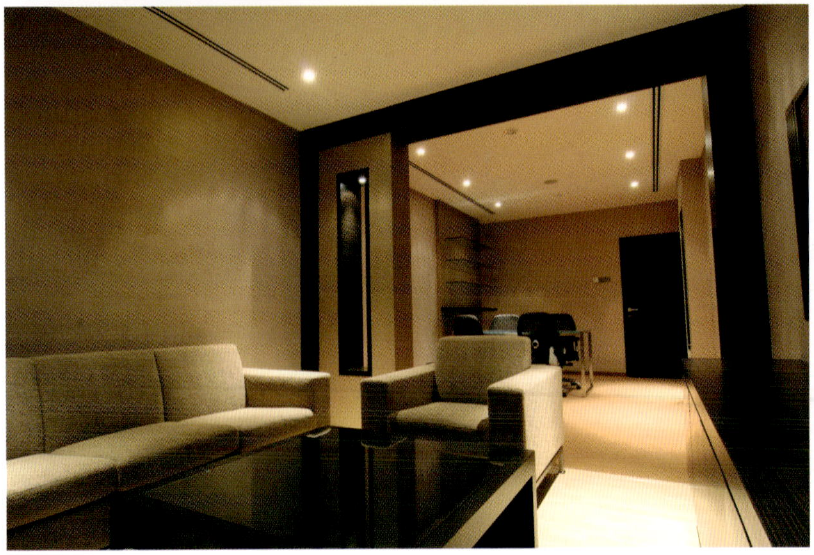
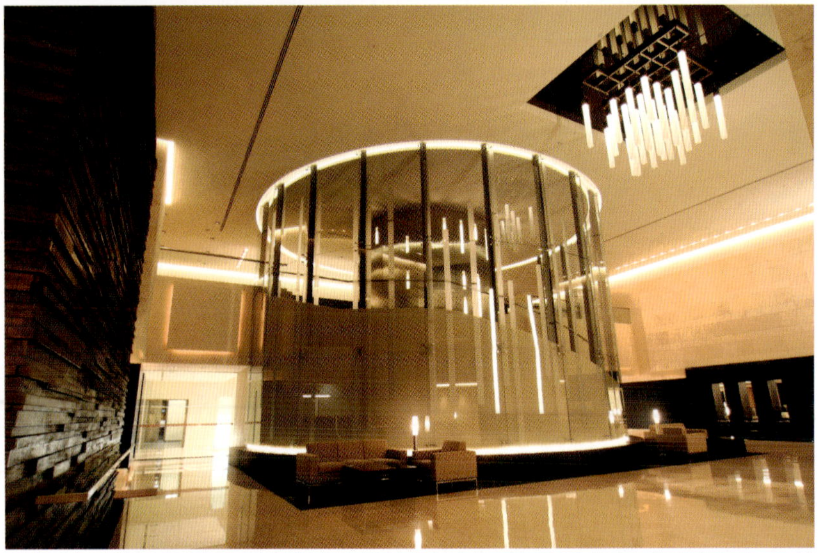

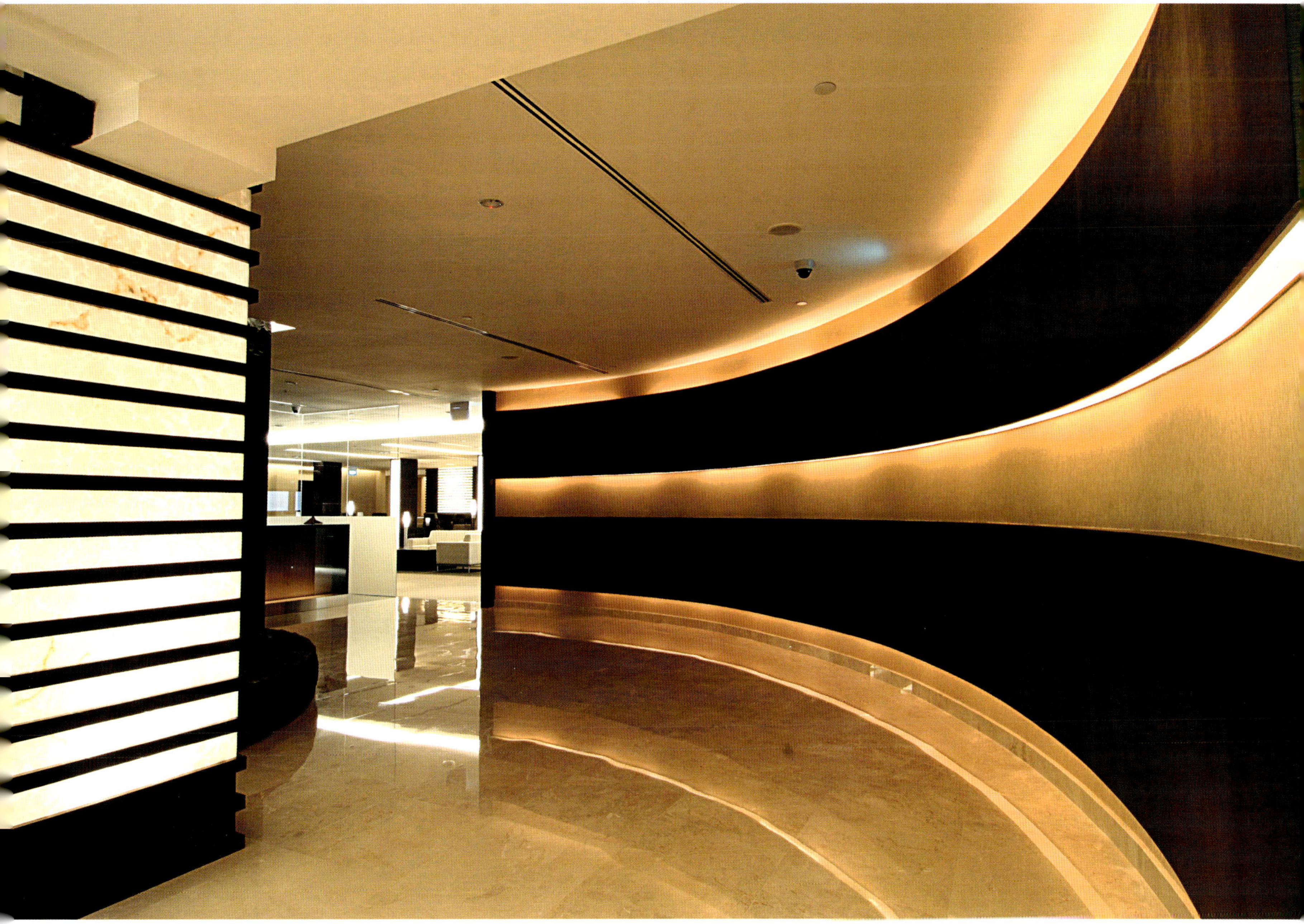

OSIM ChairSpa

where Hong Kong SAR, China

Covering a space of 176 sq. m., the OSIM ChairSpa is a showroom open in a new upmarket shopping arcade. The interior space is decorated in a modern style and endorses the concept that simplicity can be beautiful and elegant.

The colour palette consists of sophisticated earth tones, complemented by wood flooring, stone walls, glass partitions and fabric curtains. The refined lighting, floral arrangements and natural stones add a personal touch to the space.

The decor of each section in the spa reflects the cultural background of the nation featured in the area. The mood is comfortable and relaxed. Traditional accents and the warm lighting calm visitors' minds. This spa is different from any other OSIM operation in that it is structured as a modern rather than traditional sanctuary.

The ambiance is outstanding and distinctive, blending European, Thai and Japanese styles into a unique environment, evoking different local flavours to create a one-of-a-kind space.

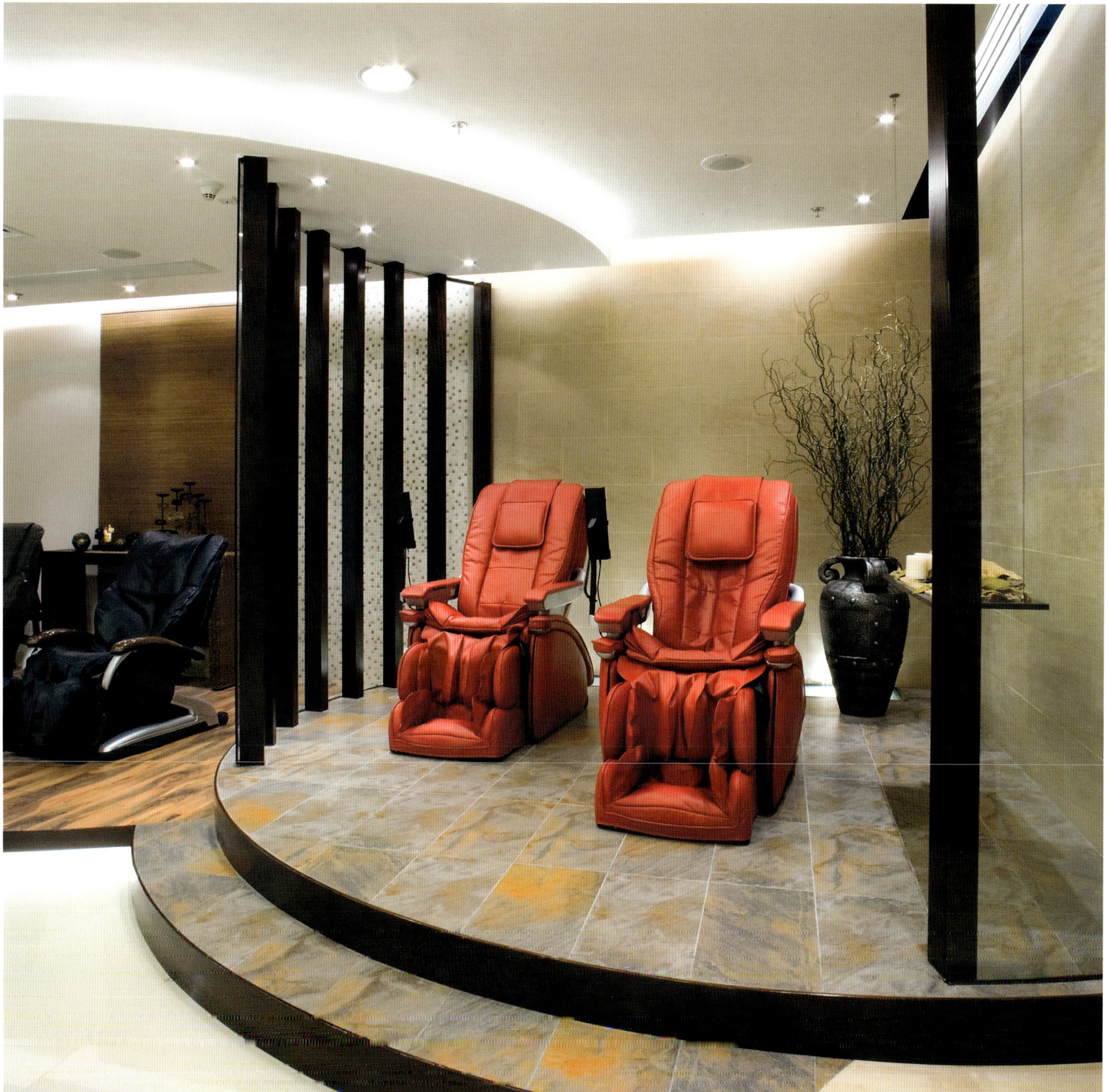

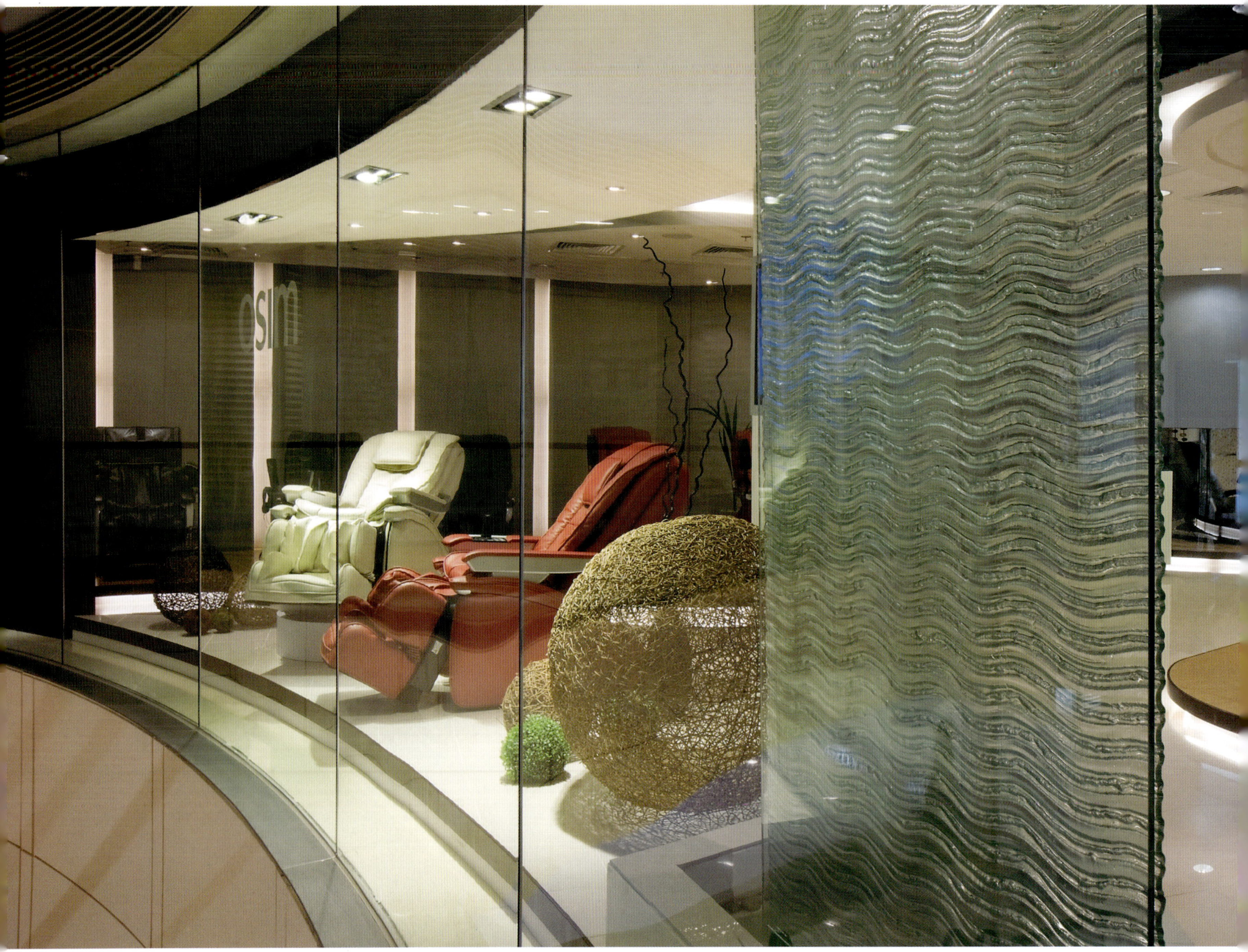
osim

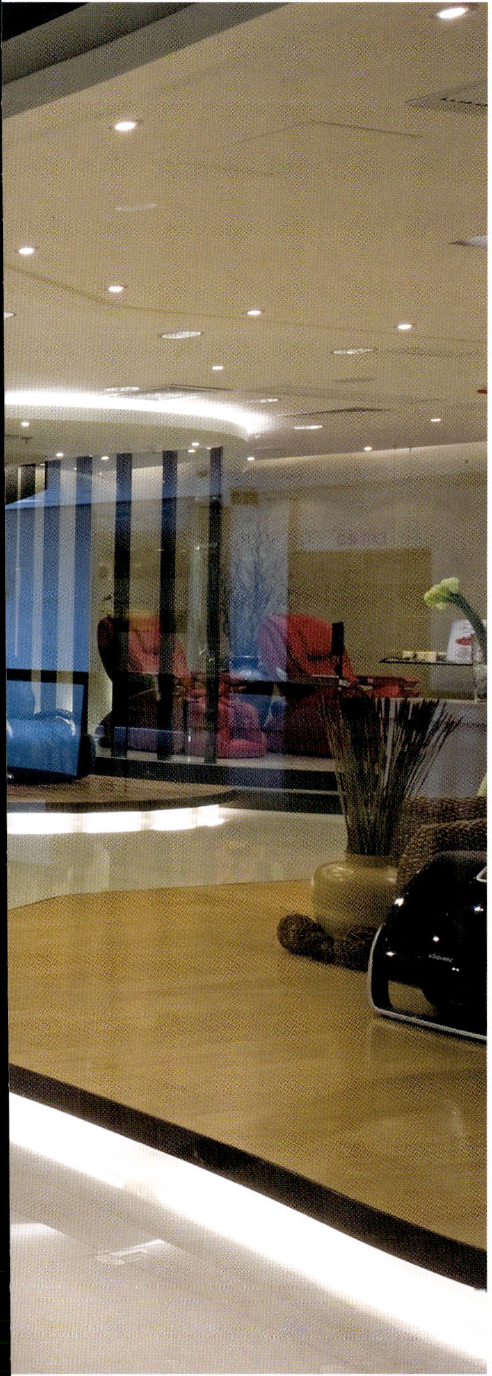

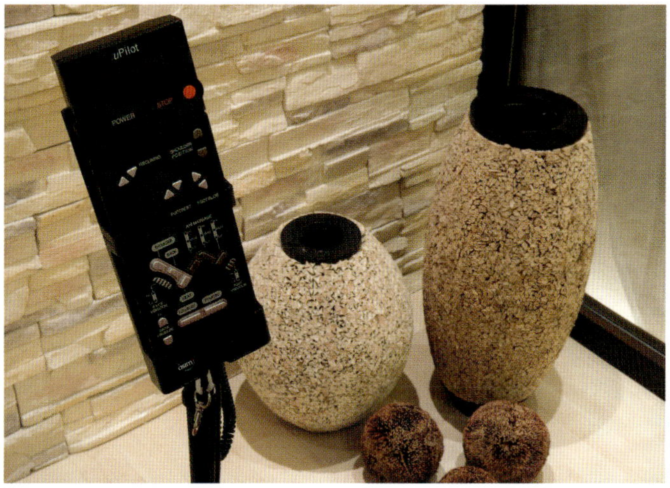
uPilot
POWER
STOP

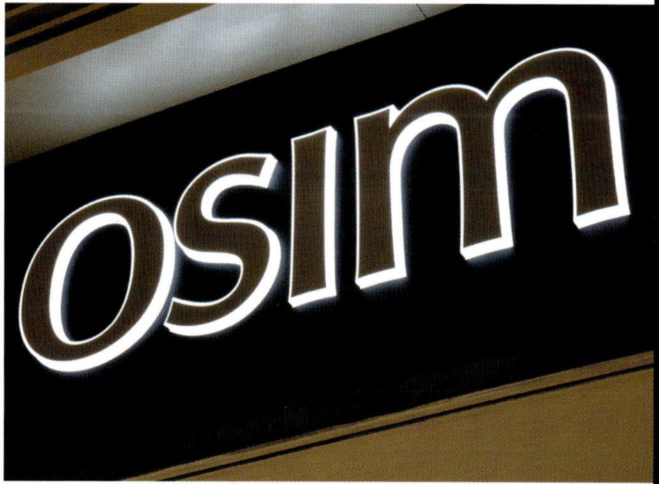
osim

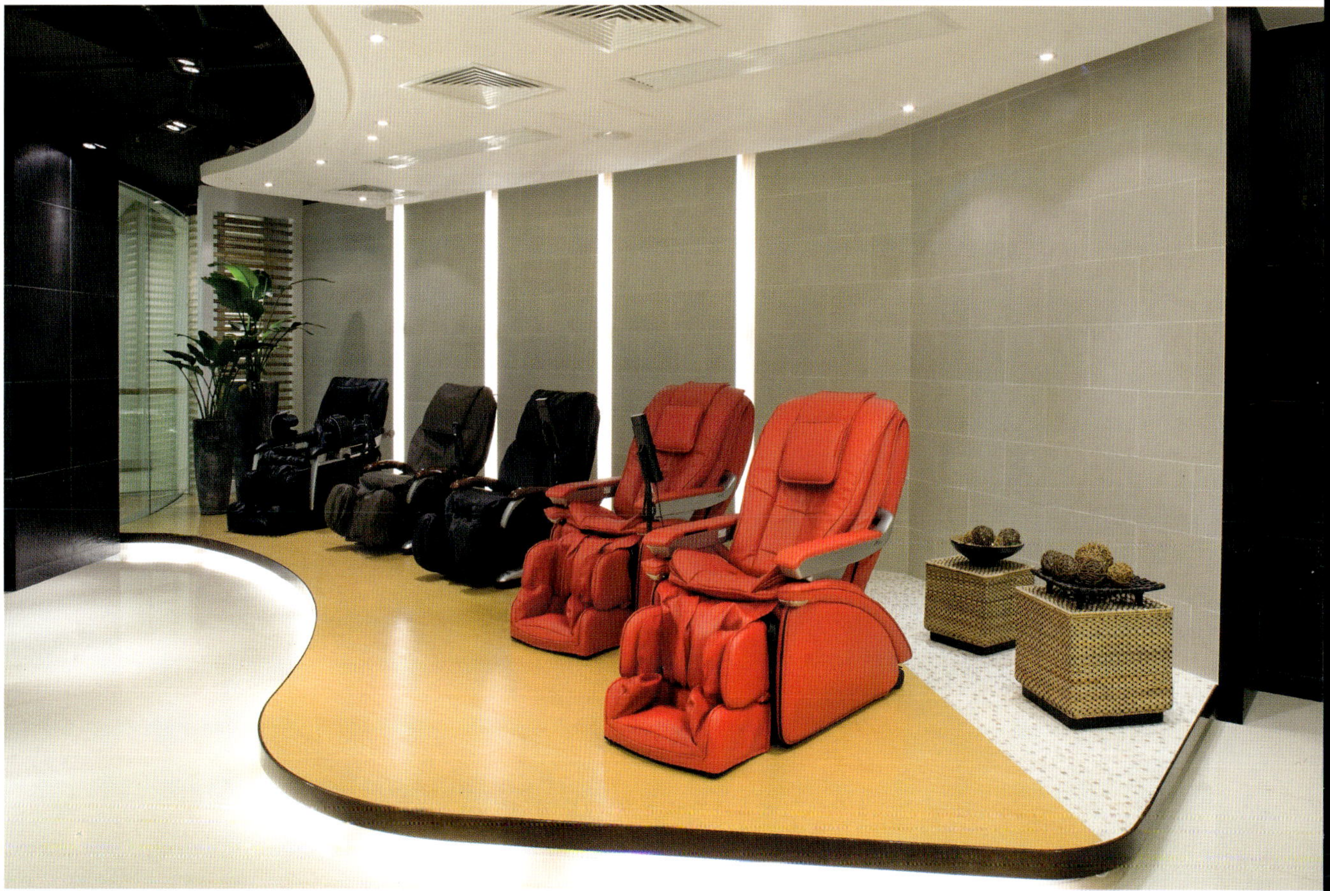

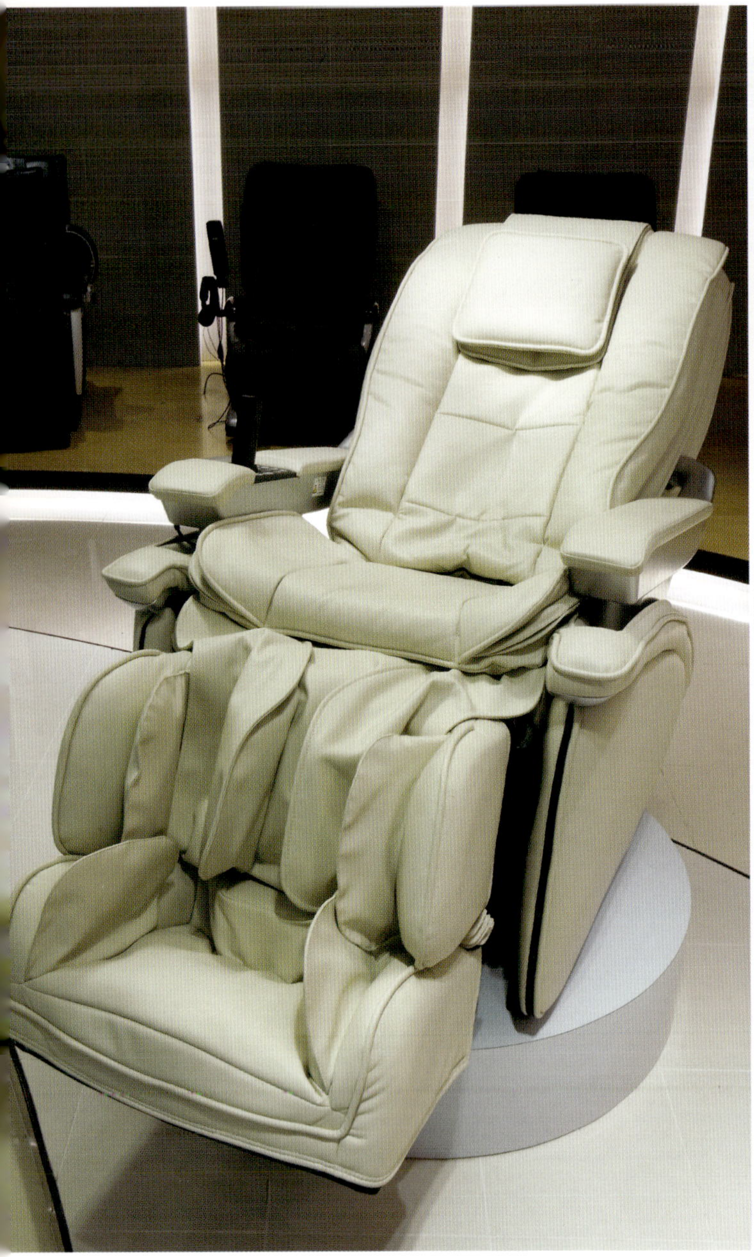
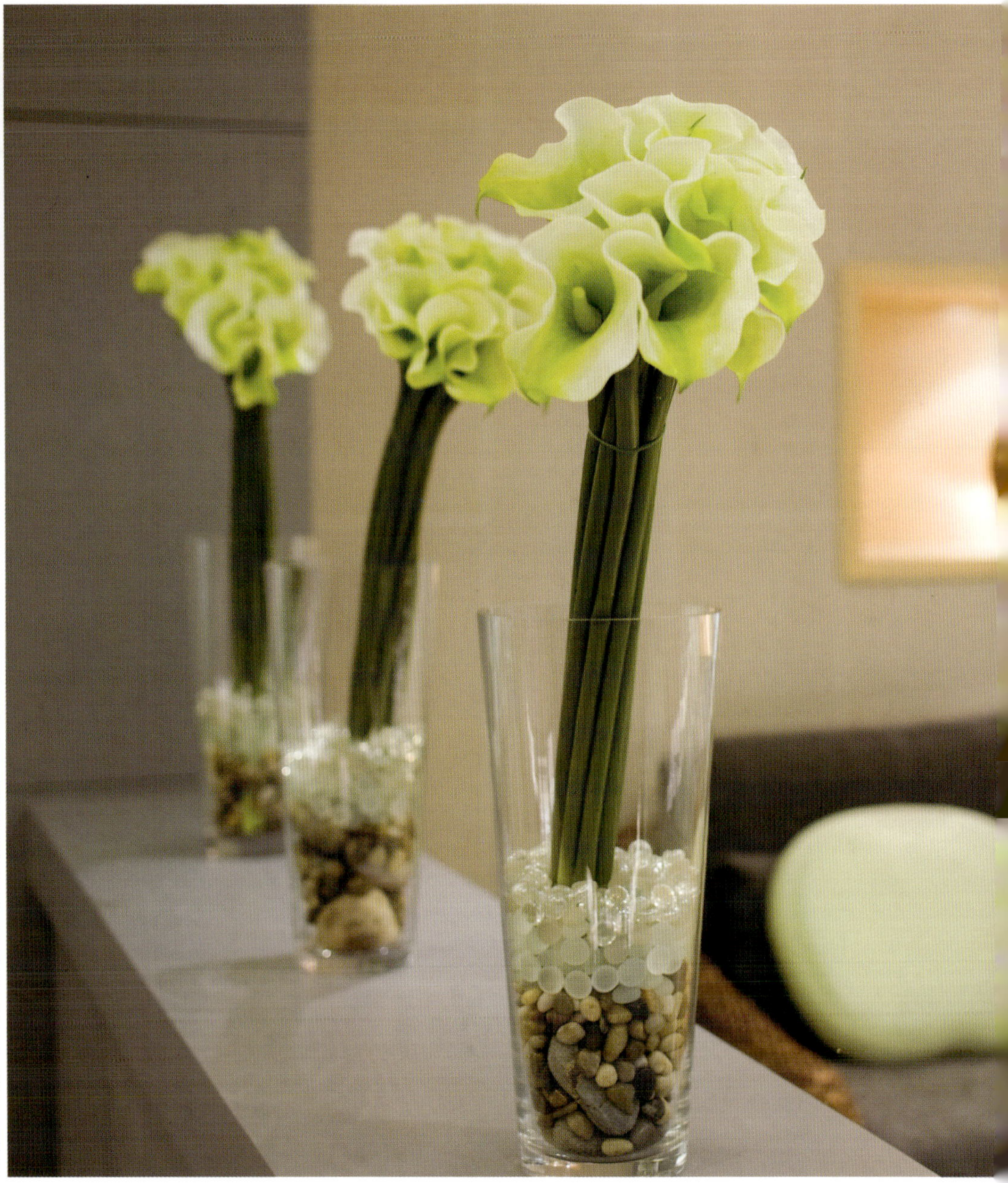

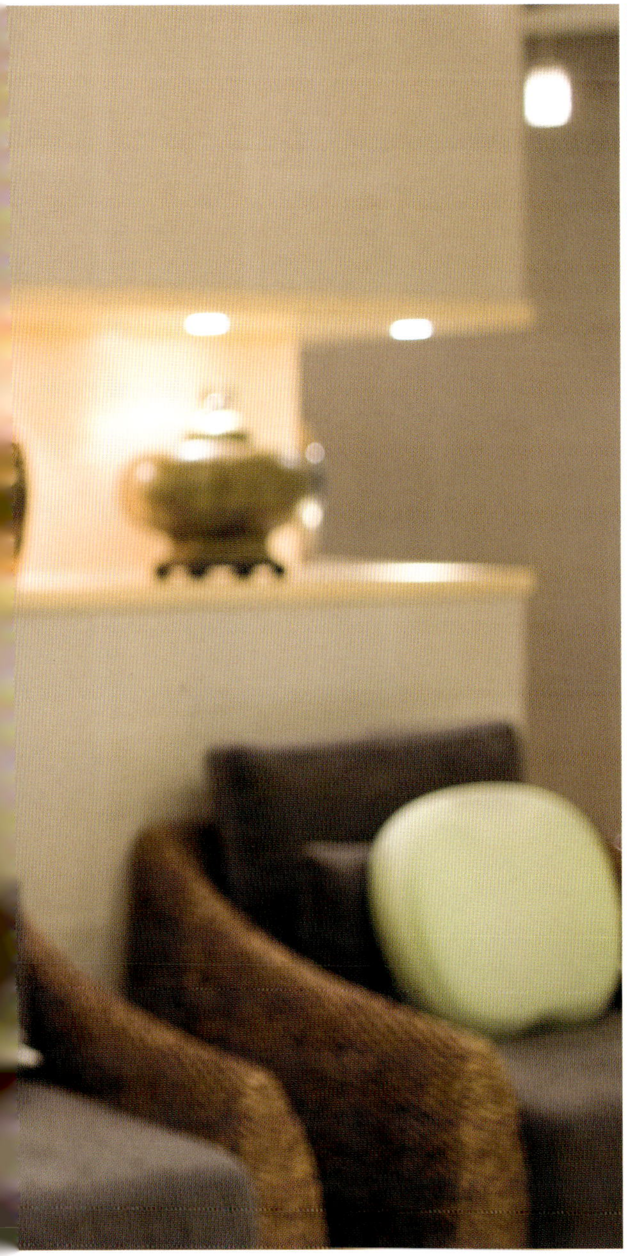

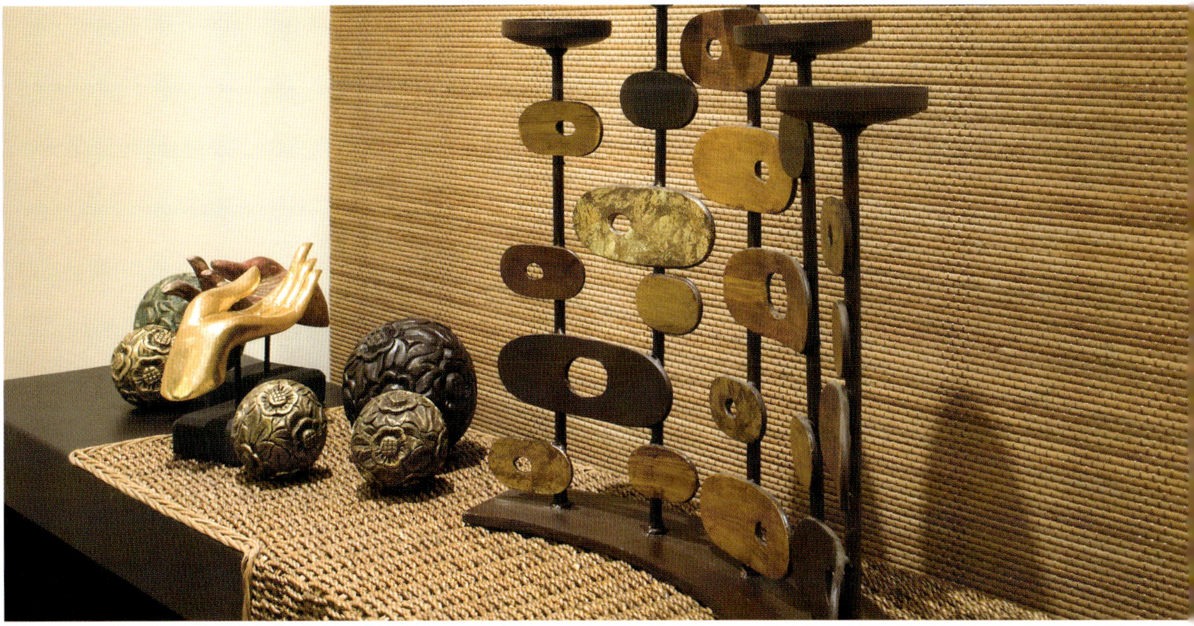

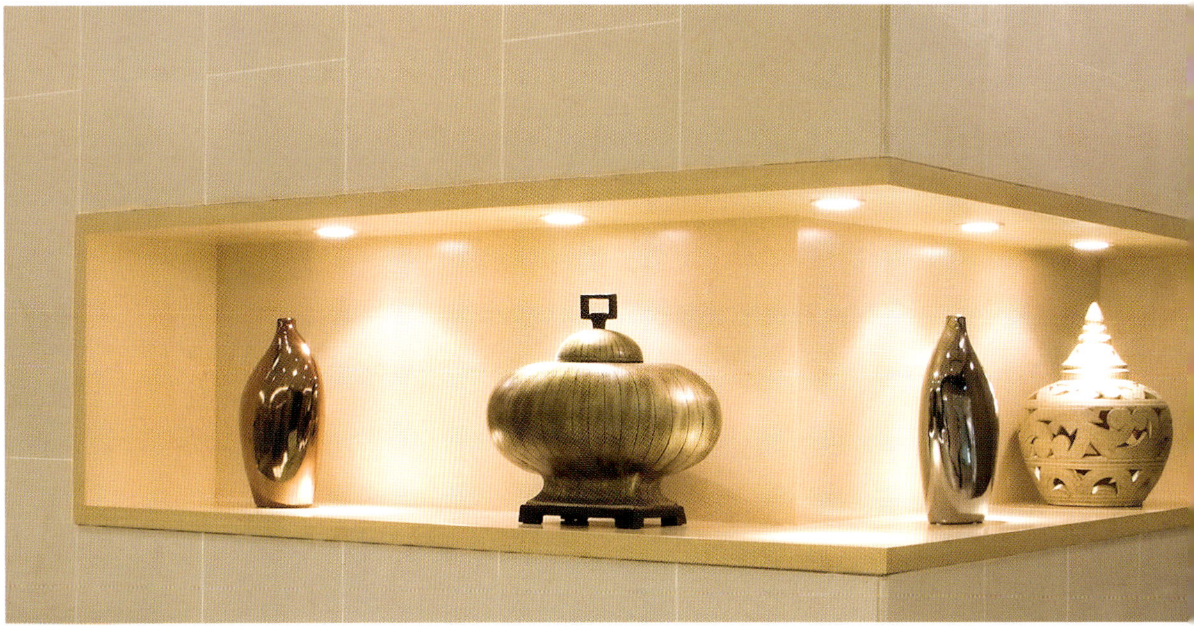

Leica Flagship Shop

where Taipei, Taiwan

In an area totalling 300 sq. m. throughout five floors, a new flagship shop for Leica was designed and constructed in Taipei, Taiwan.

The designers effectively used materials to furnish the space with glass, paints, iconic materials, stackable board and polished enamel bricks, giving a sense of elegance and refinement.

To establish harmony between the old exterior of the building and the new interior, the design team utilised dark brown shelves and pure white walls. The lighting system combined overhead spotlights, LED lighting and flameproof LED lighting. The upper floors were used as galleries for shows curated by the clients.

The flagship shop has its own atmosphere and unique appearance – trendy and modern, with an easy and flexible use of display space.

The effective and unique design has proven most popular with both Leica management and clientele.

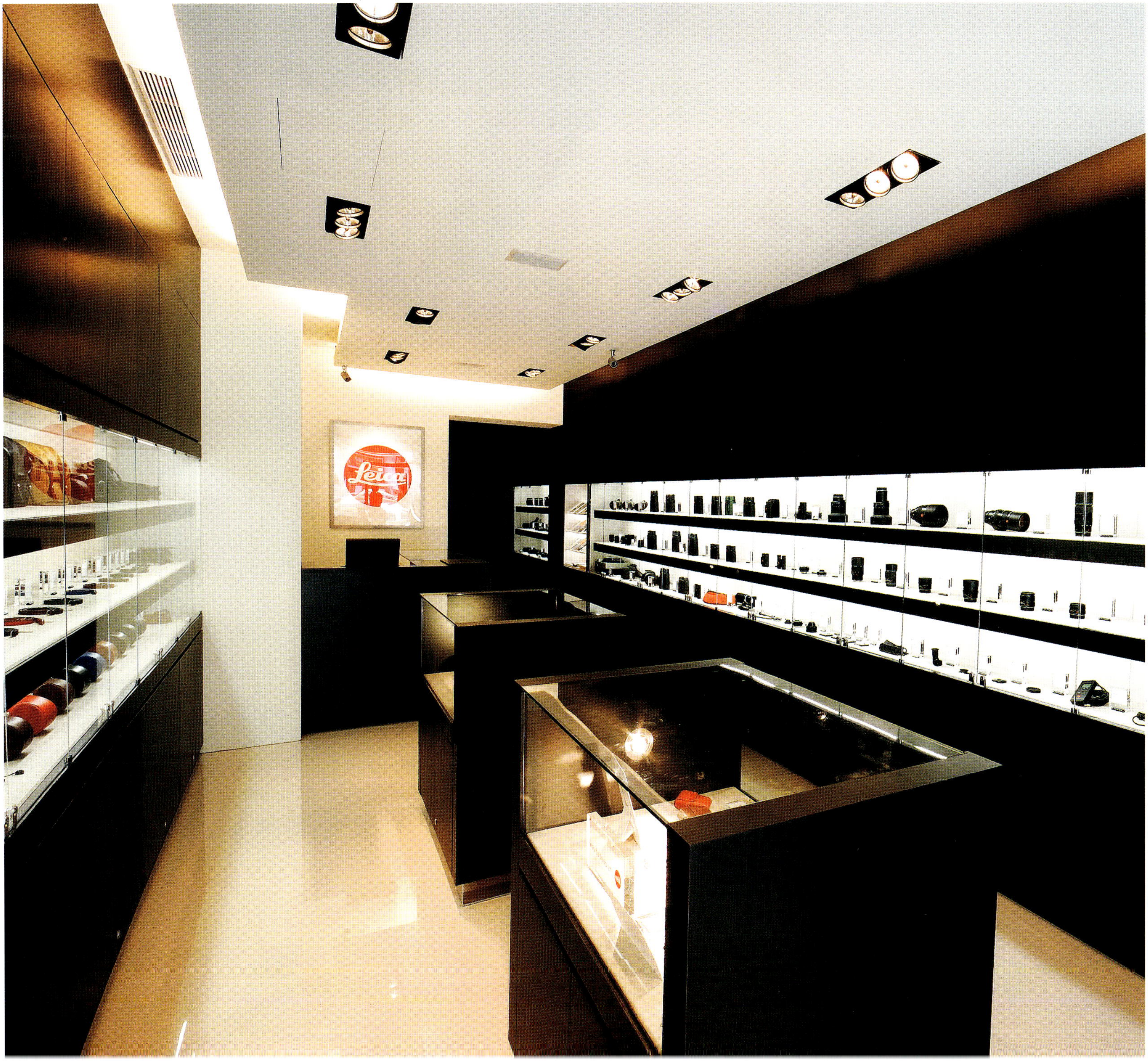
Leica

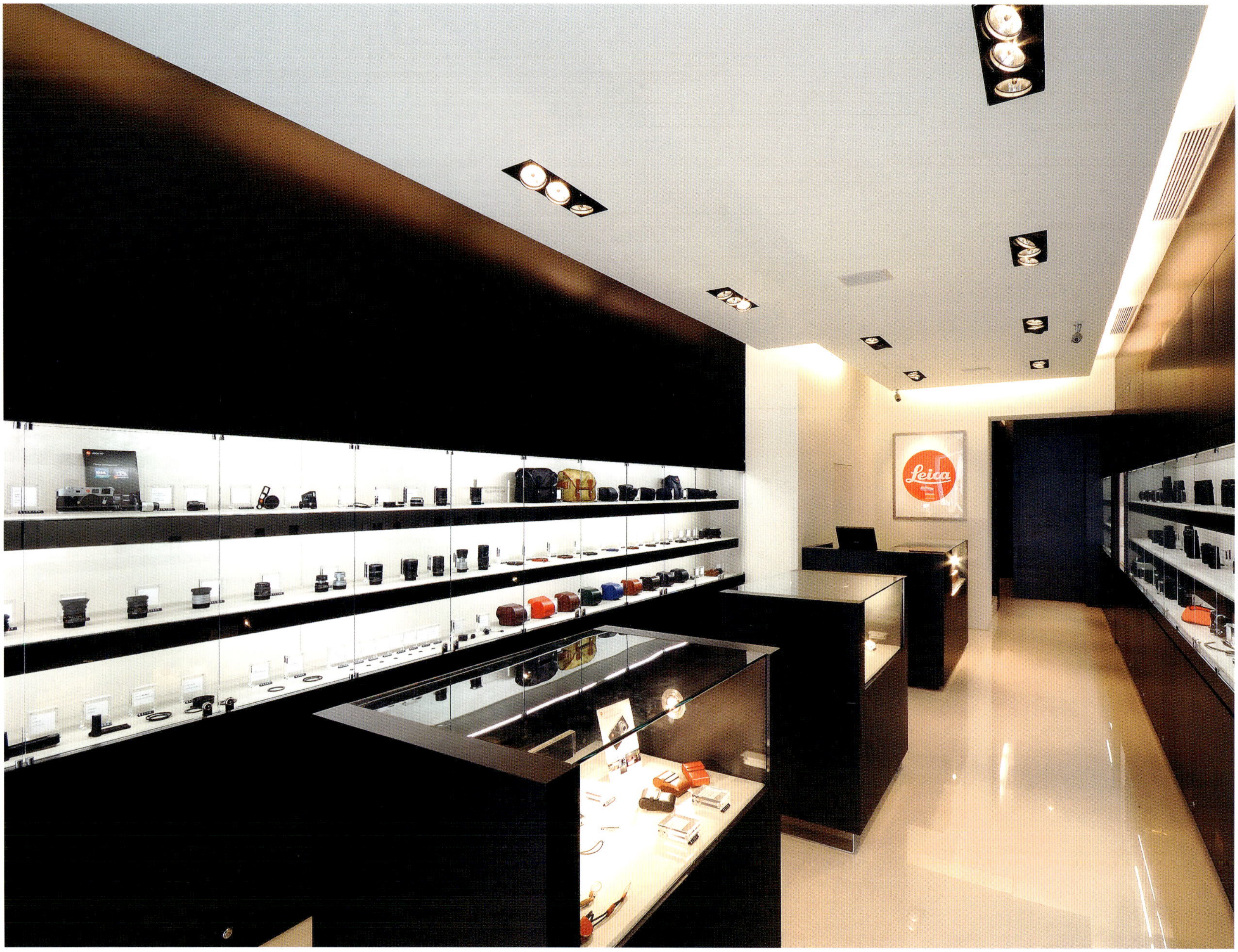
Leica

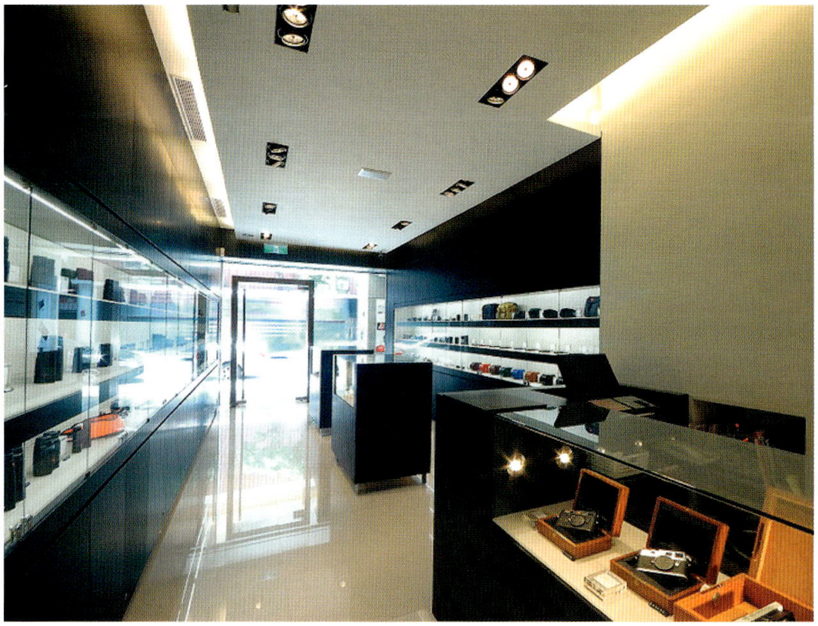
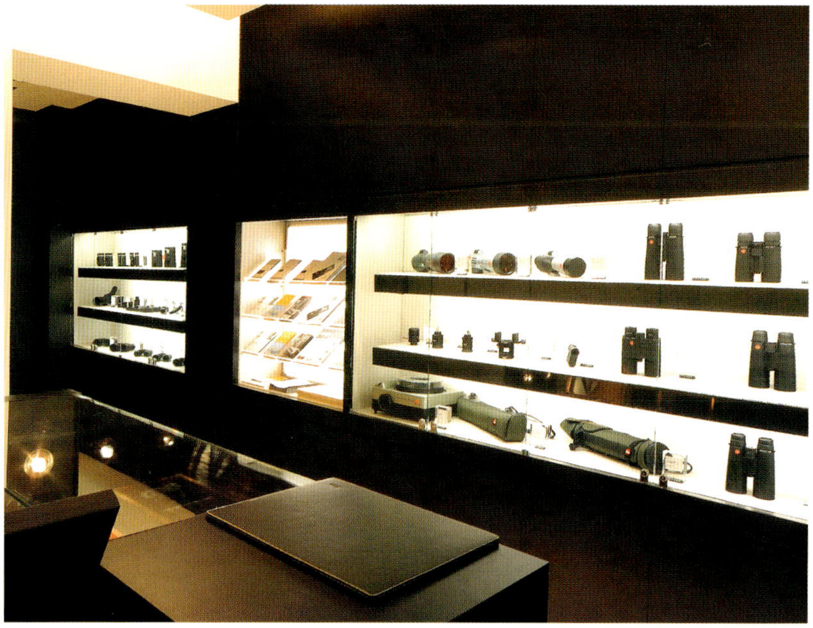
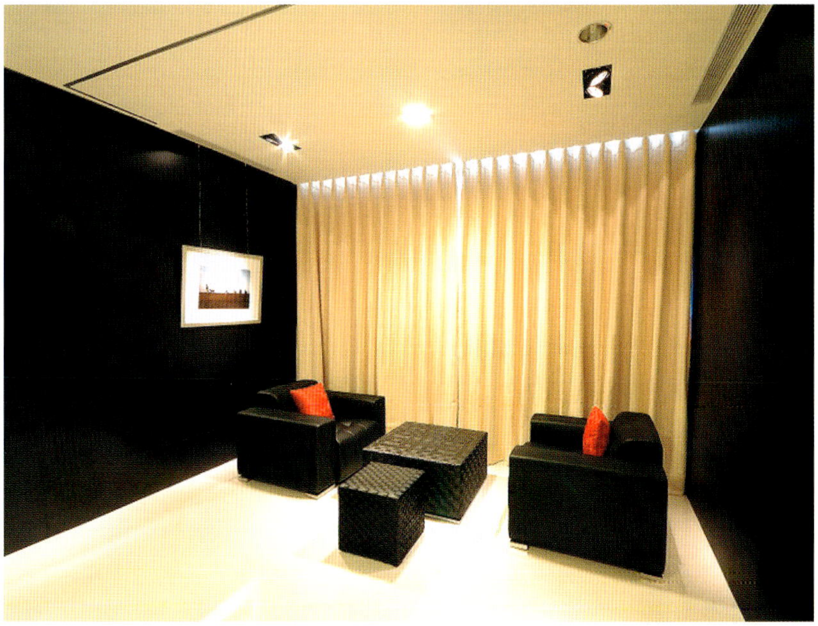
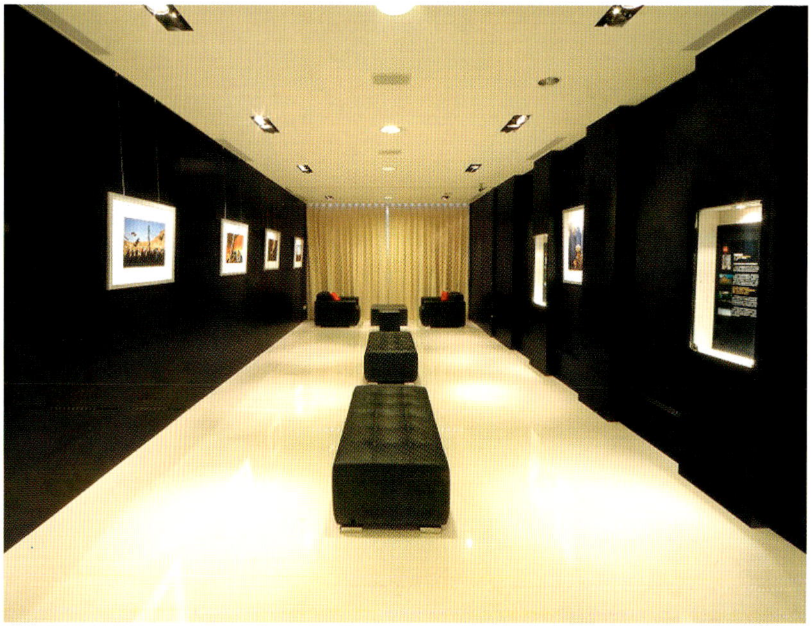

Mercedes-Benz Accessories Shop

where Busan, Korea

Mercedes-Benz Korea required the design, fabrication and project management for their new accessories store, the first Mercedes-Benz accessories shop to be located in Korea. In a space of 73 sq. m., the goal was to create a striking impact for the Mercedes-Benz brand.

In order to create the perfect showcase for the range of top quality accessories, the countertops and display units were decorated in a luxurious laminated black. The area was furnished with wood and metal frame materials. The dominant colours are black and red. The illuminated Mercedes-Benz logo is suspended from the ceiling and mirrors the round-shaped black display of the panel below.

The response has been outstanding for this first Mercedes-Benz accessories showroom in Busan, Korea.

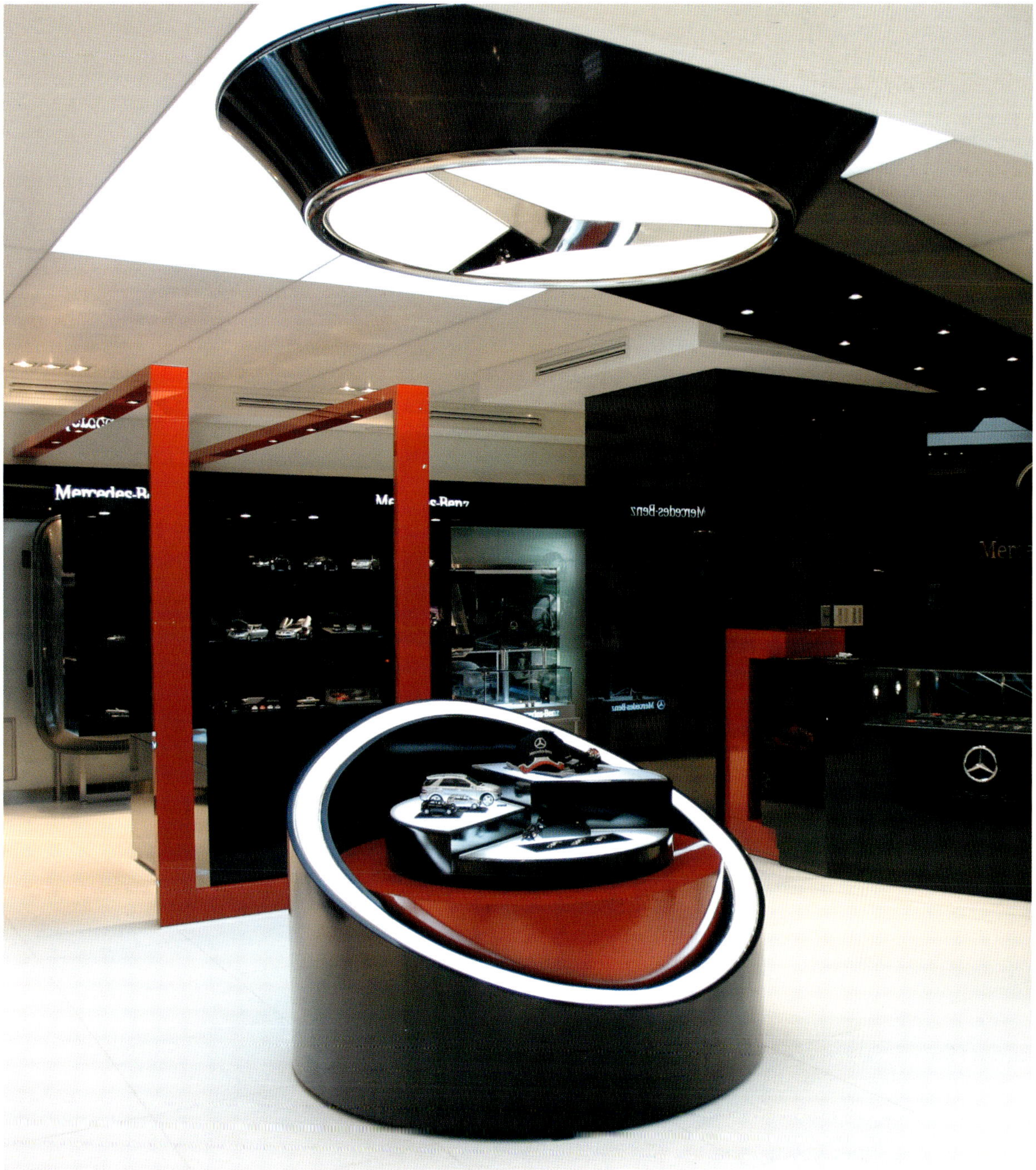

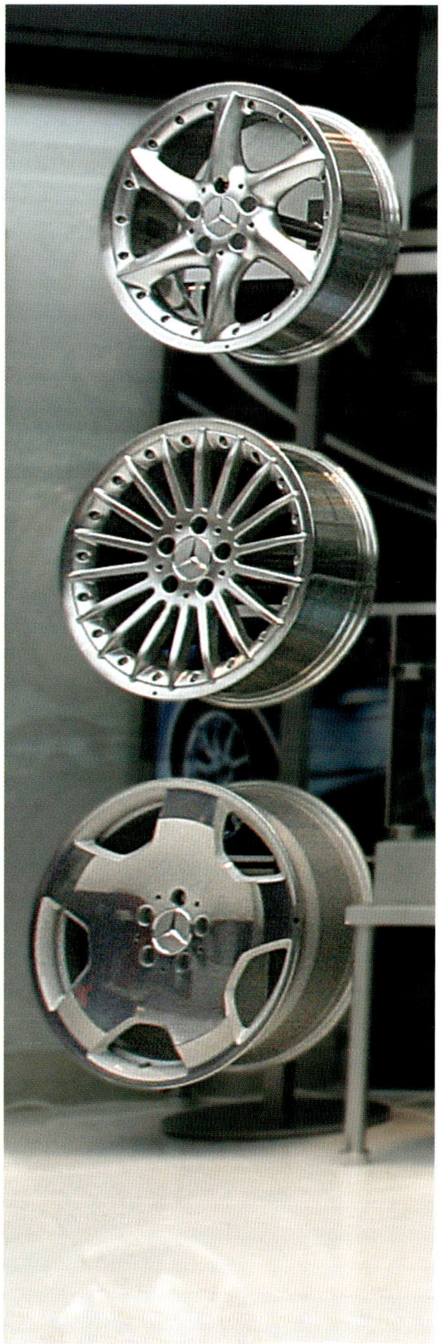

Qingdao CNC Centre

where Qingdao, China

To publicise sailing events in the 2008 Beijing Olympics, China Netcom Group Corporation had this exhibition centre designed and constructed in Qingdao, China. The Centre not only presents the company's latest business developments in China, but promotes its image, improves public relations and raises awareness to the public.

The designers developed the project by dividing the centre into three main areas: the first shows the development of CNC and its network, while the other two areas guide visitors in understanding the applications of the CNC network.

Guests travel a curved route that brings them through the space. Netcom's corporate colours, blue and green form the colour palette accented by an effective lighting system with LED, glass materials, and steel. An interactive system was created to provide synchronous presentations with displays and information in a tight space.

The design firm performed extensive research before commencing work on the project, and China Netcom Group Corporation took an active part to ensure whilst a cost-saving approach was effected, various criteria were met as well.

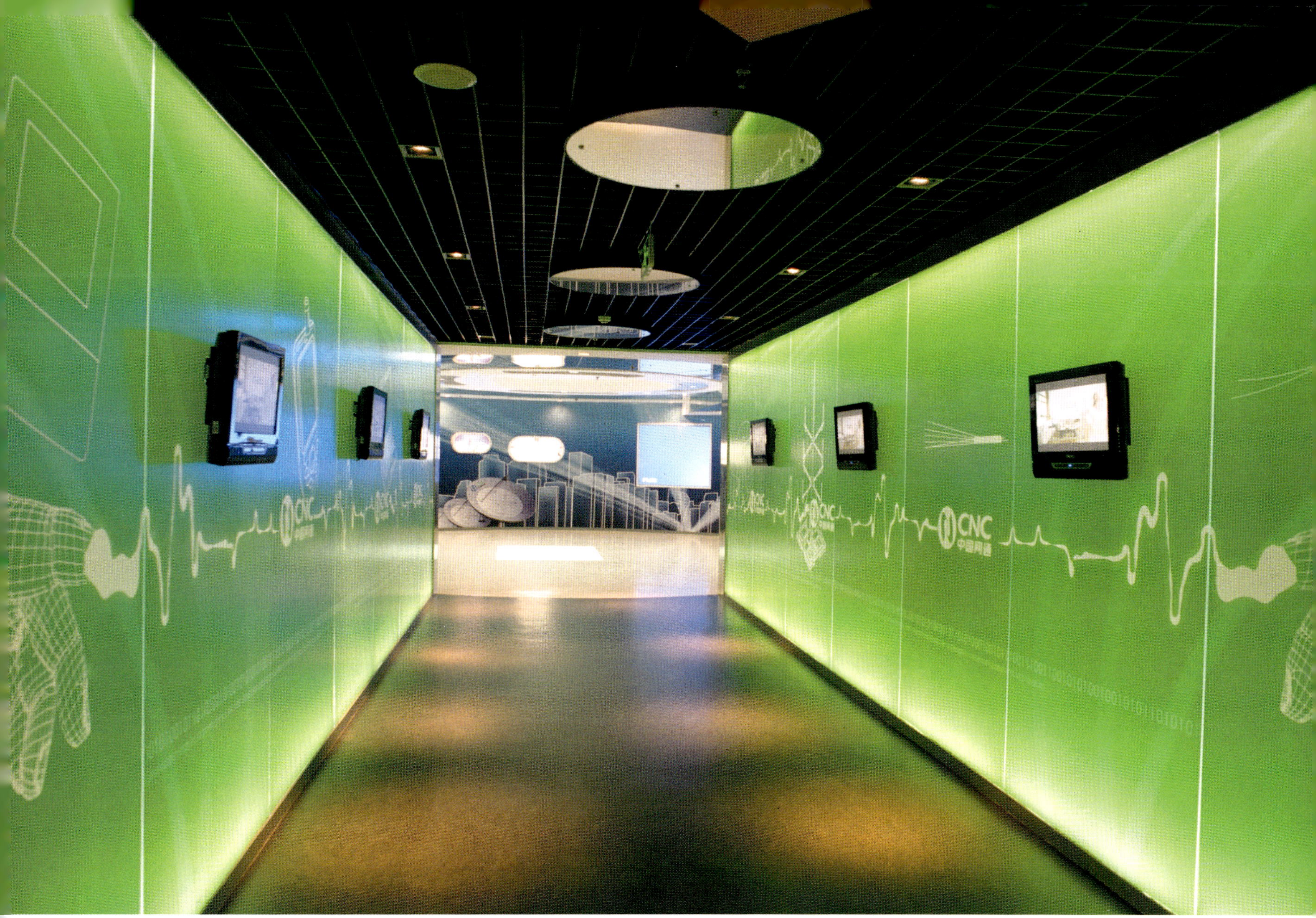
CNC

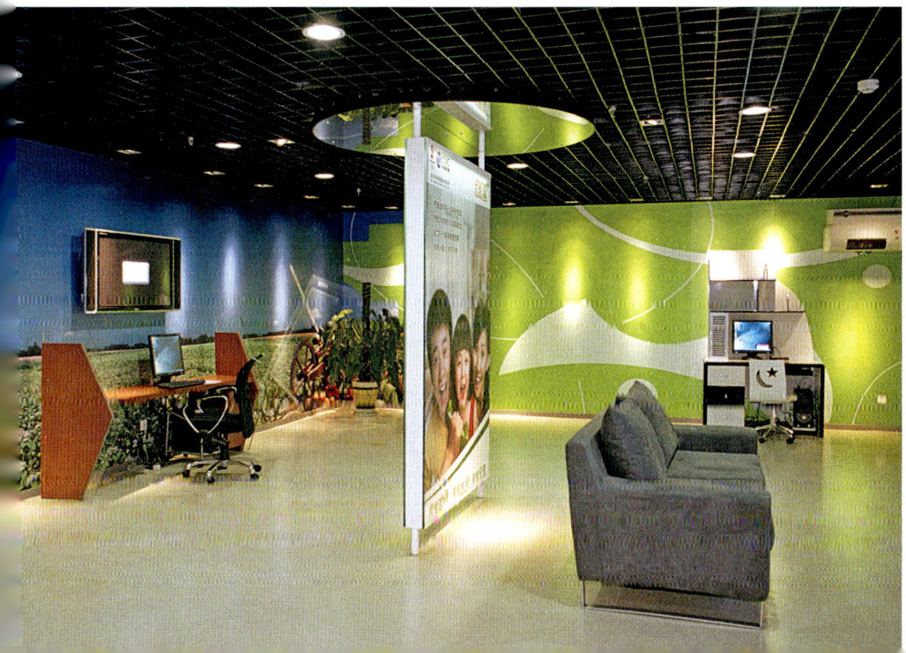

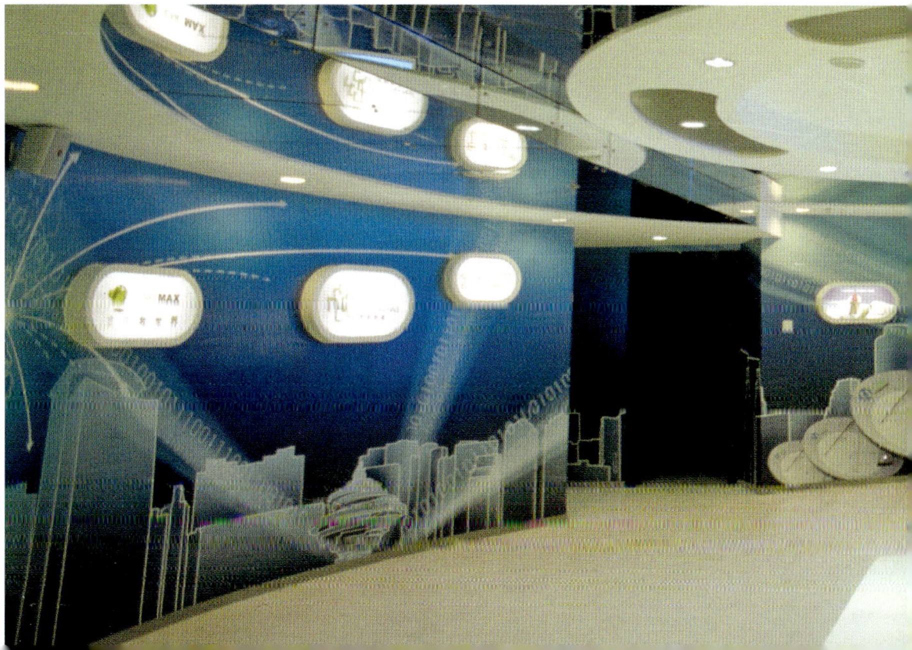

Motorola Facilities Branding Projects

where various cities in North America

During the past few years, Pico has developed many large scale branding projects for Motorola, to bring to life the corporate-wide re-branding of Motorola facilities throughout the U.S. This entailed close coordination with Motorola's facilities management group, Jones Lange LaSalle. The key sites included Motorola's corporate headquarters in Schaumburg, IL, as well as locations in high-profile cities such as Washington, DC; Chicago, IL; Seattle, WA; Holtsville, NY; Austin, TX; Boston, MA and San Diego, CA.

Each site is a unique open space. The challenge for the designers was to create a uniform corporate branding environment that was a simple, functional and elegant environment without compromising the surroundings.

Starting with the front desk, direct, immediate contact with visitors is made, a positive first impression. Visitors' eyes are directed toward large-scale dynamic images.

Leveraging eye-catching Motorola product displays, photos, brand evolution timelines, and the instantly identifiable Motorola logo, the design team created refreshing new environments that strengthened the client's branding strategies.

Spaces have not only been transformed into productive work environments, but have also strengthened brand awareness amongst both employees and visitors.

event. exhibit. interior. themed.

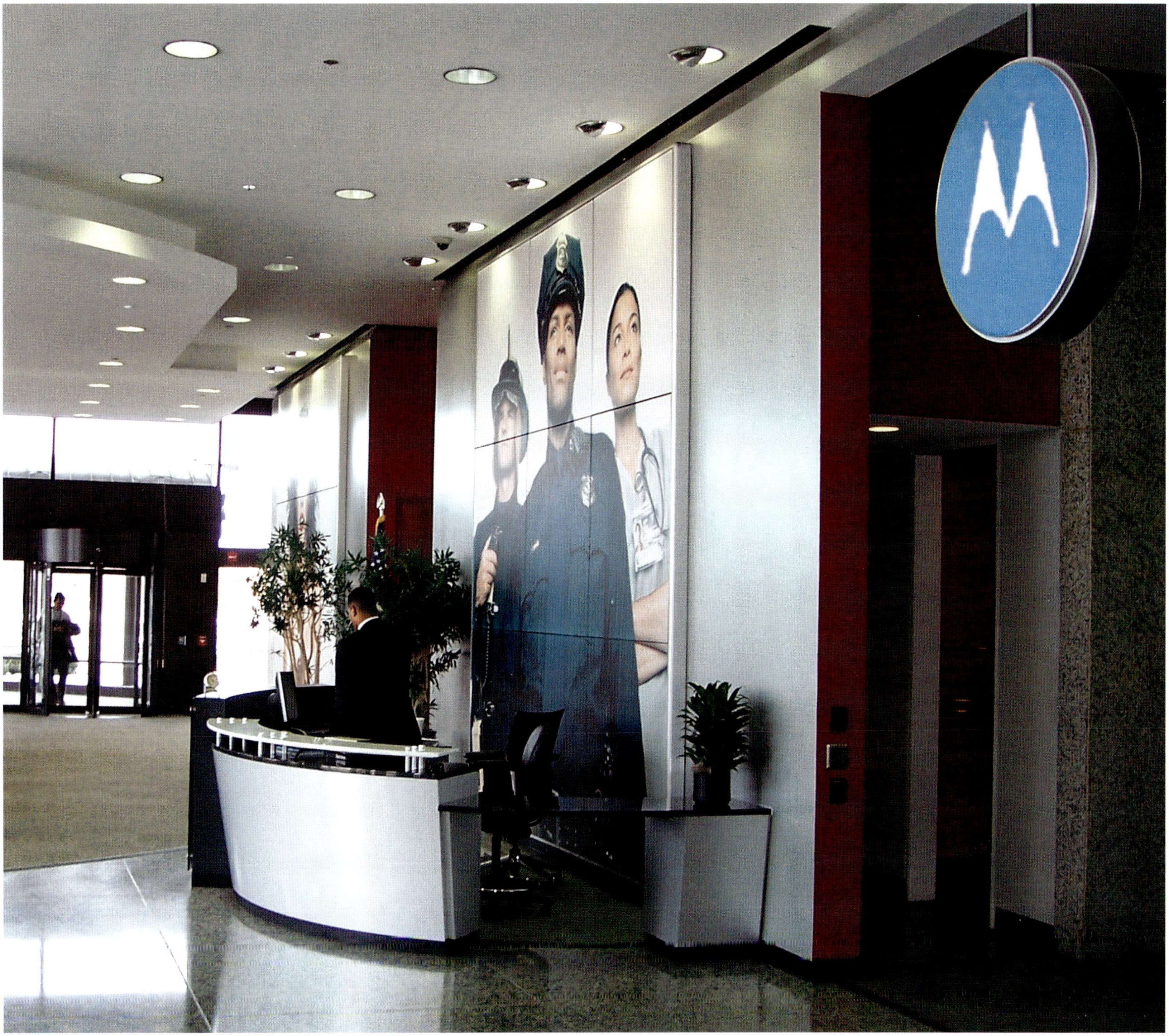

Siemens Automation Showroom

where Thuan An, Binh Duong Province, Vietnam

A new design has been completed at Siemens Automation Systems Ltd. for the Siemens Automation reception area, at their showroom located at the Vietnam Singapore Industrial Park in Thuan An, Binh Duong Province, Vietnam.

The design concept consists of a simple but elegant look, using materials such as imported laminates, including the floor system in the bar area. The design incorporates the use of Siemens products, showcasing the client's lighting fixtures and switches. Siemens corporate colours of blue and orange are used to add flair and strengthen corporate identity.

Contributing to the outstanding quality of this project was the clever use of Siemens products, creating a cohesive and effective environment that engages visitors. Some of the items are on display, while others are functional, controlling the lighting system.

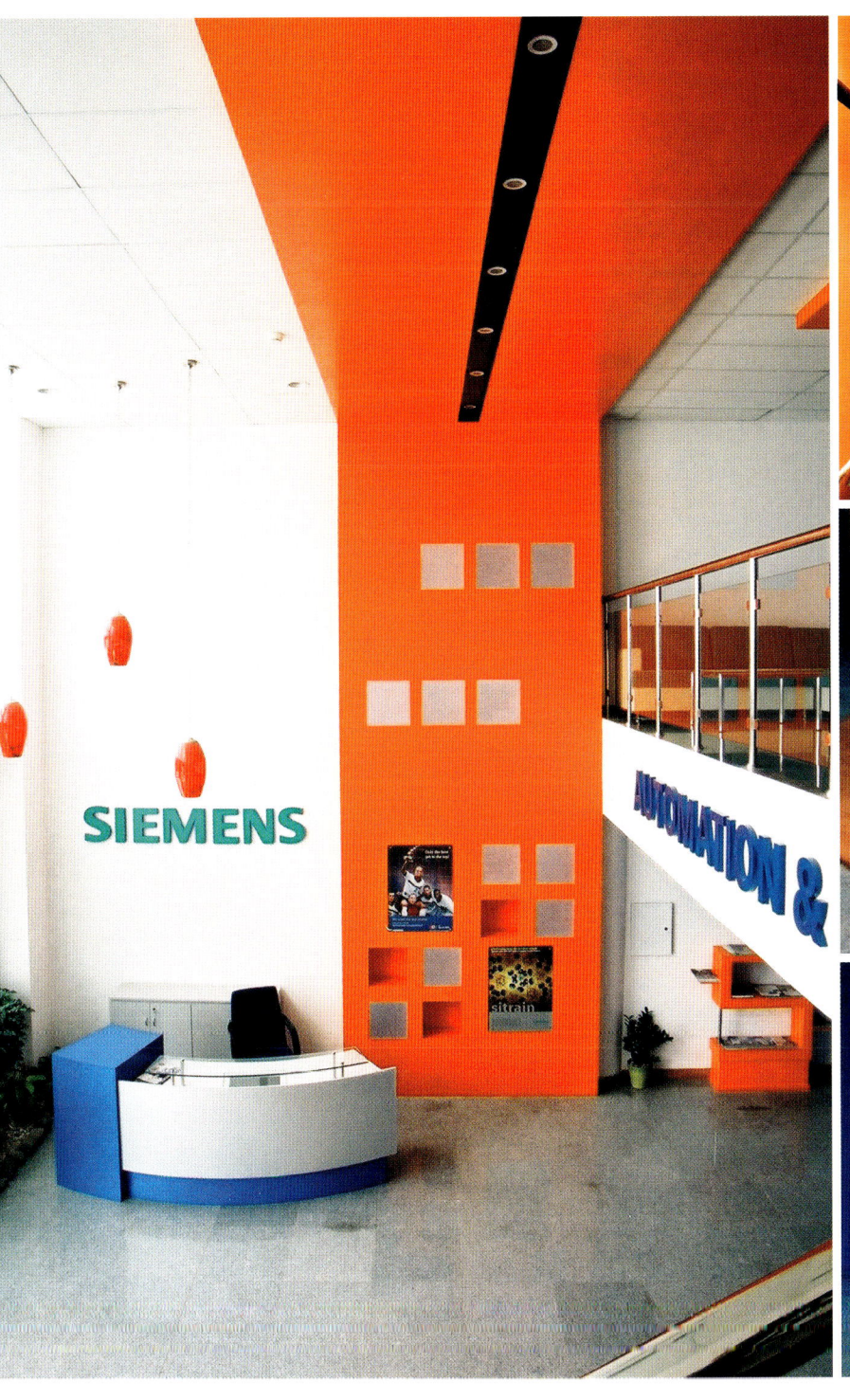

SIEMENS

AUTOMATION &

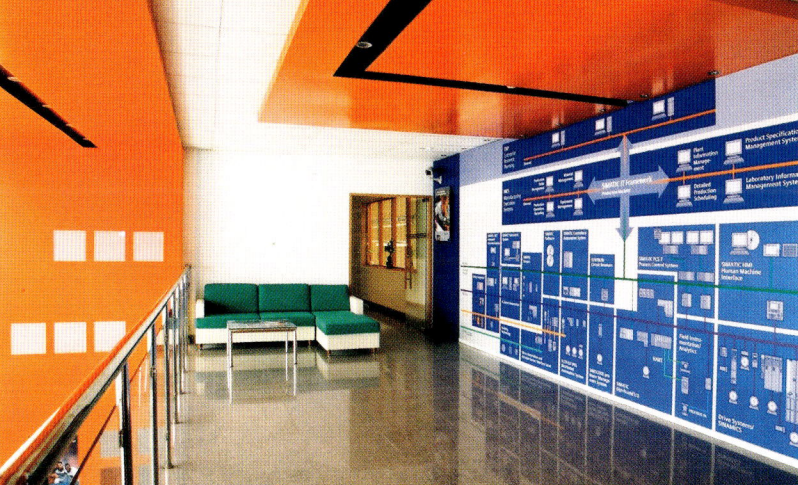

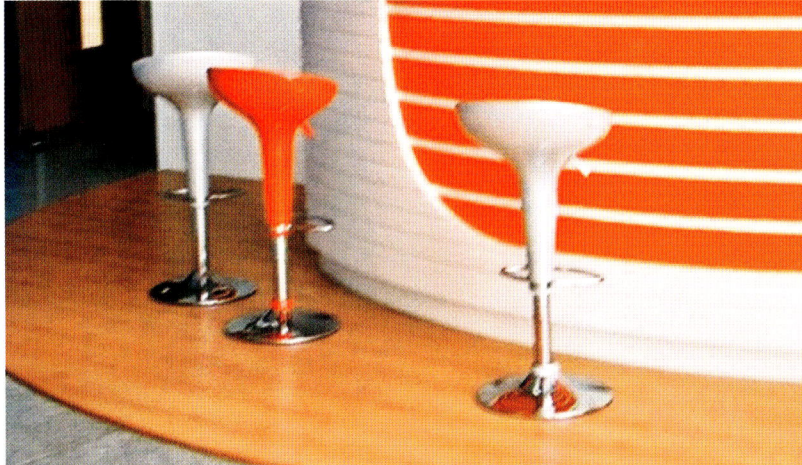

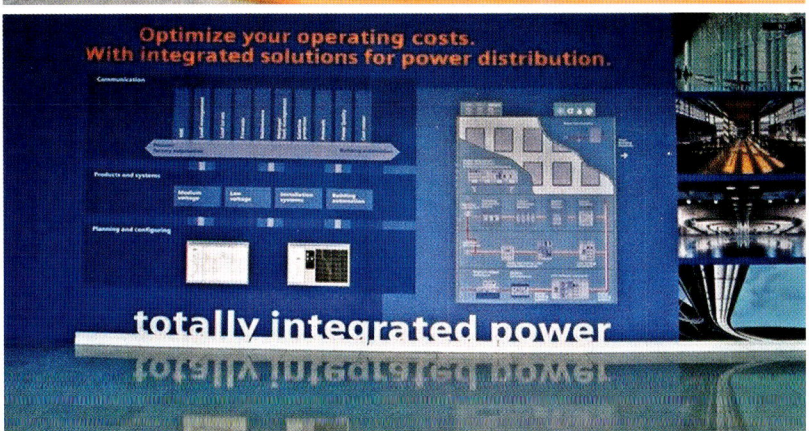

Optimize your operating costs.
With integrated solutions for power distribution.

totally integrated power

Siemens Visitor Centre

where Shanghai, China

The design solution divided the Siemens Power Transmission Visitor Centre into three areas: a business introduction area, a high voltage zone and a medium voltage zone. Electronic "flip page" sensors and touch screens presented the history of Siemens. In addition, a model wall with thousands of LED bulbs completed the highly interactive educational presentation. The space also contained a VIP conference room.

A multimedia interactive system was skilfully integrated into the environment through the use of metallic materials, brushed stainless steel flooring, kick panels and exhibit cabinets. Glass exhibit cabinets and acrylic lacquered light boxes were used throughout the space.

The creative solution was delivered on time as a result of dedicated team efforts to overcome the various challenges.

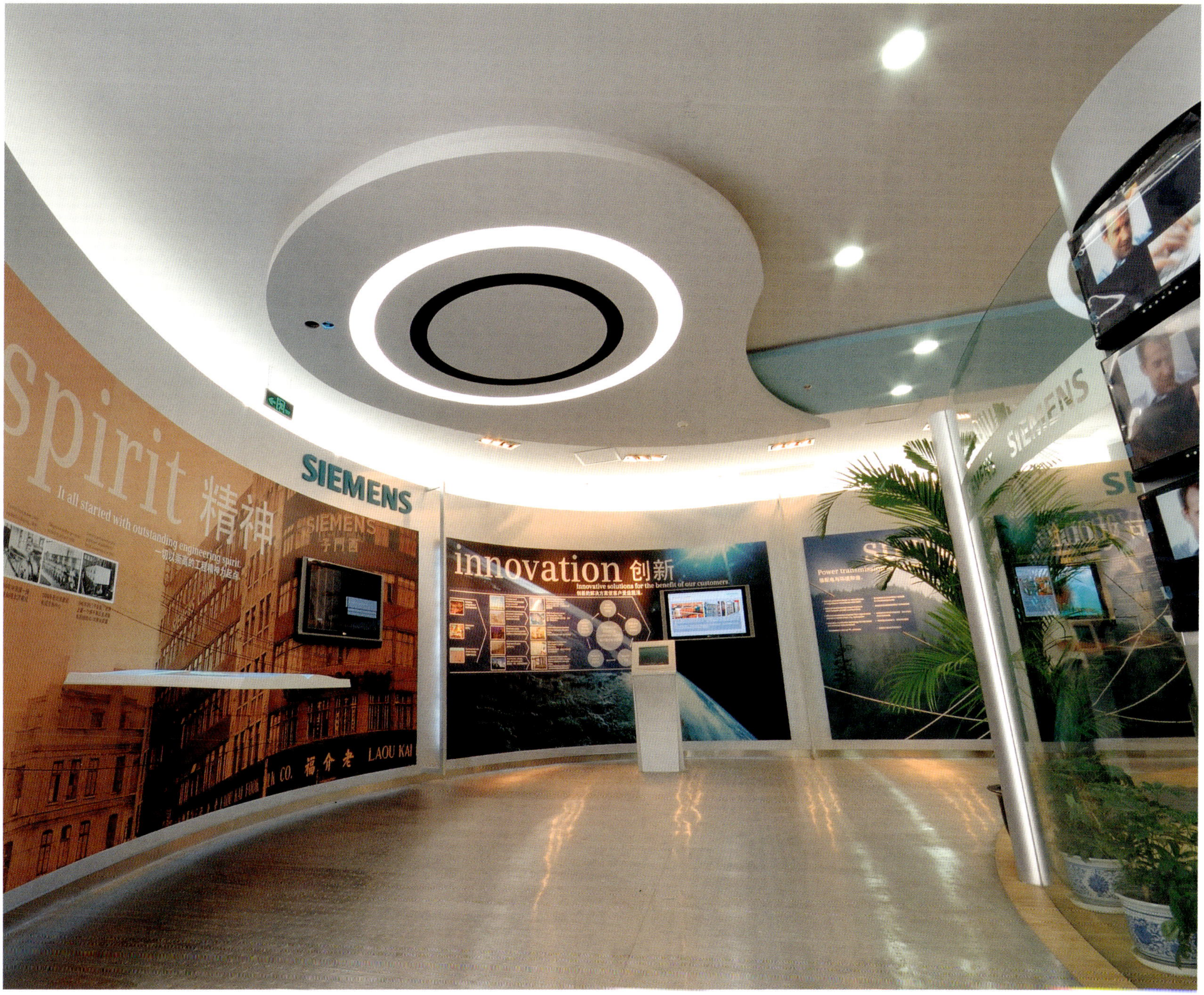
spirit 精神
It all started with outstanding engineering spirit.
SIEMENS
innovation 创新
Innovative solutions for the benefit of our customers.
LAOU KAI

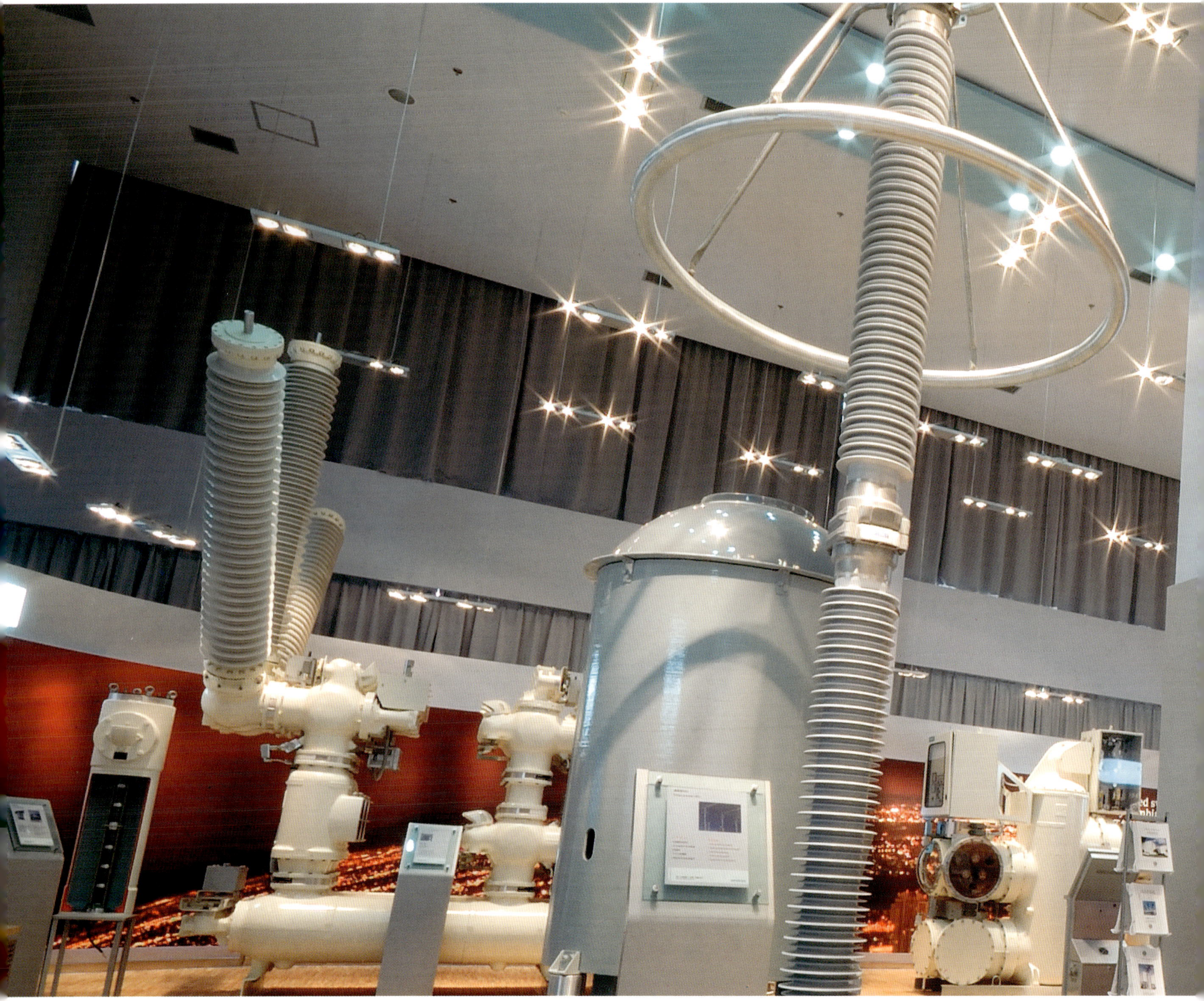

SIEMENS

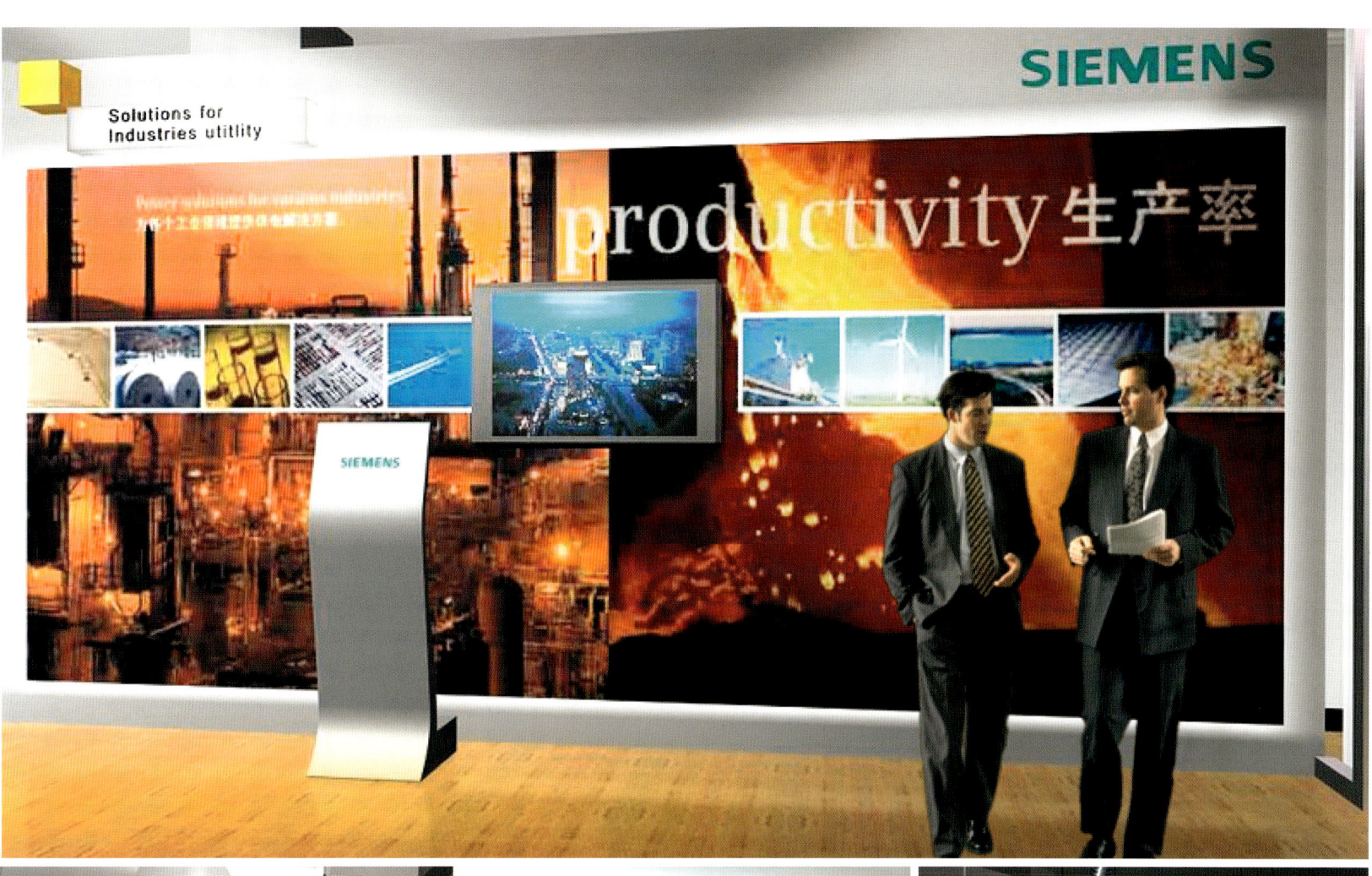

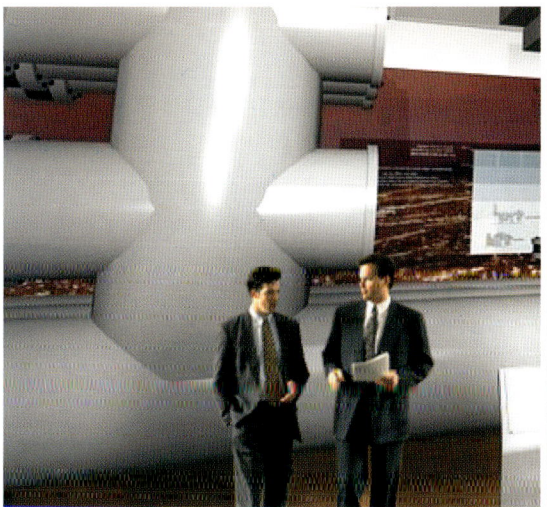

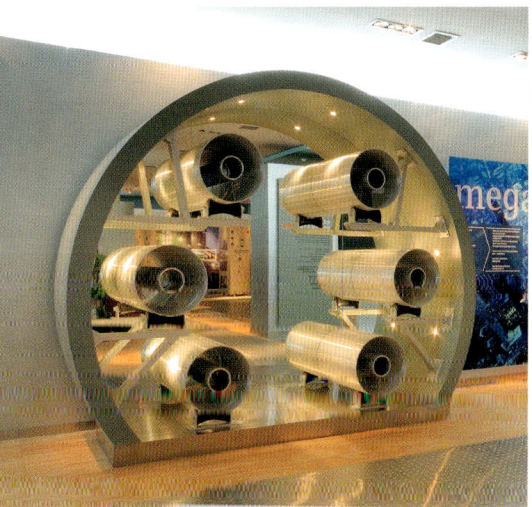

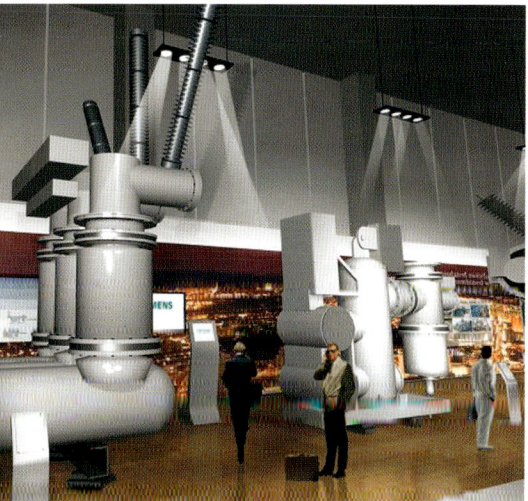

Solutions for Industries utitlity

productivity 生产率

Cellnet Executive Briefing Centre

where Alpharetta, GA, USA

Founded in 1985, Cellnet is a young, energetic company which provides wireless fixed data communication networks for the electric, gas and water utility industries. Cellnet requested the design of a unique conference space at the headquarters facility in Alpharetta, GA. The space of 1,728 sq. ft. is designed for high-level meetings with current or potential clients and Board of Directors' meetings.

The Centre is planned and laid out to appear and function as a permanent interior. The metres on the wall are used for working demonstrations.

The designers created the space incorporating a modular design, understated and elegant, displaying Cellnet's products and services on rear-lit, colour spectrum columns. These modular constructions permit easy dismantling and re-installation of the exhibit space at different locations and also allow for flexibility in response to changing requirements. The modular construction, which maintains a permanent appearance, makes the exhibit space versatile and unique.

The design firm's dedicated efforts produced results far exceeding Cellnet's expectations.

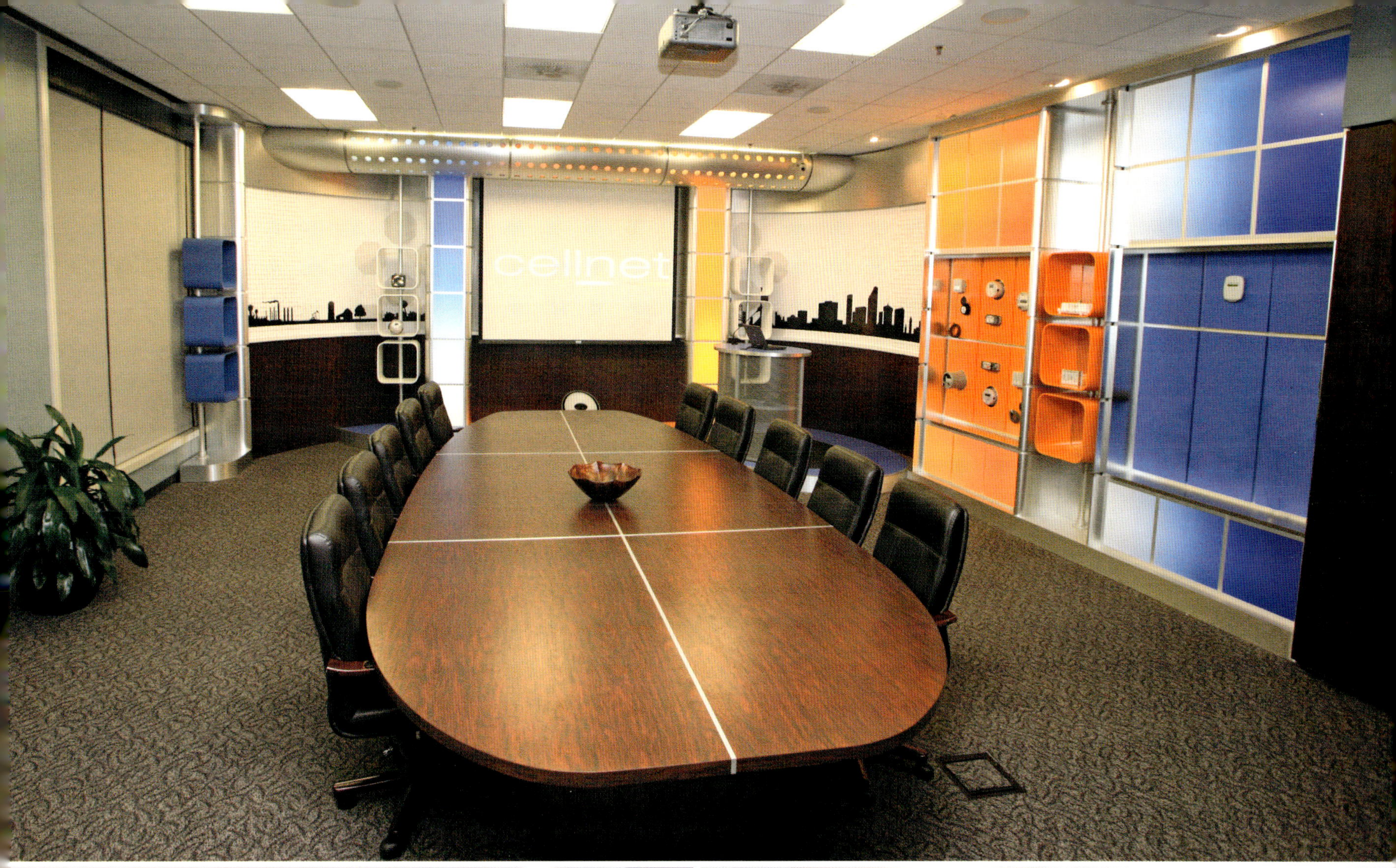
cellnet

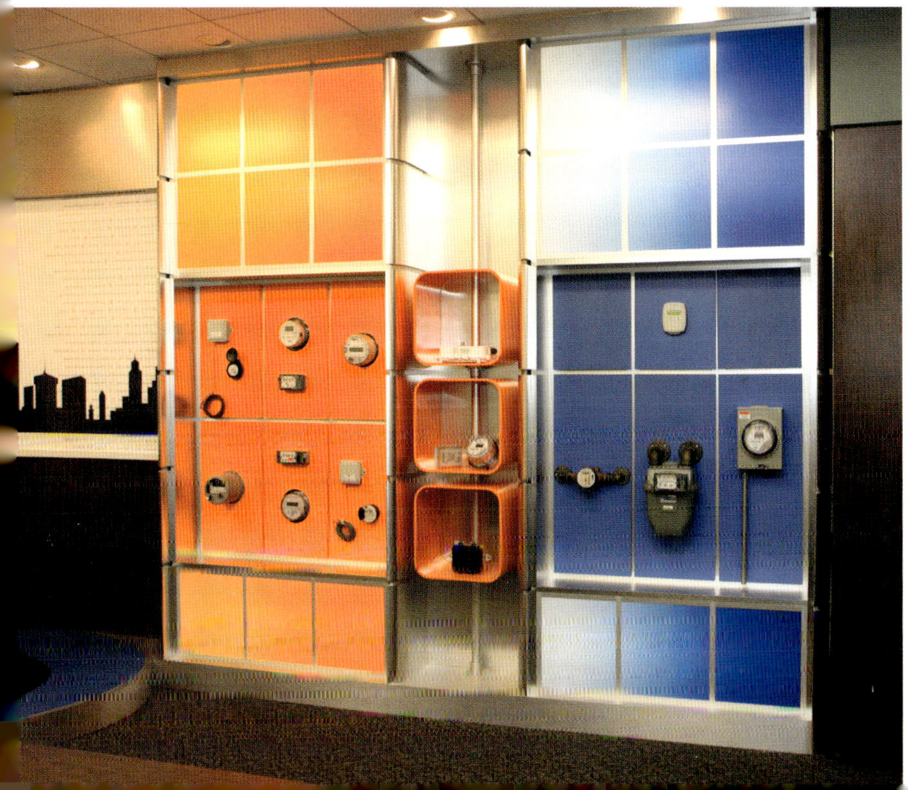

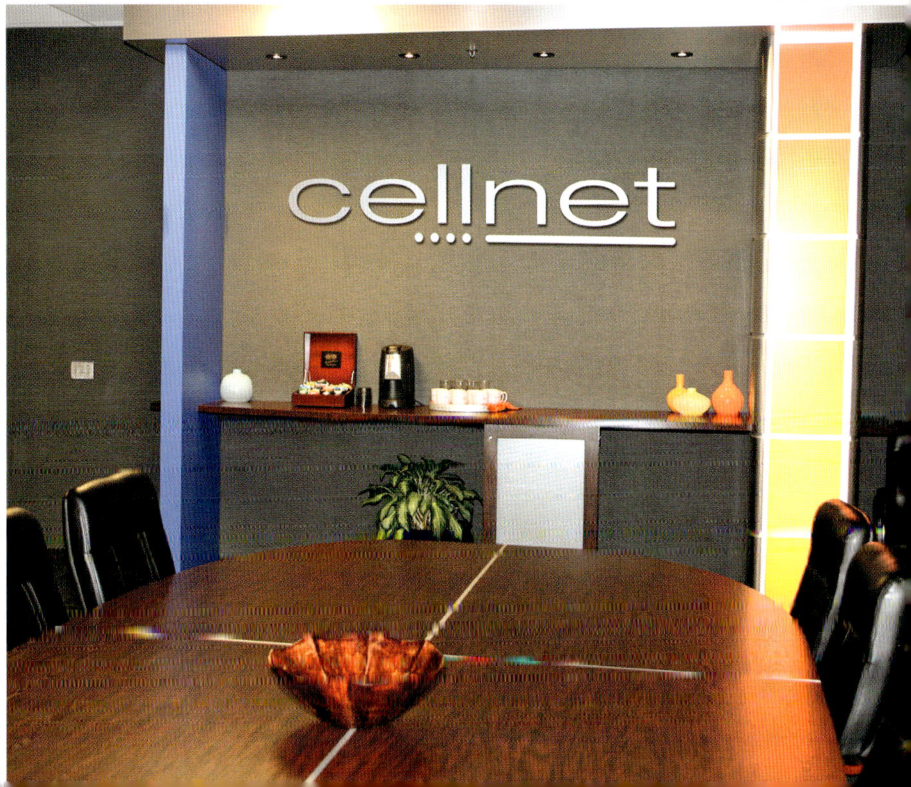
cellnet

Museums used to be repositories for old or dead things – things from the past that were visited with great solemnity. They were hallowed halls filled with a sense of awe and forbidding. That was then. Today's museums reach out to the young, the techno-hip, and the electronic-savvy with all sorts of special, interactive presentations. Corporations are forming their own visitor centres where their traditions and heritage are offered to the public.

There is nothing musty, dusty or old hat about the permanent exhibits created by Pico for museums and themed attractions. These environments sparkle with bright, smart eye-enveloping settings and high-tech accoutrements. According to Pico, "Permanent themed environments must not only be attractive – but must be timeless. Our people are well versed in creating 'stories' from concept to design that engage visitors."

Scenes of the past become meaningful when recreated dramatically in scaled dioramas or in life-sized tableaux filled with artefacts, theatrically staged and illuminated. Suddenly – what was the "past" is "now" and is here for all to experience. This technique is used in Ngong Ping Village, Hua Song Museum, as well as a variety of other visitor centres. The historic D-Day landing at Normandy is commemorated at Omaha Beach with text, photos, artefacts and interactive displays. The Malaysia Export Exhibition Centre promotes Made In Malaysia products to overseas buyers and trade organisations.

Pico tells "old stories" in new ways and utilises state-of-the-art media to turn what was the past into a fresh, new and vital experience for today – and tomorrow.

Martin M. Pegler

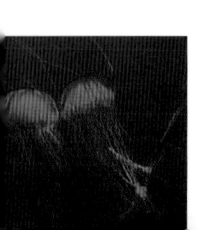

themed.

Ocean Park Hong Kong

where Hong Kong SAR, China

Ocean Park Hong Kong is an acclaimed educational theme park and the seventh most popular amusement park in the world. Within the 870,000 sq. m. park, located on the coast of Hong Kong Island, is a stand-alone jellyfish house – Sea Jelly Spectacular.

The jellyfish exhibit was designed and built in the form of eight scenes with cylindrical jellyfish tanks, textured floor finish, themed ceiling and illuminated graphics. This space was themed as a "sea atmosphere" to involve and inform visitors and raise awareness of environmental concerns.

LCD monitors on a black wall, a laser zone and mirrors focus the viewer's attention, helping people to better understand jellyfish and the importance of clean oceans. For children, there is an effective "touch and go" interactive zone to play with jellyfish, which float away when the screen is touched.

This unique exhibit shows a collection of more than 1,000 sea jellies from over ten distinct species collected worldwide. The challenge for this project was to handle the jellyfish with special care, creating a proper living environment for these fragile creatures which are most difficult to capture and maintain.

According to the Ocean Park Corporation Annual Report, "Using new interactive technologies, this magnificent attraction is a departure from the normal aquarium experience and was incredibly popular. It helped increase year-to-year attendance by more than 150,000 in its first three weeks of operation."

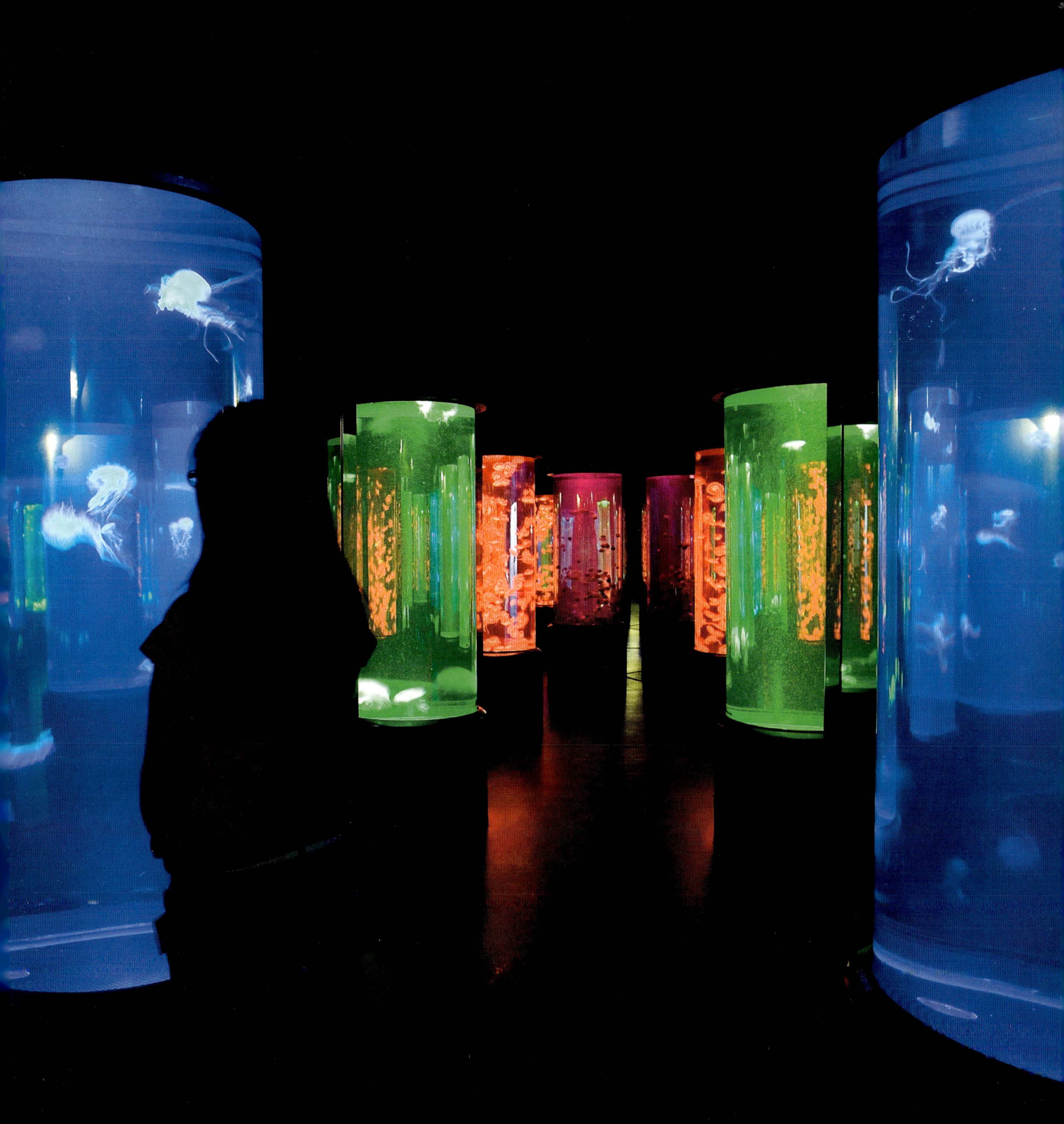

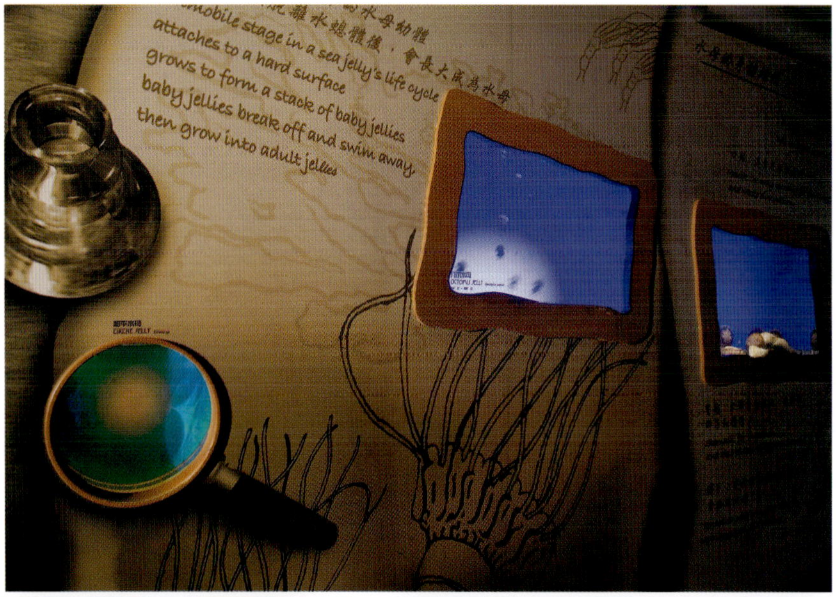
mobile stage in a sea jelly's life cycle
attaches to a hard surface
grows to form a stack of baby jellies
baby jellies break off and swim away,
then grow into adult jellies

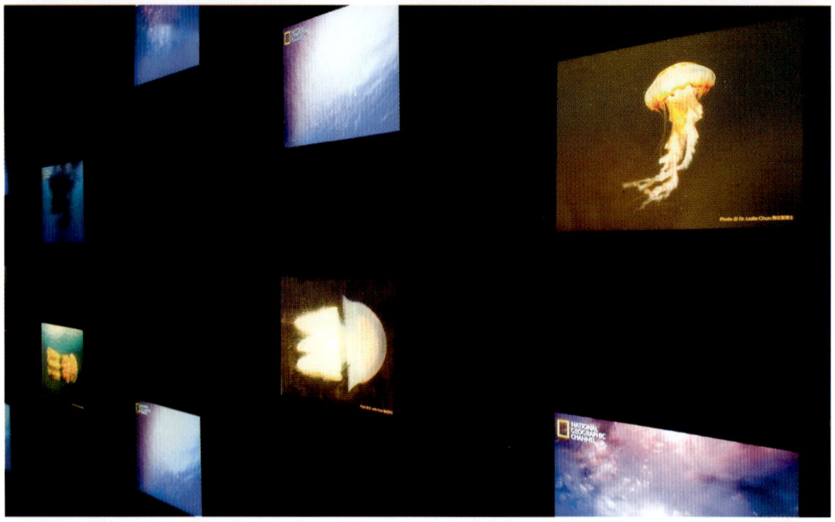

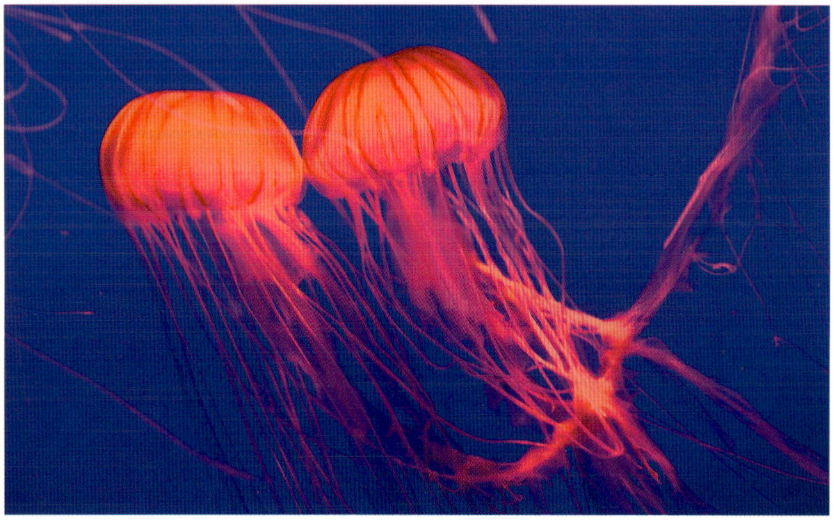

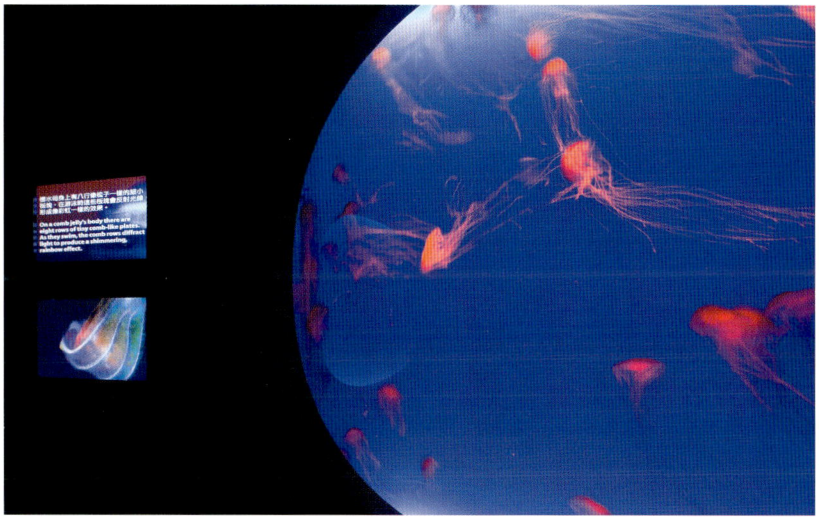
On a comb jelly's body there are
eight rows of tiny comb-like plates.
As they swim, the comb rows diffract
light to produce a shimmering,
rainbow effect.

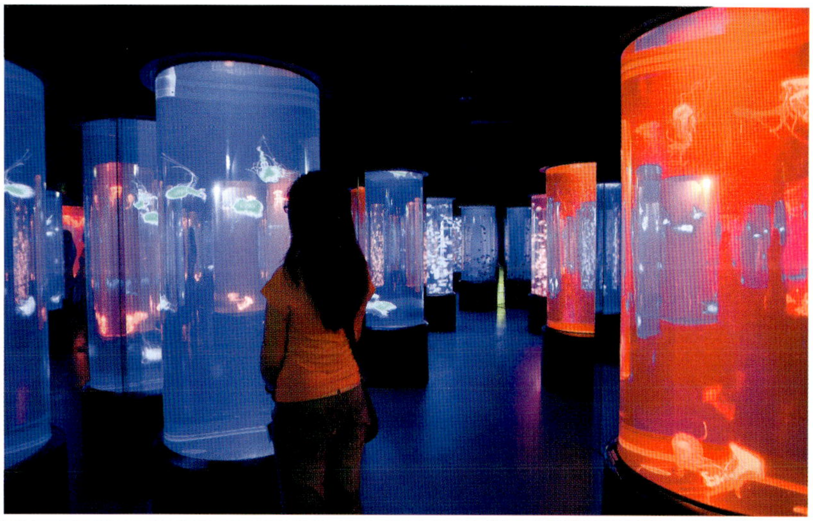

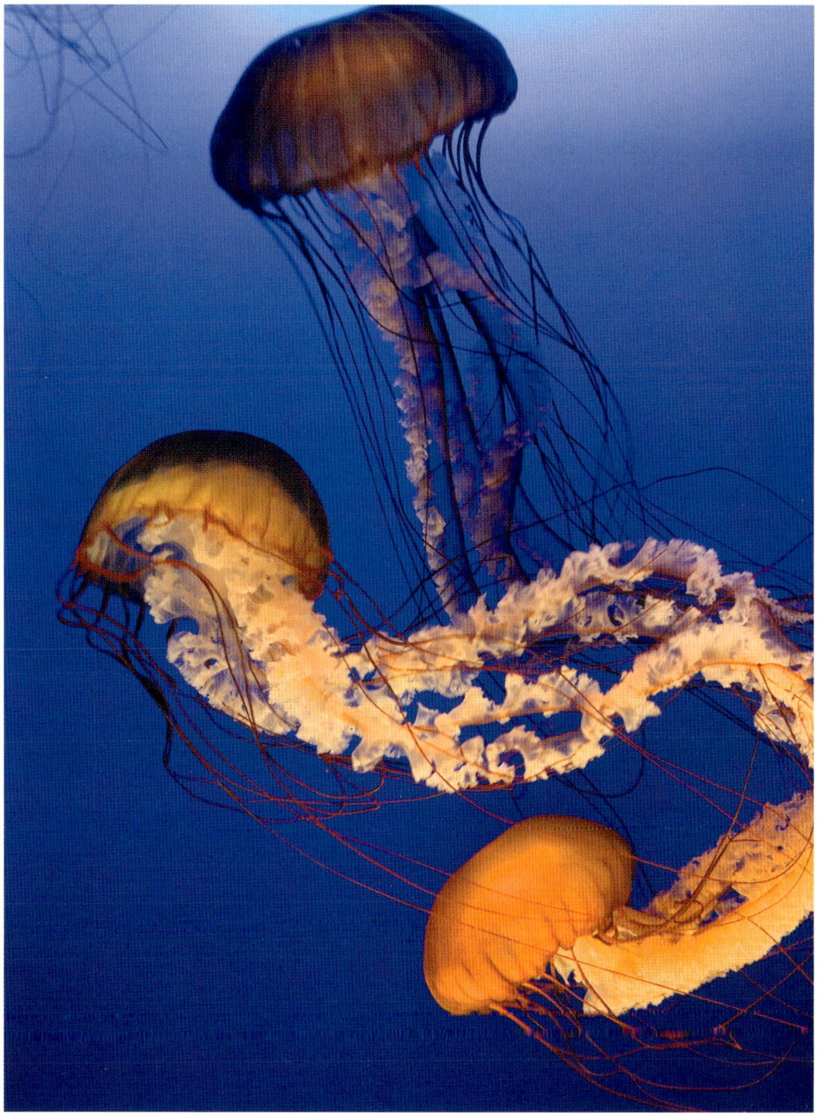

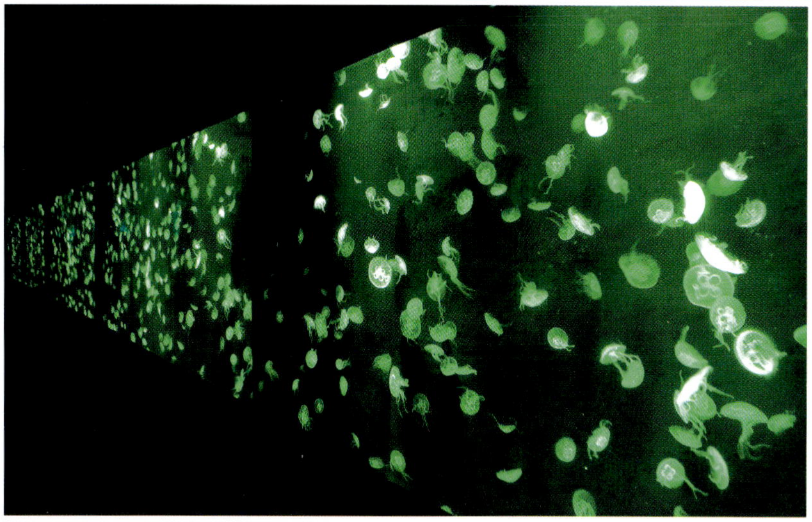

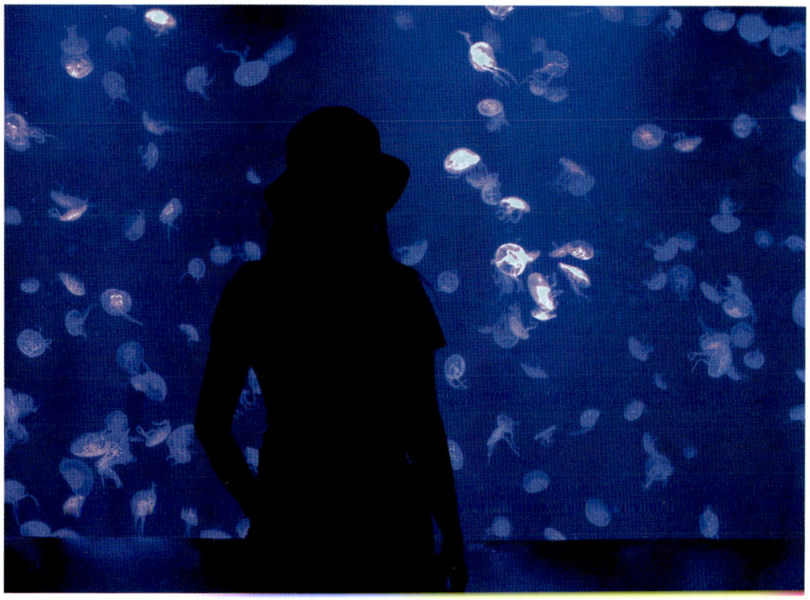

Hua Song Museum

where Singapore

The Singapore Tourism Board has opened to the public the Hua Song Museum in Singapore, the first visitor centre dedicated to the story of Chinese emigrants around the world. It is situated in the new wing of the Haw Par Villa.

Guests may view and enjoy Chinese culture through an atmosphere filled with folklore and legend. The total area allotted for the new exhibit area is 14,048 sq. m.

The work performed by the design team included interior decoration and fit-out, scene sets, props, graphics, specialty lighting, multimedia and interactive systems, copywriting and exhibit fabrication. Specialty lighting was strategically placed over showcases to highlight photographs and artefacts of significance.

The designers were responsible for the fabrication of all exhibits at the museum including the main exhibition gallery, theatre, children's learning gallery, food and beverage facilities, and souvenir shop.

The museum offers visitors the opportunity to appreciate the spirit of adventure and enterprise of early Chinese migrants in corners of the world. It is a one-stop permanent exhibit illustrating Singapore's history, culture and value. Estimated visitor count is about one million a year.

点心小품
翁譜秘笈
富貴養生
喜慶菜品

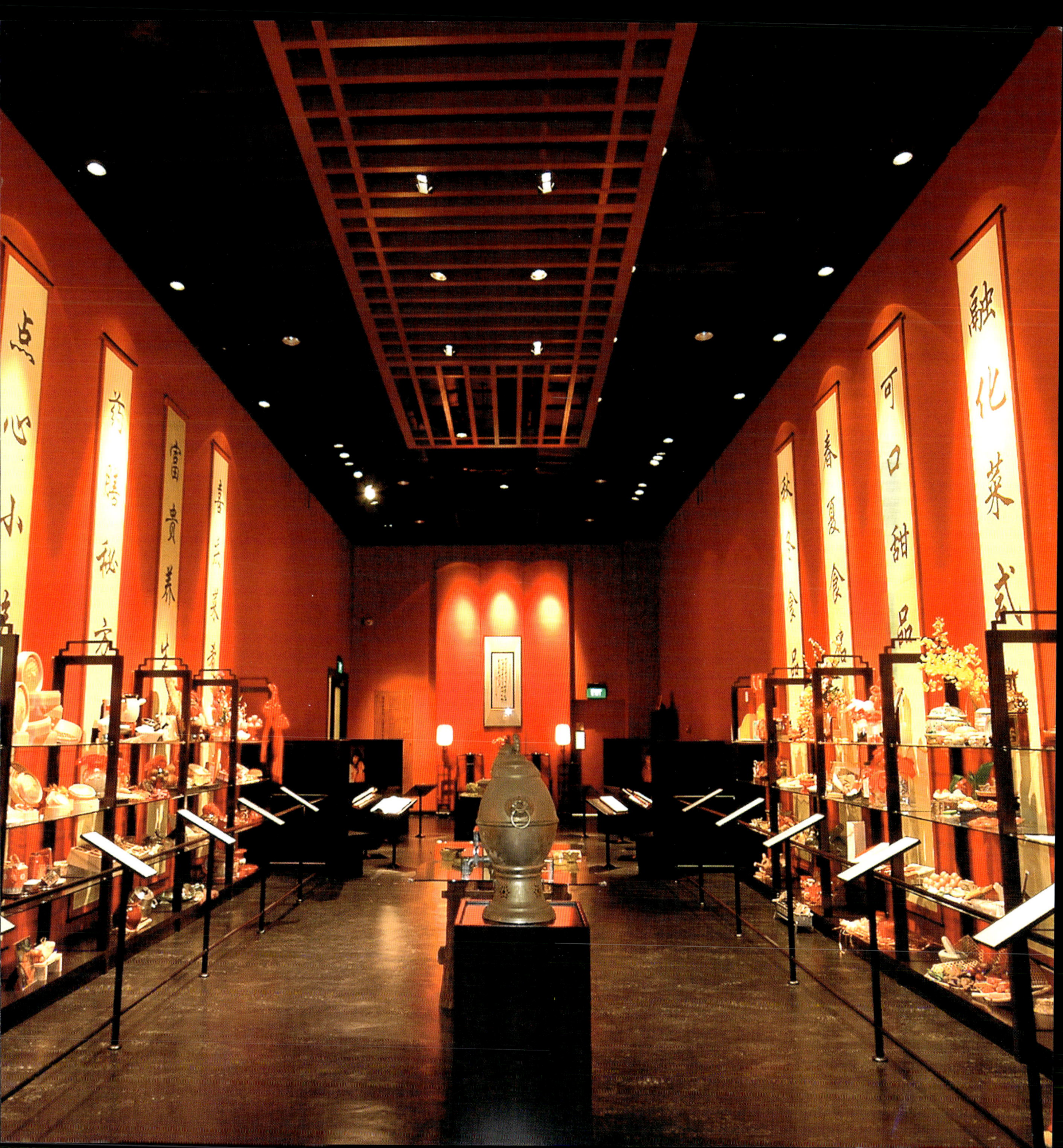

融化菜式
可口甜品
春夏食品
秋冬食品

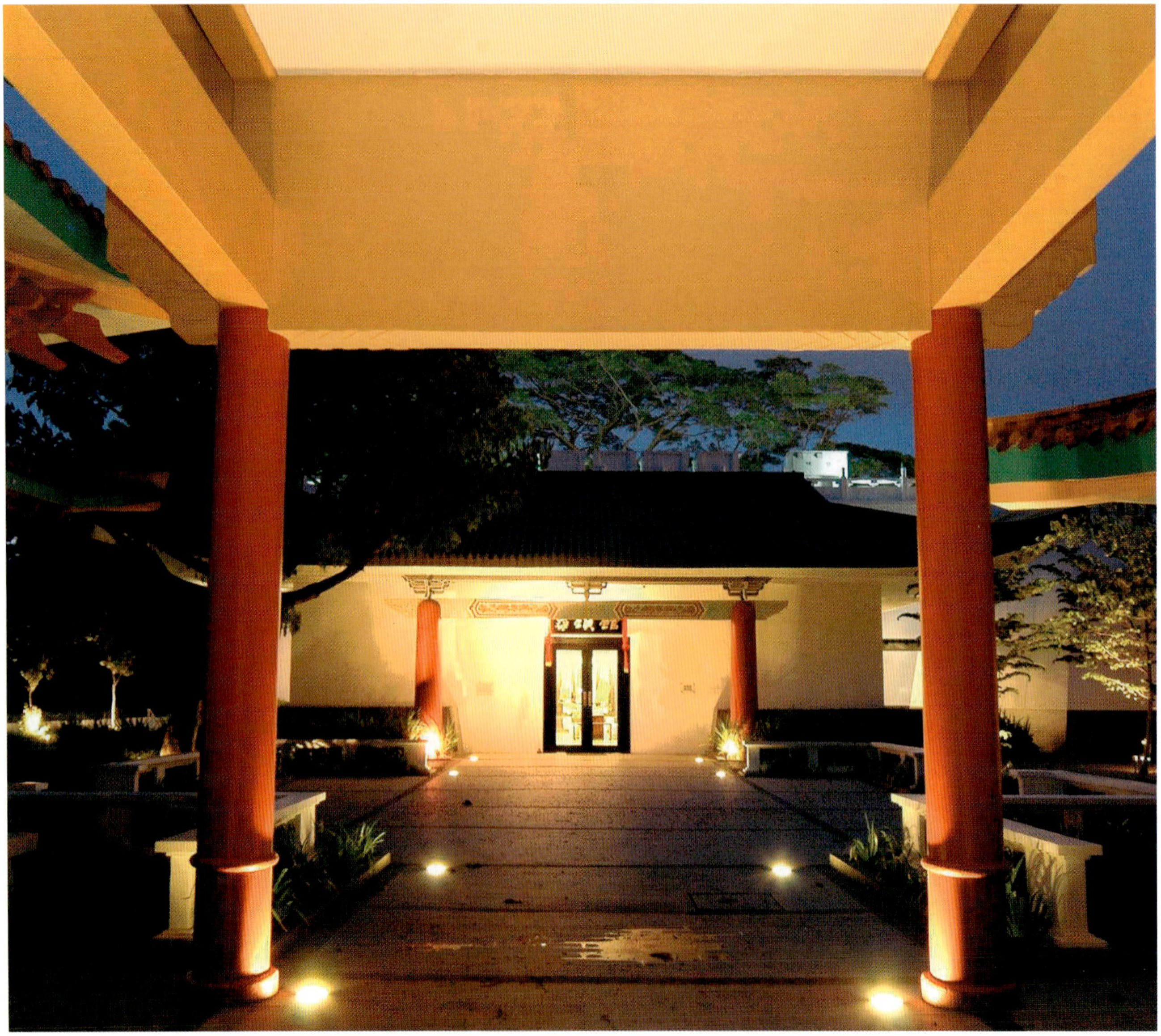

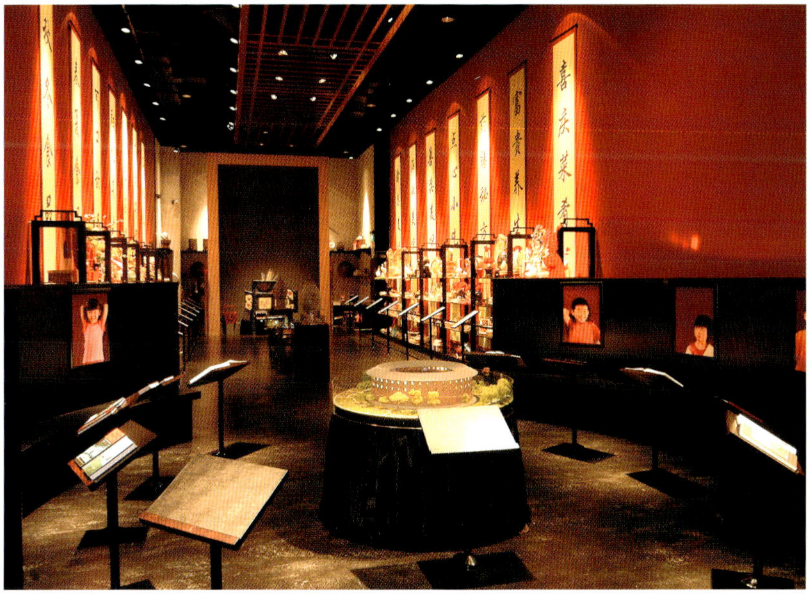

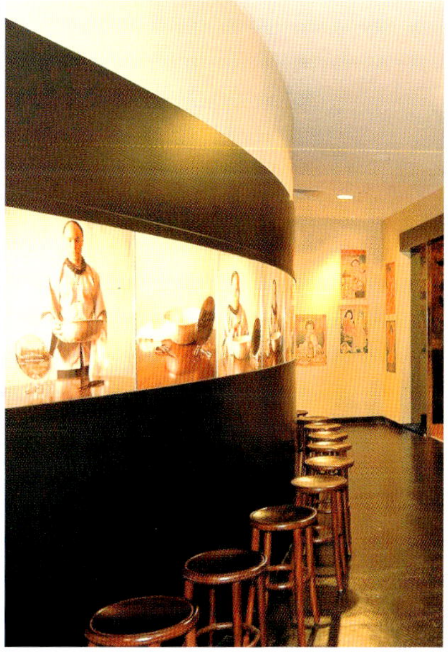

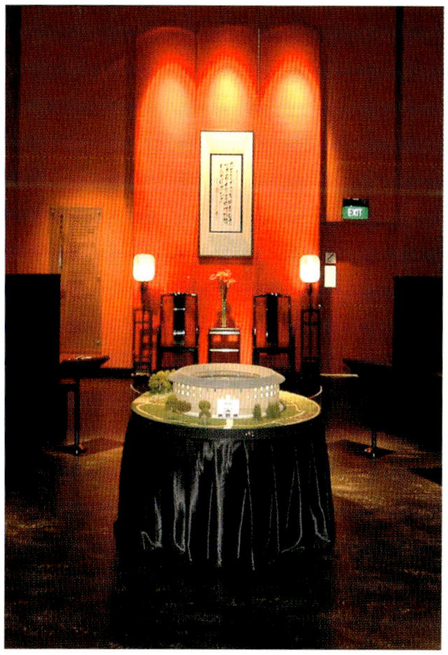

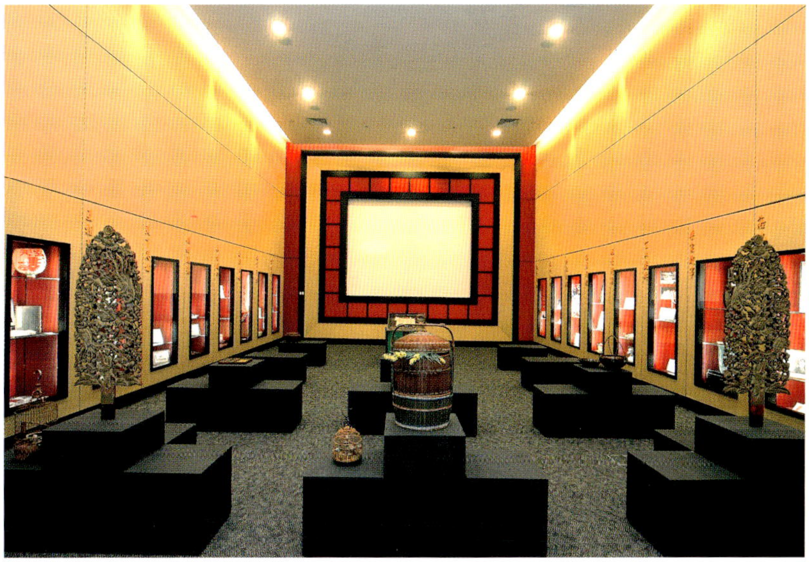

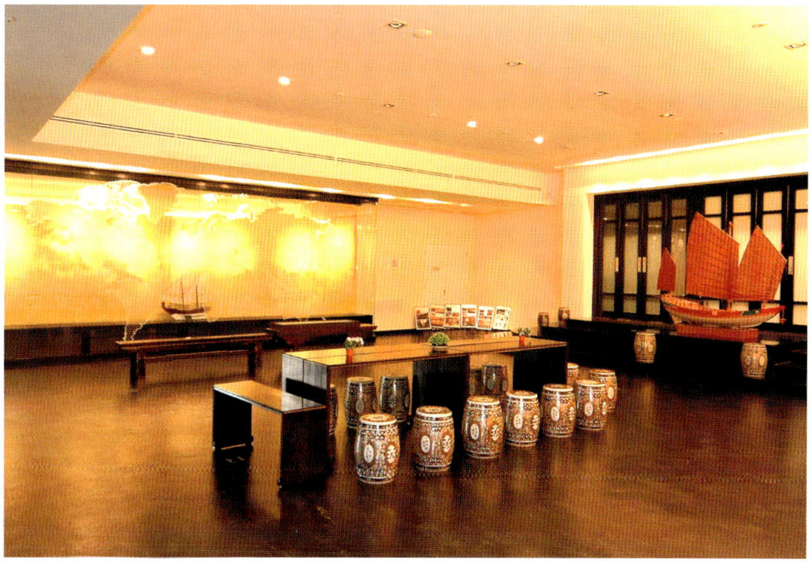

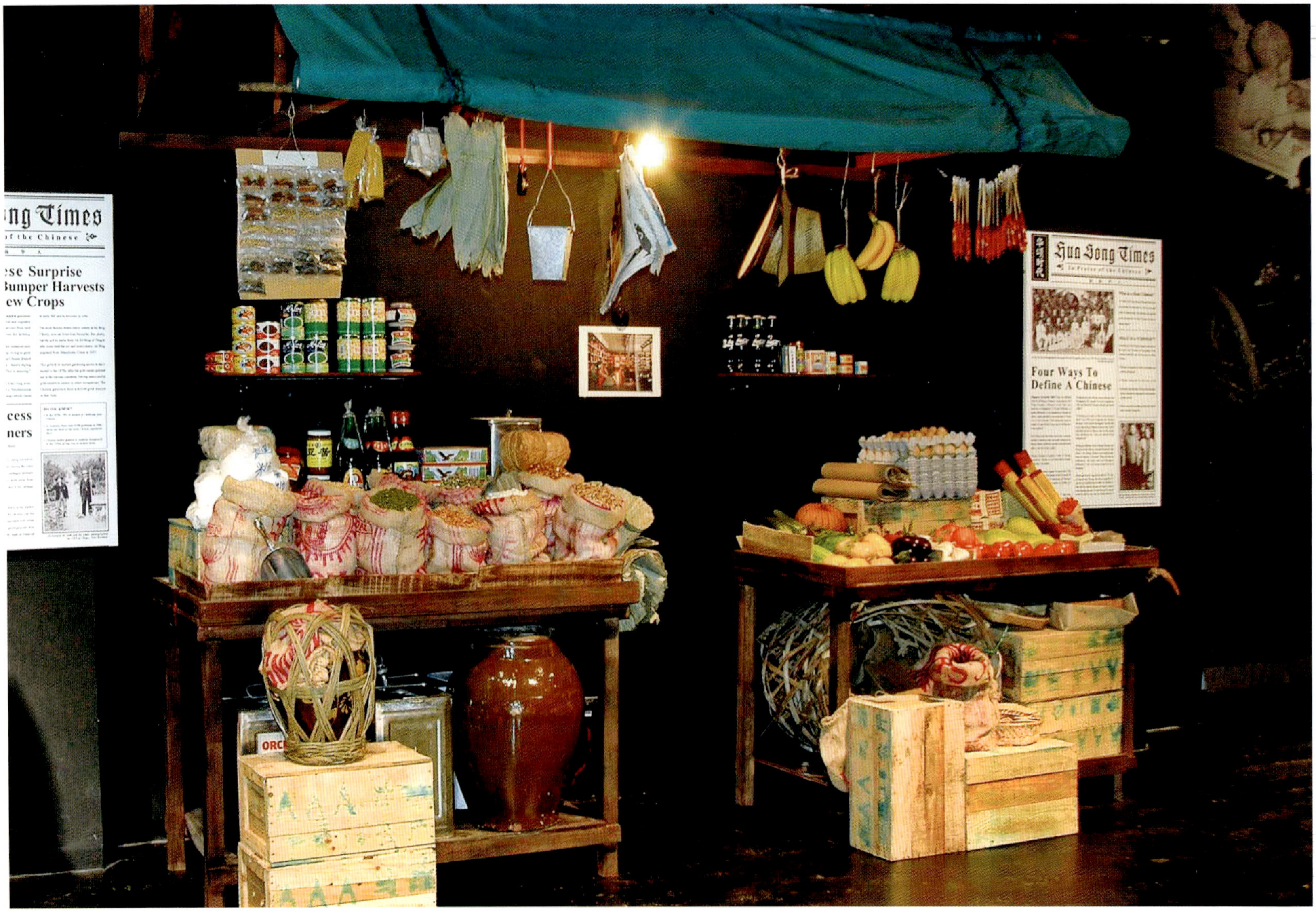
Hua Song Times
Four Ways To
Define A Chinese
Bumper Harvests

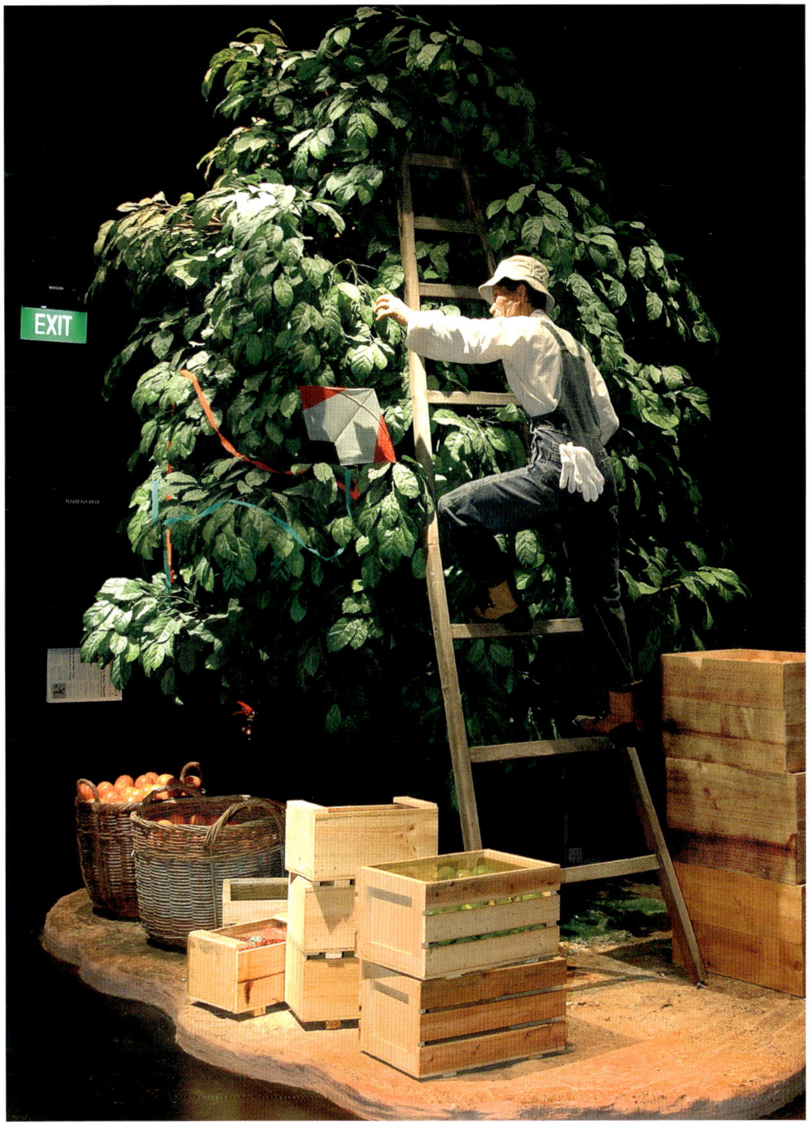
EXIT

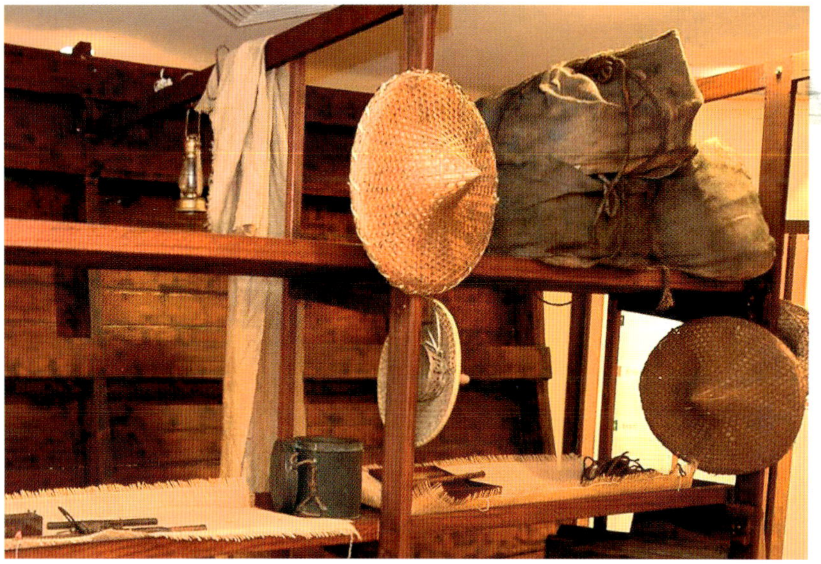

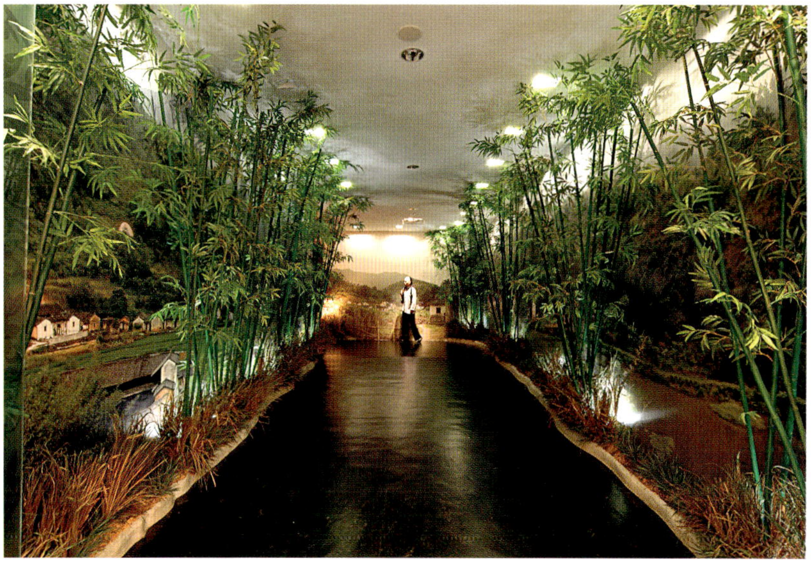

Ngong Ping Theme Village

where Hong Kong SAR, China

Covering an area of 15,000 sq. m., the Ngong Ping Theme Village, located near the famous Tian Tan Buddha Statue at the Po Lin Monastery, Hong Kong, has been architecturally designed to reflect the spiritual integrity of the Ngong Ping area. Pico, together with partners, was appointed by the MTR Corporation Limited to provide show set installations for the two major attractions in the village.

"Walking with Buddha", the multimedia attraction that portrays the life of Siddhartha Gautama and his enlightenment, was decorated with a 1.8 metres solid granite Buddha situated in the Bodhi Tree. To create the environment for the Buddha setting, the designers used furniture, scrim, graphics and decorative elements. Fibre-glass columns were incised with elegant typography, others were engraved with golden materials.

The "Monkey's Tale Theatre" is a comedy show in which the design team provided dimensional projection shapes and painted scrims. They also created a forest and cave environment, providing pipe-grid and theme lighting, creepers and leaves.

This themed-village is one of the latest tourist attractions in Hong Kong.

event. exhibit. interior. themed.

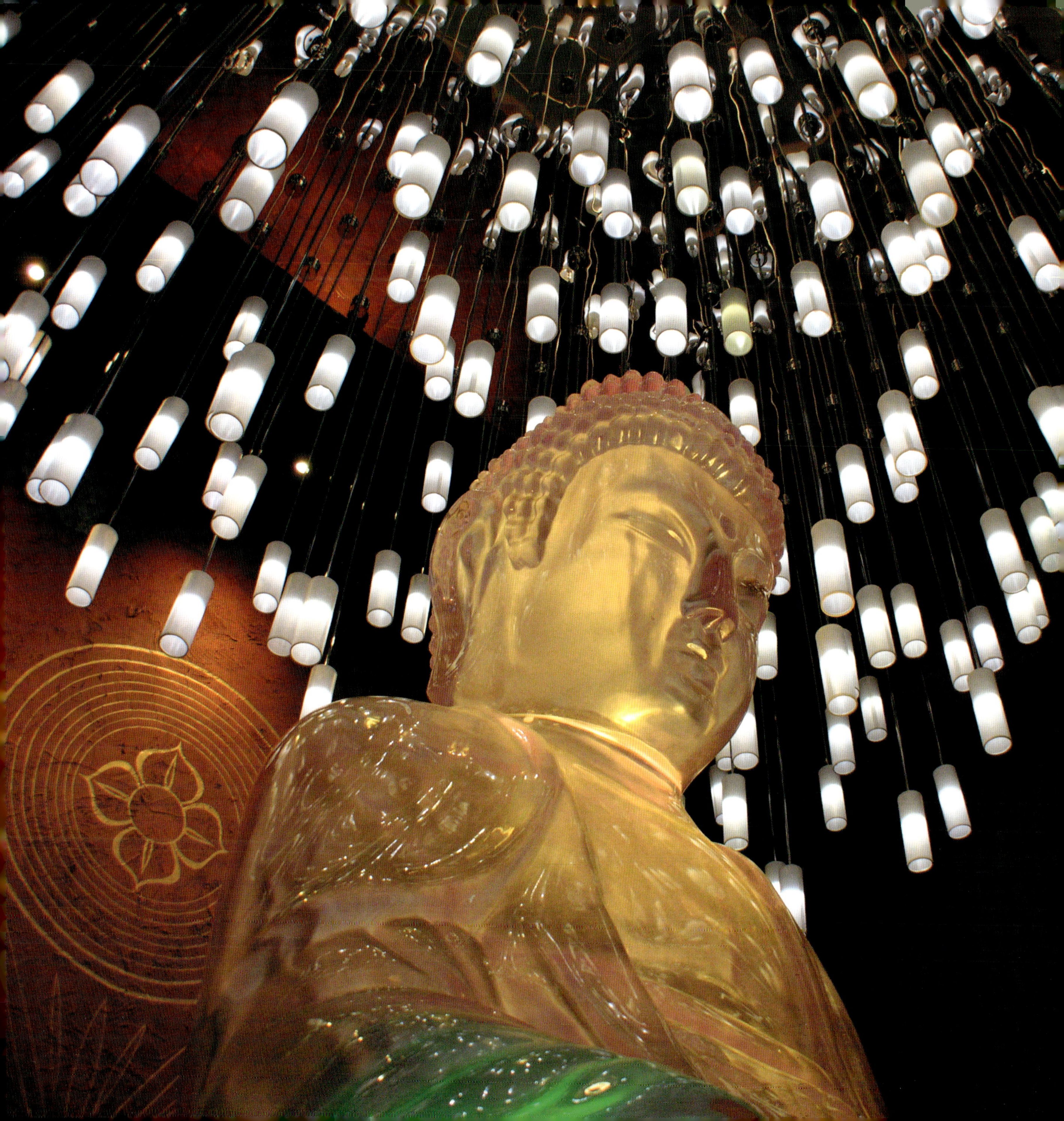

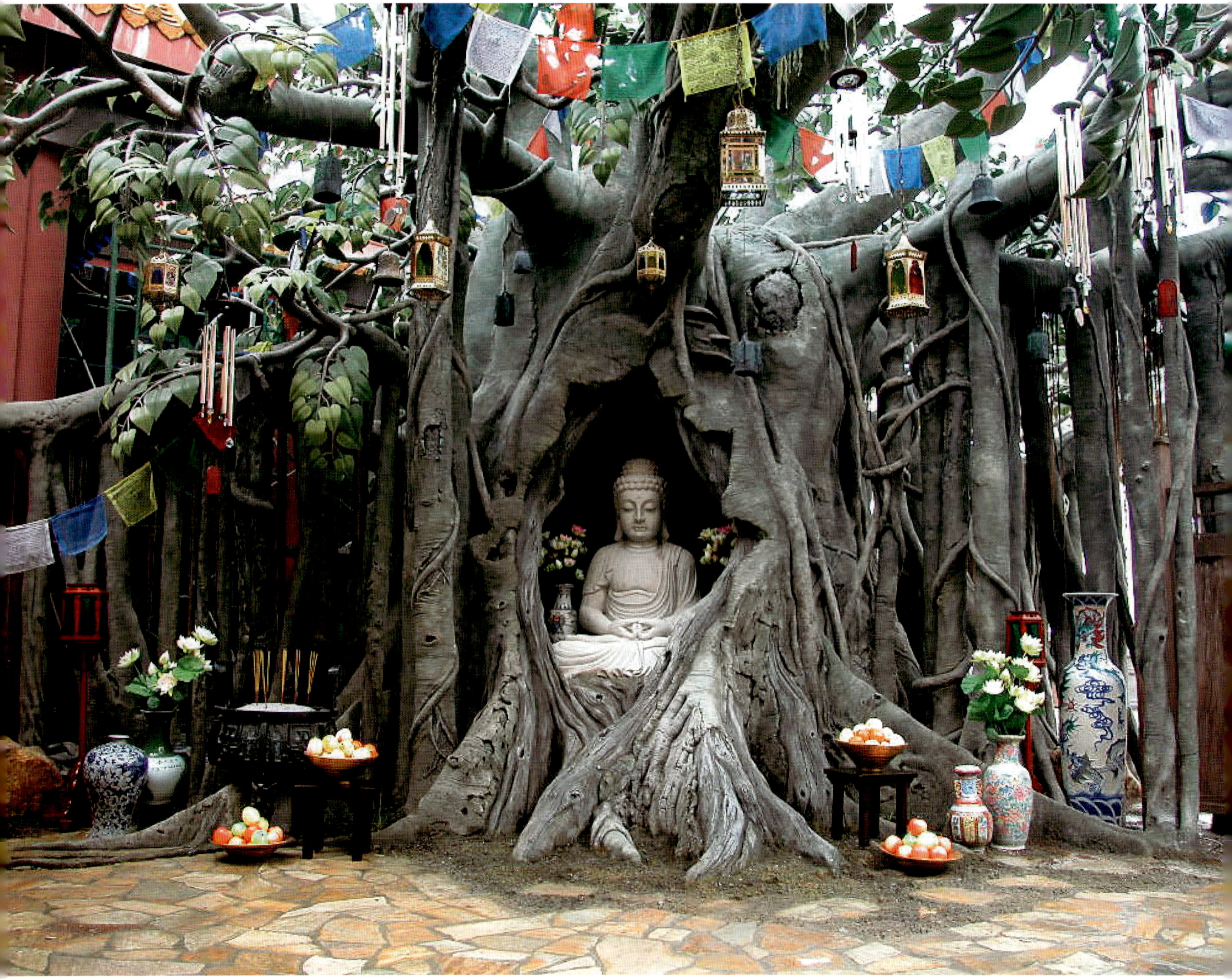

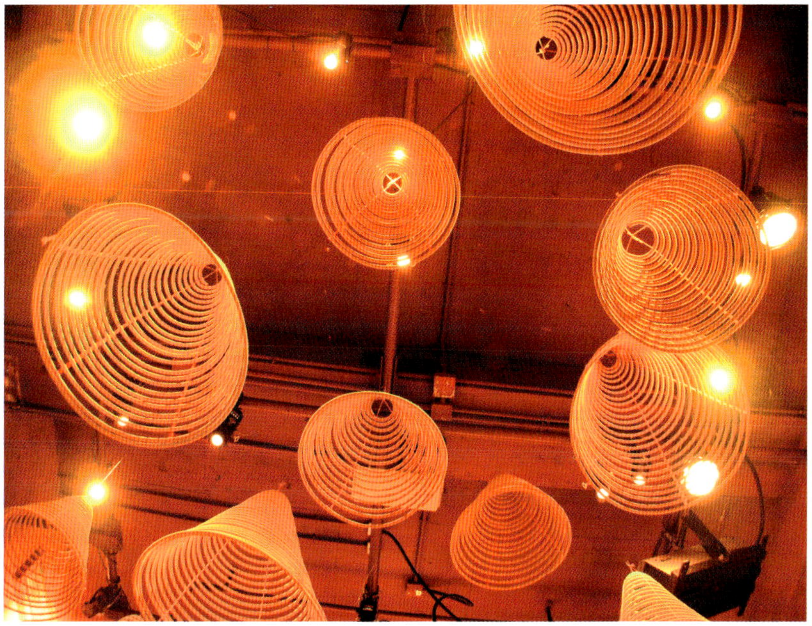

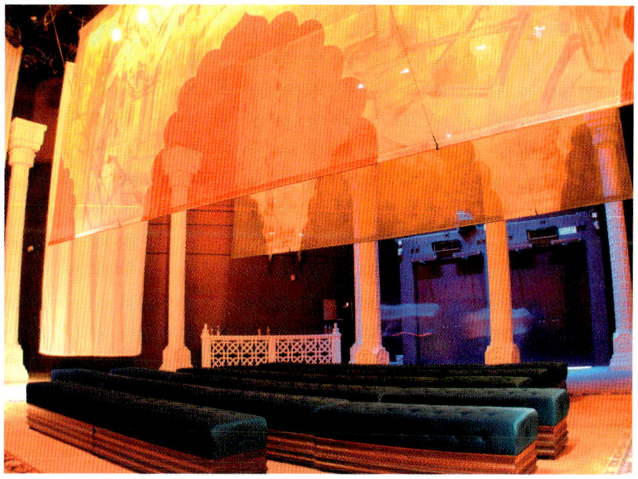

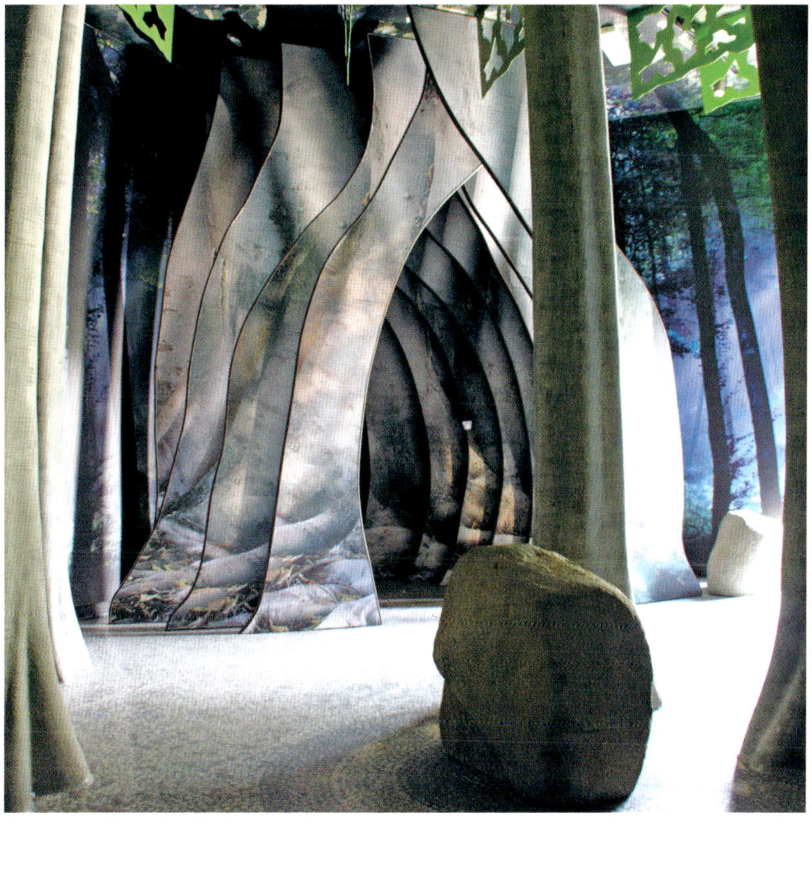

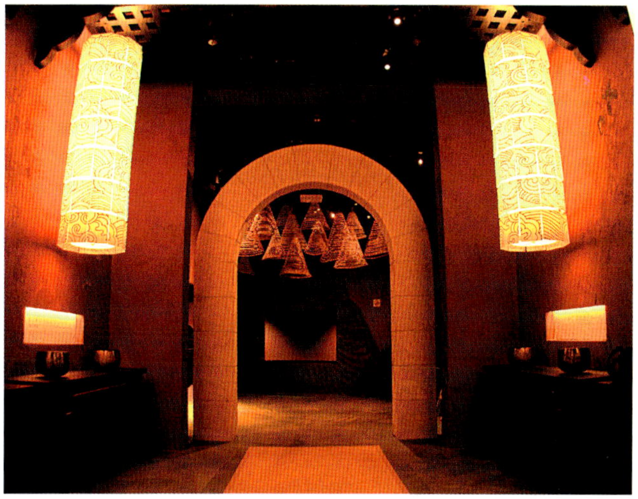

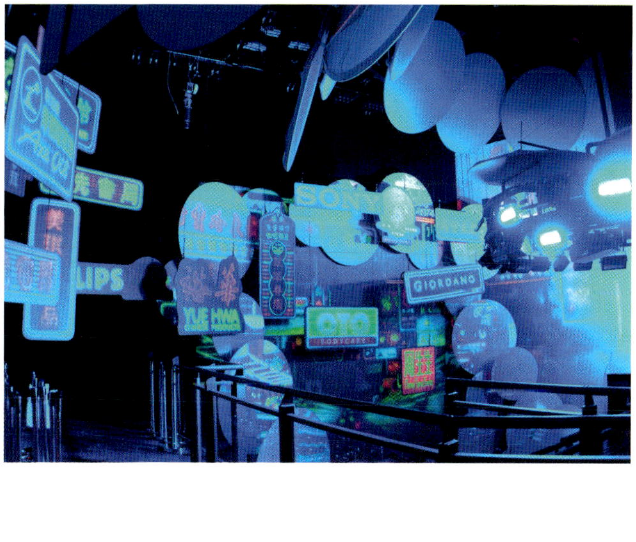
SONY
LIPS
GIORDANO
YUE HWA
OTO
BODYCARE

Cathay Pacific Experience

where Hong Kong SAR, China

Covering an area of 5,000 sq. ft., the Cathay Pacific Experience is situated at the Cathay City near the Hong Kong International Airport. With an objective to publicise the airline's history and promote its corporate image, the Cathay Pacific Experience was designed and constructed in a space consisting of several distinct galleries.

The main gallery focuses on the early stages of the airline company; the second concentrates on the development of Cathay Pacific; and the third gallery explains how the company has evolved into the airline it is today.

With the cooperation of Cathay Pacific staff members, the designers started with research and interviews for an in-depth understanding of the spirit of this airline.

Guests board a virtual flight and journey through Cathay Pacific Airways' history. The designers created a sensor activated media, graphics and artefact displays. Materials such as frosted plexiglass and stainless steel, and theatrical lighting were combined to create an immersive environment. The "magic" 1940s newspapers, an interactive flight network with globe projection, a flight loading game, multiple audio pieces and panoramic video finale engages visitors on many levels.

The predominant colours are white, light blue wash, with red and grey accents. Visitors feel as if they are taking off from the turbulent 40s, soaring through the 60's, 70's and onwards. One can appreciate how the airline operates behind the scenes through the use of interactive media technology and clever design.

Both Cathay Pacific Airways and China Civil Aviation responded positively to the successful outcome that resulted from the excellent work by the design team.

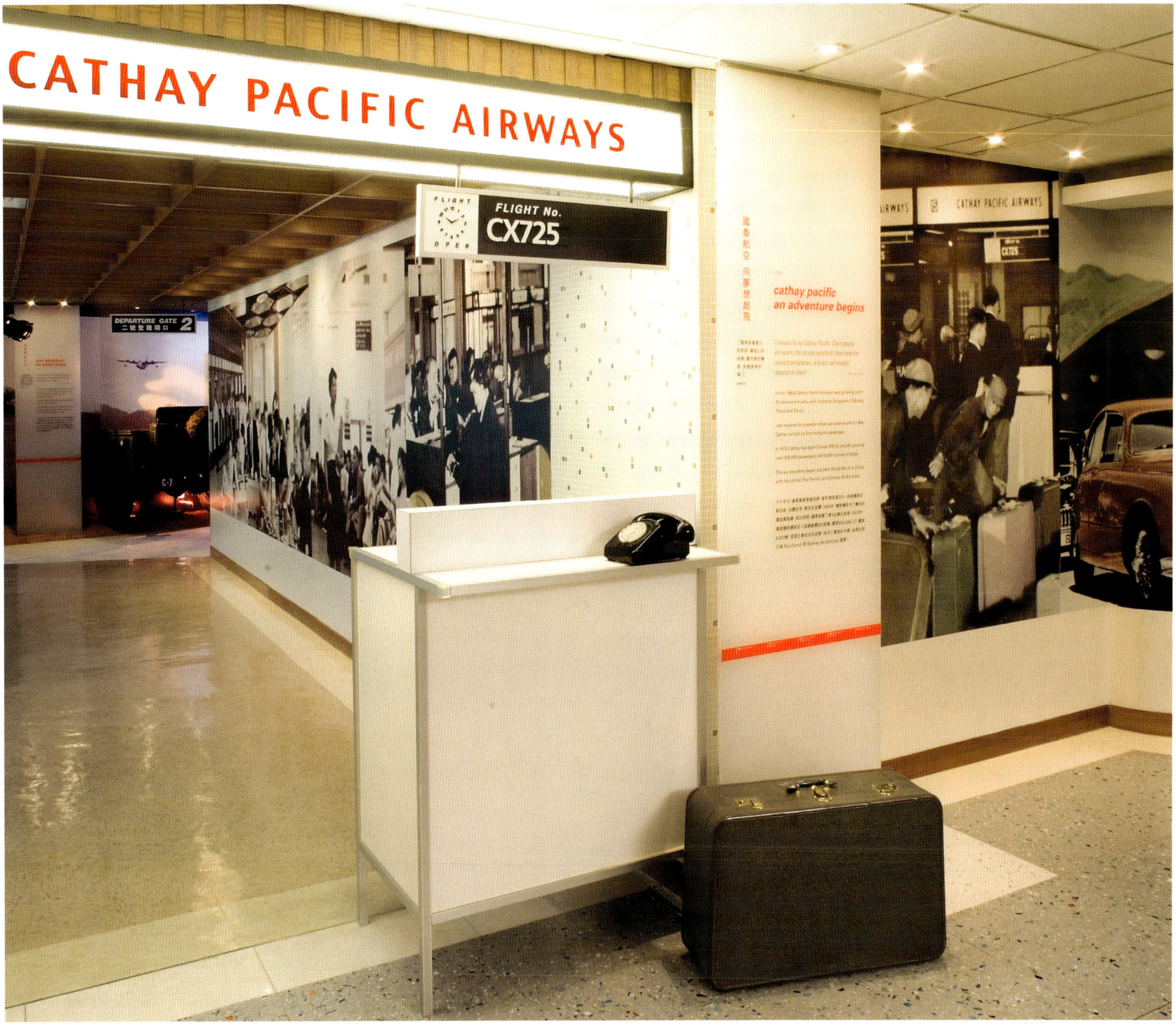

CATHAY PACIFIC AIRWAYS
FLIGHT No.
CX725
DEPARTURE GATE 2
cathay pacific
an adventure begins

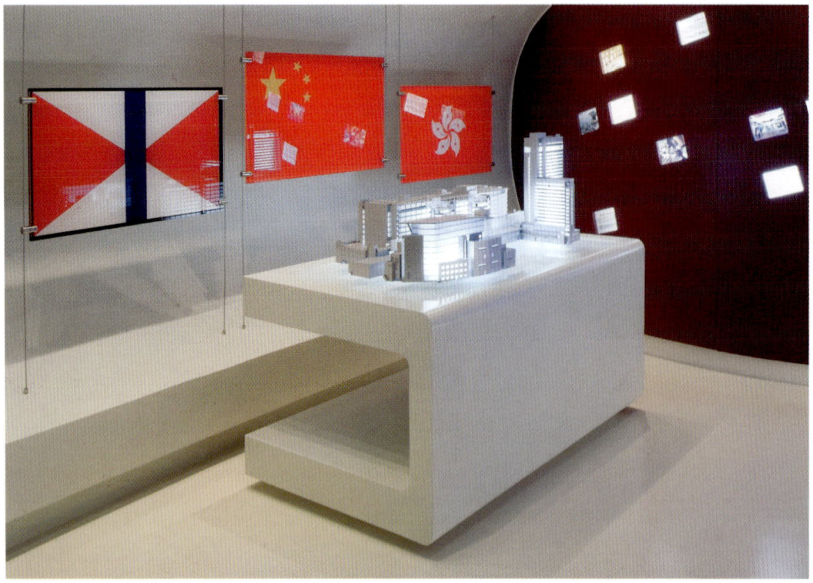

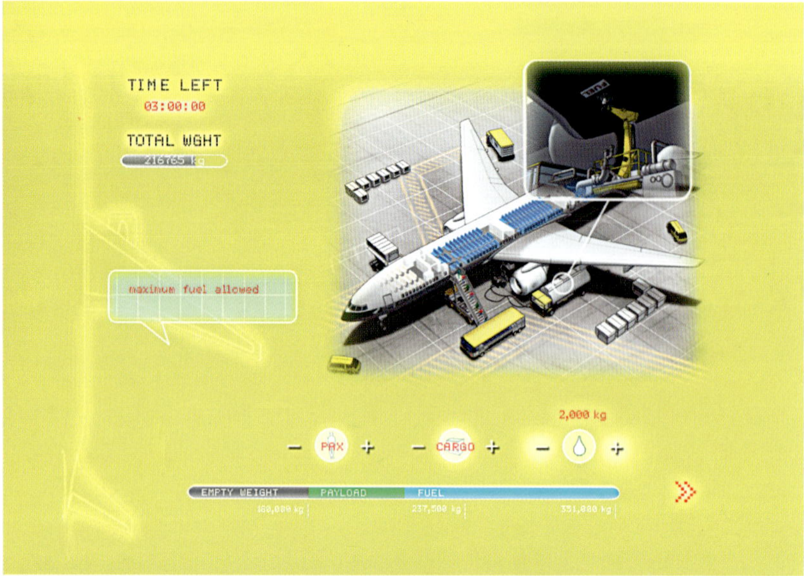
TIME LEFT
03:00:00
TOTAL WGHT
maximum fuel allowed
2,000 kg
PAX
CARGO
EMPTY WEIGHT
PAYLOAD
FUEL

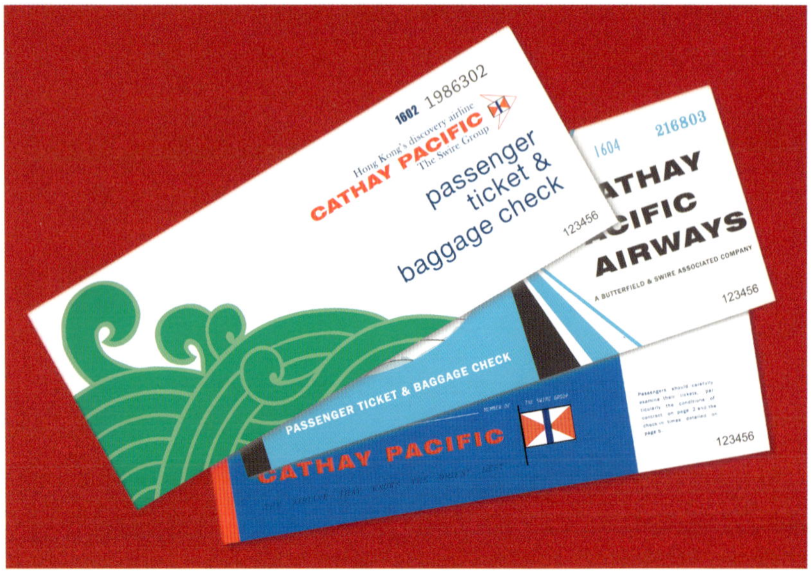
1602 1986302
Hong Kong's discovery airline
CATHAY PACIFIC
The Swire Group
passenger ticket & baggage check
123456
1604 216803
ATHAY
ACIFIC
AIRWAYS
A BUTTERFIELD & SWIRE ASSOCIATED COMPANY
123456
PASSENGER TICKET & BAGGAGE CHECK
CATHAY PACIFIC
123456

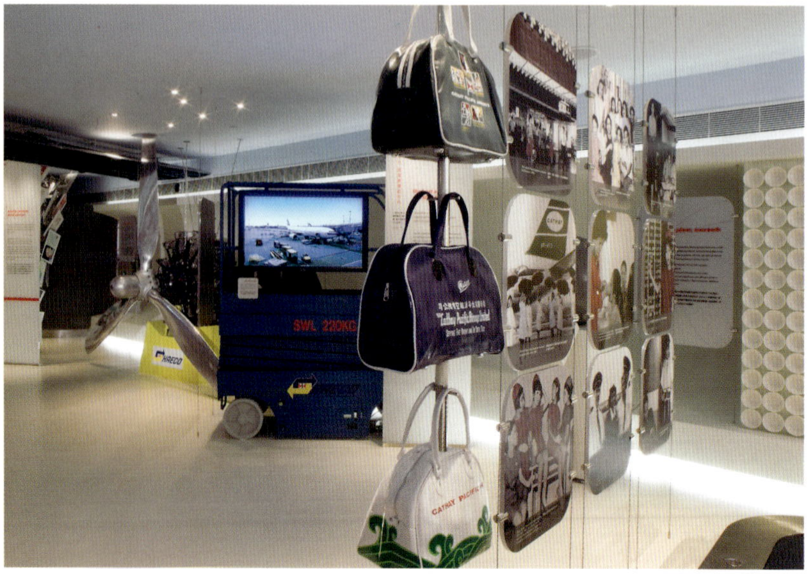

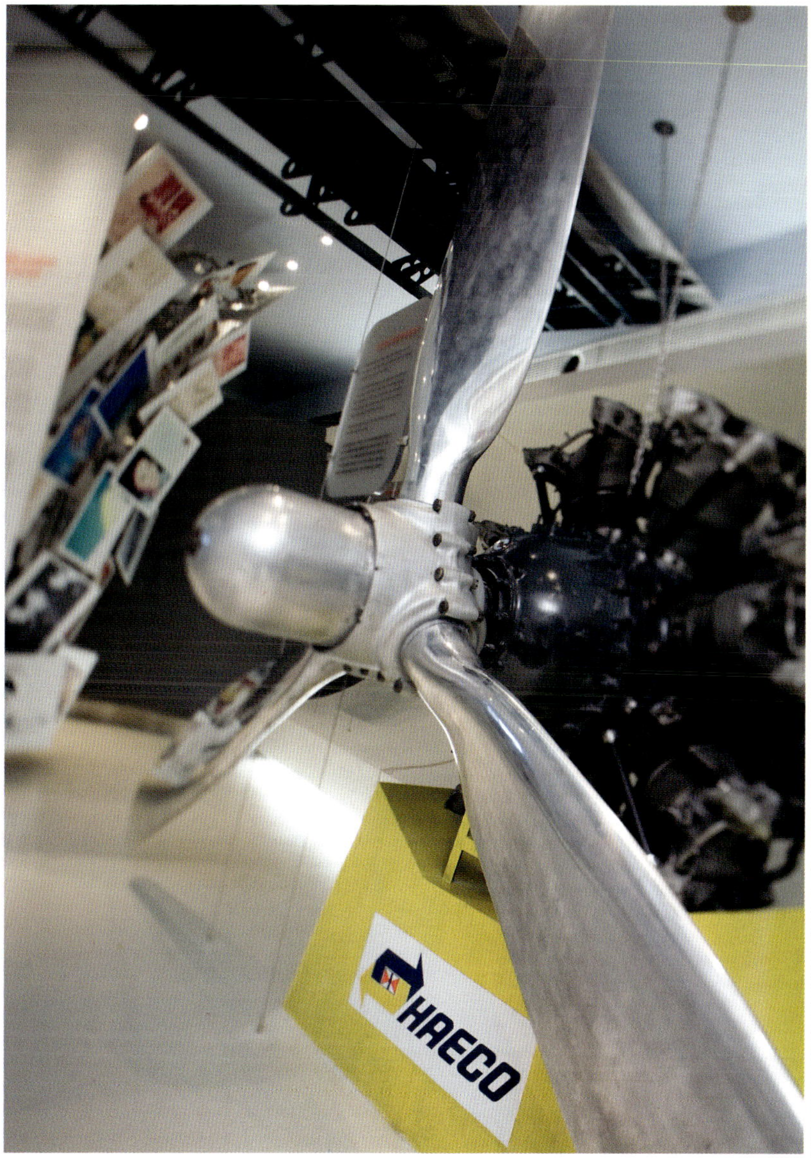
HAECO
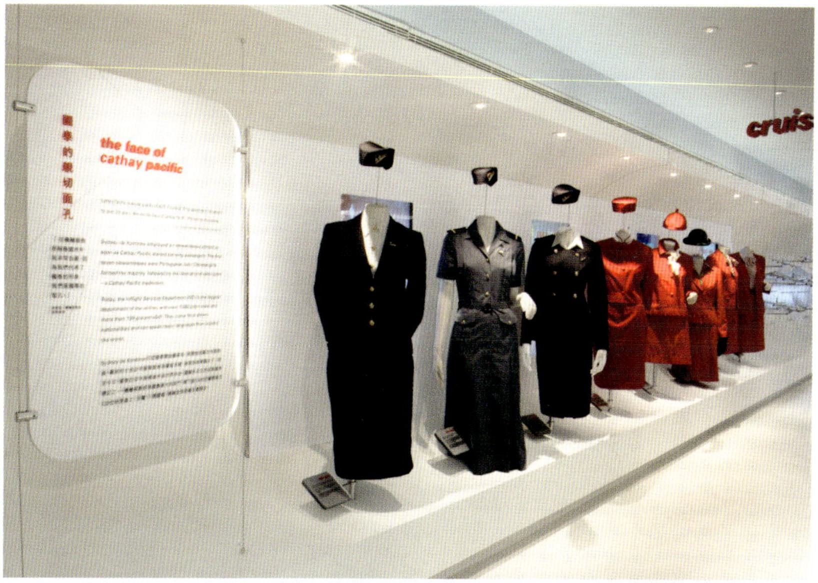
the face of
cathay pacific
cruis
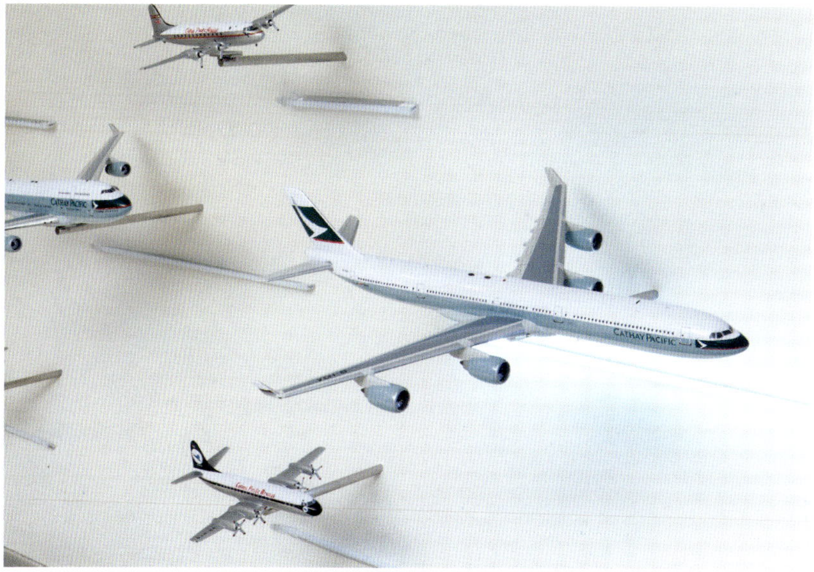
CATHAY PACIFIC

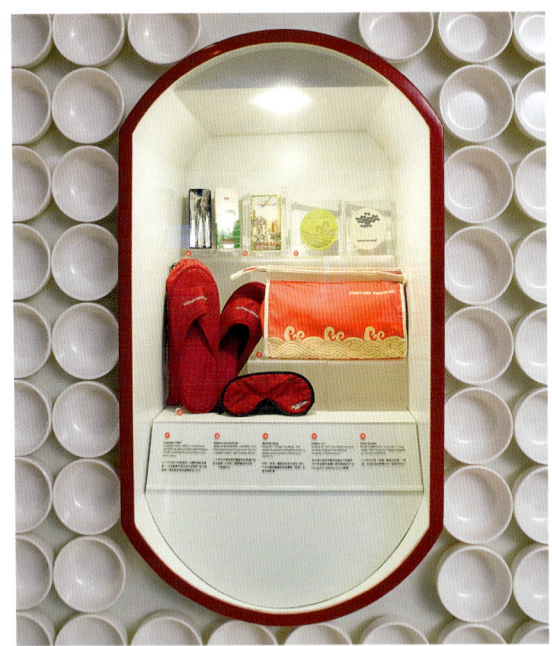

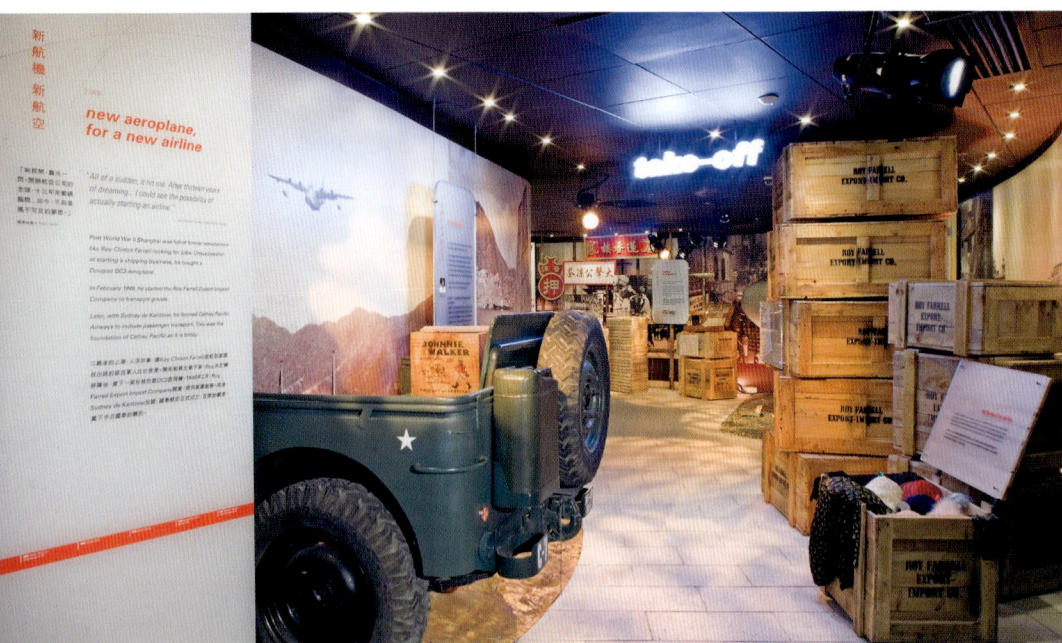

new aeroplane, for a new airline

"All of a sudden, it hit me. After thirteen years of dreaming... I could see the possibility of actually starting an airline."

Post World War II Shanghai was full of former servicemen like Roy Clinton Farrell looking for jobs. Unsuccessful at starting a shipping business, he bought a Douglas DC3 aeroplane.

In February 1946, he started the Roy Farrell Export-Import Company to transport goods.

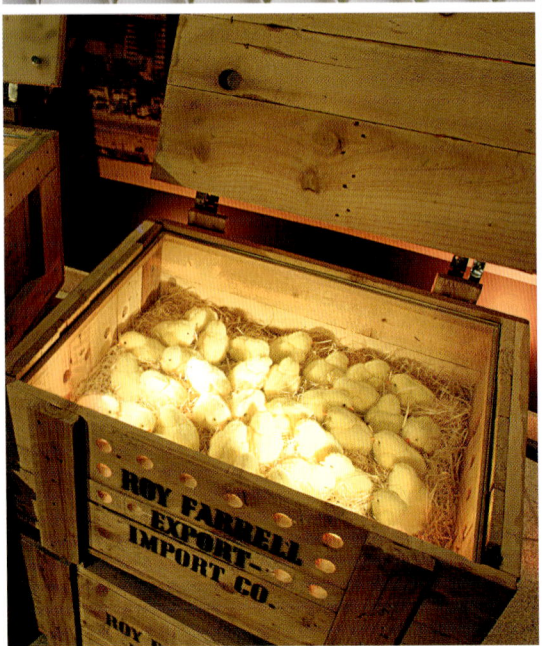

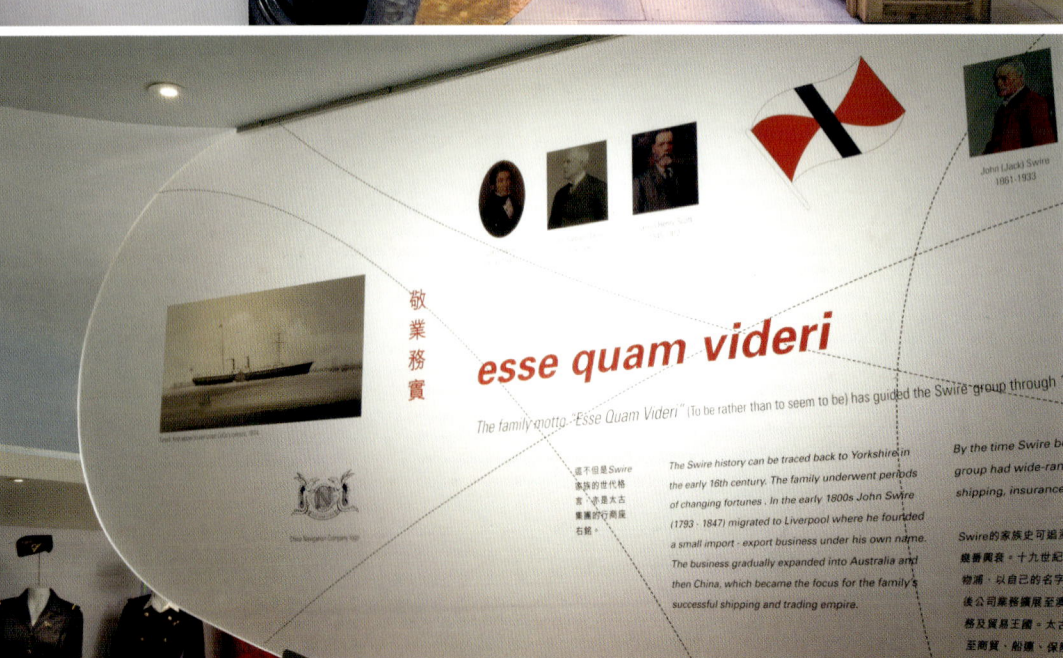

Later, with Sydney de Kantzow, he formed Cathay Pacific Airways to include passenger transport. This was the foundation of Cathay Pacific as it is today.

esse quam videri

The family motto "Esse Quam Videri" (To be rather than to seem to be) has guided the Swire group through

The Swire history can be traced back to Yorkshire in the early 18th century. The family underwent periods of changing fortunes. In the early 1800s John Swire (1793 - 1847) migrated to Liverpool where he founded a small import - export business under his own name. The business gradually expanded into Australia and then China, which became the focus for the family's successful shipping and trading empire.

By the time Swire bo group had wide-ran shipping, insurance

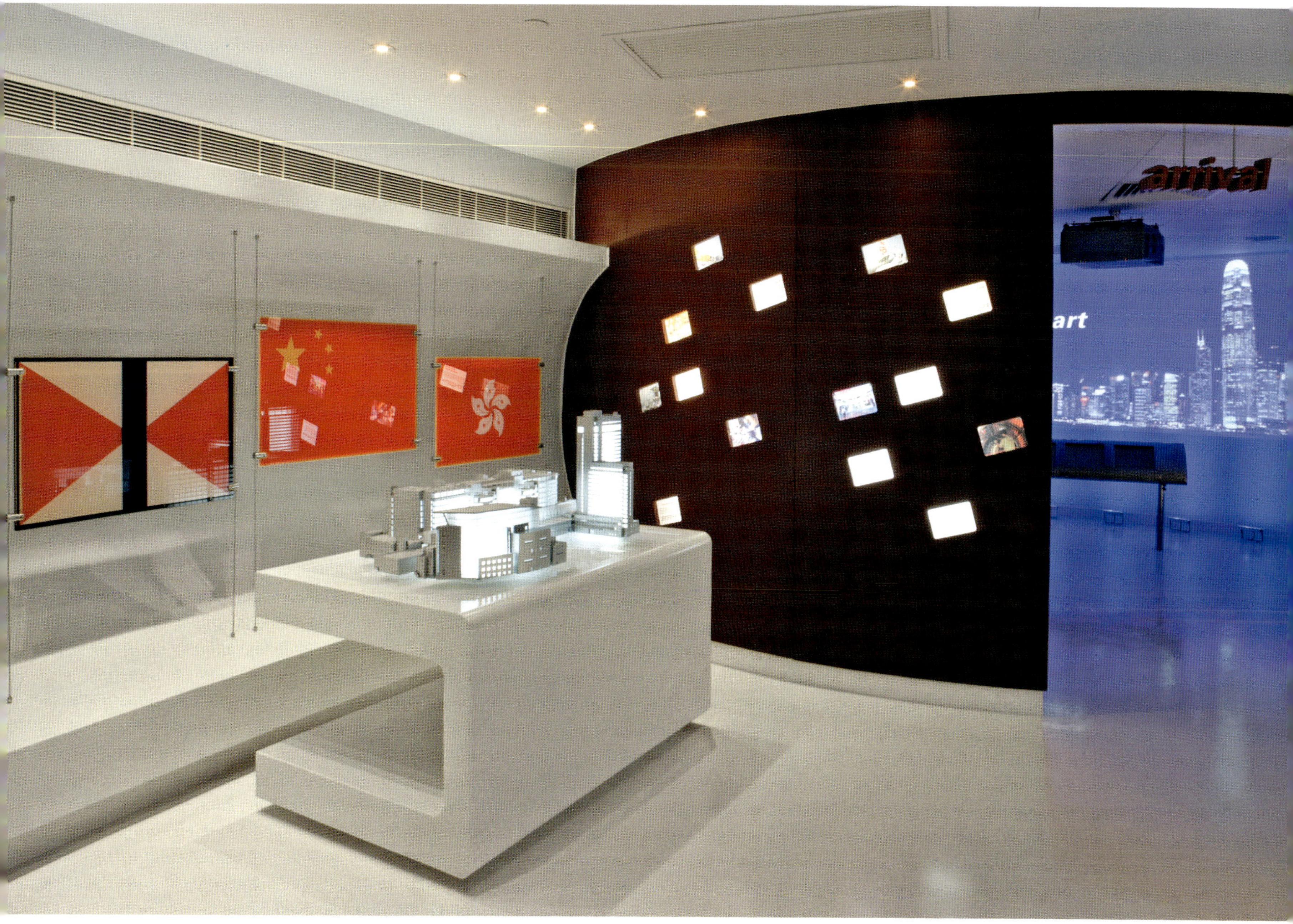
arrival

Kiang Saket Energy Centre

where Rayong, Thailand

Built for the CTCI Thailand Company Ltd., the Kiang Saket Energy Centre of 1,800 sq. m. is the largest visitor centre in the Map Ta Phut Industrial Estate located in Rayong, Thailand. The centre contains several areas of exhibit space including a lobby, the auditorium, a reception area and meeting rooms.

Particular attention was given to the conceptual design, the interior design of the space, the control of the audio visual system, multimedia and interactive software production, and the development of thematic landscapes. The design theme conveys the concept of the harmony between nature and technology.

The space was divided into four areas. The "Main Lobby," located at the centre of the building, represents the origin of life. Here, the atmosphere is friendly and welcoming. The Gallery "24" displays human activities for every hour of the day and the Gallery "Why Coal?" presents the generation of electricity in Thailand. Galleries three and four, "Who BLCP Is" and "Green Power Plant," through the effective use of interactive models and graphics, show the importance of coal power plants and explain topics such as energy conservation and environmental control.

The effective use of 3-D interactives audio visual and multimedia systems made this space a unique and exciting exhibit to visit. It helped the designers develop the true message of the centre: every single activity involves electricity.

This project succeeded in creating a peaceful environment to better the relationship between the community and the mega-scale technology of the power plant.

event. exhibit. interior. themed.

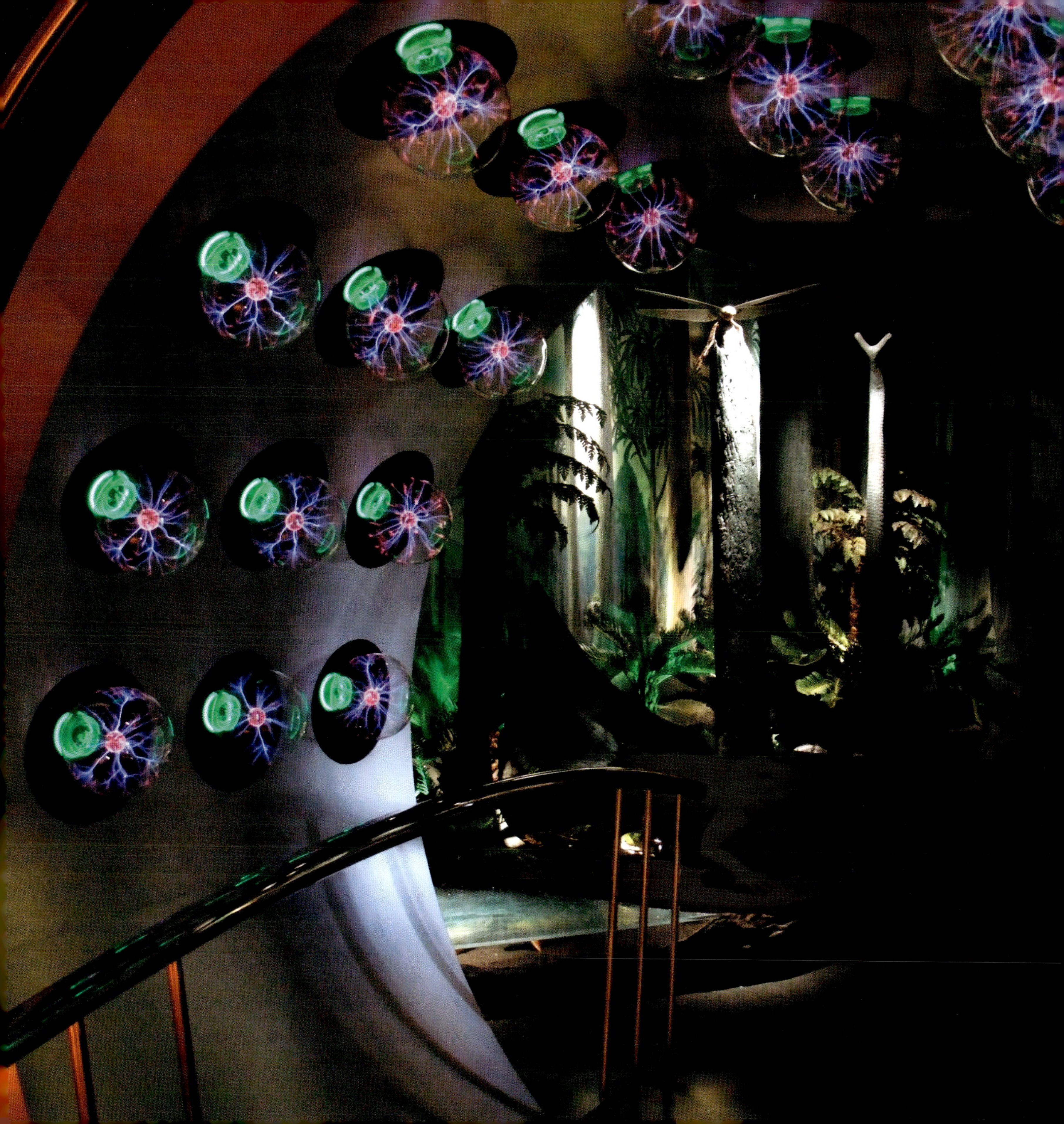

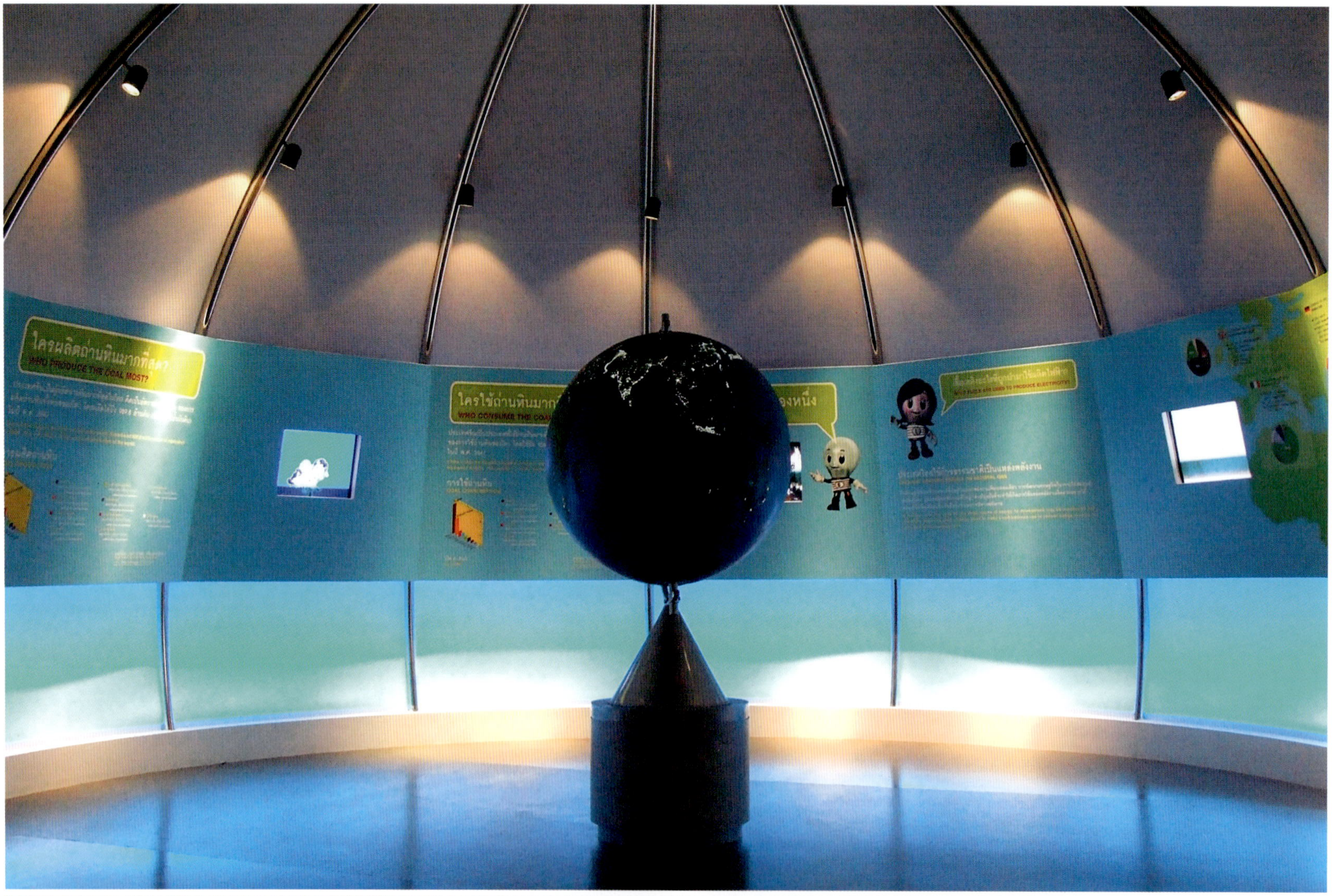
ใครผลิตถ่านหินมากที่สุด?
WHO PRODUCE THE COAL MOST?

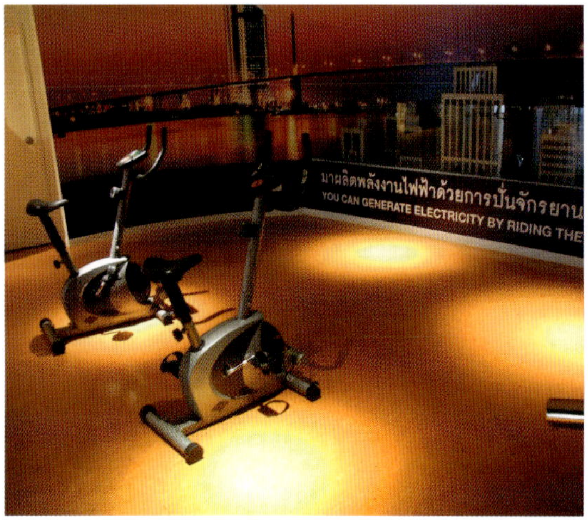
YOU CAN GENERATE ELECTRICITY BY RIDING THE

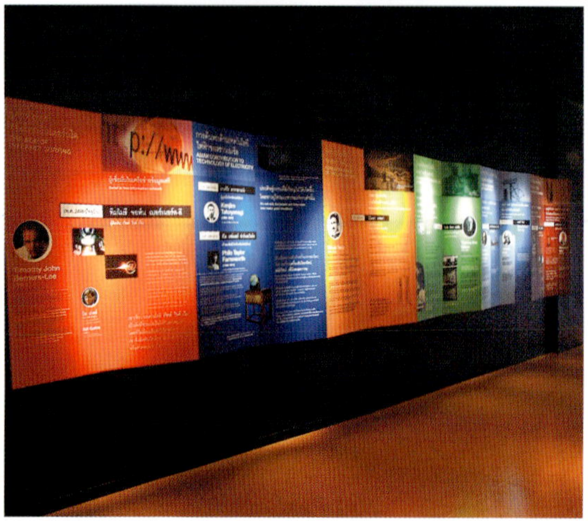

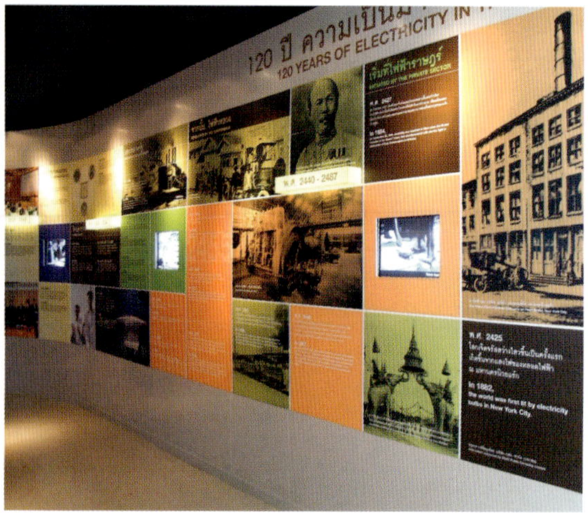
120 YEARS OF ELECTRICITY

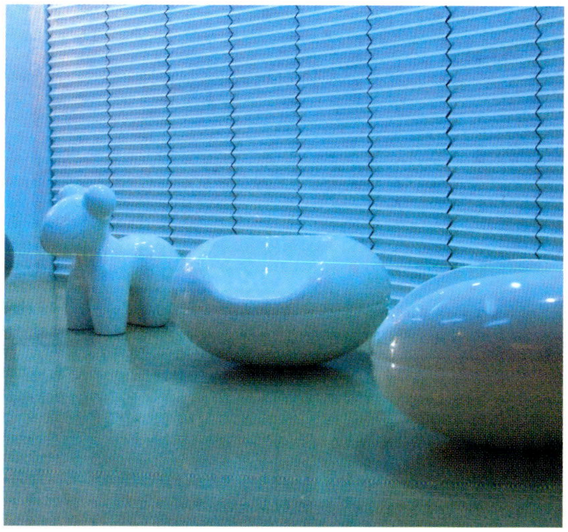
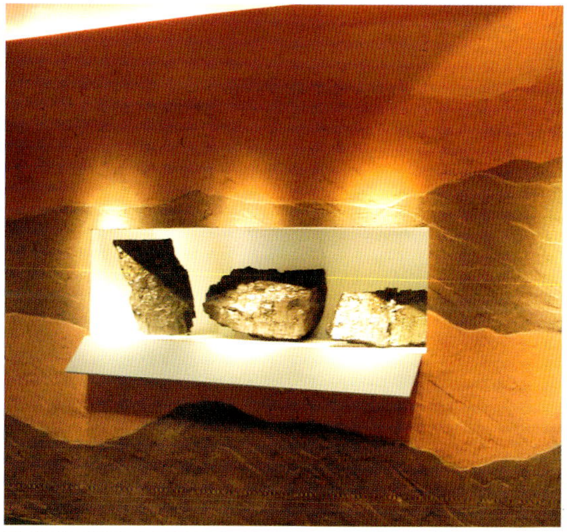
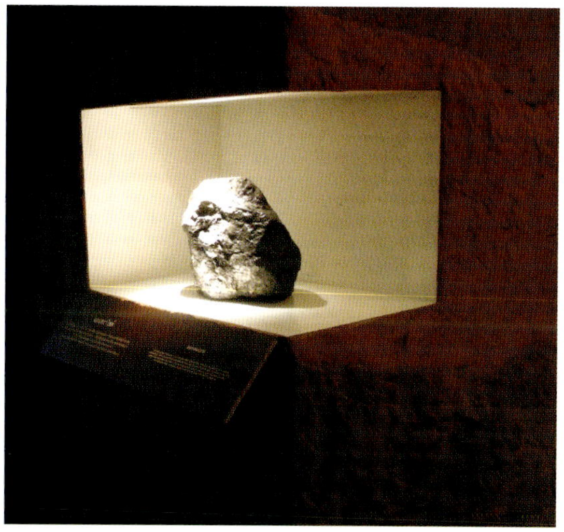
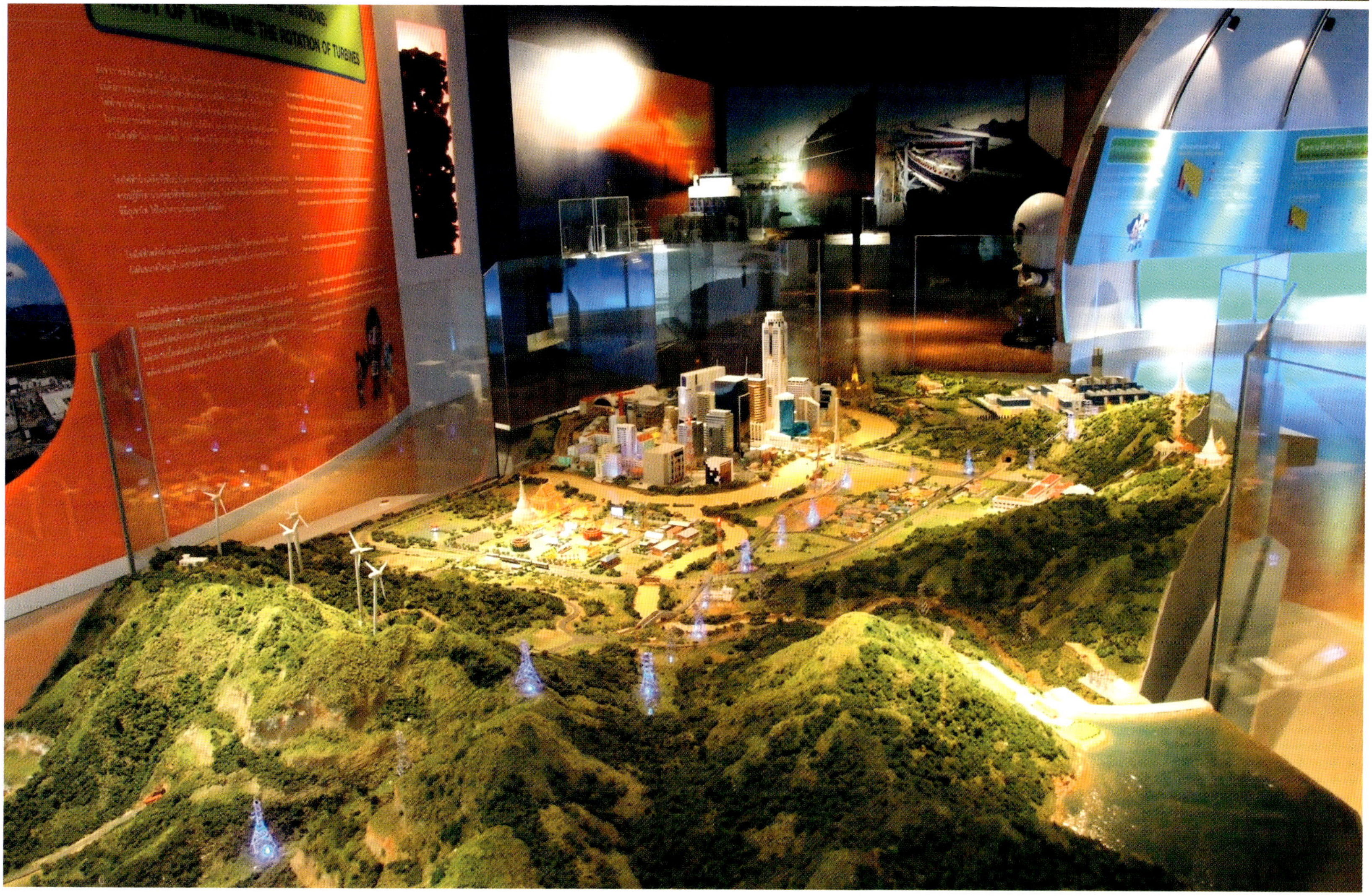

APB TigerLIVE Gallery

where Singapore

The St. James Power Station in Singapore features a permanent exhibit space of 14,000 sq. ft. for Asia Pacific Breweries entitled the TigerLIVE Gallery. The gallery is divided into eight designated zones: Tiger Tales, Tiger Universe, Tiger Allure, Beginnings, Tiger Nation, Grain to Gold, Super Cold Experience and Tiger Den.

The project was created and developed to feature special effects including green laser rays and clouds of fog. Real soap bubbles were used to give visitors the opportunity to view a 3-D, multi-sensory experience of the beer-making process. Via a rotating theatre platform and dual-screen projections, the visitors are led from area to area, along street scenes, to the factory, to the brewing chambers, and finally, to a night club.

What makes this space such an unusual exhibit is that guests, with the use of state-of-the-art technology, have the opportunity to review historical promotional campaigns and observe the evolution of Tiger beer from its beginnings to its production today. The Gallery is an exciting and strong assault on the senses, an experience that captures the imagination of visitors as they journey through the space.

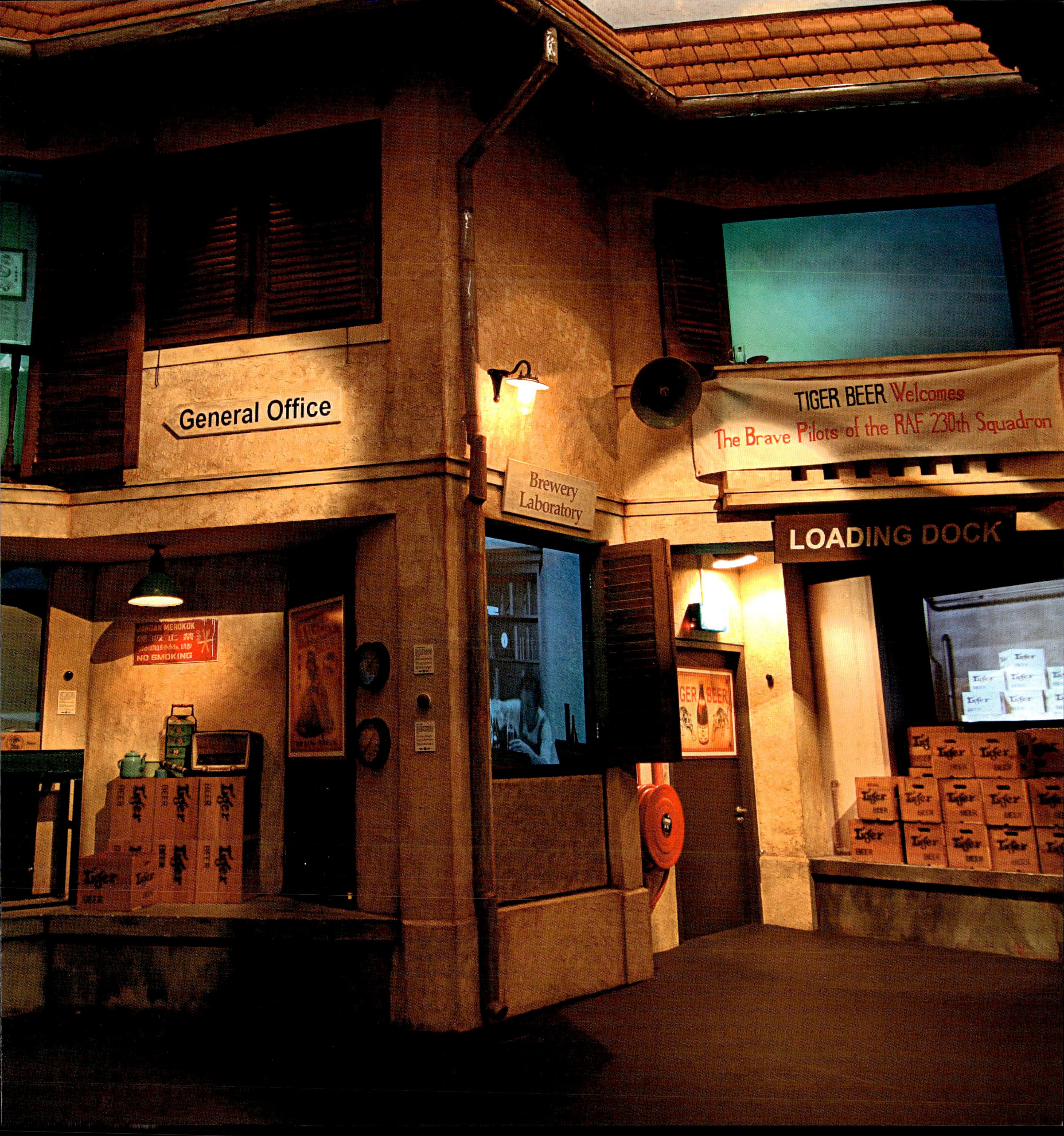
General Office
Brewery Laboratory
TIGER BEER Welcomes
The Brave Pilots of the RAF 230th Squadron
LOADING DOCK
NO SMOKING

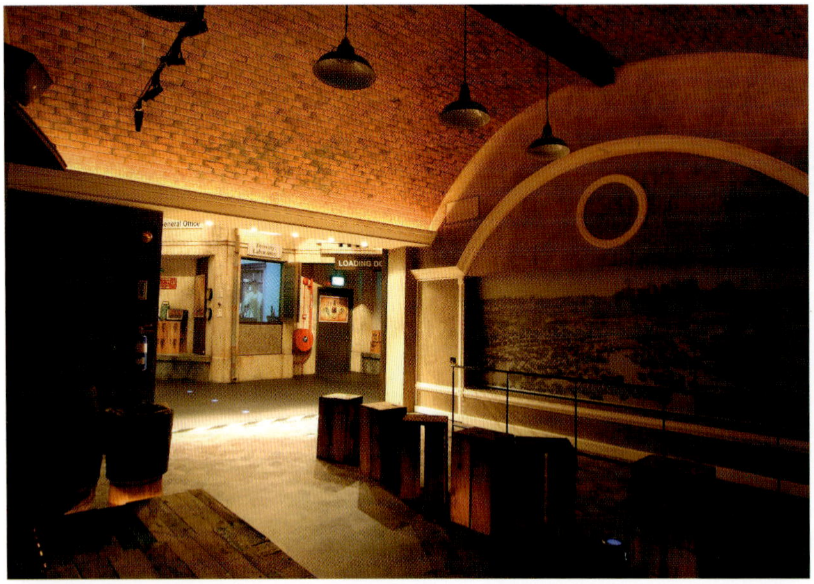
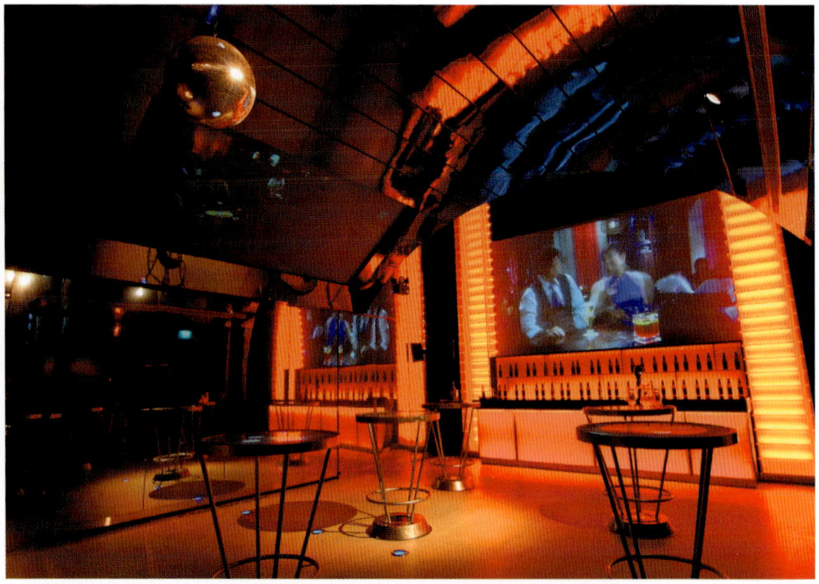
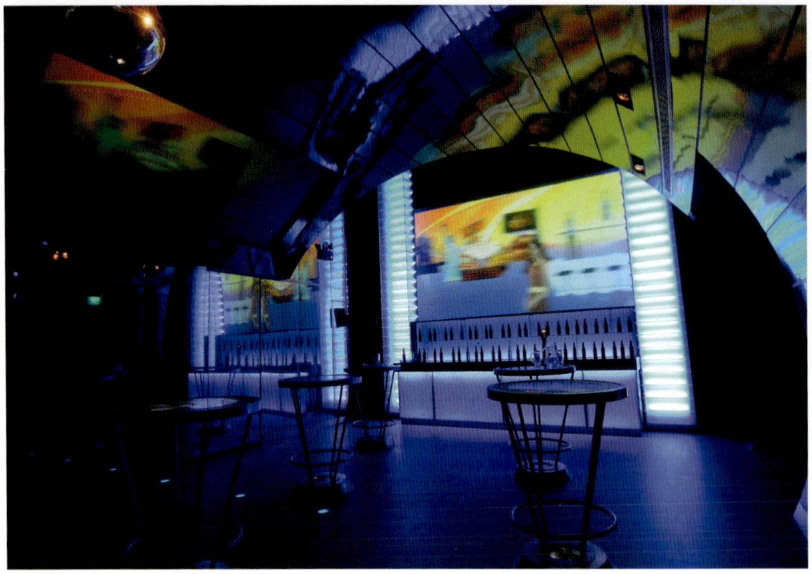
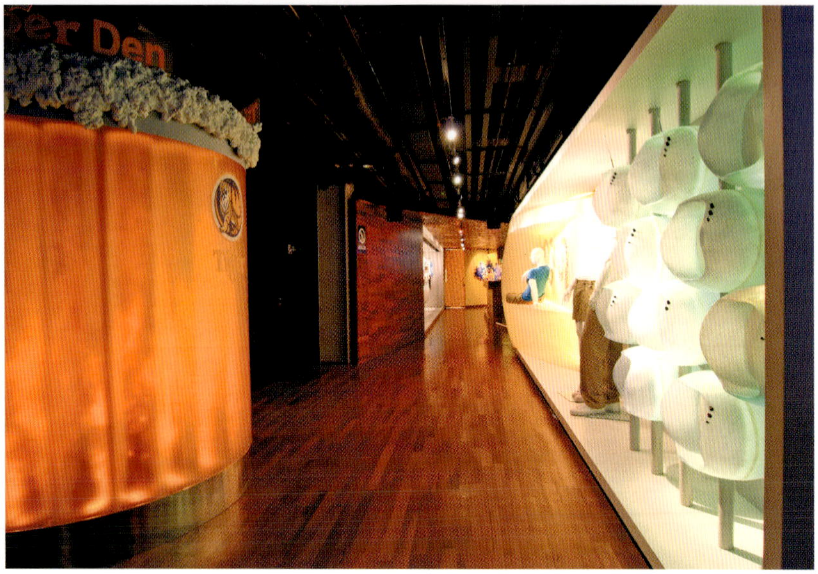

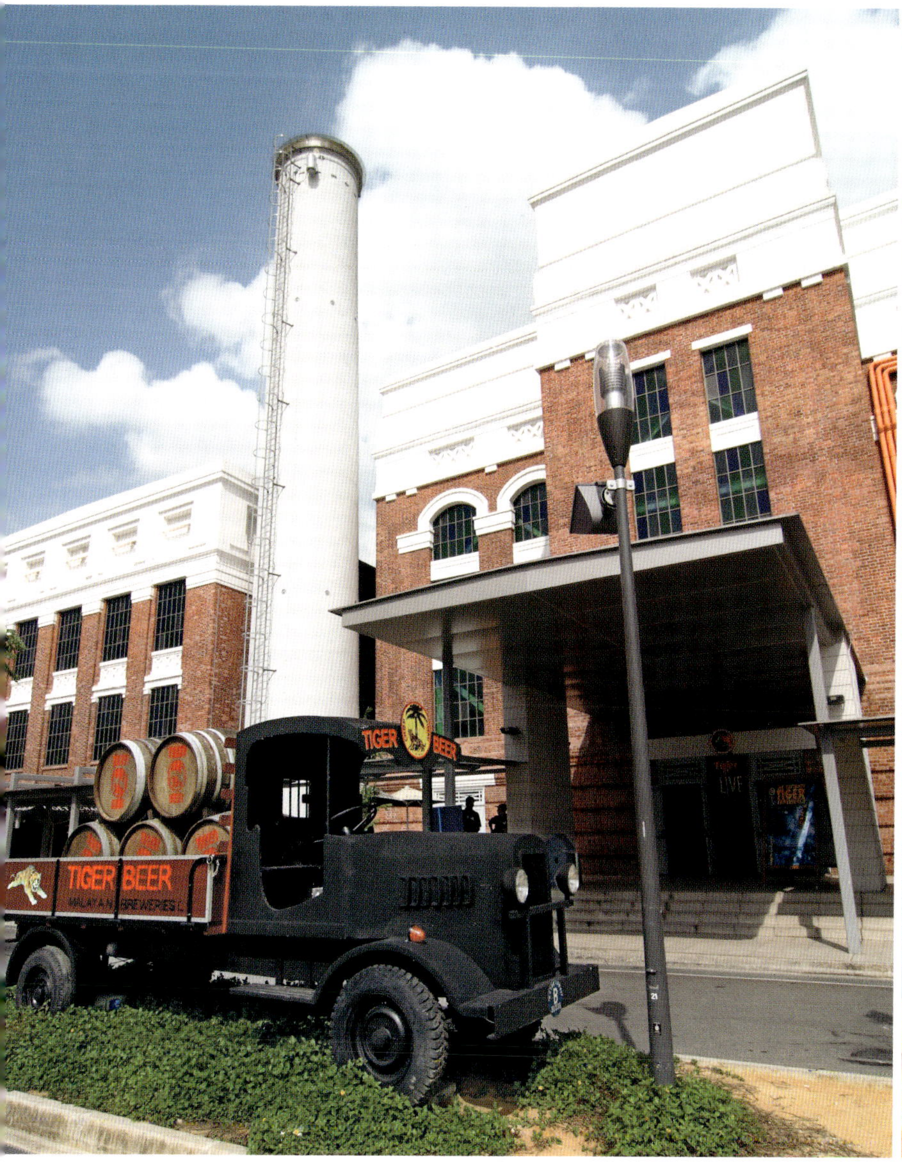
TIGER BEER
TIGER BEER
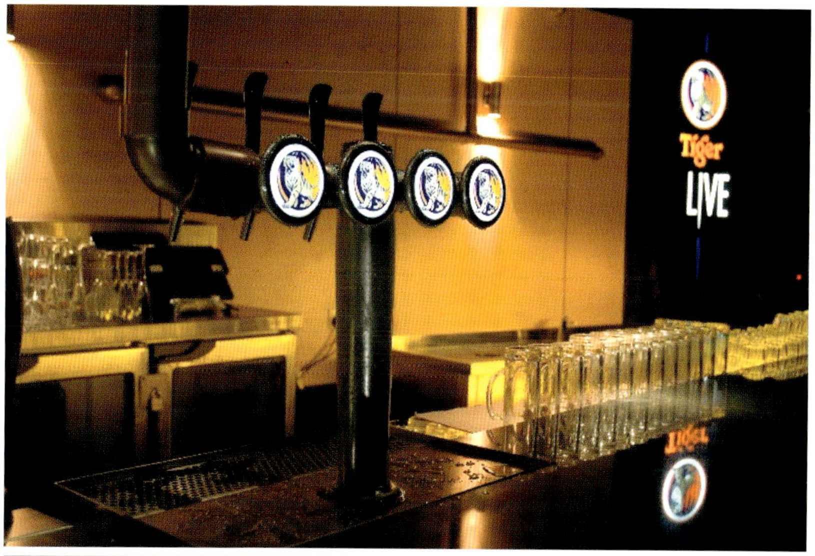
Tiger
LIVE
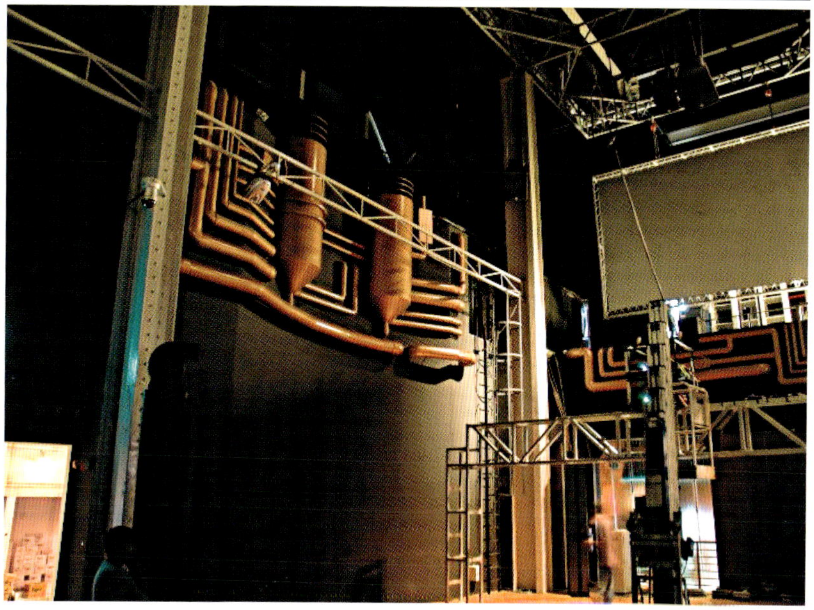

Malaysia Export Exhibition Centre

where Kuala Lumpur, Malaysia

Malaysia's External Trade Development Corporation provides and supports trade promotional services for Malaysian products. The Malaysia Export Exhibition Centre in Kuala Lumpur is a purpose-built, 3,000 sq. m. facility to display "Made in Malaysia" products. To facilitate viewing of products prior to purchase decisions, custom-made showcases and thematic displays were designed and installed. A modular display system allows for variation in display style. Products are shown in unique self-explanatory settings, divided into three themes: Indoor, Outdoor and Lifestyle.

The designers chose an illuminated, custom-designed circular framework that extends over the displays. Use of graphics, plywood laminate furniture, wallpaper, tiles, timber laminate frames, emulsion paints and stainless steel created an impressive, elegant and stylish display.

The effective design emphasises and differentiates the broad range of goods manufactured in Malaysia.

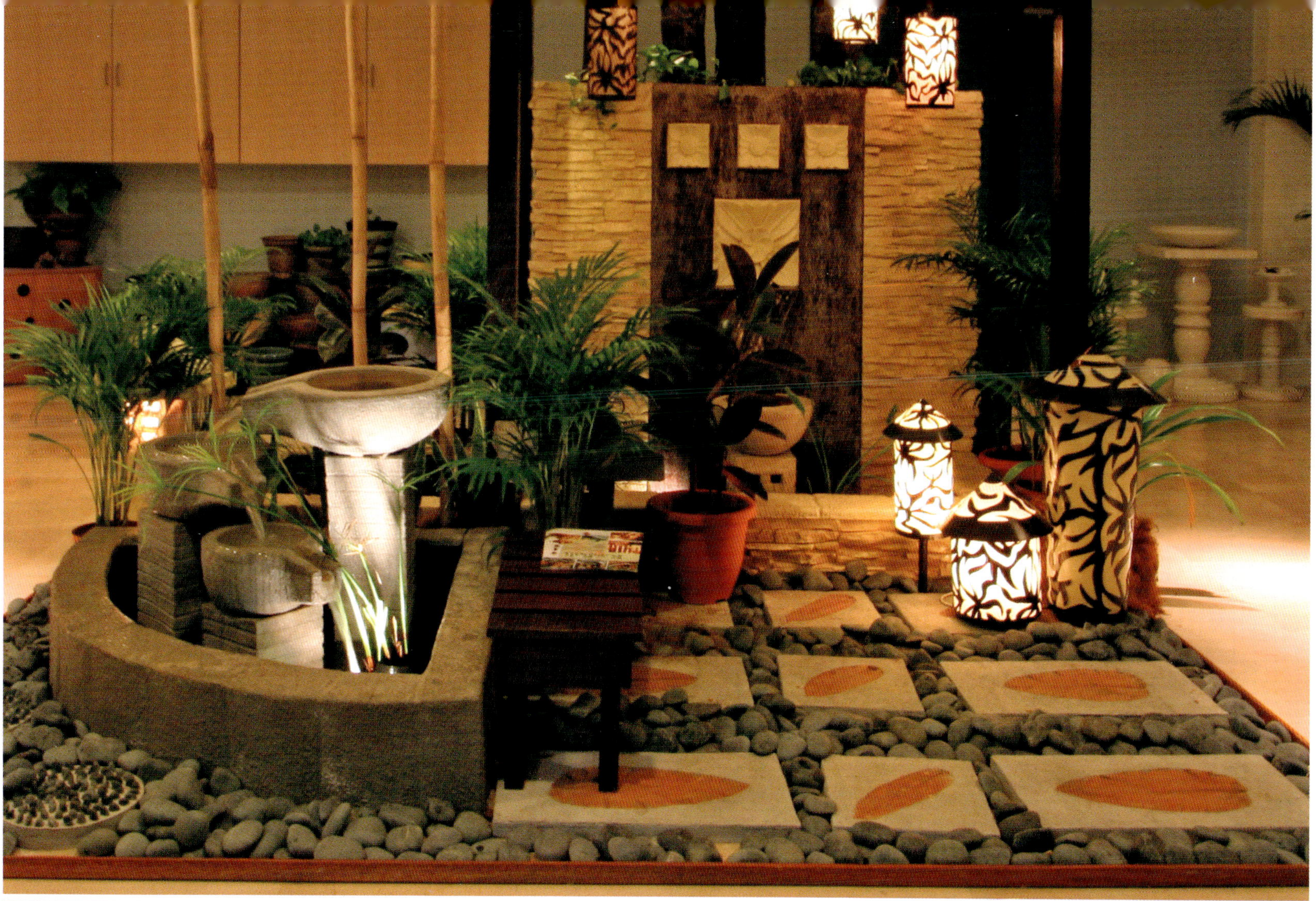

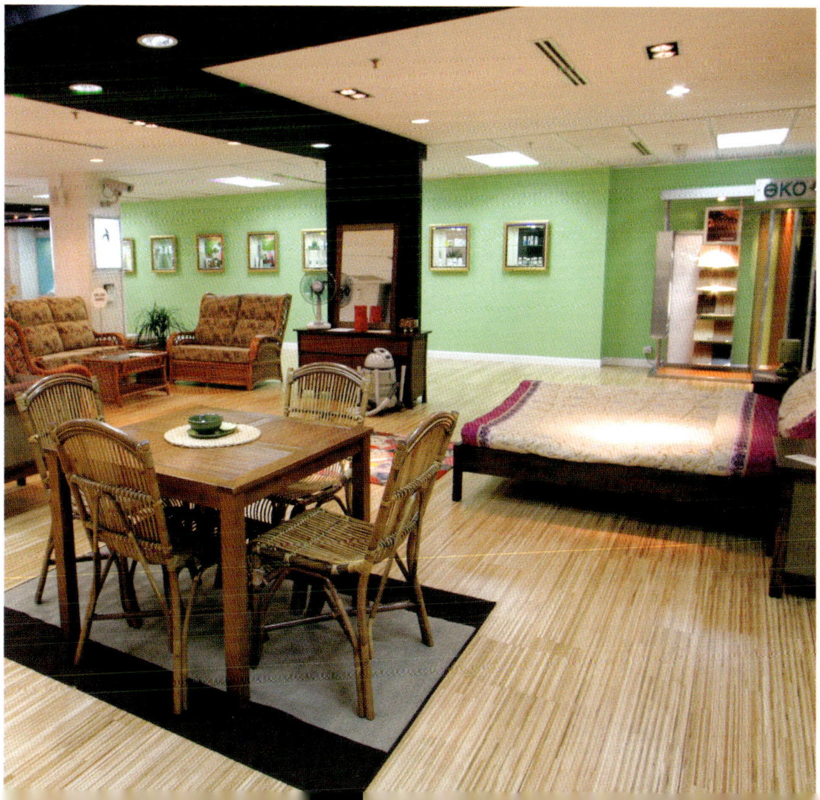

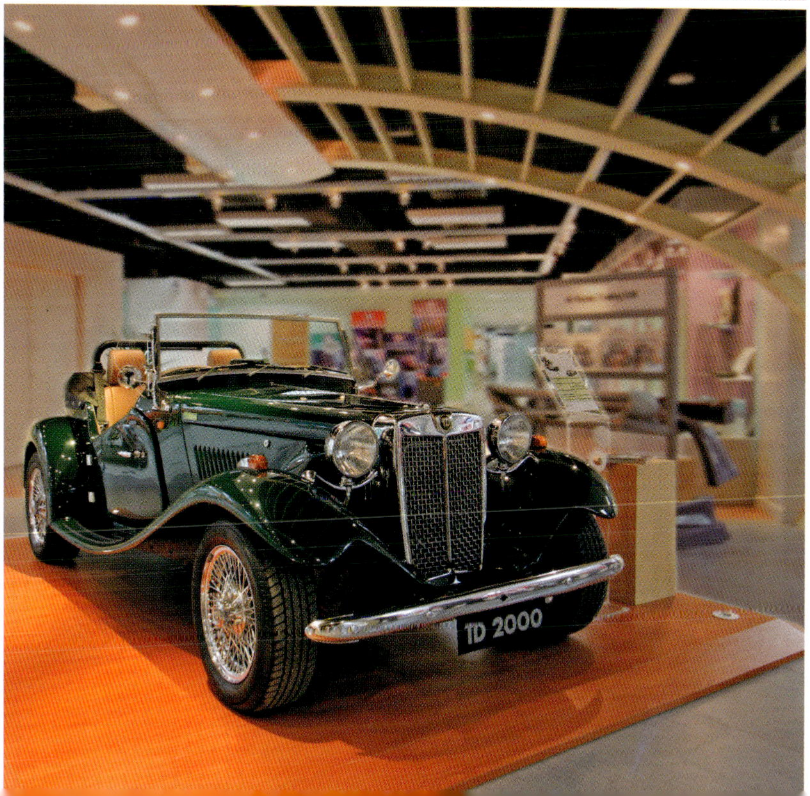
TD 2000

Normandy American Cemetery Visitor Centre

where Normandy, France

In a space of 2,000 sq. m., a permanent exhibition was constructed to pay tribute to sacrifices made some sixty years ago and celebrate the historic D-Day Landings. The centre offers the opportunity for visitors to remember the brave soldiers who helped change the course of World War II during the Allied assault on 6 June, 1944.

Pico was in charge of the scenography at the centre. The solution entailed massive steel structures, printed, engraved and acid etched glass panels, acrylic showcases and panels, projection and audio theatres, and inkjet printed aluminium panels.

The space features narrative texts, photos, films, interactive displays and artefacts to create a sensitive blend of stories, paying tribute to the soldiers' sacrifice. The designers created more than 140 large laminated glass panels, which were printed with an inkjet technique and then acid etched.

The visitor centre's official inauguration was held on the 63rd anniversary of D-Day. The American Secretary of Defence, the US Ambassador and representatives from the French Ministry of Defence attended the event along with 2,500 VIP guests.

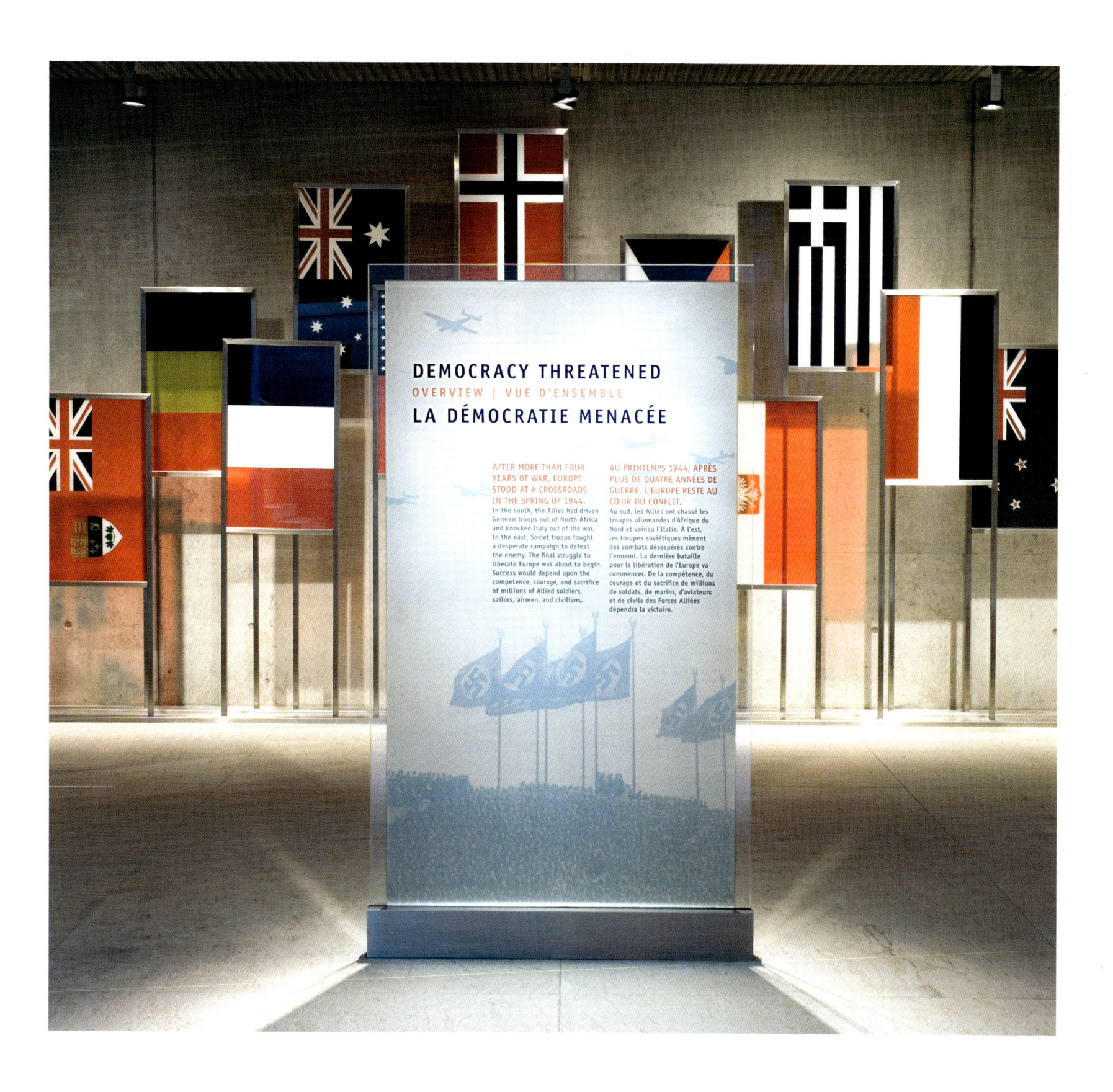

DEMOCRACY THREATENED
OVERVIEW | VUE D'ENSEMBLE
LA DÉMOCRATIE MENACÉE

AFTER MORE THAN FOUR YEARS OF WAR, EUROPE STOOD AT A CROSSROADS IN THE SPRING OF 1944.
In the south, the Allies had driven German troops out of North Africa and knocked Italy out of the war. In the east, Soviet troops fought a desperate campaign to defeat the enemy. The final struggle to liberate Europe was about to begin. Success would depend upon the competence, courage, and sacrifice of millions of Allied soldiers, sailors, airmen, and civilians.

AU PRINTEMPS 1944, APRÈS PLUS DE QUATRE ANNÉES DE GUERRE, L'EUROPE RESTE AU CŒUR DU CONFLIT.
Au sud, les Alliés ont chassé les troupes allemandes d'Afrique du Nord et vaincu l'Italie. À l'est, les troupes soviétiques mènent des combats désespérés contre l'ennemi. La dernière bataille pour la libération de l'Europe va commencer. De la compétence, du courage et du sacrifice de millions de soldats, de marins, d'aviateurs et de civils des Forces Alliées dépendra la victoire.

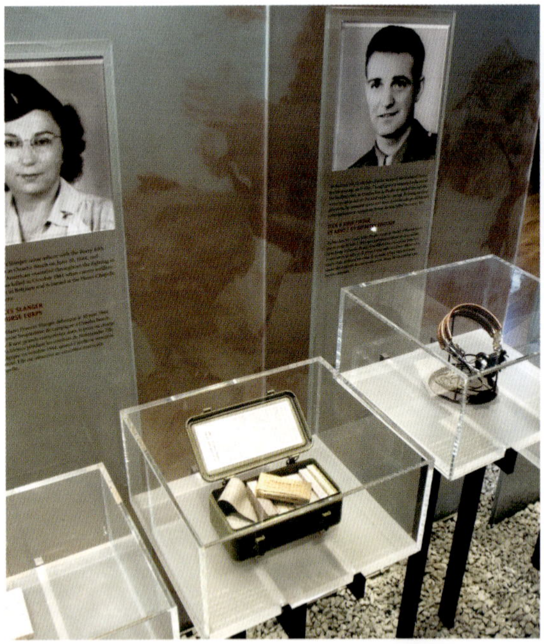

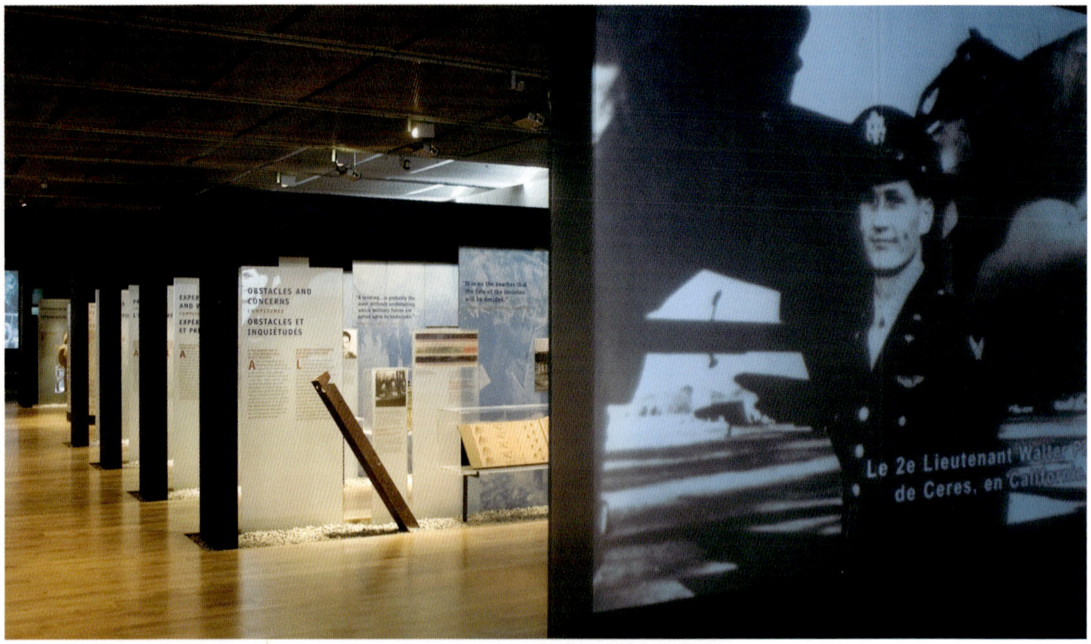
OBSTACLES AND CONCERNS
OBSTACLES ET INQUIÉTUDES

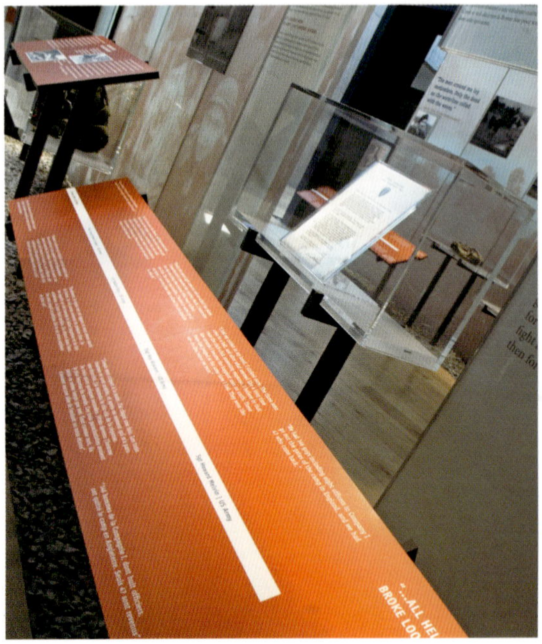

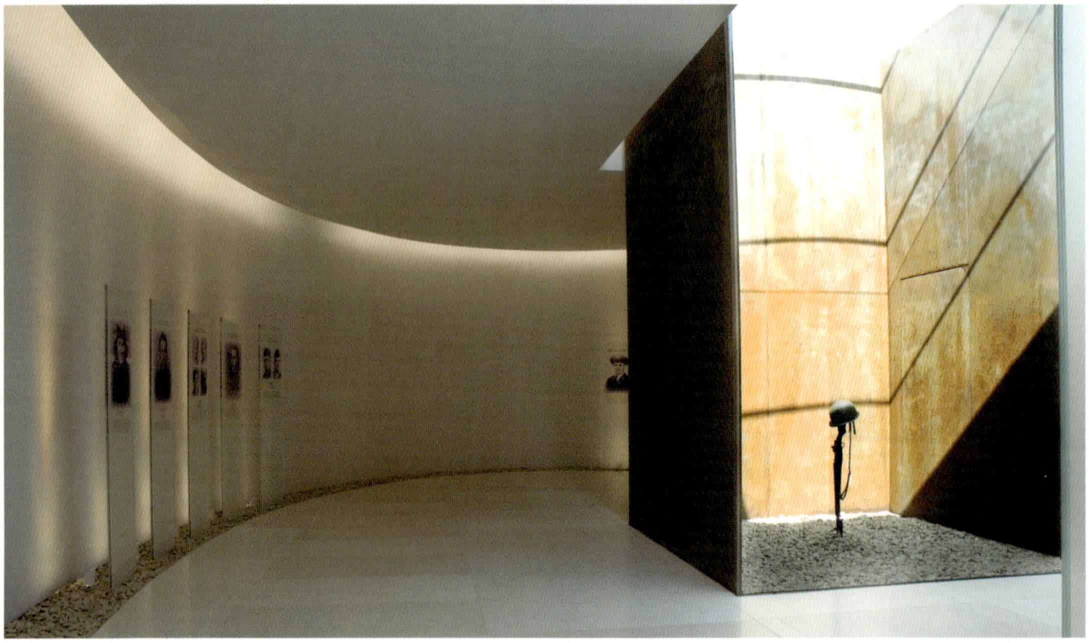

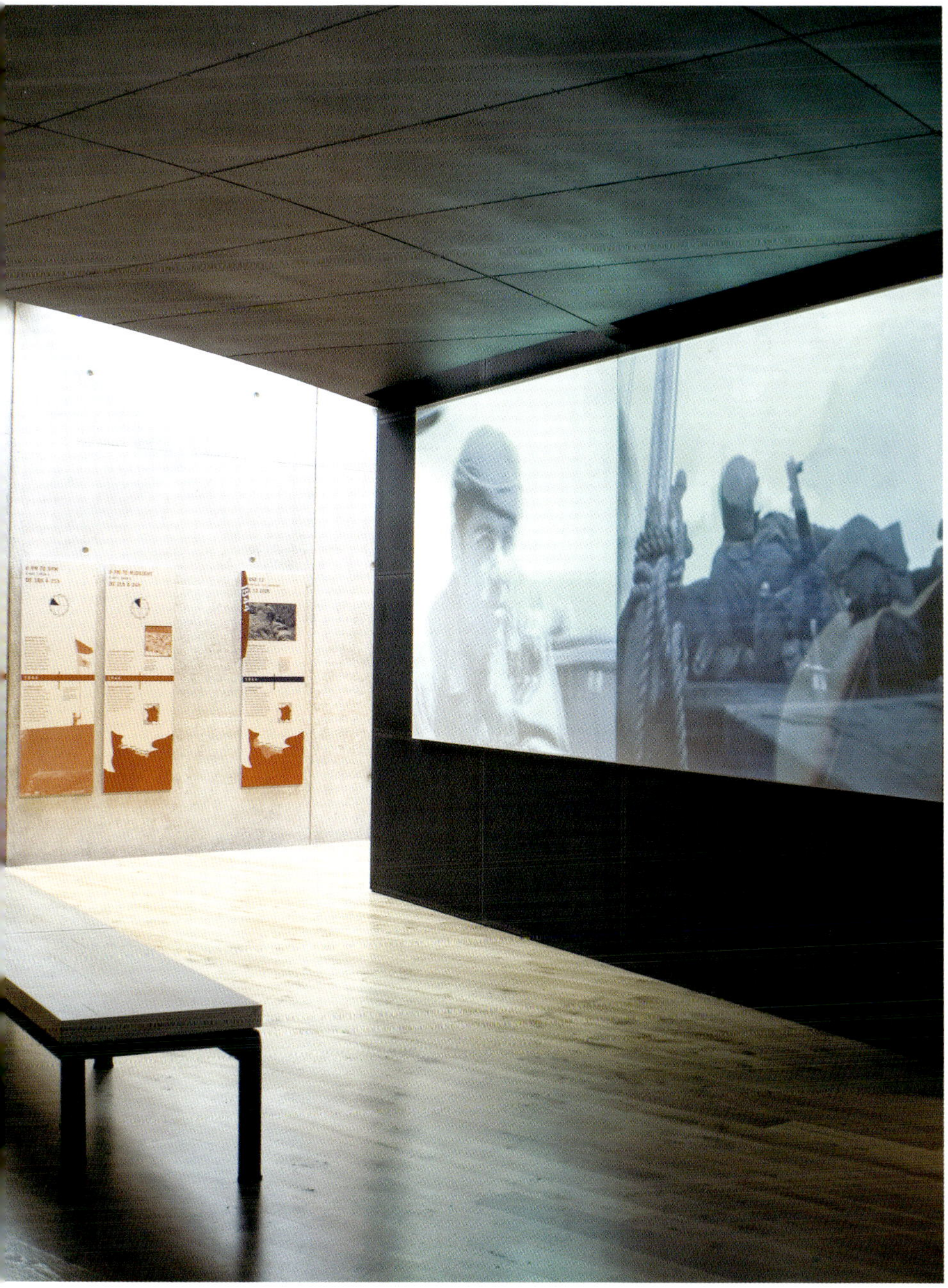

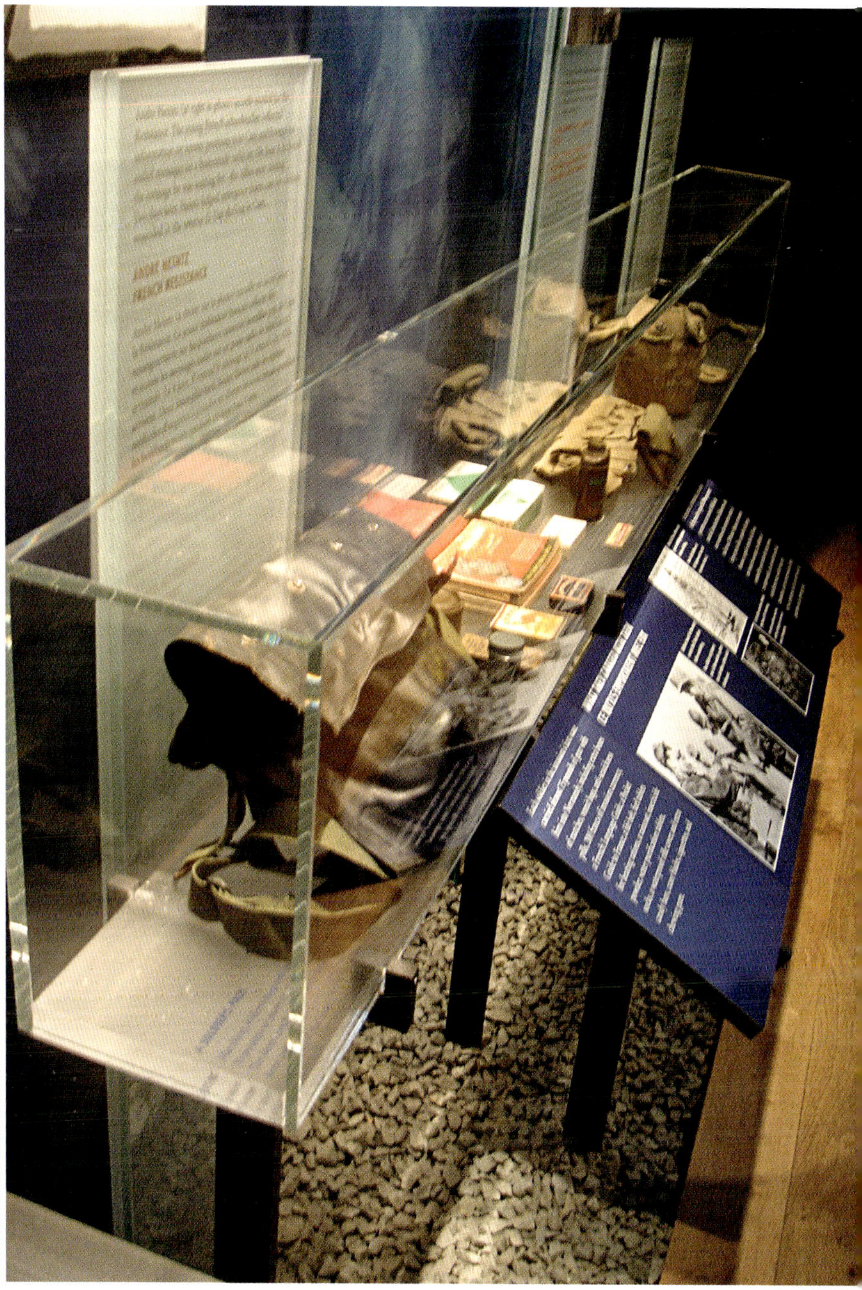

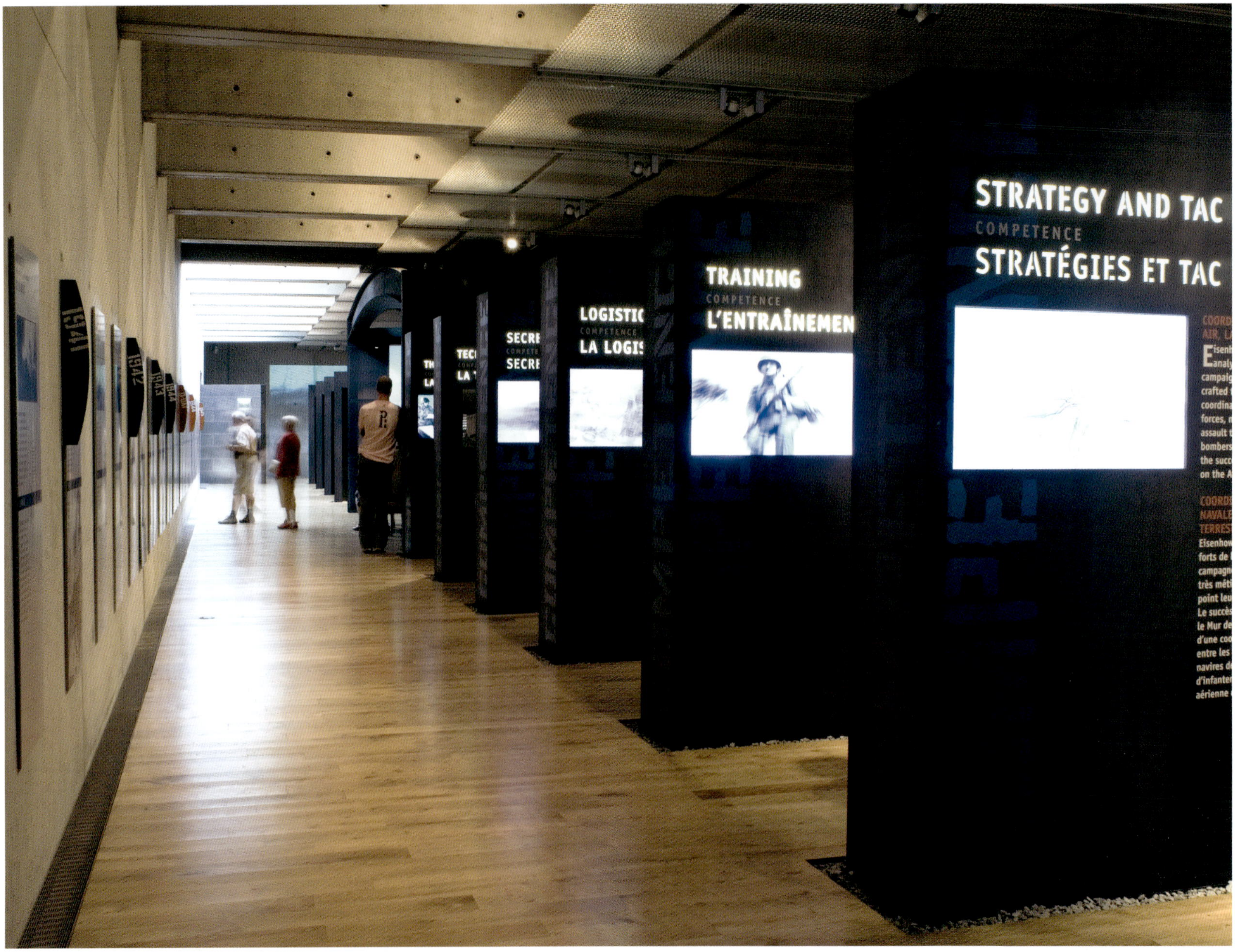
STRATEGY AND TAC
COMPETENCE
STRATÉGIES ET TAC
TRAINING
COMPETENCE
L'ENTRAÎNEMEN
LOGISTIC
COMPETENCE
LA LOGIS
1941
1942

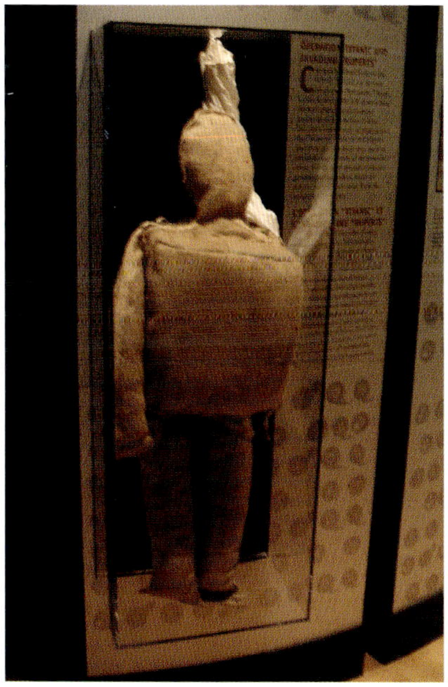

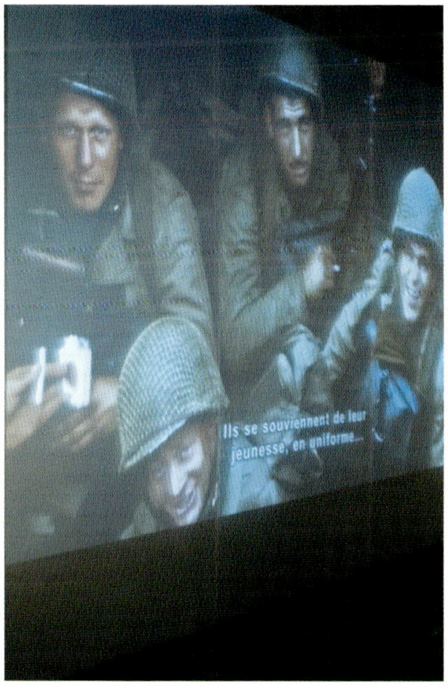
Ils se souviennent de leur jeunesse, en uniforme...

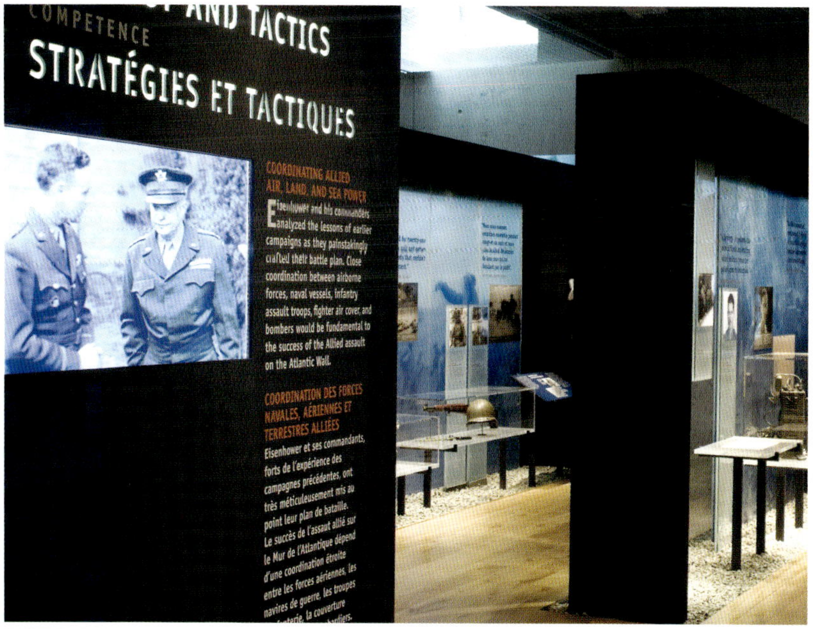
AND TACTICS
COMPETENCE
STRATÉGIES ET TACTIQUES
COORDINATING ALLIED AIR, LAND, AND SEA POWER
Eisenhower and his commanders analyzed the lessons of earlier campaigns as they painstakingly crafted their battle plan. Close coordination between airborne forces, naval vessels, infantry assault troops, fighter air cover, and bombers would be fundamental to the success of the Allied assault on the Atlantic Wall.
COORDINATION DES FORCES NAVALES, AÉRIENNES ET TERRESTRES ALLIÉES
Eisenhower et ses commandants, forts de l'expérience des campagnes précédentes, ont très méticuleusement mis au point leur plan de bataille. Le succès de l'assaut allié sur le Mur de l'Atlantique dépend d'une coordination étroite entre les forces aériennes, les navires de guerre, les troupes

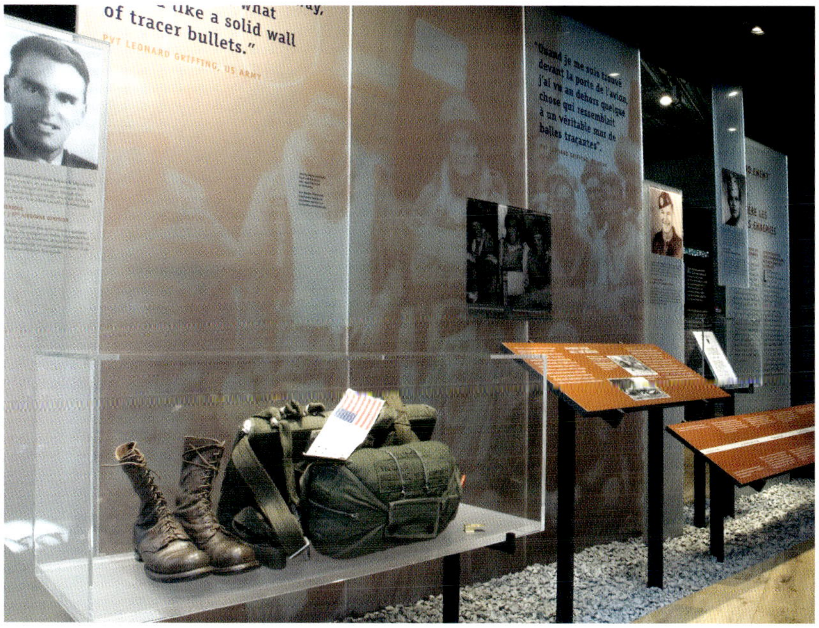
of tracer bullets."
PVT LEONARD GRIFFING, US ARMY
"Quand je me suis trouvé devant la porte de l'avion, j'ai vu au dehors quelque chose qui ressemblait à un véritable mur de balles traçantes".

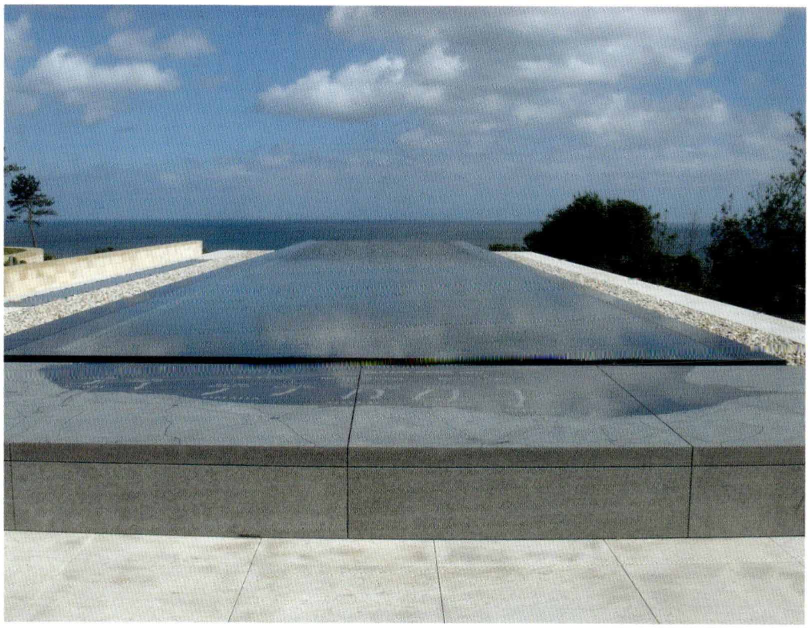

"thanks"

to our valued clients and partners for giving Pico the opportunity to be part of your success

American Battle Monument Commission
Asia Pacific Breweries
Bacardi Global Travel Retail
Blue Co., Ltd.
Caritas Bianchi College of Careers
Cathay Pacific Airways Ltd.
Cellnet
Chevrolet Sales (Thailand) Ltd.
China Netcom (Group) Company Ltd. - Qingdao Branch
Chu Kong Optical Manufactory Ltd.
CTCI (Thailand) Co., Ltd.
DaimlerChrysler (Thailand) Ltd.
DaimlerChrysler Taiwan Ltd.
Dedica Group
Design 360
DesignLab Misc.
DongFeng Peugeot Citroen Automobile Co., Ltd.
GALLAGHER & Associates
GE Capital (Thailand) Ltd.
HKSAR Leisure and Cultural Services Department
Hong Kong Taoist Association
IMG Fashion Asia Pacific
Hong Kong Tourism Board
JetQuay Pte Ltd.

Jones Lang LaSalle
Kohler China Investment Co., Ltd.
LANXESS Pte Ltd.
Malaysia External Trade Development Corporation
McCann Erickson
Meadow Creative
MediaAV International Pte Ltd.
Mercedes-Benz Korea
Micron Eyewear Manufactory Co., Ltd.
Mind & Media
Ministry of Finance, Singapore
Ministry of Science and Technology, Thailand
Motorola Inc.
MTR Corporation
Multi Design Company Ltd.
Singapore National Day 2007 EXCO
NEC Corporation
NEC Media Products
NTP Architects and Planners Co., Ltd.
Ocean Park Corporation
OSIM (HK) Co., Ltd.
Raytheon Company
Reed Tradex Company Ltd.

Royal Thai Government
Schmidt Marketing (HK) Ltd. Taiwan Branch
Shanghai Mizuno Corporation Ltd.
Siemens (China) Ltd.
Siemens Automation Systems Ltd.
Singapore Tourism Board
Siong Ann Engineering
Toshiba Corporation
US Army
Yearfull Contracting Ltd.

Andrea Teo
Andrew Loh
Candy Lo
Cathy Ho
Charles Doyle
Charlie Stewart-Cox
Charlie Yu
Chic Eather
David Price
Echo Pang
Fumiko Kataoka
Gareth Watkins
Helee Hillman
Henry Chen

Hiroshi Shoda
Ian Wilkinson
Iris Lim
Jarrad Clark
Jenny Yip
Jim Wright
Jodi Pritchard
Judy Kwan
Kelvin Tan
Keri Atchley
KK Kwan
Koichi Teramoto
Korphong Tramote
Lee Yen Miin
Maggie Ma
Mak Kam Hang
Makisan K.E. Yap
Mark Tindall
Michael Olson
Myra Lee
Nopadol Limwattanakul
Pamela Lee
Preecha Sanunwattananont
Simon Lock
Simon Siu
Tracey Kwong
Tsuyoshi Ikegami

"thanks"

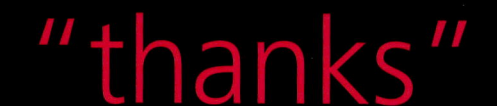

to our Pico designers and project managers for your vision, precision and excellent work

Abdul Wahab	David Poe	Kazuhiko Ishikawa	Ployrudee Pholpok
Akkapol Phanyadilok	Derek van Dugteren	Kelly Guan	Racy Ngan
Alvin Leong	Derrick Teo	Kelvin Tan	Renee Long
Amy Hui	Dirk Nicolay	Kemachart Kantirattanawong	Robert Kang
Andy Liu	Duangsamon Nachaisin	Kenny Kan	Rossetti Ho
Andy Wong	Eddia Li	Keri Atchley	Saichon Daengsopha
Ann Shelley	Edmund Ooi	Kevin He	Sam Lim
Anne Li	Edward Chan	Khanittha Chaipetch	Sam Wang
Arch William	Effie Chou	Korpong Tramote	Samson Lam
Ashley Churcher	Eric Cheng	KP Chua	Sarah Kim
Azmi Tarmuji	Eric Law	Lam Kwong Yuen	Sharon Soh
Barbara Yoong	Erika Lui	Laurie Aklinski	Shirley Hsu
Beau Lockwood	Eva Leung	Li Jie	Shirley Li
Bonz Or	Frankie Yeung	Li Xiao Lei	Silchai Kiatpapan
Burnice Ip	Harris Chan	Lim Kian Meng	Sim Ban Kok
Busarin Sriwachirawat	Hay Cheung	Lim Pei Pei	Song Ji Fang
Carol Liu	He Yuan	Lim Shu Nee	SP Chia
Caroline Kwauk	He Zhi Mei	Lim Tien Yong	Stephanie Soon
Chanida Cholmaitri	Helen Bui	Liu Wu	Steven Kwok
Charlie Liew	Hijiri Ishii	Magdalene Ho	Suee Poon
Chatchawal Praditsatien	Isamu Takano	Maggie Ma	Sun Wen Rui
Chayaphol Kalapaphong	Ivy Lau	Margaret Wong	Supaporn Sawangjitt
Chen Jiong	Jack Chia	Mariah Suthira Silakote	Tack Roberts
Chew Theng Meng	James Chen	Martin Lo	Tanaphon Boonmark
Chia Chee Wee	Jaruwan Koedamrong	Mary Ann	Tham Chee Kong
Chim Wei Yee	Jasper Narcisco	Mattayan Eampaiboon	Thanida Prachanok
Chito Ignacio	Jay Zou	Michelle Fong	Thitiphongdech Rongkavong
Chokchai Vatcharanirankul	Jeerasak Adam	Mike Chua	Waily Liu
Chua Meng Kiat	Jespher Tsao	Myra Lee	Warang Rodpol
Cissy Jiang	Jessica Luk	Nancy Ha	Wittaya Penparkkul
Clarence Fong	Jiang Yun Ming	Nelly Soo	Wu Chin Wei
Colin Yeo	Jiggs Ibarrola	Ngew Thye On	Xu Ye
Collin Shin	Joseph Lee	Nopadol Limwattanakul	Yap Jin Cung
Damon Ding	Josh Cho	Pakkhanat Rojkhajornsiri	Yen Cheng
Daniel Wu	Kanas Tang	Pang Zhuo Feng	Yu Fu Cai
Daren Chia	Karen Lee	Patrick Yang	Yuthachai Veerataveeporn
Dave Caswell	Karl Du	Pattamate Watthanasakulcharoen	

\<index\>

APB TigerLIVE Gallery, **162**
Bombay Sapphire Martini Glass Exhibition Display, **102**
Caritas Bianchi Fashion Show, **28**
Cathay Pacific Experience, **152**
Cellnet Executive Briefing Centre, **134**
Chevrolet at the 28th Bangkok International Motor Show, **52**
Chinese New Year Parade, **30**
Chu Kong at the Hong Kong Optical Fair, **80**
The Daodejing: Its Editions and Versions, **78**
GE Money at Money Fair, **34**
Hua Song Museum, **142**
IMF and World Bank Group Annual Meetings, **26**
JetQuay – CIP Terminal, **108**
Kiang Saket Energy Centre, **158**
Kohler at China Building & Construction Trade Fair, **62**
LANXESS at ChinaPlas, **66**
Leica Flagship Shop, **118**
Malaysia Export Exhibition Centre, **166**
MasterCard Luxury Week Hong Kong, **16**
Mercedes-Benz Accessories Shop, **122**
Mercedes-Benz at Taipei Auto Show, **76**

Mercedes-Benz at the 28th Bangkok International Motor Show, **70**
Mercedes-Benz C-Class Launch, **20**
Micron at the Hong Kong Optical Fair, **58**
Mizuno at the 5th International Golf Trade Fair, **84**
Motorola at ITU Telecom World, **48**
Motorola Facilities Branding Projects, **126**
National Science and Technology Fair, **38**
NEC at ITU Telecom World, **44**
Ngong Ping Theme Village, **148**
Normandy American Cemetery Visitor Centre, **168**
Ocean Park Hong Kong, **138**
OSIM ChairSpa, **112**
Peugeot at Auto Shanghai, **88**
Qingdao CNC Centre, **124**
Raytheon at the 47th International Paris Air Show, **92**
Siemens Automation Showroom, **128**
Siemens Visitor Centre, **130**
Singapore National Day Parade, **22**
The 60th Anniversary of His Majesty's Accession to the Throne, **10**
Toshiba Private Show, **98**

about Martin

A leading authority on store design, visual merchandising and exhibit design, Martin M. Pegler has worked as a designer, manufacturer, display person, store planner and consultant for over 40 years.

He has lectured on these subjects for industry and small business groups, at shopping centres and chains nationwide and internationally. He is a former professor of store planning and visual merchandising at the Fashion Institute of Technology in New York.

Martin is the author of more than 80 books published by Visual Reference Publications including, the Stores of the Year series, Store Windows series, Store Presentation and Design Series, Cafes & Coffee Shops series, Café Design series, Designing the World's Best Bars, Storefront & Facades series, Designing the World's Best Supermarkets, Christmas Advertising, Marketing & Display, and the Contemporary Exhibit Design series.

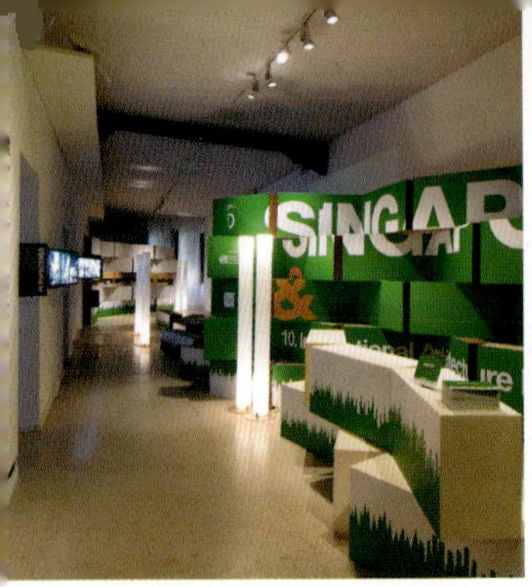

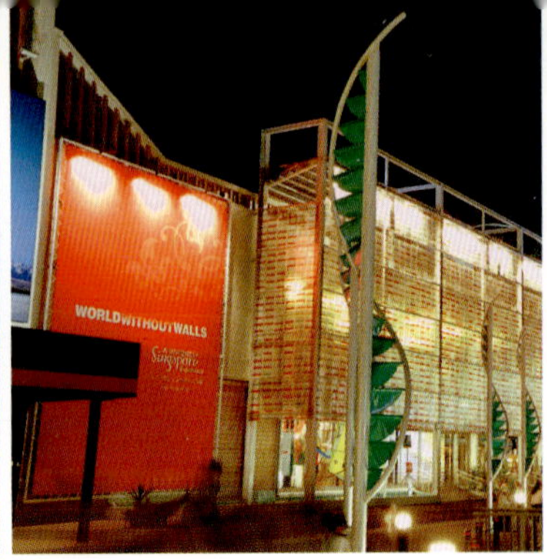
WORLDWITHOUTWALLS

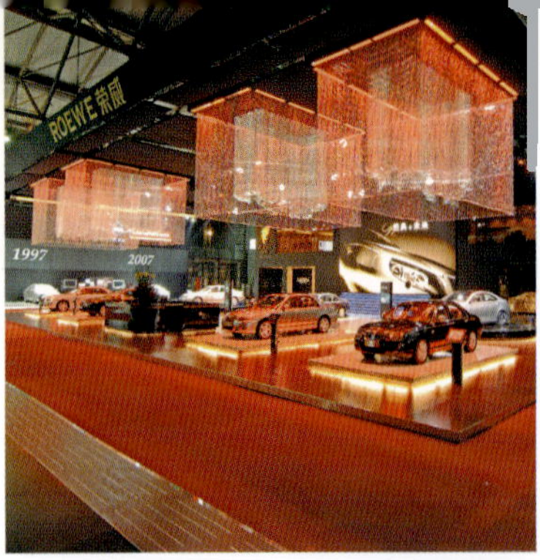
ROEWE荣威
1997
2007

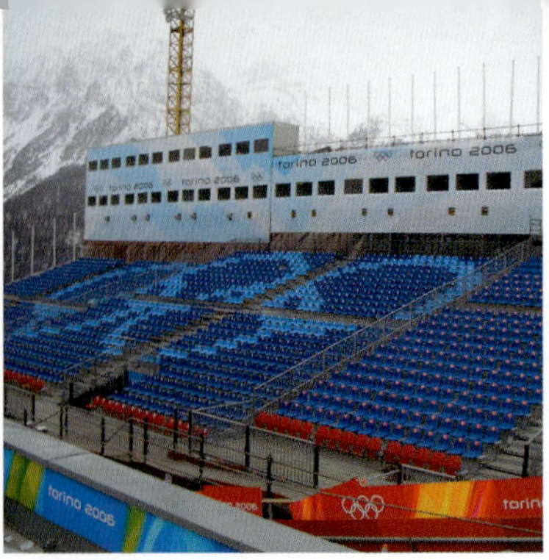
torino 2006

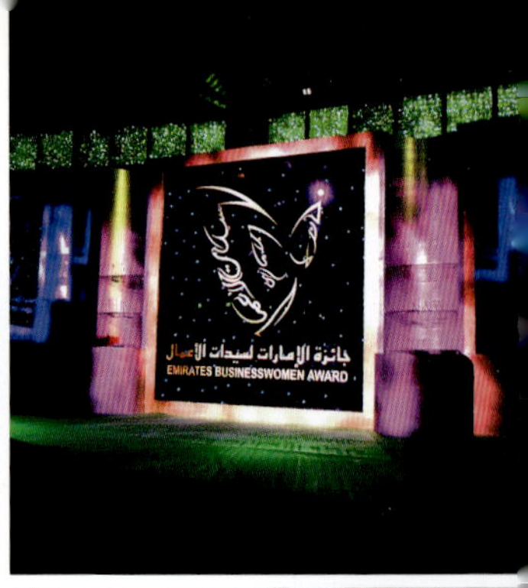
EMIRATES BUSINESSWOMEN AWARD

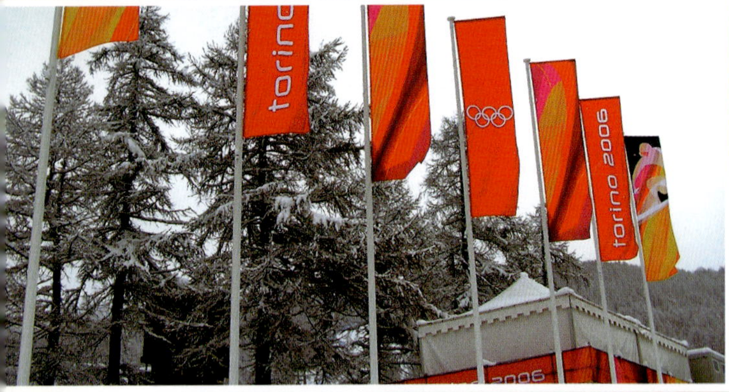
torino
torino 2006

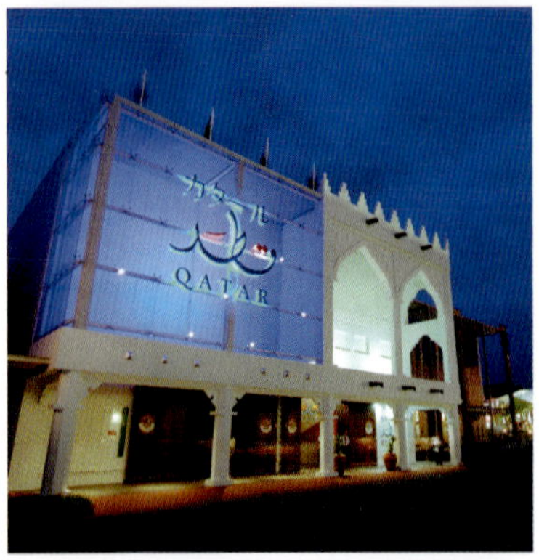
QATAR

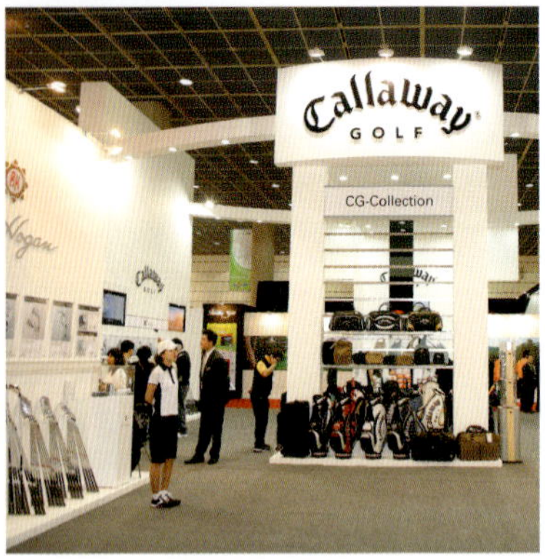
Callaway
GOLF
CG-Collection

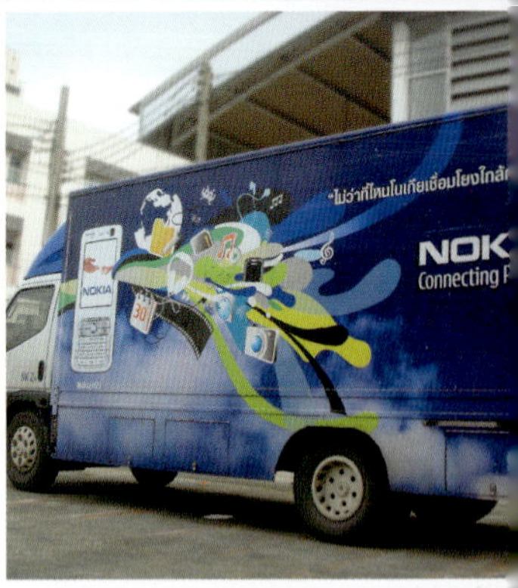

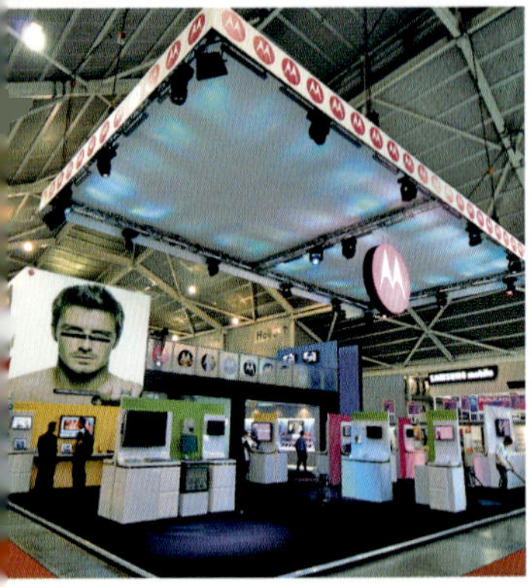

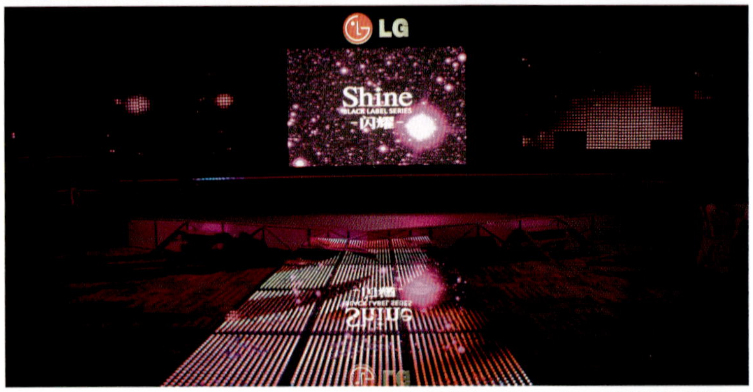
LG
Shine

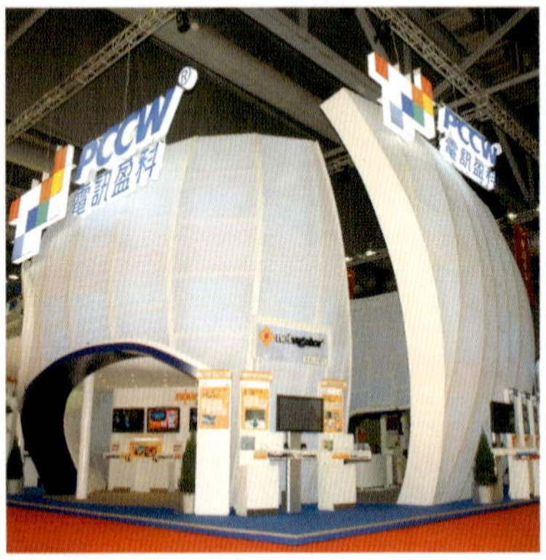
PCCW

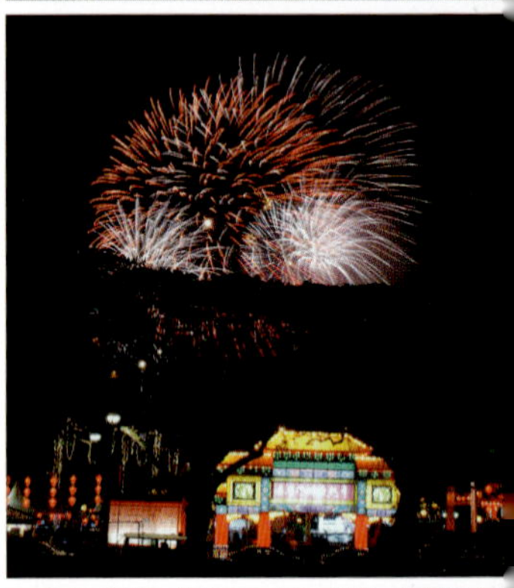

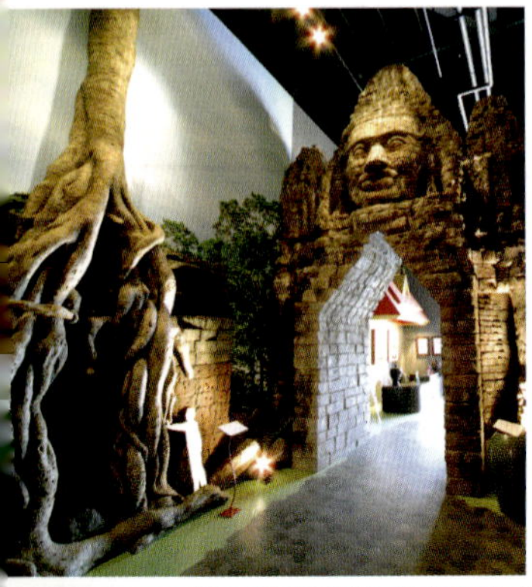

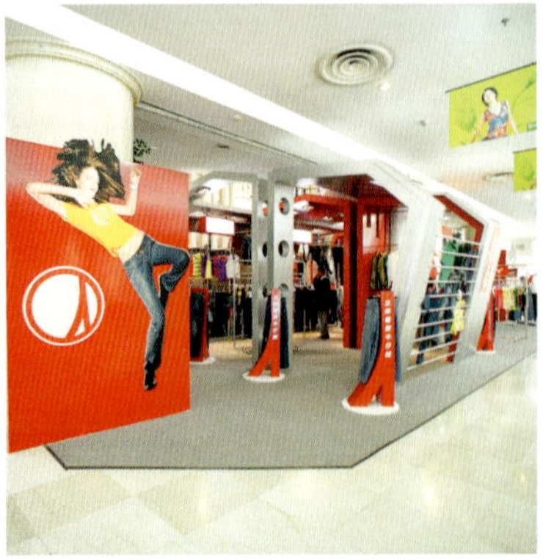

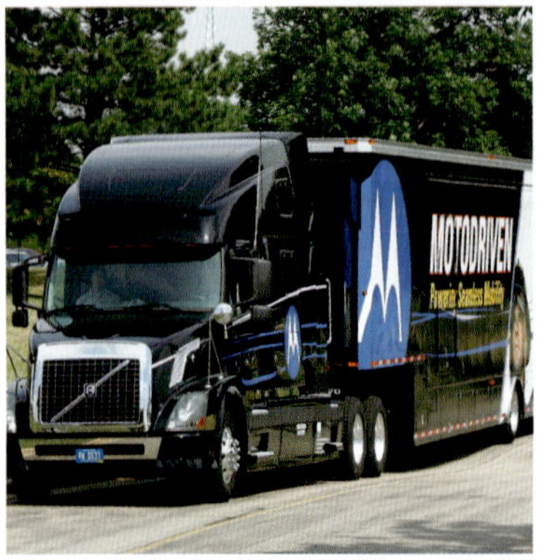
MOTODRIVEN

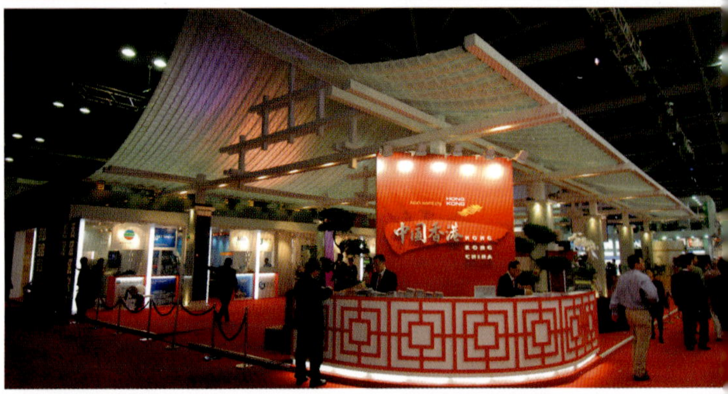

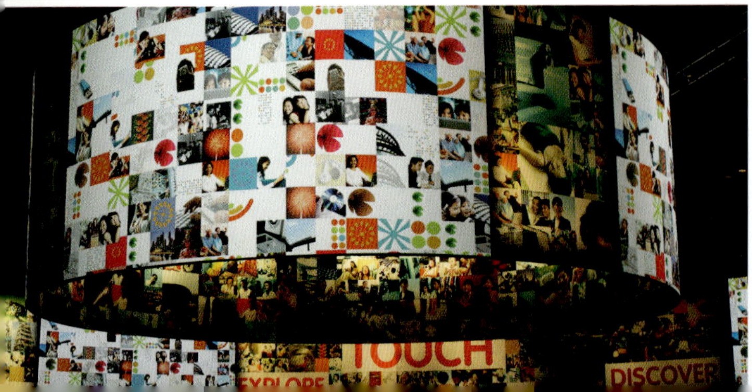
TOUCH
DISCOVER

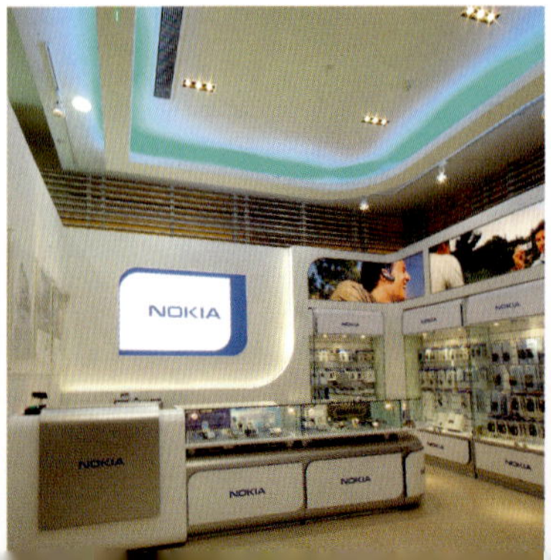
NOKIA

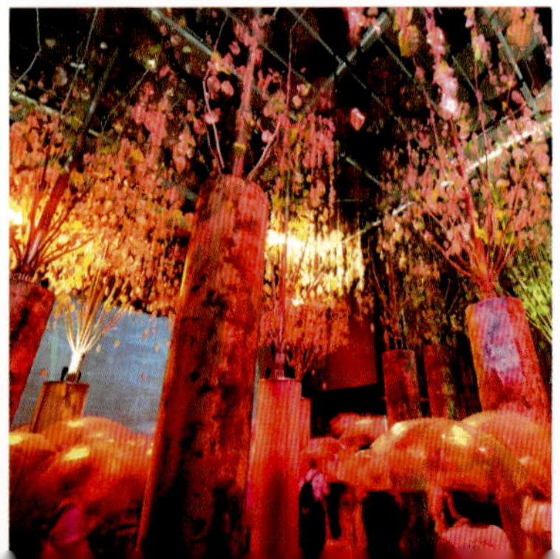

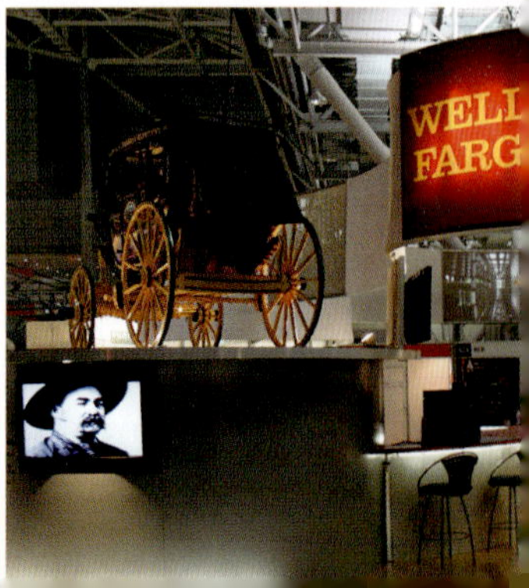